Extending the Table . . .

. . . A World Community Cookbook

j oetta Handrich Schlabach

k ristina Mast Burnett,
Recipe Editor

*Commissioned by Mennonite
Central Committee (MCC),
Akron, Pennsylvania, to
promote global understanding
and celebrate the variety of
world cultures.*

*MCC is the service and relief
organization of the Mennonite
and Brethren in Christ
churches of Canada and the
United States.*

H ERALD PRESS
**Scottdale, Pennsylvania
Waterloo, Ontario**

Library of Congress Cataloging-in-Publication Data
Schlabach, Joetta Handrich.
    Extending the table : a world community cookbook / Joetta Handrich Schlabach.
        p.   cm.
    Recipes and stories in the spirit of *More-with-less cookbook.*
    "Commissioned by Mennonite Central Committee"—T.p.
    Includes indexes.
    ISBN 0-8361-3561-X
    1. Cookery, International. I. Mennonite Central Committee. II. Title.
TX725.A1S4214 1991   91-14756
641.59—dc20

Scripture is from the New Revised Standard Version Bible, copyright 1989 by the Division on Christian Education of the National Council of Churches of Christ in the USA; used by permission.

Map on pp. 10-11 is based on World Map: Peters Projection, Friendship Press, N.Y.; copyright Akademische Verlagsanstalt, Graz, Austria; used by permission.

Back cover photo, Mark Beach; spiral edition: inside front cover, Julie Kauffman; inside back cover, Dan Marschka.

EXTENDING THE TABLE
Copyright © 1991 by
Herald Press, Scottdale,
Pa. 15683

Published simultaneously in
Canada by Herald Press,
Waterloo, Ont. N2L 6H7.
All rights reserved
Library of Congress Catalog
Card Number: 91-14756
International Standard Book
Number: 0-8361-3561-X
        (spiral edition)
International Standard Book
Number: 0-8361-9264-8
        (paperback edition)

Printed in the United States of
America

Design by Ken Hiebert,
Merrill R. Miller,
Julie Kauffman

To order or request information,
please call 1-800-759-4447
(individuals);
1-800-245-7894 (trade).
Website: www.heraldpress.com

Shehzad Noorani:
Bangladesh

Contents

Many, many people helped "set the table" for this book. The following list of names by no means includes everyone who supported and encouraged the project to completion.

I am first indebted to Kristina Mast Burnett, who, along with Reg Toews of Mennonite Central Committee (MCC) and representatives from Herald Press, initiated this project and invited me to be the author. Tina worked closely with me throughout the process of planning and compiling the book, although we were miles apart. While I worked from my home in Indiana, writing chapter introductions, editing stories, testing and revising recipes, Tina worked in the MCC office in Akron, Pennsylvania. She assisted in selecting, testing, revising, and editing recipes, coordinated the recipe testing done by volunteer testers, researched unfamiliar ingredients, and efficiently coordinated administrative details.

Eight people served as an advisory committee to this book. The group met for a weekend at the onset of the project to help shape and direct it. They provided ongoing support and counsel.

International members of the committee included Sadie Campbell of Jamaica, Cynthia Peacock of India, and Ezra Sigwela of South Africa. North American members were Karen Klassen Harder of Kansas, Jessie Hostetler of Oregon, Carol Loeppky of Kentucky and Ontario, Willard Roth of Indiana, and Ingrid Schultz of British Columbia.

Approximately 250 people contributed more than 1,000 recipes and nearly 300 stories. Although we were only able to include a portion of these, each item helped shape and confirm the value of the book.

Every recipe selected was tested several times, in both a Canadian and a U.S. kitchen whenever possible. A large group of home economists, nutritionists, and experienced cooks volunteered to help with this enormous task. Although there is not sufficient space to list all their names or recount all their stories, their evaluations and recommendations were invaluable. They accepted the challenge of testing unfamiliar recipes with a sense of adventure and enthusiasm, and often extended hospitality by inviting friends to share in the resulting meal.

The following people did additional specialized recipe testing and gave technical assistance for recipe development: Carolyn J. Grasse, Herb

Hoover, Margaret Loewen, Sarah E. Myers, Dawn Russell, Joann Burnett and Goshen College foods and nutrition students, Janet Harder and Eastern Mennonite College dietetics students, Mary Ann Mihok and Messiah College dietetics students, Evie Shaar and the MCC dining hall staff, Barbara Stettler and Bluffton College home economics students, and Marge Warta and Bethel College home economics students.

Helen Alderfer, Amy Dueckman, Jan Enns, Suzanne Franz, Karen Klassen Harder, Nancy Heisey, Jessie Hostetler, Mary Beth Lind, Catherine Mumaw, Willard Roth, and Ingrid Schultz carefully read and commented on parts of the manuscript.

Cheryl Zehr Walker and Andrea Schrock Wenger copyedited the manuscript, and Carol Brubaker assisted with proofreading. Larry Litwiller provided valuable staff assistance in the last months of the project.

My husband and sons supported me in numerous ways—with humor during low points, patience when I put in extra hours, honest yum-to-yuk evaluation of recipes, and love.

—Joetta Handrich Schlabach

The Author

Joetta Handrich Schlabach has worked in various writing, educational, and administrative capacities with Mennonite Central Committee (MCC). From 1980-1982 she worked in the Food and Hunger Concerns office, and from 1982-1987 she and her husband, Gerald, were on assignment in Nicaragua and Honduras.

Joetta grew up in Grand Marais, Michigan. She graduated from Goshen (Indiana) College in 1980 with a degree in home economics, and received a master's degree in family economics and management from Michigan State University in 1989. She and her husband have two sons, Gabriel and Jacob.

Since returning from Central America, Joetta and her family have continued to enjoy the diversity of international living. They have resided in student apartments, also home for many foreign families, at Michigan State University, Associated Mennonite Biblical Seminaries (Elkhart, Indiana), and the University of Notre Dame. She worked on this project from her home in the latter two settings.

Joetta and her husband are members of Kern Road Mennonite Church at South Bend, Indiana, where they live.

The Recipe Editor

Kristina Mast Burnett has worked as an editor, writer, and administrator with MCC since 1976. She is currently the MCC U.S. Women's Concerns Coordinator. From 1978 to 1989 she was director of MCC Information Services. Prior to that she served with MCC as editor of a Native American economic development newsletter in Washington, D.C.

Kristina grew up in Clarence Center, New York, and graduated from Eastern Mennonite College (Harrisonburg, Virginia) with a degree in English. She has been a journalist and a high school English teacher.

She and her husband, Tom, are members of the Pilgrim Mennonite Church at Akron, Pennsylvania, where they live. They have two children, Kevin and Kathryn.

Joetta Handrich Schlabach (left) and Kristina Mast Burnett

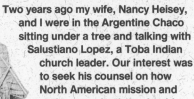

*Shehzad Noorani:
Bangladesh*

Two years ago my wife, Nancy Heisey, and I were in the Argentine Chaco sitting under a tree and talking with Salustiano Lopez, a Toba Indian church leader. Our interest was to seek his counsel on how North American mission and service organizations should work in the years ahead. We asked how, in Argentina or neighboring countries, *he* would begin to share the gospel with other indigenous people who do not have churches among them. He paused for a moment, and then responded, "I would go and eat their food." He began to weep, and the missionary couple who were our translators wept with him. Nancy and I were also overcome with his simple but powerful response. We knew that these forty-year missionaries and their colleagues had acknowledged the dignity of the indigenous people of the Chaco by eating their food, sleeping in their houses, and learning and recording their languages.

Extending the Table is an invitation to follow Salustiano Lopez's counsel and enjoy the gifts of people from Argentina and Bangladesh to Yugoslavia and Zambia. The stories and recipes help us enter into the lives and situations of these people and to be changed by them in significant ways. Food is a medium of communication, but it is more; in a mysterious way, it is part of the message, as Jesus so vividly portrayed in the breaking of bread and distribution of the cup.

Extending the Table follows in the tradition of Doris Janzen Longacre's *More-with-Less Cookbook,* and especially her *Living More with Less,* which I, as her husband, completed after her death. Both books challenged us to learn from the world community, to celebrate with joy, and to care for the earth. *Extending the Table* presents recipes and stories of people around the world. Many of them live with few material resources, yet they share gifts which point us toward a different and freer way of life.

Extending the Table is much more than a cookbook. It will most often be found on the kitchen shelf, but it could just as well fit comfortably on the bedside stand or coffee table for inspirational reading. Let it also find its way onto the pastor's shelf for its excellent sermon illustrations and stories.

For all of us, it provides repeated opportunities to take part in the lives of people around the world and to delight in the wealth they have to offer. As we are able to treat other peoples and traditions with respect and tenderness, we too are changed.

—Paul Longacre
December 1990

to *Angela Silva*
and *Sonia Esperanza Chávez,*

friends who cook
without cookbooks,
but whose lives inspired this one.

A new world map

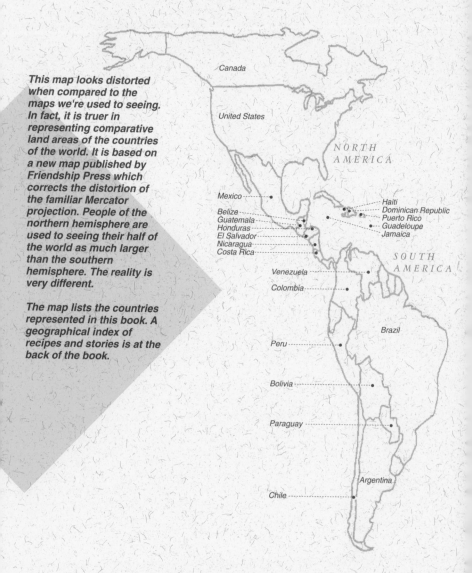

This map looks distorted when compared to the maps we're used to seeing. In fact, it is truer in representing comparative land areas of the countries of the world. It is based on a new map published by Friendship Press which corrects the distortion of the familiar Mercator projection. People of the northern hemisphere are used to seeing their half of the world as much larger than the southern hemisphere. The reality is very different.

The map lists the countries represented in this book. A geographical index of recipes and stories is at the back of the book.

Canada

United States

NORTH AMERICA

Mexico

Belize
Guatemala
Honduras
El Salvador
Nicaragua
Costa Rica

Haiti
Dominican Republic
Puerto Rico
Guadeloupe
Jamaica

Venezuela

Colombia

SOUTH AMERICA

Brazil

Peru

Bolivia

Paraguay

Argentina

Chile

Ireland
England
Spain
France
Netherlands
Switzerland
Germany
Norway
Sweden

Italy
Austria
Poland
Finland
Hungary
Croatia
Bosnia
Serbia
Romania
Ukraine
Greece
Armenia

EUROPE

Russia

Turkey

Japan
Korea

China

Nepal

Algeria
Libya

Egypt

India

Bangladesh
Taiwan
Hong Kong

ASIA

Philippines

Iran
Iraq
Lebanon
Jordan
Saudi Arabia
Israel
West Bank

Niger
Chad
Sudan

...na
...so

...ria
...na
...Coast
...eroon

Ethiopia

Laos
Thailand
Cambodia
Vietnam
Malaysia

Melanesia

AFRICA

Somalia
Uganda
Kenya

Zaire

Indonesia

Tanzania

New Zealand

...bia
...awi

...babwe
...rambique
...swana

Madagascar

Swaziland

Australia

...otho
...th Africa

AUSTRALIA

Michael Knowles: Thailand

11

Harvey Harmon: South Africa

—A credit line at the end of each recipe acknowledges the valuable participation of the individuals who contributed them. However, like other folk materials, most recipes do not "belong" to any particular individual. They represent entire communities, regions, and countries. Many North Americans contributed recipes they received from international guests or collected while living in other cultural settings. Whenever possible we included in the same credit line the name of the person who originally shared the recipe with them.

We took some liberties in combining similar recipes and making revisions based on suggestions of testers. In some cases we sacrificed a degree of authenticity to make recipes more accessible to North American cooks.

—The availability and price of some ingredients vary by season and geographical region. Individual cooks may choose to omit a locally expensive ingredient or use a substitute. Many of the less-common ingredients, such as cardamom, *garam masala*, sesame oil, and fish sauce, are sold at lower prices in ethnic food stores. These shops may not be on regularly traveled routes, but seeking them out can be an occasion to meet people of other cultures living in our communities.

—Recipe headings include several symbols for quick reference:

—indicates recipes with timesaving or prepare-ahead advantages for busy cooks.

—indicates recipes that are spicy hot. People with tender palates may bypass these recipes, or decrease or omit the spicy ingredients, labeled +!. Some recipes have a small amount of hot pepper or other hot and spicy ingredients, labeled +!, but because the overall recipes are not particularly spicy, they do not have the - *H* - label.

—indicates recipes with instructions for preparing part or all of the recipe in a microwave oven. We have provided such instructions for a sample of recipes where microwave cooking was most advantageous in terms of timesaving and/or flavor or texture enhancement. Many more recipes could be prepared in a microwave, and people experienced with microwave cooking can do so. Because cooking times vary according to the wattage of different ovens, we list a range of cooking times. Begin with the lowest time to determine which time best suits your oven.

—Unless otherwise stated, *flour* refers to white all-purpose flour and *sugar* refers to white, granulated sugar. We have generally used *margarine* instead of butter, and *milk* instead of specifying skim, low fat, or whole milk. Individuals may use the ingredient they prefer.

—Flavoring ingredients such as soy sauce (common in Asian recipes), bouillon cubes, and salt are high in sodium. These items should be used with moderation in one's overall diet.

—Abbreviations for standard measurements throughout the book are:

centimeter	—cm
cup	—c.
gallon	—gal.
gram	—g
kilogram	—kg
liter	—L
milliliter	—ml
pint	—pt.
pound	—lb.
quart	—qt.
tablespoon	—T.
teaspoon	—t.

—Metric measures are based on the official metric standards used in Canada and are intended for use with standardized metric measuring utensils.

—Recipes are like maps and picture books. They lead and provide an idea of how particular foods are prepared. They cannot, however, capture the graceful art of chopping vegetables or the rhythmic kneading of bread dough. Neither can they offer the friendships that develop while learning to cook from another person. Use the recipes, but look for opportunities to cook with and learn from others.

The recipes in this book contain a number of spices and other ingredients that may be unfamiliar. Many are readily available in spice and specialty shops, natural food stores, and supermarkets. Some of the spices and seasonings are expensive, but since recipes generally call for small amounts, the price is spread over many uses. Spices used only occasionally should be tightly sealed and stored in the freezer to preserve freshness. We list some possible substitutes below to make recipes more flexible, but using the real ingredients will allow you to experience international foods at their best.

Anise—Star anise is the star-shaped fruit of a small evergreen tree native to China. The dried stars add a delicate flavor to soups and stir-fried dishes. Star anise, anise oil, and anise seed are available on spice shelves and in specialty stores.

Basmati rice—*See* p. 142

Bean thread—*See* Cellophane noodles

Bulgur—Bulgur is the common name for whole wheat kernels that have been heated in water, dried, and cracked, with some of the bran removed. A staple food in Middle Eastern countries, bulgur is used in combination with meat dishes, in pilafs, soups, salads, desserts, and as a hot cereal. Purchase in natural food stores or stores that sell dried products in bulk.

Cellophane noodles— Also called bean thread or bean thread vermicelli, these fine transparent noodles are made from the starch of mung beans. They are used in recipes such as Vietnamese Spring Rolls (p. 264) and sold in Asian food stores.

Cardamom—This perennial herb in the ginger family is a common ingredient in Asian and African curries, and in breads and cookies. Many grocery stores sell ground cardamom, but the pods which contain small seeds are more likely to be found

in Asian food stores. Whole cardamom pods used in stews or curries are removed before serving.

Chilies—Chilies are members of the capsicum family of peppers native to South America. There are many varieties, ranging greatly in size and in spiciness from mild sweet green peppers to extremely hot chili peppers. Chilies vary in color from green to yellow to orange to red as they vine ripen. Vine peppers that give us ground black pepper are not from the capsicum family. Common chili peppers include the jalapeño used in Mexican cooking, and long, slim, green chili peppers used in Indian cooking.
Hot chilies are readily available year-round in most North American communities. Check Asian and Spanish food stores if the local grocery store does not carry them. It is also easy to grow your own and chop and freeze or dry a winter supply. Frozen peppers maintain their flavors, but lose much of their crispness. Chilies keep well in the refrigerator, stored in a paper bag. Since some chilies are extremely hot, handle them with respect. Generally, the smaller the chili, the hotter it is. Most of the heat is in the seeds and membranes. You can carefully remove them before use. Protect hands with plastic gloves, and avoid touching fingers to eyes or mouth while washing and chopping hot chilies. Dried whole chili

peppers are generally not as hot as fresh ones. Ground red pepper (cayenne) or Tabasco pepper sauce can be substituted for fresh chilies.

Cilantro—The pungent leaves of this hardy annual are used in Latin American, Asian, and Middle Eastern cooking. If it is not available in a local supermarket, check Spanish and Asian food stores. Or buy seeds and grow your own. The plants are similar to parsley. Cilantro is also called Chinese parsley or fresh coriander.

Coconut milk—*See* p. 280

Coriander—In this book coriander refers to ground coriander, readily available on spice shelves. Coriander seeds are used in curries, pickling, and sausage making. *See also* Cilantro

Fenugreek—The fenugreek seed is used in curries, North African cooking, and some Mediterranean cuisine.

Feta cheese—This Greek cheese made of goat milk has a strong, salty flavor and crumbly consistency. It is most likely found in the supermarket delicatessen.

Fish sauce—Made from salted fish, this watery brown sauce, also called *patis*, is to Vietnamese and Thai cooking what soy sauce is to Chinese cuisine. Purchase in Asian food stores. *See also* Seasoned Fish Sauce, p. 282

Garlic—Common in cooking on every continent, the bulb of the garlic plant consists of a number of wedge-shaped cloves. When shopping, look for firm cloves without discolored spots. To use, peel away outer papery skin, remove discolored spots, and crush or mince. The broad, flat side of a wooden handle on a kitchen knife works well for crushing. Garlic keeps indefinitely in a tightly closed container in the freezer. Separate cloves before freezing for easy access. Peel and mince while still frozen. Powdered garlic can be substituted for garlic cloves in some dishes.

Garam masala—This Indian spice mixture is available in spice and Asian food stores. *See* p. 289

Ginger root—Ginger gives a unique flavor to Asian dishes and a spicy bite to cold and hot beverages from a number of continents. Look for smooth outer skins; ginger wrinkles and roughens with age. Peeling before grating is not usually necessary. Keeps four to six weeks in refrigerator in brown paper bag. Or grate or thinly slice, cover tightly, and freeze. Ground ginger can be substituted for ginger root in some recipes, but when possible use fresh ginger root for truest and best flavor.

Ghee—This clarified (purified) butter is used in Indian cooking. Purchase in Asian food stores.

Cooking oil generally can be substituted for all but the fanciest feast dishes.

Groundnuts—The traditional African name for peanuts is groundnuts. African and some Asian recipes commonly use ground raw and roasted peanuts in soups, sauces, meat, and vegetable dishes. They can be stored in the freezer; frozen peanuts grind in the blender more easily than at room temperature when oil may gum the blades. Chunky peanut butter is a common substitute for freshly ground peanuts, although some of the unique flavor is lost.

Laos—This member of the ginger family is also called galangal, galangale, galanga, or galingale. It is used in Indonesian cooking and found in some Asian food stores.

Lemon grass—Also called citronella, this common tropical grass is used in parts of Asia, Africa, and Latin America. It has the strong taste and smell of lemon and can be replaced by lemon peel, cut in thin strips or grated. Available fresh and dried in Asian food stores.

Lentils—Lentils, like beans and peas, are legumes, but they require less cooking time. There are many varieties widely used in Middle Eastern and South Asian cooking. Brown lentils are most common. Red (orange) lentils make attractive, bright-colored stews, soups, and curries.

15

Masa harina—Commonly labeled with the Spanish name, this tortilla flour is made of finely ground corn that has been treated with lime water. It can be used interchangeably with white cornmeal in some recipes. Available in Spanish food stores and with other flours in some supermarkets.

Mushrooms, specialty—Dried Chinese mushrooms are fragrant mushrooms available in Asian stores. Soak before using; once soaked they have a chewy, firm texture. Shiitake mushrooms, available dried, fresh, and canned in Asian stores, are a similar fragrant mushroom used in Japanese cooking. Dried fungus, used throughout Asia, is also called cloud ear fungus and wood ears. It has little aroma or taste and takes on the flavors of other ingredients. Dried mushrooms will keep indefinitely if stored in closed container in cool place. Substitute other varieties of mushrooms if these are unavailable.

Oyster sauce—This Cantonese-style seasoning, packaged under many brand names, is available in Asian food stores and specialty aisles. Refrigerate.

Pepper—We use *pepper* to refer to ground black pepper. Ground red pepper is also known as cayenne or red chili powder. *See also* Chilies

Phyllo—This extremely thin dough produces a flaky pastry when baked. It is used in Greek and other Mediterranean cooking. Sold in Greek food stores and specialty aisles of many grocery stores. Also called filo or fillo dough.

Pine nuts—Also called pignolias or *piñon*, these tender seeds from pine trees are used in Mediterranean cooking and by Native American groups in the U.S. Southwest. Look for pine nuts on specialty shelves with Italian, Greek, or Spanish items. May substitute almonds.

Plantain—This large, hard, green member of the banana family is common in West Indian, Latin American, and African cooking. The green fruit is fried or boiled and eaten as a vegetable. Ripe plantains, which turn black, are fried and used as a snack food or vegetable, or cooked in a variety of dessert dishes.

Red oil—Sometimes called hot oil or pepper oil, this fiery combination of sesame oil and red pepper is used in Asian cooking. Available in specialty aisles. To make your own add 1 T. ground red pepper (15 ml) and 1 t. sesame oil (5 ml) to 1/4 c. heated vegetable oil (50 ml).

Rice noodles—Also called rice vermicelli or rice sticks, these are very fine rice flour noodles sold in Asian food stores and many supermarkets. They cook much more quickly than noodles made from wheat flour.

Rice paper—Vietnamese Spring Rolls (p. 264) are wrapped in this paper. Sold frozen or refrigerated in Asian food stores. If not available, substitute Chinese spring roll paper.

Sesame—Sesame products include sesame seeds, oil, paste, and butter. Sesame seeds and oil are readily available in supermarket specialty aisles. The oil is an important flavoring in Chinese cooking. Sesame paste, a rough, crushed seed mixture commonly called tahini, and sesame butter, a more finely ground paste, are used in Middle Eastern dishes. In many recipes the two can be interchanged. Look for these ingredients in Greek or Asian food stores or specialty stores.

Teff—This ancient grain of Ethiopia is a member of the millet family and reportedly the smallest grain in the world. It is ground into a fine dark flour and used in Ethiopian Injera (p. 47). Look for teff in health food and specialty stores.

Tempeh—The flavor and texture of this fermented soybean product, commonly used in Indonesian cooking, are distinct from tofu, another soy product available in many grocery stores. Look for tempeh in health food and Asian food stores.

Wild rice—*See p. 142*

**... extending
the table**

David Merchant: Laos

As I was growing up, Sunday was a day when my family put an extra board in the dining room table. My father was a pastor in a remote village on the Michigan shore of Lake Superior. My mother routinely prepared extra food, sometimes for invited guests, other times for unexpected visitors we would invite home from church.

Sunday dinner, as we called it, was the best meal of the week. Mother fixed her finest foods, and my father, able to relax with the sermon delivered, livened the table conversation with his stories. The visitors who came to our table—some from next door, some from around the globe—brought their own stories, pushing back the boundaries of our small world.

Years later I traveled to Honduras as a college student in an international study service program. There I found myself in the home of another pastor in another small village. This time the table was turned. I was the guest, and the hospitality I received was of a variety I had never before encountered.

Gonzalo and Lilian Alemán lived with their six children in a small, two-bedroom house. For seven weeks they gave me one of their three beds, all to myself. Doña Lilian had neither a kitchen sink nor indoor plumbing, no counter space, and only a two-burner gas stove. Her table was not large enough and she did not have enough dishes to feed the entire family at one time. But she graciously served food to any who stopped by at mealtime. Amid their unending routine of household tasks, work at a *cacao* plantation, and church responsibilities, Lilian and Gonzalo patiently answered my questions, introduced me to neighbors, and told me about their dreams and struggles.

I thought I knew what it meant to be hospitable and generous before I went to Honduras, but the Alemán family taught me much more. To learn from them required the uncomfortable task of simply being a guest and receiving their sacrificial gifts.

Two tables. One in a setting of plenty, the other in a setting of poverty. At one I learned to give, at the other I learned to receive. At both I learned that taking time to share the stories of our lives is as essential as sharing food and shelter.

—jhs

1

●●●●●●●●●●●●●●●●●●●●●●●●●

Extending the Table

In 1976, prompted by what came to be called the world food crisis, Doris Janzen Longacre compiled the *More-with-Less Cookbook*. Her narrative and recipes invited North Americans to take a look at their connections to world hunger and to explore alternative patterns of eating. She challenged readers to reduce high levels of consumption and share the abundant resources of North America with hungry people in other parts of the world.

Doris knew that genuine sharing is two-way and that material goods are not the only form of wealth to be shared. In a sequel, *Living More with Less*, she invited readers to "learn from the world community" about patterns of living that respect the environment and nurture personal relationships.

Learning from others, especially people we do not know, is often difficult. We find it easier to give than to receive, to teach than to learn. This changes, however, as we enter the lives of others and come to know them well enough to see their strengths and weaknesses, their needs, and the wealth they have to offer.

When Mary Yoder Holsopple went to Uganda to work in rural community development, she was prepared to try some new flavors. She did not realize, however, that she would return home with a whole new understanding of generosity, hospitality, and the meaning of food within a community.

> One of the things I enjoyed most about Uganda was the opportunity to walk on meandering paths through gardens, up and down hills, and along streams. Walking was almost synonymous with conversing because invariably I would meet someone along the path or at work in their garden and we would talk.
> One afternoon I came across my friend Ruth, busy pulling weeds. After chatting a while, she took me to one corner of her garden to see what she had grown. She was excited because she had planted eggplant for the first time and

they were just beginning to bear; two lovely fruits dangled
on the stem.

Later that evening two unexpected visitors arrived to spend
the night in my home. Word soon spread that we had
guests, and before long Ruth appeared at the kitchen
door. In her hands were the two eggplants. She gave them
to me, saying, "Please prepare these for your friends
tonight."

I wanted to say, "No! No! You must keep your eggplant. We
have plenty of food, and you have so little." But I could not
do that. I could not deny Ruth the opportunity to give of
her literal firstfruits. She was giving so joyously.

So I accepted the eggplants with much gratitude, a tear in my
eye, and a new humbleness, for once again a Ugandan had
taught me a lesson of generosity.

Stories of people like Ruth are not sensational enough to make
the evening news. They are frequently lost behind pictures of poverty
and stories of crisis. Yet we have much to learn from them.

Fifteen years after the *More-with-Less Cookbook* was first
published, it is important to note changes and trends in North
American eating patterns. Nutrition consciousness is at an all-time
high. Words like sodium, cholesterol, saturated fat, and fiber—once
relegated to the fine-print section of food packaging—are now
common vocabulary.

The number of people involved in food production is at an
all-time low. Only 2 percent of the U.S. population over age 18 owns
agricultural land,[1] and only 4 percent of Canadians are classified as
rural.[2] People are busier, demanding convenient, no-fuss food, and
eating more of it away from home.[3]

Yet in 1987 North Americans spent less than 15 percent of
personal disposable income on food. By comparison, food
expenditures accounted for approximately 35 percent of disposable
income in Thailand and 52 percent in the Philippines.[4]

The subtle outcome of these trends has been a diminishing
respect for food among people with greatest access to it. By reducing
food to good, bad, fast, and affordable, people lose sight of the fact
that food is first of all sacred—a precious gift of the earth to be
enjoyed with others and shared by all.

The intention of this book is to take us to the tables of people
for whom food is the staff of life. This collection of recipes and
stories invites us to sit with people we have never met, taste the
flavors of their food, feel the warmth of their friendship, and learn
from their experiences.

If this feels somewhat strange and uncomfortable, the example of Jesus can encourage and guide us. We may remember him best as the host who multiplied a few loaves and fish to feed a hungry crowd. But receiving food, water, and blessing from others was also important in his ministry.

The Jesus of Luke's Gospel "always enters upon the scene as a guest in need of hospitality. He has nowhere to lay his head (9:58), unless a kind host obliges," noted John Koenig, author of *New Testament Hospitality*. "But on another level this man without a home is obviously the supreme host, the welcomer par excellence to God's kingdom."⁵

Ted Koopmans: Indonesia

Mark Beach: Soviet Armenia

I believe the experience of preparing new foods and meeting people through stories can broaden our understanding of other people and their problems and of our own selves. That is why this is more than a recipe book.

We did not glean recipes from a refined list of the world's best dishes. These are recipes that people learned to eat as they lived, worked, and grew to know others in settings as diverse as the winding paths of Uganda, the mountains of Appalachia, a rice table in Indonesia, and an international center in London. Since each recipe represents a relationship, we must share the stories and friendships that first gave flavor to the foods.

Many of the recipes and stories were contributed by well-educated, financially secure people such as Mary Yoder Holsopple. They crossed a cultural boundary, intending to transfer some of their knowledge, skills, or resources for the betterment of a "less developed" or "needy" community.

In most cases, however, they soon found themselves on the receiving end. Their new friends and hosts did not let limited material resources and educational opportunities keep them from sharing liberally of themselves and their possessions. In conversations, through proverbs, and by example, they taught lessons about hospitality, generosity, and being thankful in the midst of poverty; about living in community, forgiving, and celebrating in the midst of uncertainty.

Generosity and poverty, celebration and uncertainty. For people accustomed to plenty, these may seem like mismatched pairs. But Jesus also preached these paradoxes. His example of generosity was a poor widow giving away her last few cents (Mark 12:41-44). His recipe for security was to lose one's life for others (Matthew 16:25).

Many of the stories told here are cause for celebration, but some tell the harsh reality of trying to make ends meet when resources are scarce. Some are faith renewing, telling of the amazing resilience of the human spirit, while others evoke despair. The stories and recipes are interspersed to acquaint you with people and places as you cook. Share a story during your meal with family or guests.

Telling children stories and involving them in food preparation are good ways to introduce them to new foods. On a number of occasions, I was not sure how our five-year-old son would react to some of the recipes I was testing. A simple introduction was enough to pique his curiosity and whet his appetite: "This is Japanese food that [our friend] J. J. ate when he lived in Japan," or "This is the kind of food that Jabulani and Mazoe [former neighbors from South Africa] ate before they came to the United States."

In their own way, the recipes also tell stories. They reflect the pace of life, the important seasons and celebrations, and the resources available in the settings where the recipes originated.

Many of the recipes in their original form were extremely time consuming to prepare. Food preparation is still the main activity for a large sector of the world's women. Using only a few basic utensils and primarily unprocessed foods, they prepare at home most or all of the food their families eat.

None of the recipes came with instructions for preparing the dish in a microwave oven. In fact, far more recipes called for frying than for baking. For many families in the world, a one- or two-burner hot plate is a luxury; a frypan or black cooking pot cradled over an outdoor three-stone fire is more common.

The recipes also tell a story about health. In much of the affluent world today—where people eat more than they need, ride more than they walk, and where stress levels are high—fat and cholesterol are a curse. They contribute to heart disease, a leading cause of death.

In contrast, fat and oil still represent health and prosperity in less-affluent areas of the world. They are welcome flavoring agents and energy-producing components for people whose feet are their primary means of transportation, whose work involves vigorous physical labor, and whose meager incomes afford meat and other rich foods only on rare occasions. For them, a glistening ring of floating oil indicates the richness of a stew.

We have adapted some recipes, especially reducing the fat and adding some timesaving features, but our "hosts" invite us to consider their eating patterns. Perhaps we will regain an appreciation for the "oil of gladness" (Psalm 45:7) when we moderate our daily diet and reserve richer foods for special times of celebration. Our respect for what nourishes us can deepen as we occasionally devote extra time to preparing food, thinking about where it has come from and those who have produced it, and then enjoying it in the company of others.

Those who contributed would caution us not to follow their recipes too meticulously. Cookbooks are a mystery to many of the world's finest cooks, who add ingredients to the pot until "it looks and tastes right." A number of recipes in this collection came with qualifiers like "I watched someone prepare this dish, and I have tried to estimate the handfuls and pinches. . . ."

Duplicating the flavors of any region is difficult since each cook has personal taste preferences and favorite preparation methods. We have diligently tested each recipe, revising some to make them more adaptable to North American kitchens and tables. Yet we encourage you to cook from this book following the advice of Milkah Terman, a Nigerian visitor to the United States. She submitted a recipe with precise measurements, but explained, "We don't use all the measurement items you use here. We just approximate it." Then she quoted a Hausa-language proverb from her country: "*Da gwadelawa ake san na kwarai* (trials make perfect)."

Take liberties as you cook, allow the stories to touch you as you read, and joyfully extend the table as you eat.

— *Notes*

1. Gene Wunderlich, "The Evolution of Land Ownership," *Our American Land: 1987 Yearbook of Agriculture*, ed. William Whyte (Washington, D.C.: U.S. Government Printing Office, 1987), p. 125.

2. Statistics Canada, Ottawa, Ontario.

3. Ewen M. Wilson, "Marketing Challenges in a Dynamic World," *Marketing U.S. Agriculture: 1988 Yearbook of Agriculture*, ed. Deborah Takiff Smith (Washington, D.C.: U.S. Government Printing Office, 1988), p. 3.

4. Statistics Canada, cited in *Food Market Commentary*, July 1989; and World Agricultural Trends and Indicators 1970-1988 (Economic Research Service, USDA, *Statistical Bulletin No. 781*, July 1989).

5. John Koenig, *New Testament Hospitality: Partnership with Strangers as Promise and Mission* (Philadelphia: Fortress Press, 1974), p. 90.

... beverages

Dave Klassen: Nigeria

About 4:30 one afternoon we arrived unannounced at Abraham and Nebyat's home. Abraham promptly found some chairs and we sat under the *racuba*, a grass shelter outside their round grass hut. Nebyat fanned the charcoal fire and brought out raw coffee beans, a roasting pan, and a flask-shaped coffeepot.

We talked quietly, easily. When Nebyat finished roasting the coffee beans, she put them in a heavy wooden cup. With her baby tenaciously nursing at her breast, she pounded the beans with an iron rod until they were ground. Putting the grounds in water in the pot on the fire, she boiled them three times and served us each a tiny porcelain cupful.

As we drank two, three, eventually four of these little cups, each one-fourth filled with sugar, we talked of refugee resettlement. Abraham dreamed of leaving war-torn Sudan and going to the United States, but knew his chances were small. We asked what he heard from his friends who had gone to the United States, what they noticed as most different from Africa. He thought for a minute, then answered simply, "Time is golden."

Time in North America and other industrialized societies is as valuable as gold. People there try not to waste it, plan how best to use and manage it, convert it into money, results, and knowledge. They count it and use it for what seems most important. But like money, they never seem to have enough of it.

In rural Sudan time is not golden. It is as plentiful as sheep and goats. People treat it as casually as trees, hacked down and not replaced, as if the supply of both were infinite.

Progress and development require people to treat time as a valuable resource. As they master time, they progress. But when time becomes a commodity and they worry about not having enough, it then masters them.

In much of Africa, time still grows wild like the lilies of the field.

—Janice Armstrong and Ray Downing, Musoma, Tanzania

During the first three years we lived in Lesotho, in southern Africa, we were disturbed by children who came to our door on Christmas Eve, chanting, "Give me Christmas!" Since we lived and taught in a vocational school compound, we thought they were singling us out as white people who had a long-standing reputation of giving handouts.

When we moved to a rural village, we found the entire community taking part in this activity. All had prepared extra food and were gladly sharing it with those who came to their door. "Give me Christmas" was not an expression of begging, but of identity with the clan. People who belonged to one another had the right and the confidence to ask for food or assistance. The children at our door had not singled us out as white people, but had treated us as members of their community.

Sometime later I was carrying water home from a spring when I met two women I had seen, but never personally met. They stopped me, saying, as they would to any member of their community, "Give us water."

I was elated. I felt like I belonged, as though I were in the Bible. All at once I knew how the Samaritan woman, rejected by her community, felt when Jesus asked her for water. You only ask for something of those to whom you belong. Jesus was telling the Samaritan woman she belonged to his group. These women didn't know me, but they were saying that I was part of them.

—Brenda Hostetler Meyer, Millersburg, Indiana

2

• •

An Invitation to Friendship

will never forget the morning I was offered, and drank,
six large glasses of satiating corn drinks, all within an hour. It was one
of my first initiations into Nicaraguan hospitality, occurring just
weeks after my husband and I arrived as service volunteers.

José Durán, a pastor and community development worker,
invited us to spend a weekend in the rural community where he and
his family lived. It turned out to be a weekend of much walking. He
took us to meet his parents and several brothers who lived in
neighboring communities, all several kilometers apart.

On Saturday morning José led us up a steep hill to a village
named Zonzapote. As soon as we reached the top and momentarily
caught our breath, he led us down a path on the other side of the hill
to show us the enclosed well and clothes washing-bathing area that
the community had built.

In an arid region, this was a prized source of water, even if it did
not reach directly to people's homes. On our return ascent to
Zonzapote, we huffed and puffed alongside teenage girls effortlessly
carrying three- and five-gallon tins of water on their heads—water
that would soon help quench our thirst.

José took us from home to home, introducing us to various
members of the community. People welcomed us warmly, offering us
the one or two chairs or benches that they had. Within minutes we
had glasses of *chicha* or *pinolillo* in our hands to drink as we conversed.
Although the visits were brief, no host ever asked if we cared for
something to drink; each simply presented the gift of friendship.

I soon learned that my experience in Zonzapote was not unique.
Even in the busy capital city where we lived, many people kept a
ready bucket of homemade fruit or grain drink in the refrigerator, or
in a shaded spot if they did not have a refrigerator. People welcomed
visitors and always served a drink, even to the unexpected caller.

Some of the drinks tasted strange to me at first—sweet, grainy,
and heavy. Before long I realized that people consumed little sugar in
other forms, and the heaviness of a grain drink was added
nourishment for some who might not always have an adequate diet.
Over time I began to find these drinks satisfying, both for their full
flavors and for the way they drew me into the circle of people's lives.

In many parts of the world, serving a beverage is synonymous with extending friendship. Be it a corn drink in Latin America, a cup of tea in Asia, or a ginger drink in Africa, a beverage is an invitation to stay awhile, to sit and refresh one's body, to share the recent events of one's life.

Cynthia Peacock of Calcutta, India, says that in Indian culture, offering a cup of tea is a symbol of accepting and identifying with another person. Hospitality offers us the opportunity to "deepen and broaden our insight in our relationships to our fellow human beings," writes Henri Nouwen. In many Bible stories, "guests are carrying precious gifts with them, which they are eager to reveal to a receptive host."[1]

Shehzad Noorani: Bangladesh

Often in these accounts, however, the guest arrived unexpectedly. Abraham did not send an invitation to the three strangers who brought the news that he and Sarah would have a son (Genesis 18:1-15). The widow of Zarephath had an almost empty larder when the prophet Elijah arrived. Extending hospitality to him resulted in sufficiency and life for her son (1 Kings 17:9-24). Zacchaeus was merely trying to climb into viewing and listening range of the teacher when Jesus suddenly told him that he wanted to go to his house (Luke 19:1-10). And what a life-changing visit that was!

Do we find the unexpected caller a welcome guest or a frustrating interruption? The following recipes and stories invite us to make more time for giving and receiving the precious gift of friendship. We deprive ourselves and others if we feel we must have the house free of clutter and our desks cleared of urgent business before we entertain guests. A simple beverage and an attentive ear will honor a stranger or a friend.

....

**Lord, today you made us known to friends
we did not know,
And you have given us seats in homes
which are not our own.
You have brought the distant near,
and made a brother of a stranger.
We thank you, Lord; your love be praised.**

—Mozambique prayer[2]

t here is no joy in eating alone.

—The Buddha, 543 B.C.

Stan Reedy: Vietnam

Asha's Ginger Tea (Kenya)

Chai Cha Tangawizi
(chai chah
tahn-gah-WEE-zee)

This is a rich tea with a sting. Testers report that using fresh ginger and black tea leaves makes it something out of the ordinary.

• Options:
Substitute 4 tea bags for black tea leaves.
•
Substitute 1 T. ground ginger (15 ml) for ginger root.

Boil:
2 c. water (500 ml)
Add:
1 T. ginger root, diced (15 ml)
4 t. sugar (20 ml)
Simmer 10 minutes (or longer, for more flavor).
Add:
5 t. black tea leaves (25 ml)
Simmer 3-5 minutes, stirring as needed.
Add:
2 c. milk (500 ml)
Heat until very hot, but do not boil. Strain to remove ginger and tea.

—*Asha Juma, Migori, Kenya; and Sylvia L. Hess, Bausman, Pennsylvania*

The path leading to Asha's mud house was lined with zinnias and marigolds. She regularly welcomed me and offered a chair for me to sit and watch as she made ginger tea and meat-filled pastries called *sambuzas.*

Living in a community where jobs and food were in short supply, Asha supported herself, her daughter, and two nieces. She tended a cornfield, wove baskets and mats to sell at market, and went to town each day at noon to sell her *sambuzas.* Occasionally she traveled to northern Kenya to obtain ginger that she dried for sale in the Migori market.

As she worked we talked of food, our families, and God. A devout Muslim, Asha was surprised to learn of our shared belief in the Torah—the first five books of the Bible. After talking about how we both trace our faith history to Abraham, whom God called to be a blessing for all peoples, we agreed that "our God is one."

—*Sylvia L. Hess, Bausman, Pennsylvania*

*W*ar iyo la cuno, baa lagu nool yahay.
Communication and food are the things that one lives by.

—*Somali proverb*

• •

Spiced Tea (Nepal)

Serves 6

Chiah
(chee-ah)

Many variations of this sweet tea are served in India, Bangladesh, Nepal, and parts of Africa. A perfect ending to curry meals.

Steep:
  3 T. black tea leaves (45 ml) or 3 tea bags
  5 c. boiling water (1.3 L)
Add:
  1 1/4 c. milk, heated (300 ml)
  1/3-2/3 c. sugar (75-150 ml)
  4 whole cloves
  2-3 cardamom pods, cracked open, or 1/2 t. ground cardamom (2 ml)
  1 cinnamon stick
Simmer 10 minutes to blend flavors.
Strain and serve hot.

—*Selma Unruh, North Newton, Kansas*

....

T ea is the national drink in Somalia. Each day almost every household prepares a thermos or two of hot, spicy tea for family members to drink during the day or to serve to guests who drop by. It is considered poor manners not to offer visitors something to drink, and tea is most frequently served, often with zamboosies (Samosas, p. 270).

• •

Ginger Tea (Dominican Republic)

Serves 4

Té de Genjibre
(TAY day hayn-HEE-vray)

This tea, made with double the ginger in the Dominican Republic, is reportedly good for colds and stuffy heads. Dominican hosts serve it to guests who visit on cool evenings.

• *Option:*
For more zing, increase ginger root to 2-inch piece (5-cm).

Combine in saucepan:
  1 qt. water (1 L)
  1-inch-square piece ginger root, sliced (2.5-cm)
  4 whole allspice or 1/4 t. ground allspice (1 ml)
Bring to a boil. Simmer 30 minutes.
Add:
  approx. 1/4 c. brown sugar (50 ml)
Serve hot. Sip slowly.

—*Carmen Martinez, Juan Barón, Dominican Republic; and Nelson Weber, Reading, Pennsylvania*

Turkish Coffee
(Middle East)

Ahweh
(AH-hway)

Turkish coffee, common
throughout the Middle East,
is usually served very sweet.
The happier the occasion, the
sweeter the coffee. Bitter
coffee is served at funerals.
Many coffee grinders in
grocery stores and specialty
shops have a Turkish setting
that pulverizes coffee. One
contributor recommends
using French roast coffee.

Measure into saucepan with pouring spout:
   6 demitasse cups water
   scant 6 T. pulverized coffee (90 ml)
   scant 6 T. sugar (90 ml) (or less to taste)
   2 cardamom pods or pinch of ground
      cardamom (optional)
Bring to a boil. As foam comes up, remove saucepan from
heat. Repeat process until coffee has boiled three times.
Rinse demitasse cups in hot water. Put a teaspoon of foam
in each cup. Pour coffee and serve hot. Allow coffee to
settle a bit before sipping it. Do not stir. Sip only off the top
to avoid the coffee sediment. For best results, do not make
more than 6 small cups at a time.

—*Yehuda Ben Yehuda, Yemen; and Mary Berkshire Stueben, Seattle,*
   Washington
—*Alice W. Lapp, Akron, Pennsylvania*

Turkish coffee is the drink of preference in the Old City of Jerusalem. Throughout the marketplace and in most food shops, merchants sell special small coffeepots to brew the coffee. Kitchen stove tops come with a special burner sized for these small pots.

When entertaining guests at home, the host serves Turkish coffee at the close of a meal. In the marketplace shopkeepers offer coffee to customers considering a purchase. The viewing and haggling over price may take a while, so shopkeepers flag down young boys who serve as runners through the marketplace. They run and fetch a tray of Turkish coffee. Whether or not they successfully make a sale, it is the shopkeepers' honor to treat the customers with hospitality.

*I*n the remote Ethiopian village of Bedeno, women
prepare fresh-ground, aromatic coffee without the
luxury of automatic grinders and coffee makers.
Inside a simple, thatched-roof home with an earthen
floor, a hostess works over the fire in the center of the
room as her guests visit and look on. She begins by
roasting coffee beans in a large pan shaped like a
hubcap. Next she grinds the roasted beans with a
mortar and pestle. After boiling and brewing the
coffee, she serves each guest. The room is filled with
rich aroma and the warmth of conversation.

—*Miriam Housman, Lancaster, Pennsylvania*

In Turkey it is a great virtue to be known as someone who loves company and has a lot of it. Although there are many ways to visit in a Turkish home, often it is the guests who inform the host that they will be coming at a set time.

When guests arrive, the host greets them at the door, where they remove their shoes. They are given a pair of slippers, ushered into the guest sitting room, and seated. The host kisses each guest on both cheeks and sprinkles lemon cologne on their hands before asking about the health, jobs, schooling, and activities of their family.

After these formal greetings, the host asks if they like coffee with or without sugar. She soon brings small cups of strong Turkish coffee and offers cigarettes and chocolates.

When conversation flows freely and everyone has finished the coffee, the host takes the empty cups to the kitchen and prepares tea—fresh black tea grown along the Black Sea. The tea must simmer 17 minutes and is always made fresh when a guest arrives. One may serve warmed-up tea to family, but only fresh tea to guests.

Tea is served in clear tea glasses along with sweet and salty pastries. The host quickly refills each emptied cup until the guests insist that they absolutely cannot drink any more.

After tea, women visit and do needlework; men watch television and discuss the news, politics, and religion. When the guests first speak of leaving, the host insists that it is still early. But when they offer a credible explanation of why they must leave, the host hurries to the kitchen and brings individual plates of fresh fruit for everyone.

When the guests insist that they have eaten enough, the host brings damp washcloths, and then arranges their shoes with toes pointed toward the door. They part with kisses, handshakes, and an exchange of invitations for future visits.

—Jewel Showalter, Irwin, Ohio

Cornmeal Cocoa Beverage (Nicaragua)

Pinolillo
(pee-noh-LEE-yoh)

Little known in North America, grain beverages are common in many countries of Latin America and Africa. Some are prepared by cooking the grain. Others, like Pinolillo, are made with raw or roasted grains. Nicaraguans traditionally make Pinolillo by roasting whole corn kernels and cacao beans, then grinding them finely. To authentically drink Pinolillo, one must regularly twirl the glass to keep the cornmeal suspended.

• •

Makes 5 cups (1.3 L)

In heavy frypan, toast until light brown, 3-5 minutes:
   1 c. white cornmeal or *masa harina* (250 ml)
Transfer toasted cornmeal to pitcher.
Add:
   2 T. cocoa (30 ml)
   1/3 c. sugar (75 ml)
   1/4 t. ground cinnamon (1 ml)
   dash of ground cloves
   5 c. water (1.3 L)
Beat until cornmeal and cocoa are well mixed. Chill. Stir before serving.

   • *Option:*
Although Pinolillo is a cold, unstrained drink in Nicaragua, it also makes a lovely hot drink, similar to hot chocolate. Simply strain and heat.

—Angela Silva, Managua, Nicaragua

33

Cinnamon Coffee (Mexico)

(ts)

Serves 4

Café con Canela
(cah-FAY kohn cah-NAY-lah)

This dressed-up coffee gives a nice final touch to a Mexican meal. Serve on any cool evening.

Before brewing coffee, place in coffeepot:
1 cinnamon stick
3 T. sugar (45 ml)
Brew 4 c. medium to strong coffee (1 L) as usual. Keep hot and allow to steep 10 minutes before serving.

• *Options:*
May omit sugar, allowing each person to sweeten as desired.
•
Replace cinnamon with 2 cardamom pods, cracked open, or 1/4 t. ground cardamom (1 ml).

—*Author's recipe*

Hot Creamy Fruit Punch (Mexico)

Serves 8-10

Atole de Fruta
(ah-TOH-lay day FROO-tah)

Atoles are hot drinks traditionally offered during the Mexican Christmas posadas, when people go from house to house in remembrance of Mary and Joseph's search for a birthplace for Jesus. They are a warm gesture of hospitality on any chilly night.

• *Option:*
Substitute 1 c. strawberry jam (250 ml) for fresh fruit; decrease sugar to 1/2 c. (125 ml).

Combine in large saucepan:
2 T. cornstarch (30 ml)
2 c. water (500 ml)
Heat until mixture begins to thicken.
Add:
1 qt. milk (1 L)
2/3 c. sugar (150 ml)
Remove from heat and set aside.
Puree in blender:
1 1/2 lb. fruit (750 g) (strawberries, mangoes, peaches, raspberries, or blackberries)
Strain.
Return milk mixture to heat and add:
pureed fruit
1 c. cream or evaporated skim milk (250 ml)
1 t. vanilla (5 ml)
food coloring to match fruit (optional)
Bring to a boil over medium heat, stirring constantly.
Serve warm.

• *Variation:*
For a hot chocolate atole, omit fruit. Add 2 squares unsweetened chocolate or 6 T. cocoa (90 ml), 1 t. ground cinnamon (5 ml), and 1/2 t. ground nutmeg (2 ml).

—*Maria Teresa Nava de Sierra and Celine Vatterott Woznica, Oaxaca, Mexico*

● ●

Spicy Cinnamon Cup (Israel)

Serves 4

Finjan Erfeh
(fin-juhn EHR-fuh)

Finjan Erfeh is a festive drink traditionally served by Nazareth's Arab families to visitors who come to see a new baby.

Boil until dark colored:
 1 qt. water (1 L)
 1 T. whole anise seeds (15 ml)
 1-inch piece ginger root, crushed (2.5-cm)
 2 whole cloves
 2 cinnamon sticks
Strain and add:
 2-4 t. sugar (10-20 ml)
Place in each cup:
 walnut or almond, shelled
Pour hot tea over nuts and serve.

—*Badia Howa, Nazareth, Israel; and Margaret Dyck, St. Catharines, Ontario*

....

A very full taxi transported us over the winding road from Jerusalem to Hebron one evening. The brilliant starlight, with no competition from streetlights, heightened our anticipation of a visit with Palestinian friends.

Upon arrival our mutual greetings communicated a message of welcome, even though we could not understand each other's language. Our hosts seated us on the floor around a *tubuk*, a round woven mat, piled high with rice and chicken, garnished with pine nuts, and accompanied by bowls of gravy, yogurt, and pita bread. The aroma was wonderfully inviting.

As soon as I sat down, a daughter who was engaged to be married came and took my hand,

motioning me to stand up. With ample instructions and comments, she insisted that I put on her new full-length wedding dress. She helped me slip on the beautiful black satin dress with intricate, colorful embroidery on the bodice, down the sides, and around the hemline. Proudly she stood back and admired me, clasping her hands together with satisfaction and delight.

After I was seated again, the same daughter came and spread towels across our laps. I found it awkward to eat rice, chicken, and pita bread dipped in gravy and yogurt with my fingers as was customary, fearing that some might spill on the gorgeous dress. So I pulled the towel up and tucked it under my chin into the dress. Seeing what I had done, the young woman came and

pulled it out, placing it across my lap. Her reprimand clearly meant I was covering up the beautifully embroidered bodice.

When we stepped back out into the starlit night following a wonderful meal and translator-assisted visit, the *tubuk*, woven by the grandmother, lay in my arms. Our hosts had made us feel like true friends, members of their family. In their presence they honored me with the wedding dress, and as we departed they sent a part of themselves, their eating mat, with us.

—*Naomi K. Lederach, Mt. Gretna, Pennsylvania*

Country Compote (Poland)

(ts)　M　　　　　　　　　*Makes 2 qt. (2 L)*

**Kompot
(KOM-poht)**

Poles serve this beverage with dessert. Fruit pieces are eaten with a spoon. Each cook varies the amount of liquid and sugar; some Kompots are thick and very sweet, others are mostly juice.

Combine in saucepan:
> **2 c. fresh, canned, or frozen fruit, cut in cherry-sized pieces (500 ml) (plums, strawberries, gooseberries, red or black currants, rhubarb, cherries, apples)**
> **6 c. water and juice from canned fruit (1.5 L)**
> **1/2 c. sugar (125 ml) or to taste**

Bring to a boil, cover and simmer until fruit is soft and juice is flavorful. Serve warm in winter and chilled in summer. (If using canned fruits, do not simmer; just warm or chill.)

• *Microwave:*
Combine ingredients, reducing water by 1/2 c. (125 ml), and cook covered on high for 8-10 minutes, until fruit is tender.

—*Krystyna Król, and Eileen and Merlin Becker-Hoover, Warsaw, Poland*

Philippine Punch (Philippines)

Makes 1 1/2 gal. (6 L)

**Inumin ng Prutas
(ih-noo-MIHN nahng PROO-tahss)**

This tropical punch adds a colorful and flavorful touch to festive occasions. Make it when fruits are in season for best economy.

Mix and bring to a boil:
> **3 qt. water (3 L)**
> **3 c. sugar (750 ml)**

Add:
> **2 c. lemon or lime juice (500 ml)**
> **4 c. strawberry juice or pureed strawberries (1 L)**
> **2 c. orange juice (500 ml)**
> **4 c. pineapple juice (1 L)**
> **2 c. strong black tea (500 ml)**

Mix well. Chill before serving.

—*Norrie del Fierro and Fanny P. Miray, Nueva Vizcaya, Philippines*

On the fourth Friday of Lent, the people of Oaxaca, Mexico, celebrate the feast of the Samaritan woman. Families, friends, churches, and businesses offer fruit drinks to passersby. This "giving of water" commemorates the woman at the well, who gave water to Jesus, and in return received the water of life.

Grapefruit Drink (Somalia)

(ts)

Makes 6 cups (1.5 L)

Isbamuto
(iss-bah-MOO-toh)

Isbamuto is a favorite Somali drink in the hot season when grapefruit is plentiful and sweet. Somalis like it very sweet. They consume little sugar except in beverages; cakes and cookies, eaten only occasionally, are not very sweet. Adjust sugar and concentration of grapefruit juice to taste.

Mix:
   2 c. grapefruit juice (500 ml)
   1 qt. water (1 L)
   1/2 c. sugar (125 ml)
Serve chilled.

—Barbara Witmer, Dayton, Ohio

Grapefruit Dream (Dominican Republic)

(ts)

Serves 4

Morí Soñando
(moh-REE soh-NYAN-doh)

The unusual combination of milk and tart grapefruit makes a silky, smooth drink that is a true delight. Dominicans usually serve Morí Soñando (Spanish for: I died dreaming) in the evening. The typical naranja agria *(sour orange) is replaced by grapefruit juice in this recipe. The juice will not curdle the milk if you follow directions.*

Chill:
   1/2-2/3 c. grapefruit juice (125-150 ml)
   3 c. milk (750 ml)
Slowly add juice to milk while stirring.
Add:
   3 T. sugar (45 ml) or to taste
Serve cold.

—Carmen Martinez, Juan Barón, Dominican Republic; and Nelson
   Weber, Reading, Pennsylvania

....

𝒲hen someone stops to visit in a Dominican Republic home, the host typically offers a drink, extending the visit to at least an hour. Hot coffee or a chilled fruit drink—the preferred beverages—are never served casually. The host brings chilled drinks in glass tumblers (rarely plastic), carrying them on a tray, and provides a saucer or coaster to rest them on.

Water

Water sustains life. There is nothing quite so refreshing to the thirsty person, animal, or land as pure, sparkling water. In some parts of the world, it is available at the turn of a faucet. In many other places, water must be carried home from a spring, river, or communal well which may be located several miles away. The following reflection comes from one who has lived in both settings.

Jim King: Bangladesh

5:46 a.m. Sehonghong, Lesotho

The colors are beginning to flood the mountains as if a bucket of the most brilliant pure gold paint was tipped over from somewhere beyond them and is now dripping down the valleys. The gold seeps gently into the sky the way a drop of paint spreads on wet paper.

She loops her arm through the handle of the bucket and walks up the rise to the tap for water. Reaching the top, she sets the bucket down on the small pile of rocks placed there for that purpose.

When she turns on the tap, a trickle that swells to a single directed torrent slaps the bottom of the bucket and jumps to splash the sides with a noise that startles the morning. The song of the singing water deepens as the bucket fills.

The water level reaches the top of the bucket and she turns off the tap, grasps the handle on each side where it joins the bucket, and lifts it in a single concentrated effort onto her head. One hand supports the top of the bucket and the other steadies the bottom. She hasn't yet learned to balance the water with no help from her hands the way the women of the mountain village do.

She stands straight and walks slowly and gently,

38

. . . trying to move like the water she carries, . . . with controlled yet liquid movements, . . . knowing that what she carries is precious.

She reaches the door of the house, lowers the bucket, carries it inside, then carefully lays a towel over the top to keep out the dust. Each drop has its purpose: some for washing, some for drinking, some for cooking. The cloudy wash water will travel to the garden later in the day to nourish the vegetables.

Tomorrow she will again take the bucket and walk to the tap, and the ritual of the water will continue.

7:30 a.m. Cleveland, Ohio

She walks briskly to the stainless-steel sink in the kitchen, turns on the cold faucet with an efficient flick of the wrist, and rapidly fills a glass of water, letting some overflow the sides. She turns off the faucet and glances out the window at the cars and houses and then looks at her watch. She gulps half a glass of water, pours the other half down the drain, sets down the glass, and hurries out the door so as not to be late for work. The filling of the glass will be repeated over and over and over again.

—*Nicki Petrone, Cleveland, Ohio*

Carrot Orange Juice (Honduras)

Jugo de Zanahorria y Naranja (who-go day sah-nah-OH-reeah ee nah-RAHNG-hah)

This creative, colorful blend of vegetables and fruit is an excellent source of vitamins A and C. Such combinations are common throughout Central America and the Caribbean.

● ●

Makes 2 qt. (2 L)

Place in blender:
4-5 medium carrots, uncooked, cut in 1-inch chunks (2.5-cm)
Cover with:
3 1/2 c. water (875 ml)
Blend until pulverized. Strain if desired.
Combine:
carrot juice
4 1/2 c. orange juice (1.1 L)
2-4 T. sugar (30-60 ml) (optional)
Chill and serve. If unstrained, serve with a spoon to eat the carrot pulp.

● *Option:*
Substitute lemon or grapefruit juice for orange.

—*Linda Bonilla de Rovelo, San Pedro Sula, Honduras; and Joel and Patricia Ebersole Zwier, Santo Domingo, Dominican Republic*

*A*n onion offered by a true friend is like a whole lamb.

—*Egyptian proverb*

Tropical Fruit Shake (Latin America)

●●●●●●●●●●●●●●●●●●●●●●●●●●●●●●●●●

Serves 4-6

Batido de Fruta
(bah-TEE-doh day FROO-tah)

There are many variations of this refreshing cold drink. Names include batido, jugo, vitamina, sorbete, *and* merengada. *Older children can easily make nutritious Batido de Fruta using fruits in season. This makes a nice breakfast drink.*

Fill blender 2/3 full with any combination of fruit:

strawberries, bananas, oranges, cantaloupe, papayas, peaches, pineapple, mangoes, berries, watermelon, tomatoes, or avocados

Add water to cover (or slightly less). Whip.

Add:

several ice cubes
sugar to taste (optional)
lemon or lime juice (optional)

Whip again.

• *Variation:*
For a creamy shake, chop 1 1/2 c. fruit (375 ml) in blender. Gradually add 3 c. milk (750 ml) instead of water. Omit ice and lemon juice; add sugar to taste. Blend until frothy. Avocado shakes made this way are a favorite in Brazil.

—*Leslie Book, Managua, Nicaragua*
—*Martha Giles, Caracas, Venezuela*
—*Mary Hobe Stucky, Bogota, Colombia*
—*Goldie Kuhns, Akron, Pennsylvania*

In many parts of Latin America, a blender is one of the most sought-after and often-used household appliances. It quickly liquefies the wide variety of tropical fruits that people make into refreshing drinks on hot days. It also simplifies the task of pureeing cooked beans (see p. 162).

A blender is an economic asset. It allows homemakers to supplement their income by making large quantities of fruit drink to sell to neighbors. Those fortunate enough to have a refrigerator with a freezer may also freeze the drink in small plastic bags to sell to neighborhood children.

Nothing is wasted where resources are limited. When Honduran cooks buy fresh pineapple, they extract flavor from the peelings before discarding them. They simmer the peelings in water with a small amount of rice and several cinnamon sticks for 30 minutes. After pureeing, straining, sweetening, and chilling the mixture, they have a flavorful, full-bodied drink.

● ●

Festive Fruit Punch (Guatemala)

Serves 10

Ponche de Frutas
(POHN-chay day FROO-tahss)

Guatemalans serve this unique hot punch for special occasions like weddings, Christmas, or the New Year, when the climate is cool. It can be costly to make if you use fresh ingredients not in season or locally available. Experiment with local fruit combinations.

Boil:
  2 qt. water (2 L)
Add:
  1 medium pineapple, chopped finely or liquefied in blender
  1 papaya, not too ripe, chopped (optional)
  1 c. pitted prunes, chopped, or raisins (250 ml)
  5 apples, chopped
  1 bunch grapes
Add:
  1/2 c. sugar (125 ml)
  1/2 t. ground cinnamon (2 ml) or 4 cinnamon sticks
  1/4 t. ground cloves (1 ml) or 4 whole cloves
  pinch of salt (optional)

Boil until fruit is soft. Just before serving, add a bit of rum flavoring (optional). Serve hot with a spoon.

—*Leonor de Danila and Fanny Ellen Yoder, Guatemala City, Guatemala*

● ●

Ginger Cooler (Ivory Coast)

Makes 1 gal. (4 L)

Gnamakoudji
(nya-mah-COO-jee)

This drink originates in rural African villages where there is no refrigeration. The ginger refreshes and rehydrates on hot, humid days. People in urban areas with refrigerators make flavored ice by freezing Gnamakoudji in small plastic bags. Children bite out a corner and slowly suck the frozen drink.

Soak in water 20-30 minutes, then scrape outer peeling from:
  3 pieces of 4-inch ginger root (10-cm)
Cut ginger root into 1/2-inch pieces (1-cm).
Combine in blender:
  1 c. ginger root pieces (250 ml)
  1 c. water (250 ml)
Liquefy and pour into 1-gal. container (4-L). Repeat process until all ginger root is liquefied.
Add:
  water to make 1 gallon (4 L)
  1 1/2 c. sugar (375 ml)
  juice of 1 lemon (optional)
Refrigerate at least a half day or overnight. Before serving, strain with cheesecloth or a fine strainer. Dilute with water or adjust sugar according to taste. Serve over ice.

—*Sita, daughter of Chief Moumouni, Yocoboué, Ivory Coast; and Jeanette Krabill, Elkhart, Indiana*

41

Yogurt Mint Drink (India)

 (ts)

Makes 2 qt. (2 L)

Lassi
(LAH-see)

This cold mint beverage is a variation of a common South Asian drink, often flavored with rose water. Similar drinks are served in parts of the Middle East. Lassi is a nice accompaniment to hot, spicy foods. Children will enjoy making and drinking it as a refreshing snack. All proportions may be varied to taste.

Mix together:

1 qt. milk (1 L)
1 qt. yogurt (1 L) (p. 295)
1/2-3/4 c. sugar or combination of sugar and honey (125-175 ml)
4 t. vanilla (20 ml)

Immerse into Lassi:

6-8 fresh mint stalks (bruise leaves and tie ends of stalks together)

Let stand in refrigerator at least 5 hours to allow mint flavor to permeate the Lassi. Remove mint before serving.

• Option:
Substitute 2-3 T. dry mint (30-45 ml) in a tea ball or cheesecloth for the fresh mint.

—*Nancy Brubaker, Lancaster, Pennsylvania*

....

***A** crazy guest eats and leaves right away.*

—*Arabic proverb*

You are always with us, Lord,
You are water in the desert,
the fruit of life in the garden,
light at evening time.
In that way you are with us, Lord.

You are always with us, Lord,
You are the face reflected in the mirror,
the wine of joy at the celebration meal,
the sharing between friends.
In that way you are with us, Lord.

You are always with us, Lord.
You are the pilot in the boat,
the healer of the injured,
the parent in the home.
In that way you are with us, Lord.

—*Fr. Pierre-Etienne*[3]

....

—Notes
1. Henri J. M. Nouwen, *Reaching Out: The Three Movements of the Spiritual Life* (Garden City, N.Y.: Doubleday, 1975), p. 47.
2. From a letter the Manica regional council of the Christian Council of Mozambique presented to a visiting delegation from Mennonite Central Committee, April 1989.
3. "Nos cœurs te chantent" (71250 Cluny, France: Taïzé, 1977); in *With All God's People: The New Ecumenical Prayer Cycle*, comp. by John Carden (Geneva, Switzerland: WCC Publications, 1989), pp. 89-90.

... breads

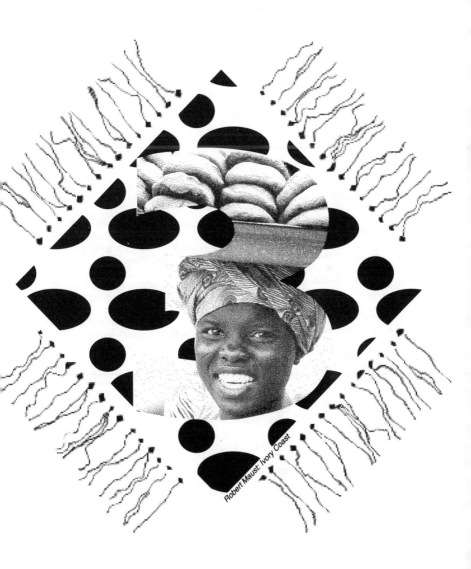

Robert Maust: Ivory Coast

With his 50-year-old son Don Chayo, 70-year-old Don Jesús spent eight days during a guerrilla offensive trapped in his sister's home in a poor barrio in the capital of El Salvador. During the first days, they lived on weak soup and small tortillas made from half-ground corn. When that was gone, they drank tea made from orange leaves.

When the two men were able to return to their rural community and talk about what had happened, they realized that they had been prepared for such an experience. "We've both known hunger in our lives," explained Chayo. "I can remember when I was a boy. Dad was away earning 25 centavos a day. Between the five of us at home, we shared one egg. So we are able to withstand hunger."

This latest experience had reinforced the men's convictions about how to use scarce resources. "It doesn't make sense to eat everything you have at lunch and then go hungry at dinner," continued Chayo. "In fact, with us, gluttony is sin because if I eat everything I have, maybe making myself sick, and then someone comes to the door asking for food, I won't have anything to give him.

"I tell my wife, 'If you're eating chicken and someone comes by asking for a tortilla, don't just give him the tortilla; give him a tortilla with a piece of chicken.' You should never hide good food away just for yourself. Whatever you have, you should share with others."

Don Jesús concluded, "When we pray, we shouldn't ask for a long life. We should pray for the strength to do what is right."

—Noel Wiggins, San Francisco Gotera, El Salvador

During the 1989 Lenten season, hundreds of men, women, and children in detention cells throughout South Africa began to refuse to eat. Many had been jailed for months, some for years, without being charged with a crime. They asked either to be charged or released.

The news media reported the action as a hunger strike, but it was not a well-planned, coordinated event. One group of young men and women in a Johannesburg jail began to fast, and the news spread to other prisons. By Holy Week, hundreds in jails and thousands more outside had joined the fast.

Many people saw the spontaneity of the fast and the response of the authorities as the work of God. Lawyers, doctors, family members, and co-workers had struggled unsuccessfully through legal means to obtain the release of these people. Then these "helpless" prisoners used their only tool, their bodies, to declare to their jailers, the rulers of their jailers, and the world, that they must be free.

The prisoners' resolve and commitment frightened the authorities, who did not want anyone to die. So they began releasing prisoners. Easter celebrations were especially jubilant that year as children, parents, sisters, and brothers walked out of jail, haggard and hungry, but free.

—Dale and Gann Herman, Maseru, Lesotho

3

. . . .

Rising, Breaking, Reconciling

Bread is one of the most simple, basic foods we know, yet it offers a wealth of images. In the Judeo-Christian tradition, bread is a symbol of such widely contrasting concepts as suffering, hope, liberation, and reconciliation.

Before the captive Israelites made their exodus from Egypt, they prepared an unleavened "bread of affliction" (Deuteronomy 16:3). It symbolized the suffering of their soon-to-end slavery and the difficult road they would walk to freedom.

During their 40-year wilderness pilgrimage, God provided manna, a bread that liberated them from desert hunger. Many years later when Jesus multiplied a few barley loaves to feed a crowd of Jewish people living under Roman occupation, the people connected this bread with the manna their ancestors ate and longed for their own liberation.

Jesus ate bread with friends and multiplied it for the poor. He described his kingdom as yeast that penetrated and expanded the gluten of grain. But most importantly he took for himself the identity of bread. In order to bring reconciliation between peoples, and between people and God, he allowed others to break his body and take his life.

Much of the power of these images is lost in the bread aisles of modern supermarkets where factory-made bread lies in sterile wrap. We eat it without a trace of the aroma of fresh loaves leaving the oven. We buy flour, but seldom meet the farmers or walk the land that produced the grain; we may never touch the grains or observe how they are crushed and ground.

But many people in the world still touch the raw grains each day—planting, picking, grinding, and then shaping the resulting dough into their tortillas, *injera, chapatis, arepas,* or pitas. This is their literal daily bread, a revered and cherished staple in their diet.

While living in Turkey, Jewel Showalter observed how Turkish people treat bread with great respect. "If a piece falls to the floor, it is picked up and kissed before being put back on the plate or in the trash can. If people find bread on the street, they pick it up, kiss it, and put it in a trash can so it won't be trampled on."

Some people still make the "bread of affliction." They work in the fields all day, but because the fields are not their own, they cannot enjoy the full product of their labor. They and their families know days and seasons when there is not enough bread to fill their stomachs and meet their energy demands.

Others are "eating manna" and finding ways to multiply the few grains that they have. They hope against hope and survive against great odds. Kori Leaman-Miller wrote from El Salvador that people who have lived through house-to-house searches, death threats, torture, and war can say, "Isn't God good!" and know it to be true.

"Old Lucia was one who said it. With tears in her eyes, she told of fleeing army repression seven years earlier. An old woman, she went without food or companionship for 17 days. She recalled her fear and hunger, but then added that somehow she had been able to sleep soundly every night. 'Isn't God good!' she said."

Others also live in the midst of hostilities and long-standing mistrust due to cultural differences and historical conflicts. Yet they are breaking bread, both literally and figuratively, in acts of reconciliation. In most traditional economies, children take part in many of the tasks of agriculture and food preparation; they also join in peacemaking.

Several years ago pupils from a Christian Palestinian school in the Israeli-occupied West Bank town of Zababdeh went door-to-door collecting donations for a neighboring Muslim village that was under military curfew. Although unemployed themselves for over three months because of the uprising in the occupied territories, the people of Zababdeh donated some $1,500. The students bought rice, sugar, powdered milk, biscuits, and other foods, and sent them to families with young children. Each box carried the message, "With love, from the children of Zababdeh to a child in Qabatiyeh."

The bread recipes and stories that follow help us understand more fully the suffering of crushed grain, the hope of rising bread, and the liberation and reconciliation of broken bread shared with others.

*b*e who shares my bread and salt is not my enemy.

—*Arabic Bedouin proverb*

Y ou have come from afar
and waited long and are wearied:
Let us sit side by side
sharing the same bread
drawn from the same source
to quiet the same hunger
that makes us weak.
Then standing together
let us share the same spirit,
the same thoughts
that once again draw us together
in friendship and unity and peace.

—Prières d'Ozawamick, Canadian
Indian liturgical text[1]

Ethiopian Flat Bread

Injera
(in-JEH-rah)

Injera, a spongy crepe-like bread, is eaten with Ethiopian stews. In Ethiopia, Injera are layered on top of a mesob, a round basket-like table, and spicy stews are heaped on top. Family members and guests sit on stools around the mesob, and pull off pieces of a stack of Injera that they use to scoop up and eat the stew. Hosts honor special guests by placing the first bite in the guest's mouth. Authentic Injera is made with teff, a kind of millet, and sourdough starter. The batter is fermented two to three days. This is a close imitation developed by Ethiopians living in North America. It takes time to fry the individual Injera, but it is not difficult.

• *Option:*
For a more authentic Injera, add 1/2 c. teff flour (125 ml) and reduce whole wheat flour to 1/4 c. (50 ml).

● ●

Makes 20 12-inch Injera (30-cm)

Mix:

3 c. self-rising flour (750 ml)
1/2 c. whole wheat flour (125 ml)
1/2 c. cornmeal or *masa harina* (125 ml)
1 T. active dry yeast (15 ml) (1 package)
31/2 c. warm water (875 ml)

Let set in large bowl, covered, an hour or longer, until batter rises and becomes stretchy. It can sit as long as 3-6 hours. When ready, stir batter if liquid has settled on bottom. Then whip in blender, 2 c. of batter (500 ml) at a time, thinning it with 1/2-3/4 c. water (125-175 ml). Batter will be quite thin.

Cook in nonstick frypan without oil over medium or medium-high heat. Use 1/2 c. batter (125 ml) per Injera for 12-inch pan (30-cm) or 1/3 c. batter (75 ml) per Injera for 10-inch pan (25-cm). Pour batter in heated pan and quickly swirl pan to spread batter as thin as possible. Batter should be no thicker than 1/8 inch (1/3 cm). Do not turn. Injera does not easily stick or burn. It is cooked through when bubbles appear all over top. Lay each Injera on a clean towel for a minute or two, then stack in covered dish to keep warm. Finished Injera will be thicker than a crepe, but thinner than a pancake.

To serve, overlap a few Injera on large platter and place stews on top. Or lay 1 Injera on each dinner plate, and ladle stew servings on top. Give each person 3 or more Injera, rolled or folded in quarters, to use for scooping up the stews.

—Mary Jane Wehibe, Elizabethtown, Pennsylvania; and Blanche Horst, Stevens, Pennsylvania

Indian Flat Bread (India)

Makes 10

●●●●●●●●●●●●●●●●●●●●●●●●●●●●●●●

Chapati
(chah-PAH-tee)

Chapatis are made in varying sizes and thicknesses in South Asia and East Africa. Pieces of Chapati are used instead of utensils to scoop up curry dishes or chutney.

Combine:
2 c. whole wheat flour (500 ml)
1 t. margarine, melted (5 ml)
pinch of salt
Gradually add:
1/2 c. (or more) lukewarm water (125 ml)
Knead until dough is soft. Cover with damp cloth and let rest 1 hour. Divide dough into 10 pieces. On floured surface, roll each piece into 4-inch circle (10-cm), 1/4-inch thick (3/4-cm).
Heat heavy ungreased frypan. Cook each Chapati until it starts to bubble on bottom, turn, fry other side, and remove. Stack in tea towel to keep warm.

● *Options:*
Substitute white flour for half the whole wheat flour.
●
After turning Chapati, rub with a few drops margarine or oil. When second side is finished, turn over again and cook briefly on first side. Rub oil on second side and fry briefly.

—Cynthia Peacock, Calcutta, India

....

Poverty often means that people have limited choices. In some cases the few choices they do have are cruel and dehumanizing.

One afternoon while I was living in Bangladesh, my best friend Monie took me to visit Ramona. Ramona greeted us at the door and invited us into her bamboo hut, surrounded by trees. It was nice to be out of the bright summer sun and heat.

As my eyes adjusted to the dimmer light inside, I saw the daughter Ramona was carrying on her hip. The girl's hair was almost white. Her eyes peered lifelessly at me from sunken sockets. The child appeared to be desperately ill. Nearly two years old, she was not strong enough to walk.

When Ramona stepped into the kitchen to make some tea, I whispered to Monie, "What's wrong with Ramona's daughter?" She replied quietly, "Ramona and her husband can no longer feed all the children they have, so they have chosen this daughter to die."

—Charmayne Denlinger Brubaker, Lancaster, Pennsylvania

....

*t*he hungry dream of the bread market.

—Egyptian proverb

● ●

Whole Wheat Bread Puffs (India)

Makes 20-25

Puris
(POO-reess)

This is a common bread in India, eaten with curry dishes or sometimes as a snack with sauce.

Mix:
   2 c. whole wheat flour (500 ml)
   1 c. white flour (250 ml)
   1 t. salt (5 ml)
   1 T. shortening (15 ml)
   1 c. milk (250 ml)
On floured board, knead until smooth and elastic. Divide dough into 20-25 pieces and roll each into thin, 3-4-inch circle (7.5-10-cm), or roll out entire piece of dough and cut into circles. Heat oil in deep saucepan. Fry 1 Puri at a time, turning once as they puff and rise to top of oil. Remove and drain on paper.

—*Selma Unruh, North Newton, Kansas*

● ●

Native American Fry Bread (United States)

Makes 8

Variations of this recipe are common in many Native American communities, including the Cheyenne, Choctaw, and Navajo. Children will enjoy patting out the dough and watching it puff as it fries, but should stay away from hot oil.

Combine in large mixing bowl:
   3 c. flour (750 ml)
   1 1/4 t. baking powder (6 ml)
   1 t. salt (5 ml)
   2 T. dry milk powder (30 ml) (optional)
Gradually stir in:
   1 1/3 c. warm water (325 ml) (or slightly less)
Mix until dough forms ball and comes clean from edge of bowl. Knead on lightly floured surface until well mixed and elastic. Divide dough into 8 pieces and roll into balls. Using palms of hands, pat into circles about 1/2-inch thick (1-cm). Heat 3/4 inch oil (2 cm) to 450°F (230°C) in frypan. Carefully slip rounded, flat piece of dough into hot oil. Bread will start to rise to top of hot oil. When underside of bread is brown, turn over and brown other side. Drain well on paper, then place in baking pan in 200°F oven (100°C) and cover with damp towel to keep warm and chewy. Repeat with remaining dough.

—*Betty E. Hart, Clinton, Oklahoma*
—*Velma Heisey, Mount Joy, Pennsylvania; and Nancy Heisey, Ephrata, Pennsylvania*
—*Myrtis Morris, Philadelphia, Mississippi; and Elaine Maust, Meridian, Mississippi*

During the Vietnam War, U.S. bombing missions wiped out entire mountain villages in Laos, killing many people. Survivors were airlifted by U.S. planes to refugee camps in the hot valleys. After the war the people returned to their villages to rebuild their lives.

They were like pioneers needing to start from scratch. But their land was neither virgin nor empty. Bombs the size of tennis balls were buried in the fields where the people wished to plant rice, prepare gardens, and build homes. They first had to clear the land of the "bombies," as they called them. Hoeing into a bomb could kill or maim them.

In 1985, twelve years after the end of the war, an MCC peacemaking team from the USA visited one of these mountain villages named Ban Ponsovan. The villagers graciously prepared a feast for their guests. The hosts served food on banana leaves and gave each guest a large soupspoon crafted from metal salvaged from a crashed U.S. plane. One large common soup bowl served every four people;

a common bowl of sticky rice was between every two people. Everyone reached and ate from meats and hot sauces in the middle of the table.

A government official commented to the U.S. team, "Look at those men down there eating with you people from America. They could be very angry with you for what your country did to them in the war, but instead they receive you in friendship and eat with you. They accept you as people just as you are—people who want peace and friendship in the world so we can all live together."

—Martha Zimmerly, Orrville, Ohio

Henry Neufeld: Thailand

●●●●●●●●●●●●●●●●●●●●●●●●●●●●●●●●●

Pita Bread
(West Bank)

Makes 12

450°F 230°C

5-6 min.

Khubiz Arabi
(KHUH-biz AH-rah-bee)

Pita Bread is a staple throughout the Middle East where people fill it to eat as sandwiches, or break off bits of the thin crust to spoon up other food. Pita rounds that do not puff up when baked can be used as bases for individual pizzas. Testers note that variations in ingredients are not as important as technique in making good pitas; we recommend following procedure closely.

• Variations:
For whole wheat pita bread, reduce water to 1 1/2 c. (375 ml), salt to 1/2 t. (2 ml), and use 4 c. whole wheat flour (1 L) instead of 6 c. white flour (1.5 L). Omit oil.
•
To make thalamae, a thicker bread without a pocket, divide dough into 6 pieces and roll out twice as thick. Prick rounds with fork to keep from puffing up. Brush with egg white or olive oil and sprinkle with sesame seeds, oregano, chopped green peppers, or other toppings. Bake 8-10 minutes.

Combine in large bowl, stirring occasionally for about 5 minutes until yeast is dissolved:
   1 T. active dry yeast (15 ml) (1 package)
   2 c. warm water (500 ml)
Stir in:
   1 T. oil (15 ml)
   6 c. flour (1.5 L)
   2 t. salt (10 ml)
Knead on lightly floured board until smooth and satiny. Place in greased bowl, turning greased side up. Cover and let rise about 45 minutes. Return to floured board and cut into 12 pieces. Shape into slightly flattened balls. Cover and let rest 20 minutes. (Keep dough pieces covered at all times when not working with them, to keep dough from drying out.)
Preheat oven to 450°F (230°C). Heat cookie sheets (it is important to place dough on heated sheets). Carefully roll rounds of dough into 6-inch circles (15-cm), turning a quarter turn with each roll. Take care not to stretch, puncture, or crease dough. Place 4 rounds on hot cookie sheet. (Tester recommends baking on upside-down cookie sheet on bottom shelf of oven.) Bake 3-4 minutes until puffed and set. Turn over with spatula and brown 2 minutes more. Remove from sheet with hot pad or turner, leaving sheet in oven to stay hot while rolling next batch. (Bake 1 batch before rolling the next.) Place bread rounds on cloth and cover with another cloth while cooling (covering keeps pita soft). When cool, store in plastic bags in refrigerator up to 1 month. To serve, warm briefly in microwave or conventional oven. Cut slit and fill as desired.

—Alice W. Lapp, Akron, Pennsylvania

Jerry Martin: Jordan

In the early hours before sunrise when the roosters are just beginning to crow, the gentle sound of grinding and patting fills the air in many Central American villages. In her rural Nicaragua home, Doña Petronila lights a small kerosene lamp which casts shadows across the smoke-covered wooden poles that are her kitchen walls. Next she lights a fire under the *comal*, a heavy piece of round metal built into a homemade clay stove.

Petronila takes the corn that soaked through the night and puts it through a manual food grinder. She transfers this *masa* to a flat stone and grinds it more finely with strong, even stokes, using a cylindrical stone.

When the cornmeal is fine and smooth, Petronila pats it into tortillas. Her grandmother and mother always did it *a mano*, forming a perfectly rounded tortilla using only their hands. Petronila has adopted the modern version of placing the meal on a piece of plastic and patting the tortilla out on a table. She places the tortillas on the hot metal plate and turns them with her bare fingers. When the tortillas are ready, she moves them from the *comal* to a large basket lined with a cloth that covers the tortillas.

As Petronila works, she drops pieces of the cornmeal to the chickens that enter the kitchen looking for food. Her hands move swiftly as she pats out a full day's supply of tortillas. Her family will eat the fresh hot tortillas and bits of dry cheese for breakfast. At noon reheated tortillas will accompany soup, rice and beans, yucca, and if someone in the community has butchered, perhaps some meat. In the evening there will be more rice and beans, perhaps an egg or cheese, and certainly tortillas. Petronila's husband says you haven't eaten if you haven't had a tortilla.

—jhs

● ●

Hominy Cheese Patties (Colombia)

Makes 12

Arepas con Queso (ah-RAY-pahss kohn KAY-soh)

Arepas, a typical Colombian bread substitute, are made in various ways. Some are the shape of small balls with no salt. Others have a slice of cheese between two thin patties. Arepas are regaining popularity because they are made from corn, a local product, which is less expensive and nutritionally superior to imported, refined wheat products.

Grind until smooth in blender or food processor:
  1 1/2 c. canned hominy (375 ml) with
  1/4 c. liquid from can (50 ml)

Transfer to mixing bowl and add:
  3/4 c. yellow cornmeal (175 ml)
  1 c. cheese, grated or crumbled (250 ml)
  1 T. brown sugar (15 ml)
  1/4 t. salt (1 ml)

Mix well. Form into 12 small balls and carefully flatten into 2-3-inch patties (5-7-cm). Fry on lightly greased griddle over medium-high heat, or roast on grill, turning as first side begins to brown. The cheese will make Arepas chewy. Serve in place of bread with meal or as a snack.

—Saúl Murcía, Brownsville, Texas
—Mary Becker Valencia, Bogotá, Colombia

Señor, dadles pan a los que tienen hambre,
y hambre de justicia, a los que tienen pan.
Lord, to those who hunger, give bread.
And to those who have bread, give the hunger for justice.

—Latin American prayer

●●●●●●●●●●●●●●●●●●●●●●●●●●●●●●●

Flour Tortillas (Mexico)

Makes 8-11

Tortillas de Harina (tor-TEE-yahss day ah-REE-nah)

Flour and corn tortillas are readily available in most supermarkets. Neighborhood Mexican stores often sell better-quality tortillas, and at lower prices. A properly cooked Flour Tortilla remains mostly white, but is flecked with brown and puffed in spots; it has a dry look but is soft and pliable.

Combine in mixing bowl:
2 c. flour (500 ml)
1 t. salt (5 ml)
Cut in with pastry blender:
1/4 c. shortening (50 ml)
When particles are fine, add gradually:
1/2 c. lukewarm water (125 ml)
Toss with fork to make stiff dough. Form into ball and knead thoroughly on lightly floured board until smooth and flecked with air bubbles. To make dough easier to handle, grease surface, cover tightly, and refrigerate 4-24 hours before using. Let dough return to room temperature before rolling out.

Divide dough into 8 balls for large tortillas, 11 balls for 8-inch size (20-cm). Roll as thin as possible on lightly floured board or between sheets of waxed paper. Drop onto very hot ungreased griddle. Bake until freckled on 1 side, about 20 seconds. Lift edge, turn, and bake on second side. Wrap in clean tea towel to keep warm. Refrigerate or freeze leftover tortillas in airtight wrap.

—*Adapted from* More-with-Less Cookbook, *by Doris Janzen Longacre (Herald Press, 1976; all rights reserved; used with permission).*

Mark Beach: Honduras

The following three recipes from different continents have strikingly similar ingredient lists and baking procedures. They use basic ingredients, can be mixed quickly, and were traditionally baked over an open fire.

Native Biscuit Bread (Canada)

Bannock (BA-nick)

Native Canadians have traditionally made Bannock while trapping or living in camps during berry-picking or rice-harvesting seasons. Early versions were made with wild rice flour and baked on a flat rock over an open fire. The dough can also be wrapped around a stick and baked over a fire. This heavy, moist bread with a crisp crust goes well with soup.

• **Option:**
Use half whole wheat flour.

● ●

Makes 1 loaf

400°F 200°C

30 min.

Preheat oven to 400°F (200°C).
Combine:
> **4 c. flour (1 L)**
> **1/2 t. salt (2 ml)**
> **5 t. baking powder (25 ml)**
> **1 1/2 c. water (375 ml)**

Mix to form stiff dough. Knead on floured surface, adding additional flour if necessary. Form into round or oblong loaf about 1-inch high (2.5-cm). Bake on greased baking sheet approximately 30 minutes, or fry in frypan in a little hot oil. Serve warm with margarine and jam or honey.

• *Variation:*
For modern adaptation, increase salt to 1 t. (5 ml), decrease baking powder to 4 t. (20 ml), add 1 egg, 1 T. oil (15 ml), and 3/4 c. raisins (175 ml); replace water with 1 3/4 c. milk (425 ml). Mix to form sticky batter. Do not knead. Spoon into greased tube pan. Shake pan several times to release air bubbles. Bake about 40 minutes at 375°F (190°C).

—Marguerite E. Brite, May Pitchenese, and Kate Kroeker, Dinorwic, Ontario

Stove-Top Muffins (Botswana)

Diphaphata (dee-pah-PAH-tah)

Diphaphata is most often made with yeast, but this simple baking-powder version is also common. It produces a tasty, round bread, similar to, but heavier than, an English muffin.

• *Variation:*
To make fat cakes (called *dikuku*), form the dough into small balls and deep-fat fry.

● ●

(ts)

Makes 8-12

Stir together:
> **4 c. flour (1 L)**
> **4 t. baking powder (20 ml)**
> **pinch of salt**
> **2 t. sugar (10 ml)**
> **1 c. milk or water (250 ml)**

Knead to rolling consistency on floured board. Flatten with hands or rolling pin. Cut into 3-4-inch circles (7.5-10-cm). Place heavy frypan over low heat. Sprinkle with a little flour or spray with vegetable spray to keep bread from sticking. Place bread circles in pan and brown on both sides, about 10 minutes per side. Serve immediately.

—Jean Maribe, Mochudi, Botswana; and Kathleen Roth, Akron, Pennsylvania

Outback Damper (Australia)

• •

Makes 1 round 9-inch loaf (22-cm)

375°F 190°C

30 min.

This baking powder bread is a favorite used in campfire cooking in the Australian bush, whether camp is 10 or 1000 kilometers from the next fresh bread outlet. Australian Christians sometimes use Damper in communion services.

• Option:
Use all-purpose flour; increase baking powder to 4 t. (20 ml) and salt to 1 t. (5 ml).

Mix:

4 c. self-rising flour (1 L)
2 t. baking powder (10 ml)
pinch of salt

Add:

approx. 12/3 c. warm milk or water (400 ml)

Stir until dough sticks together well. Heat cast-iron Dutch oven over campfire. When hot, put dough inside, place oven over coals, and cover lid of oven with hot coals. (It is possible to place Damper directly in coals, although only the inside of the crusty bread may be edible.) Bake approximately 30 minutes, exact time depending on heat of coals.

To bake in oven, turn dough into a greased 9-inch pie plate (1 L). Flour hands and gently pat dough to fill the plate, forming a round, flat loaf. Bake uncovered at 375°F (190°C) 25-30 minutes, or until golden brown. Let stand 10-15 minutes before cutting.

—Janet Stutzman, Lathlain, Australia

The Mokolare family in the Botswana village of Mmankgodi hosted me during two different periods of language study. I took part in many family activities. During my second visit, these included helping the father, Rra-Phakedi, chase the sparrows from the family's sorghum and maize field.

The rains were good, and the grain was growing well. But one day a large part of the sorghum was ruined—not by the sparrows, but by a neighbor's goats.

That evening the mother, Mma-Phakedi, went over to the neighbor's yard and arranged for the woman to come and assess the damage caused by her goats. The next morning I accompanied them to the field. Mma-Phakedi led her neighbor around, pointing out the damage and scolding her indirectly for not watching her goats more carefully.

After about 20 minutes, Mma-Phakedi sent me off to one corner of the field with instructions to pick the largest, best-quality watermelons I could find. I returned with three prize specimens, supposing Mma-Phakedi would be taking them home for lunch. Instead, she turned and gave them to her neighbor, sending her on her way with God's blessing.

I do not know whether the neighbor made any restitution for the damage, but Mma-Phakedi's act of forgiveness was something I'll never forget.

—Eugene Thieszen, Gaborone, Botswana

Kentucky Cornbread (United States)

•••••••••••••••••••••••••••••••••

Serves 4-6

350°F 180°C

30-35 min.

Cornbread goes with any meal in Kentucky. This basic recipe without eggs, oil, or sugar is from the cook of the Hindman Settlement School.

Preheat oven to 350°F (180°C).
Mix together to cake-batter consistency:

1 c. flour (250 ml)
1 c. cornmeal (250 ml)
1 t. soda (5 ml)
1 t. baking powder (5 ml)
1/4 t. salt (1 ml)
11/2 c. milk (375 ml)

Pour into greased 8 x 8-inch pan (2-L) or greased muffin tins. Bake 30-35 minutes. Serve warm with margarine.

—*Debbie Beverly, Hindman, Kentucky; and Carol Loeppky, Whitesburg, Kentucky*

....

Putting a meal on the table in many countries often means back-breaking, time-consuming work. For the poor in the United States, it can mean a spirit-breaking visit to the food-stamp office.

Debbie Beverly has lived most of her life in Knott County, Kentucky. Her husband, Bruce, worked in the mines until an accident disabled him. Since then, Debbie has worked full-time to support their family of three children. But her minimum-wage job does not cover all their expenses. Although Bruce has supplemented their income by farming and gardening, they have needed to use food stamps.

Debbie remembers the intimidation and humiliation she experienced when she first signed up for food stamps. It was hard because she had been raised to take care of herself. Her husband resisted taking food stamps and ten years later is still ashamed to receive them. He has never gone to pick them up nor used any to buy food.

Bruce is not unique among mountain men. "You go to the food-stamp office," says Debbie, "and there will be nine women and only one or two men. Women may be proud, too, but the Lord has given them the instinct to look after their kids."

Debbie does not let the "stigma" of food stamps keep her from being active in her community.

"People need to figure out what they can do," she says. "Everyone can do something. Bruce can do algebra and teach our children algebra. I can bake 100 loaves of bread and sell them to raise money for Kentuckians for the Commonwealth. We have to have everyone in it together. When we get ordinary people involved, then we'll see some change."

—*Carol Loeppky and Melanie Zuercher, Whitesburg, Kentucky*

Cheese Muffins (El Salvador)

●●●●●●●●●●●●●●●●●●●●●●●●●●●●●●●●

Makes 18

350°F 180°C

15-18 min.

Quesadillas
(kay-sah-DEE-yahss)

Quesadillas make a delightful snack or quick breakfast. Salvadorans make them with double the margarine, sugar, and eggs, and use a local hard white cheese. These bear no resemblance to Mexican Quesadillas (p. 257), which are cheese-filled tortillas. Both derive their name from the Spanish word for cheese—queso.

• *Option:*
Bake 20 minutes in a greased 9 x 13-inch cake pan (3.5-L). Cut in squares to serve.

Cream:

1/2 c. margarine, melted (125 ml)
3/4 c. sugar (175 ml)
2 eggs

Combine:

2 c. flour (500 ml)
2 t. baking powder (10 ml)

Add alternately to creamed mixture with:

1 c. milk or sour cream (250 ml)

Beat until smooth.

Stir in:

1 1/2 c. cheese, grated (375 ml) (mozzarella, cheddar, or combination)

Put paper baking cups into muffin pans and fill 3/4 full of batter.

Sprinkle with:

sesame seeds

Bake at 350°F (180°C) 15-18 minutes until golden, or until toothpick comes out clean. These muffins freeze well.

—Karen Canales and Dolores Braun, Saskatoon, Saskatchewan
—Angela Méndez and Edna Hohnstein, Edmonton, Alberta

I worked on the hacienda over there, and I would have to feed the dogs bowls of meat or bowls of milk every morning, and I could never put those things on the table for my own children. When my children were ill, they died with a nod of sympathy from the landlord. But when those dogs were ill, I took them to the veterinarian in Suchitoto.

You will never understand violence or nonviolence until you understand the violence to the spirit that happens from watching your children die of malnutrition.

—A peasant in El Salvador[2]

God gives blessings to all people. If people were to distribute them, many would go without.

—African Hausa proverb

Somali Egg Crepes (Somalia)

Ambabur Bed
(ahm-bah-boor bed)

Somali Muslims make these clove-flavored crepes for the holy day that marks the end of Ramadan, a month of daily fasting from dawn to sunset.

Mix into smooth, thin batter:

5 T. sugar (75 ml)
2 eggs
1/2 t. baking powder (2 ml)
1/8 t. salt (.5 ml)
1/2 t. ground cloves (2 ml)
1 1/4 c. milk (300 ml)
1 1/4 c. flour (300 ml)

Pour by 1/3 cupfuls (75 ml) onto hot, lightly greased griddle or ungreased nonstick frypan. Rotate pan quickly so batter spreads evenly. Crepes will be about 5 inches (12.5-cm). Allow to cook until bubbles break. Turn and fry other side. Remove to plate and keep warm in oven until all crepes are fried. Roll up crepes and eat with fingers. Serve plain with sweet tea.

—Marian Yussuf, Suna, Migori, Kenya; and Sylvia L. Hess, Bausman, Pennsylvania

In the language of the Iteso people of Eastern Uganda, as in many African languages, each month of the year is given a descriptive name. August—the month after the millet harvest is "the month of the big stomach"; but, in poignant contrast, the pre-harvest month of May, when the granaries are empty, is "the month when the children wait for food."

All over the vast savannah areas of Africa, where the main staple foods are cereals and legumes, the lives of millions of people are conditioned to the rhythm of the rains, the harvest, and the pre-harvest "hungry" months, when grain is scarce and often full of weevils, and when they must look to the perennially-available but low-protein cassava for their major source of food.

It is in these hungry months, when the millet crop is growing and ripening, oh how slowly, under the brazen sun, that the specter of malnutrition stalks the land. It is in these months many children, weakened by malnourishment, can die of illnesses which would hardly affect normal children. Growing children are always the first to be affected and are the most seriously affected by food scarcity. It is, perhaps, not by chance, that the month of May is called "the month when the *children* wait for food."[3]

Ninkii sun ku siiya, subag baa la siiyaa.
If a man gives you poison, give him ghee.

—Somali proverb

Crepes
(Croatia/Serbia)

Serves 4-5

• •

Palacinka
(pah-lah-CHIN-kah)

This popular evening meal is simple, yet festive. Vary the filling and you have a light meal, snack, or dessert. Palacinka makes an excellent meal for the road—there are no crumbs and minimal mess.

• *Option:*
Add 1/2 t. ground cinnamon (2 ml), 1/4 t. cardamom (1 ml), or any desired spice to the flour in the crepe recipe.

Crepes:
Mix to make very thin batter:

2 c. flour (500 ml)
2 c. milk (500 ml)
2 eggs
1/2 c. water (125 ml)
pinch of salt
1 T. oil (15 ml)

Whip with whisk until smooth, adding additional water to lighten if necessary. Pour small amount of batter into hot, lightly oiled frypan (preferably nonstick). Rotate pan until batter is evenly distributed, forming 1 large, thin pancake. Fry until slightly brown; turn and fry briefly on other side. Make stack. Serve filled or ready for guests to fill.

Fillings:
(1) Mix:

2 c. small curd cottage cheese (500 ml)
rind of 1 small lemon, grated
1 T. sugar (15 ml)

Put 1-2 T. (15-30 ml) in each Palacinka and roll shut.
(2) Mix:

2 c. walnuts, finely chopped (500 ml)
1/2 c. sugar (125 ml)

Put 1-2 T. filling (15-30 ml) in each Palacinka, fold in half, then into wedge-shaped quarter. Sprinkle with powdered sugar for an attractive dessert.
(3) Using wedge-shaped fold, pour inside and on top:

warm chocolate sauce

(4) Fill with:

peanut butter and jelly

(5) Fill with:

strawberries and cream

(6) Fill with:

fruit preserves topped with powdered sugar

—*Nena and Stevan Medarac, Bacuga, former Yugoslavia; and Sara Wenger Shenk, Harrisonburg, Virginia*

....

*M*ay I take your pain, may it be mine.

—*Armenian proverb*

Sweet Bread Twists (Russia)

Ragaliki
(rah-GAH-lih-kee)

Children will enjoy helping to mix, roll out, and twist this bread, which is similar to Rollkuchen, *a favorite among Russian immigrants in Canada. Serve sugared* Ragaliki *with tea for breakfast or as a summer snack with watermelon. Serve unsugared with Borscht (p. 81).*

• *Option:*
Omit twisting and fry in rectangles.

Mix together:
 2 eggs
 1/2 c. sugar (125 ml)
Add and stir to mix:
 1 c. yogurt (250 ml) (p. 295)
 1/2 t. baking soda (2 ml)
 1/4 c. margarine, melted (50 ml)
Stir in:
 4 c. flour (1 L)
Knead on floured board, adding additional flour until smooth and elastic. Roll out to 1/4-inch thick (3/4-cm). Cut into strips 4 inches long (10 cm) and 1 1/2 inches wide (3.5 cm). Make vertical, 1-inch slit (2.5-cm) in middle of each. Thread one end through slit and turn inside out (*see* below). Fry in hot oil until light brown, 1-2 minutes per side. Cool on paper. Serve plain or sprinkled with powdered sugar. These are tastiest if served the day they are made.

—*Mariya Onishchenko, Bowmansville, Pennsylvania; and Janice Horning, Mohnton, Pennsylvania*

  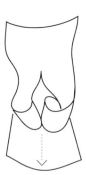

Banana Bread (Jamaica)

This Caribbean teatime specialty is quick and easy to make. Tester reported oohs and aahs from guests who tasted the loaf.

Cream together:
 1/2 c. margarine (125 ml)
 1/2 c. sugar (125 ml)
 1 t. vanilla (5 ml)
 1 egg, well beaten
Sift together:
 2 c. flour (500 ml)
 1 T. baking powder (15 ml)
  (*more* →)

60

1/2 t. ground nutmeg (2 ml)
pinch of salt

Add to creamed mixture alternately with:

3 ripe medium bananas, mashed (about
  1 c./250 ml)

Add:

1/4 c. nuts, chopped (50 ml)
1/4 c. raisins (50 ml)

Turn into greased 9-inch loaf pan (2-L). Bake 55 minutes in preheated 350°F oven (180°C) until golden brown.

—Pauline Cousins, St. Mary, Jamaica

• •

Festive Ham Bread
(Venezuela)

Makes 2 loaves

350°F 180°C

30 min.

Pan de Jamón
(pahn day hah-MOHN)

Pan de Jamón is a Christmas bread in Venezuela. It is always served at the traditional late-night meal on Christmas Eve and often on New Year's Eve. Serve it as a main dish. Leftovers make excellent after-school snacks.

• *Option:*
Substitute any favorite bread dough recipe or frozen bread dough.

Mix in large bowl:

1 1/2 c. warm water (375 ml)
1 t. sugar (5 ml)
1 T. active dry yeast (15 ml) (1 package)

Let set 10 minutes or until bubbly. Stir in:

3 eggs, one at a time
1 t. salt (5 ml)
1/4 c. sugar (50 ml)
3 T. margarine (45 ml)
6 1/2 c. flour (1.6 L)

Knead on floured board, adding more flour if necessary, until smooth and elastic. Place in greased bowl, turning greased side up. Cover with damp cloth and let rise until doubled in bulk. Punch down and divide in half. Roll out each half to 1/4-inch-thick rectangle (.5-cm). Spread lightly with margarine or bacon grease (optional). Divide following mixture and spread over top, varying amounts to taste:

1/2 lb. ham, diced (250 g)
1/2 lb. bacon, diced and fried (250 g)
1 c. raisins (250 ml)
1 c. stuffed olives, sliced (250 ml)

Roll up into shape of French bread loaves, turning ends under. Place seam side down on greased cookie sheet. Bake 30 minutes in preheated 350°F oven (180°C). Serve hot or cold in 1/2-inch slices (1-cm) without additional butter or spread. Refrigerate leftovers.

—Yajaira Andrades and Martha Giles, Caracas, Venezuela
—Ken Holderman, Caracas, Venezuela

Spicy Tea Bread (Ethiopia)

Ambesha
(ahm-BEH-shah)

Ethiopians serve Ambesha and sweet, spiced tea as refreshments for meetings and social gatherings. A delightful spicy yeast bread.

• •

Makes 1 large round loaf

350°F 180°C

30 min.

Dissolve in 1/2 c. warm water (125 ml):

1 T. active dry yeast (15 ml) (1 package)

Set in warm place until foamy and doubled in bulk.
Add:

1 1/2 c. warm water (375 ml)

Stir in:

2 T. ground coriander (30 ml)
1 t. ground cardamom (5 ml)
1/2 t. white or black pepper (2 ml)
2 t. salt (10 ml)
1/2 c. margarine (125 ml)
1 t. fenugreek (5 ml) (optional)

Add 1/2 c. (125 ml) at a time, mixing carefully until dough forms soft ball:

4 1/2-5 c. flour (1.1-1.3 L)

Knead 5 minutes, adding flour if necessary. Spread out on round pizza pan, stretching dough to reach edges. Let rise in warm place until doubled in bulk. Bake in 350°F oven (180°C) 30 minutes or until done. Baked bread will be only a couple inches high.

While loaf is still hot, spread top with:

2 T. margarine (30 ml)
dashes of Berbere (p. 288) or ground red
pepper (optional) +!

Serve with no additional toppings or spreads.

• Option:
Substitute whole wheat flour for part of the flour.

—*Blanche Horst, Stevens, Pennsylvania*

As Christmas approaches in Sweden, families make *Lussekatter*, a special sweet bread, in honor of the Christian martyr St. Lucia. Early on the morning of December 13, St. Lucia Day, the oldest girl in the family rises and prepares a pot of coffee.

St. Lucia Buns (Sweden)

Lussekatter
(loo-seh-kah-tehr)

Children will enjoy shaping and placing raisins on the curled ends of St. Lucia Buns. Serve on December 13 and introduce your family to a new holiday (see story below).

• *Option:*
Substitute 1 t. ground cardamom (5 ml) for saffron-sugar mixture.

Makes 2 dozen

350°F 180C

12-15 min.

In large bowl, combine:
1/2 c. margarine, melted (125 ml)
11/2 c. lukewarm milk (375 ml)
1 T. active dry yeast (15 ml) (1 package)
1 t. sugar (5 ml)

While yeast dissolves, grind into fine powder:
1/2-1 t. saffron (2-5 ml)
1 sugar cube or 1 t. sugar (5 ml)

Swedes use marble bowls and mallets to grind sugar and saffron together. A sturdy bowl and stone can be used as effectively. If sugar cube is not available, regular sugar can be used, but grinding must be done more vigorously.
Add to yeast mixture:
saffron-sugar mixture
1 egg, beaten
1/2 c. sugar (125 ml)
1 t. salt (5 ml)
51/2-61/2 c. flour (1.4-1.6 L)

Stir until dough is easy to handle. Knead on lightly floured surface until smooth and elastic, about 5 minutes. Place in greased bowl, turning greased side up. Cover and let rise in warm place until doubled in bulk, about 1 hour. Punch down. Roll small pieces of dough into strips 1/2-inch thick (1-cm) and 6-8-inches long (15-20-cm), curling ends in opposite directions toward center to form S shapes (*see* at left). Lay buns several inches apart (3-5 cm) on greased cookie sheet and place raisin in center of each curled end. Cover and let rise until doubled in bulk, about 40 minutes.
Heat oven to 350°F (180°C).
Brush buns lightly with mixture of:
1 egg, beaten
1 T. water (15 ml)

Sprinkle lightly with sugar.
Bake until golden brown, 12-15 minutes.

—*Birgitta Oberg and Elizabeth Hess, Jokkmokk, Sweden*

She places the coffee, some *Lussekatter*, and a candle on a tray.
Dressed in a white robe with a red sash about her waist (symbolic of the saint's blood) and a wreath of candles on her head (representing the light the saint bore), she wakens her siblings. They join her in carrying the tray of bread and coffee to their parents' bedroom. There the family begins the festive activities of this special day, marking the beginning of the Christmas season.

Cheese Strudel (Croatia/Serbia)

Sirnica
(SEAR-nee-tzah)

This cheese-filled pastry with a touch of lemon makes a delicious breakfast bread or a special treat for coffee breaks. At Christmastime, a special walnut filling is substituted for the cheese. Traditionally made in a rolled loaf, many will find this alternative assembly (at right) easier to prepare, and just as tasty.

• *Variation:*
To make traditional loaf, do not divide dough. Roll into square. Brush lightly with melted margarine. Reduce eggs in filling to 1. Spread filling over dough to within 1 inch (2.5 cm) of edges. Fold two opposing side edges over 2 inches (5 cm) to keep cheese from escaping. Then beginning with edge closest to self, fold dough over 3-4 times to enclose cheese and form oblong loaf. Pinch seam to seal. Transfer carefully, but as quickly as possible, to greased 9 x 13-inch cake pan (3.5 L) (or narrower if possible), placing seam side down. Brush with margarine and bake as directed. Serve in slices.

Dissolve:

1 T. active dry yeast (15 ml) (1 package)
2/3 c. warm milk (150 ml)

In separate bowl mix:

1/3 c. margarine, melted (75 ml)
1/2 c. sugar (125 ml)
1 egg, well beaten

Stir in:

yeast mixture
2 3/4 c. flour (675 ml)

Beat vigorously 5-10 minutes with wooden spoon. Do not knead. Cover and let rest in warm place until double in bulk, 1-2 hours. Turn dough on floured surface and gently punch down, adding a little flour to keep dough from sticking to hands. Divide dough in two parts. Gently roll first part in rectangle 1/4-inch thick (3/4-cm), adding just enough flour to keep dough from sticking. Place in greased 9x13-inch cake pan (3.5-L), stretching dough to cover entire pan. Spread filling (below) on dough. Roll remaining dough to fit pan and place over filling. Brush with 1 T. melted margarine (15 ml). Let stand 20 minutes. Bake at 325°F (160°C) 30-40 minutes or until golden brown. Cool and cut in 21/2-inch squares (6 cm) to serve.

Filling:

Press through coarse sieve or mash with a fork:

1 lb. cottage cheese, well drained (500 g)

Add and mix well:

2 eggs, well beaten
2/3 c. sugar (150 ml)
grated rind of one lemon or 2 t. lemon juice (10 ml)
1/2 c. raisins (regular or golden) (125 ml)

• *Option:*
If dry cottage cheese is available, use 12-oz. (375 g) and do not press through sieve.

—Helen Nenadof, former Yugoslavia; and Naomi Fast, Newton, Kansas
—Danica Pavlak, Brinje, Croatia; and Sanya Serpa, Notre Dame, Indiana

Serbian Orthodox Christians bake several coins into the bread they prepare for Christmas morning breakfast. When the family gathers for breakfast, one of the children says the Lord's Prayer. Before breaking bread, it is customary for family members to reconcile their conflicts. They admit the wrongs they have done and forgive one another. Then everyone stands and together they take the big round bread in their hands, all breaking off a piece at the same time.

The children are delighted if they find a coin or two in their bread as they eat. A lit candle on the table lends a special atmosphere to this meal.

—Nena and Stevan Madarac, Bacuga, former Yugoslavia

●●●●●●●●●●●●●●●●●●●●●●●●●●●●●●●●●●●

Easter Bread (Ukraine)

Paska
(PAHSS-kah)

Many families that emigrated to Canada from the former Soviet Union brought Easter bread recipes with them. This version is large, intended to serve one's family and have extra to give away. Halve the recipe for a smaller quantity.

• Option:
If dry cottage cheese is not available, use regular cottage cheese and drain in sieve or cheesecloth before using.

Makes: 1 of 3-lb. can loaf (1.5 kg)
plus 5 of 1-lb. can loaves (500 g)

325°F 160°C

50-60 min.

Bread:

Mix and set aside:
2 1/2 T. active dry yeast (35 ml) (2 1/2 packages)
1/2 c. warm water, preferably potato water (125 ml)

In large mixing bowl, beat:
2 c. sugar (500 ml)
6 eggs

Add and stir:
3/4 c. margarine (175 ml)
yeast mixture
rind of 1 orange, grated
juice of 1/2 orange
1 t. vanilla (5 ml)

Add alternately and mix:
1 c. cream or half-and-half (250 ml)
10-12 c. flour (2.5-3 L)

Knead dough on floured board until smooth and elastic. Shape into loaves and place in well-greased coffee tins. Dough should fill only 1/3 of tin; loaves will continue rising while baking. Let rise 5 hours. (This is a slow-rising bread.) Bake 50-60 minutes at 325°F (160°C). To remove loaves, run knife around edges, invert, and carefully shake out.

Icing:
1 T. margarine (15 ml)
1 c. powdered sugar (250 ml)
1/4 c. hot milk (50 ml)

When loaves cool, ice with pastry brush. Sprinkle tops with colored sprinkles or small candy Easter eggs.

Spread:
Press through coarse sieve, or whirl in blender, or beat vigorously with mixer:
16-oz. dry cottage cheese (500 g)
2 egg yolks or 1 whole egg, hard-cooked and minced

Cream together and add to cheese:
1/2 c. margarine (125 ml)
1/2 c. sugar (125 ml)

Add:
1/2 t. vanilla (2 ml)

Mix to spreadable consistency, adding light cream if too dry. Serve on slices of Paska.

—Annie and Ingrid Schultz, Aldergrove, British Columbia

65

Raisin Bread (Ireland)

Makes 2 round loaves

350°F 180°C

40-50 min.

Barm Brack

Barm Brack is an Irish favorite year-round, often served as a tea bread. On Halloween, bread makers add a gold ring to each loaf. According to tradition, the one who finds the ring will be married within a year. Barm Brack is a hearty bread that keeps well and is delicious toasted.

Mix in small bowl and let foam:
1 T. active dry yeast (15 ml) (1 package)
1 t. sugar (5 ml)
1 c. warm milk (250 ml)

Mix in large bowl:
4 c. flour (1 L)
2/3 c. sugar (150 ml)
1/2 t. ground cinnamon (2 ml)
1/4 t. ground nutmeg (1 ml)
1/2 t. salt (2 ml)

Cut in:
2 T. margarine (30 ml)

Add:
yeast mixture
1 egg, beaten

Stir until batter is stiff but elastic.

Fold in:
1 c. raisins, preferably white (250 ml)
1 c. currants (250 ml)
1/2 c. mixed candied peel, chopped (125 ml) (optional)

Knead gently on floured board, adding more flour if necessary. Place in greased bowl, turning greased side up. Cover with cloth and leave in warm place several hours until dough is doubled in bulk. Punch down. Divide into 2 portions. Shape into round loaves, adding a ring to each (optional), and place on large greased baking sheet or in 2 round pans. Cover again and let rise about 30 minutes. Bake 40-50 minutes in preheated 350°F oven (180°C).

Glaze top with:
1 T. sugar (15 ml) dissolved in 2 T. boiling water (30 ml)

Return to hot oven 3 minutes. Cool on wire rack. Slice and serve with butter or margarine, if desired.

—Pauline Fisher, Goshen, Indiana

One Sunday in a rural Haitian church the theme of the sermon was "loving your enemies." Following the sermon one of the men in the congregation stood up to explain what loving enemies meant in their local context.

"When you are at the end of your rope and your children are crying at your feet from hunger and they have all tied their stomachs to help ease the pain, you have to do something. You decide to go out to your garden a little way off to fetch the last mangoes on your tree. But when you arrive, you find they've been stolen. That's when you need to love your enemy, the thief of your children's food."

—Carla Bluntschli, Bwardlorens, Haiti

● ●

Butter Tress (Switzerland)

Makes 1 loaf

375°F 190°C

35-40 min.

Butterzopf
(BOO-tehr-TSUHPF)

Butterzopf is a popular Swiss Sunday breakfast bread. Older children will enjoy learning to braid the tresses.

Mix in large bowl:

1/4 c. butter, melted (50 ml)
1 1/4 c. warm milk (300 ml)
1 T. active dry yeast (15 ml) (1 package)

When yeast is dissolved, stir in:

3 1/2 c. flour (875 ml)
3/4 t. salt (3 ml)

Knead on floured board until dough is smooth and elastic. Place in greased bowl, turning greased side up. Cover with cloth and let rise until doubled in bulk, about 1 hour. Punch down. Divide into 2 pieces. Roll each piece into cord and braid into tress, according to diagram. Tuck ends under. Place on greased baking sheet, cover, and let rise 45 minutes.

Preheat oven to 375°F (190°C).

Brush loaves with:

1 egg, beaten

Bake 35-40 minutes. Cool on rack. Best if eaten the day it is made.

—*Margrit Ummel-Rediger, Elkhart, Indiana*

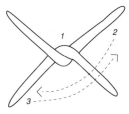

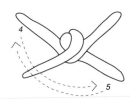

etc.

Tuck ends under

T here is no such thing as "my" bread. All bread is ours and is given to me, to others through me, and to me through others. For not only bread but all things necessary for sustenance in this life are given on loan to us with others, and because of others and for others and to others through us.

—*Meister Eckhart*

If you find no fish, you have to eat bread.

—*African proverb*

Sourdough Rye Bread (Austria)

Schwarzbrot
(schvahrtz-broht)

Austrian rye bread has a characteristic sour flavor and thick, chewy crust. Contributor learned this recipe in his father's bakery while growing up in Austria. We have adapted it so one does not need to maintain a sourdough starter.

• *Variation:*
For a more authentic sourdough bread, remove one cup of starter from first yeast mixture at end of rest period and store in refrigerator for future use. At subsequent baking, add refrigerated starter to first yeast mixture; remove 1 cup at end of rest period and store. Continue as directed, adjusting amount of white flour, if necessary to make dough smooth and elastic.

Starter:
In large bowl, mix:
3 c. warm water (750 ml)
1 T. active dry yeast (15 ml) (1 package)
3 c. rye flour (750 ml)
Stir until smooth. Cover and let rest 6-24 hours at room temperature. A longer rest period will result in a more sour bread.

Bread:
In small bowl, dissolve:
1 T. active dry yeast (15 ml) (1 package)
1 c. warm water (250 ml)
1 T. salt (15 ml)
Add to sourdough starter.
Stir in:
3 1/2 c. rye flour (875 ml)
4 c. white flour (1 L)
Turn onto floured board and knead in:
1 1/2-2 c. additional white flour (375-500 ml)
Knead until dough is smooth and elastic. Shape into 2 oblong loaves and place on greased cookie sheet. Cover with cloth and let rise until doubled in bulk, 40-50 minutes. Bake 45-50 minutes at 375°F (190°C). Cool on rack. Cut in thin slices to serve.

• *Option:*
For additional flavor and texture, add one of the following: 1/4 c. coriander seeds (50 ml); 1/4 c. fennel seeds (50 ml); 1/3 c. caraway seeds (75 ml) or 1/3 c. wheat flakes (75 ml).

—*Franz and Barbara Goller, Notre Dame, Indiana*

They shall beat their swords into plowshares,
and their spears into pruning hooks;
nation shall not lift up sword against nation,
neither shall they learn war any more;
but they shall all sit under their own vines
and under their own fig trees,
and no one shall make them afraid;
for the mouth of the Lord of hosts has spoken.

—*Micah 4:3b-4*

If all of humanity suffers together, the individual does not suffer.

—*African proverb*

Wild Rice Bread (Canada)

Manomin Baquajeegan
(mah-NOH-min
bah-KWAY-jeh-gun)

This recipe was developed for the Kagiwiosa Manomin Wild Rice project of the Ojibway community in Wabigoon, Ontario. MCC SELFHELP Crafts shops in Canada market Kagiwiosa wild rice, which is purchased from Ojibway growers and roasted in the traditional way before husking.

• Option:
Substitute brown rice for wild rice.

• •

Makes 2 loaves

400°F 200°C

30 min.

Combine:

1/2 c. wild rice (125 ml)
11/2 c. water (375 ml)
1/2 t. oil (2 ml)

Cook until rice is tender, about 30 minutes (see p. 142 on long-cooking varieties of rice).

While rice is cooking, combine:

1/4 c. warm water (50 ml)
2 T. molasses (30 ml)
1 T. active dry yeast (15 ml) (1 package)

Set aside.
Combine in large bowl:

cooked rice
1 c. cold water (250 ml)
2 T. oil (30 ml)
1/4 t. ground ginger (1 ml)
yeast mixture
11/2 t. salt (7 ml)
11/2 c. whole wheat flour (375 ml)
21/2-3 c. white flour (625-750 ml)

Mix to make stiff, smooth dough. Knead on floured surface about 10 minutes. Place in greased bowl, turning greased side up. Let rise until doubled in bulk. Punch down and knead again. Shape into 2 loaves. Place in greased pans and let rise 20-30 minutes. Preheat oven to 400°F (200°C). Bake 30 minutes, until nicely browned.

—Ruth McCaslin, Wabigoon, Ontario

• •

Hearty Wheat Bread (Germany)

Grambrot
(GRAHM-broht)

This substantial bread contains no sweetener or shortening. "It's real bread that gives you something to chew," said one tester.

Makes 2 loaves

375°F 190°C

25-30 min.

Place in large bowl:

3 c. warm water (750 ml)

Sprinkle over water:

1 T. active dry yeast (15 ml) (1 package)

When yeast is dissolved, add and mix together:

2 t. salt (10 ml)
2 c. white flour (500 ml)
6-61/2 c. whole wheat flour (1.5-1.6 L)

Knead on floured board until smooth and elastic, about 10 minutes. Place in greased bowl, cover with cloth, and let rise in warm place until doubled in bulk. Form into 2 loaves and place in greased pans. Let rise. Bake 25-30 minutes at 375°F (190°C). Cool on rack.

—Katharina Koop, Vineland, Ontario

Coconut Bread (Belize)

Makes 6 small loaves

350°F 180°C

25-30 min.

Pan de Coco
(pahn day KOH-koh)

Maud Adolphus bakes Pan de Coco inside a truck tire rim placed over an open fire. She covers the rim with a barrel lid and tops it with coals. She feeds the leftover coconut pulp to her chickens. The pulp can also be used in baking. This is a light, moist bread with the sweet taste of coconut. Directions for cracking a fresh coconut are on p. 280.

• *Variation:*
Instead of making fresh coconut milk, use 2 1/2 cups canned coconut milk (625 ml). If sweetened, omit sugar. If coconut milk comes in 15-oz. container (475-g), add water to make 2 1/2 c. liquid (625 ml). Grating your own coconut is less expensive, but time consuming. (See p. 280 for other ways to make coconut milk.)

Grate:
   1 coconut
Add 2 1/2 c. hot water (625 ml) and let stand at least 20 minutes. Drain and reserve liquid (coconut milk).
To warm coconut milk, add:
   1 T. active dry yeast (15 ml) (1 package)
   1/2 c. sugar (125 ml)
   1 t. salt (5 ml)
   1/4 c. oil (50 ml)
Let stand 5 minutes.
Stir in:
   7-8 c. flour (1.8-2 L)
Knead on floured board about 8 minutes, until smooth and elastic. Put in greased bowl and let rise 35-40 minutes. Punch down and divide into 6 balls. Shape into round loaves and press down center with heel of hand. Place on greased cookie sheet and cover. Let rise 20 minutes. Bake in preheated 350°F oven (180°C) 25-30 minutes or until golden.

• *Option:*
Instead of loaves, form into small, round individual buns. Reduce baking time to 20-25 minutes, or until golden.

—*Maud Adolphus, Valley of Peace, Belize; and Grace Weber, Reading, Pennsylvania*

After assisting the Valley of Peace Salvadoran refugee resettlement project in Belize, we transferred to Honduras to work in refugee programs there. Just before our departure, Doña Francisca, one of the refugee women who had become a good friend, baked three small loaves of sweet bread for our journey. As she gave them to us, she explained that when she fled her war-torn country of El Salvador for Belize, she had taken three small loaves of sweet bread with her. They had lasted her the entire journey—a several-day trip by bus and on foot. She hoped the three loaves would be enough for our journey. We were touched by her generosity. Our trip was a 30-minute hop by plane from Belize City to San Pedro Sula, Honduras.

—*Grace Weber, Reading, Pennsylvania*

— Notes
   1. *With All God's People: The New Ecumenical Prayer Cycle,* comp. by John Carden (Geneva, Switzerland: WCC Publications, 1989), p. 223.
   2. Quoted in the film *Witness to War: An American Doctor in El Salvador, Charlie Clements* (First Run Features, 153 Waverly Place, New York, N.Y. 10014).
   3. Jim McDowell, "The Month When the Children Wait for Food," *UNICEF News* 85, no. 3 (1975), pp. 27-28. Used with permission.

... soups

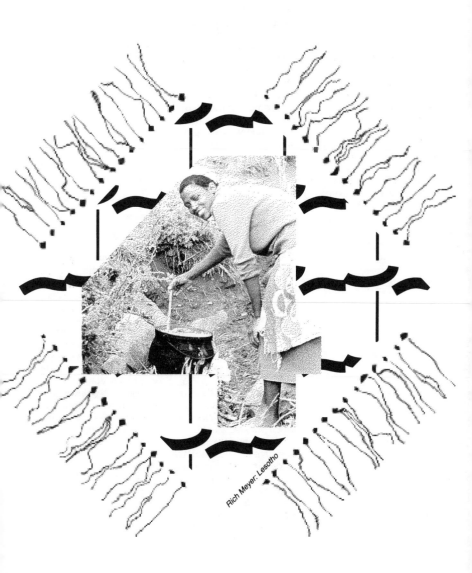

Rich Meyer: Lesotho

During the civil war that eventually ended the Somoza family rule in Nicaragua, I worked with a village of Nicaraguan fishing families who had relocated to Guapinol, a small island off the Pacific coast of Honduras. Whenever I visited the village, Paulino, one of the community leaders, invited me home for a meal.

I always felt uncomfortable being served part of their meager rice-and-beans rations, but I felt especially bad when his wife, Teresa, included a fried egg, perhaps armadillo, or fish they had caught, or maybe even some chicken.

Knowing their Red Cross food rations were limited, I tried to make excuses about why I couldn't stay to eat. I even arranged my visits so they wouldn't fall near mealtime. But Teresa was always able to put something together at a moment's notice, and Paulino insisted that I eat.

"Most of the people in our village do not want to share their food," Paulino said one day. "They say their rations barely reach from one week to the next. But we like to share with everyone who visits here, and we've noticed that even though we share, we always seem to have plenty."

I felt like I was visiting the Old Testament widow from Zarephath, whose oil jug never dried up and whose flour bin never grew empty because she shared her limited food supplies.

—*Nelson Weber, Reading, Pennsylvania*

While living in Transkei, South Africa, our Xhosa neighbor Matyani and we wished to celebrate Christmas. My husband and I were without extended family, and she was without great means. So we decided to join forces and share the day.

My husband and I provided cabbage, potatoes, and chicken, which Matyani and I cooked in her cast-iron pots. In a festive mood we tended the fire, and when the food was ready, Matyani carefully divided it so each family member would have a share.

Matyani served herself last and was just about to sit down and eat when a relatively wealthy woman from a neighboring village stopped by. The visitor had already eaten, but Matyani could not welcome her without offering food. To my astonishment, Matyani gave the visitor the plate she had prepared for herself. She gave away her Christmas dinner to one who was already well fed. And she did not even seem to mind.

—*Magdalene Andres, Maseru, Lesotho*

4

The Hospitality of Poverty

A friend of mine vividly recalls a walk one afternoon across the rural Lesotho village in southern Africa where she and her family spent three years. Brenda was going to visit her friend 'Me Malebohang. Arriving at her house, Brenda found her at a table in the courtyard cutting up a pumpkin. It was early winter, pumpkin-harvesting time. Since pumpkins keep well, they are the main vegetable the Basotho, the people of Lesotho, eat during the winter.

"What a bad pumpkin harvest!" 'Me Malebohang said after they exchanged greetings. "More than half of the pumpkins rotted in my field. These eight are the only ones I have to keep for winter."

Time passed as their conversation flowed from talk of pumpkins to other topics. When Brenda rose to leave, 'Me Malebohang reached for one of the largest pumpkins on the wall and handed it to her.

"You can't give me this pumpkin," Brenda protested. "You just told me that these are all you have!"

'Me Malebohang laughed. "We Basotho know that this is the way to do it. Next year I may have nothing in my field, and if I don't share with you now, who will share with me then?" Still smiling, she took the pumpkin back and cut it in half. "Here," she said, "you take this half and give the other half to your neighbor, 'Me Maphethetso. Go well!"

Now living in North America, Brenda recalls the things she learned in Lesotho. "No matter how much food you have or how many guests you have, food will go around. When you share it, it goes around. It always does."

....

*b*ana ba monna ba arolelana hloho ea tsie.
Children of a man share the head of a grasshopper.
(Those who are related will share their food, no matter
how little it is.)

—Sesotho proverb (Lesotho)

"It is ironic," she says, "that the more affluent we become, the less hospitable we are. We're always so busy. And we don't think we can entertain unless we have everything in order."

Brenda is right. Books and magazine articles about hospitality and etiquette abound in North America. People remodel their homes and refurbish their kitchens to make more room for entertaining. But are we really more hospitable for all the entertaining ideas we clip from magazines, and all the resources and energy we devote to creating entertaining spaces in our homes?

Finding time to give and receive hospitality is certainly not a new problem. Jesus addressed this subject some 2,000 years ago in a not-so-modern setting. One day while dining in the home of a prominent politician, he momentarily diverged from proper etiquette to tell a parable.

A man once invited many people to a great banquet. But when it came time for the occasion, the invited guests sent excuses: one had bought a field and wanted to go see it, another had purchased five yoke of oxen that needed attention, and another had just been married. The host was angered but did not cancel the banquet. Instead, he sent his servant out to the city streets to invite the poor, maimed, blind, and lame. They came at once (Luke 14:16-24).

Why did the poor and lame in Jesus' story come so willingly? Their physical hunger no doubt compelled them. But the parable indicates a more important factor: they had uncommitted time available. They were not part of a social class where being busy was a status symbol and where proper dress and appearance were essential. They were not caught up in the frenzy of buying, selling, impressing others, and getting ahead in life.

If we want to become more hospitable, we might do well to lay aside the glossy magazines, shelve the remodeling plans, and listen to these unlikely folks that Jesus elevated as model guests. Let us consult 'Me Malebohang the next time we seek advice on being model hosts.

Her example suggests that genuine hospitality does not require perfect facilities, ample resources, or hours of planning and effort. We simply need to open our doors and ourselves to others. We do not need to prepare extravagant, distinctive dishes. 'Me Malebohang offered a pumpkin. We can offer a pot of soup.

We honor guests as we focus our primary attention on them, not on the food. Hospitality will be most satisfying for both host and guest when we serve foods like soup, that are easy to prepare, serve, and eat.

Creator Lord,
through whom everything
 in this earth grows—
  sweet bananas, fat plantains,
  sour oranges, dry yams,
  rice, corn, and peanuts
  from which this good soup is squeezed—
who let the sharp red peppers grow that keep us
 healthy and burn stomachs clean;
who let fresh water burst from the ground,
 good, fresh water. . . .
Bless for us this meal,
 our loving God and Father. Amen.

—Prayer of a young Ghanaian Christian[1]

Easy Pumpkin Soup (Venezuela)

[M]

Serves 4-6

Crema de Auyama
(KRAY-mah day
ahw-YAH-mah)

This Venezuelan favorite is served in many restaurants. It is an excellent autumn soup when pumpkins and winter squash are plentiful. Save pumpkin seeds to use in African Meatballs (p. 240).

• Microwave:
In 3-qt. casserole (3-L), cook margarine and garlic on high 1-2 minutes. Add pumpkin cubes and broth and cook on high 2 minutes. Stir. Cook on medium 15 minutes to enhance flavor, stirring every 5 minutes.

Melt in large saucepan:
   1 T. margarine (15 ml)
Add and sauté:
   2 cloves garlic, minced, or 1/4 t. garlic powder (1 ml)
Add and bring to a boil:
   2 c. chicken broth (500 ml), or equivalent water with 1 chicken bouillon cube
Add:
   5 c. fresh pumpkin (1.3 L), pared and cut in 1-inch cubes (2.5-cm)
To quickly process pumpkin, cut whole pumpkin in 8 pieces. Scoop out fibers and seeds. Cut each piece, shell side down, into 1-inch cubes (2.5-cm). Cut shell from cubes.
Cook 10-15 minutes until pumpkin is transparent.
Puree for smooth soup, or serve with pumpkin chunks, adding water if soup is too thick. Serve with sandwiches or cheese and crackers.

• Options:
Substitute other winter squash for pumpkin.
•
For added nutrition, remove 1 c. soup (250 ml) and combine in blender with 1 c. dry milk powder (250 ml). Blend until smooth. Add to soup. Heat to simmer, but do not boil.

—Sherry Holland, Caracas, Venezuela

Red Root Soup
(Kenya)

Serves 4

Supu ya Mchicha
(SOO-poo yah m'CHEE-cha)

African cooks frugally forage wild leafy vegetables to add to soups and sauces. Red root (Amaranthus), a leafy weed with a bright pink root, grows plentifully in North American gardens. Instead of weeding out all the red root, allow several stalks to grow. Harvest the tender top leaves. Red root is sometimes called pigweed. It is not the same as lamb's-quarters, another nutritious plant also known as pigweed in some locales.

• Option:
Substitute 10-oz. frozen spinach (300-g), chopped. Cook it separately in 1/2 c. water (125 ml) until tender. Add spinach with cooking water in place of water in recipe.

Remove stems from leaves and chop finely:
   4 c. red root leaves (1 L)
Melt in saucepan:
   2 T. margarine (30 ml)
Add and sauté:
   red root leaves
   **2 tomatoes, chopped, or 1 c. canned tomatoes
      with juice, crushed (250 ml)**
   1 onion, chopped
Stir and fry until red root is wilted.
Stir in:
   1/2 t. salt (2 ml)
   1 T. flour (15 ml)
Continue stirring and slowly add:
   1/2 c. water (125 ml)
Cover and simmer about 10 minutes until all vegetables are tender.
Add:
   2 c. milk (500 ml)
Heat but do not boil.

• Option:
Substitute any green, leafy vegetable for red root. If greens have a lot of liquid, reduce or omit 1/2 c. water (125 ml).

—Sylvia L. Hess, Bausman, Pennsylvania

Sweet Tomato
Soup
(Germany)

• •
(ts)

Serves 4

Süsse Tomatensuppe
(zooe-seh
toh-MAHT-en-ZOOP-eh)

When surprised by unexpected guests, surprise them with this flavorful German variation of tomato soup. "It's much better than the plain tomato soup we are accustomed to," one tester wrote.

Boil:
   4 c. water (1 L)
   2 beef bouillon cubes
When bouillon is dissolved, add:
   1/2 c. uncooked rice (125 ml)
Boil until rice is almost done, about 15 minutes.
Add:
   3 c. canned or fresh whole tomatoes, peeled (750 ml)
Cook until tomatoes are heated through, stirring carefully so tomatoes remain whole.
Add:
   4 t. sugar or honey (20 ml)
   sweet cream (optional)
Garnish with parsley sprigs. Serve with fresh, crisp French bread.

*—Beate Czogalla, Germany; and Carla Kaye Jones and George
   Switzer, Hampton, Virginia*

● ●

Bean Sprout Soup (Korea)

Serves 6

Kong Namul Kook
(kohng nah-mool kook)

Cut in thin slices, then in 1-inch squares (2.5-cm):
   1/4 lb. beef tenderloin or boneless sirloin (125 g)
Add to meat:
   2 green onions, chopped (reserve uncut tops)
   1 clove garlic, minced
   dash of pepper
   1 1/2 t. Toasted Sesame Seeds (7 ml) (p. 290)
   2 T. soy sauce (30 ml)
Mix well and sear in large saucepan.
Add to meat mixture:
   3 c. fresh or canned bean sprouts, drained (750 ml)
Cook 3 minutes.
Add:
   7 c. water (1.8 L)
   2 T. soy sauce (30 ml)
Cook 30 minutes or until meat and sprouts are tender. Cut onion tops to 2-inch lengths (5-cm) and add to soup. Continue cooking 5 minutes. Season with salt to taste (optional) and serve.

—*Pat Yoder, Goshen, Indiana*

When our family lived in Burkina Faso, West Africa, one of our neighbors was a merchant who frequently traveled. One night walking home from church, I saw that he was home. I entered his yard and greeted him, asking about his family and his adventures on the road. Shortly after I seated myself, his wife came and set before me an unopened pot of *tô*, the common thick sorghum porridge, and another smaller pot of accompanying sauce.

I thanked them, opened the pot of *tô*, and noticed that none of it had been eaten. It was untouched from the moment several hours earlier when the wife poured it into the bowl to cool and harden. In surprise I asked, "Were you expecting someone to come and eat tonight?" Somewhat bewildered by my question, she replied, "We always set aside a bowl of food at night in case a visitor comes."

—*Mathew Swora, Elkhart, Indiana*

The oil lamp, though small, lights up the whole house.

—*African proverb*

Sour Vegetable Beef Soup (Romania)

Ciorba
(CHEEOHR-bah)

In Romania, this popular soup owes its unique flavor to bors, a sour liquid made by fermenting wheat bran. Bors production is a home industry. Old women sell bors to their neighbors; peasants sell it in open markets. Sauerkraut juice or lemon juice provides a similar flavor. Prepare a day in advance for best flavor.

Heat in large saucepan:
 2 T. oil (30 ml)
Add and sauté several minutes:
 1 large carrot, grated
 1 large onion, minced
Add and brown:
 1 lb. beef, cubed (500 g)
Add:
 2 qt. broth or water (2 L)
 1-2 beef bouillon cubes (if using water)
 1 t. salt (5 ml)
Bring to a boil, reduce heat, and simmer until meat is tender, about 1 hour.
Add:
 1 carrot, chopped
 2-3 potatoes, chopped
 2 stalks celery, chopped
Return to a boil and simmer 15 minutes.
Add:
 approx. 6 oz. thin noodles (175 g)
Continue simmering 10-15 minutes more, until vegetables and noodles are tender. (If making a day ahead, do not add noodles until reheating).
Add:
 salt to taste
 1/4 t. pepper (1 ml)
 pinch of dried thyme, or basil, or tarragon leaves
 1/4-1/2 c. sauerkraut juice, lemon juice, or wine vinegar, or a combination (50-125 ml)
Heat through. Serve with fresh bread, and sour cream or yogurt (p. 295) to add to soup as desired.

—Janice Friesen, Honolulu, Hawaii

....

*W*hoever is kind to the poor lends to the Lord, and will be repaid in full.

—Proverbs 19:17

Zucchini Soup (Germany)

(ts)　Ⓜ　　　　　　　　　　*Serves 4-6*

Zucchinisuppe
(zoo-KHEE-nee-ZOOP-eh)

This thick, mild soup is economical in summer when gardens are full of zucchini. Testers recommend it as an appetizer or a luncheon soup, served hot or cold.

• *Microwave:*
Cook onions, garlic, and margarine in 3-qt. casserole (3-L) 3 minutes until onions are tender. Add zucchini, cover tightly, and cook on high 3 minutes. Puree yogurt and zucchini mixture together with salt, pepper, and basil. Return to microwave oven, cover, and cook on high 8-10 minutes, stirring once, until soup is hot but not boiling.

Melt in saucepan:
  1/4 c. margarine (50 ml)
Add and sauté:
  2 onions, chopped
  2 cloves garlic, chopped
Add:
  21/4 c. zucchini, shredded (550 ml)
  2 c. vegetable stock or chicken broth (500 ml)
Simmer 12 minutes. Add:
  1/4 t. salt (1 ml) or to taste
  1/4 t. basil (1 ml)
  dash of pepper
Add:
  1/2 c. wine (125 ml) (optional)
Place soup in blender and puree until creamy. Add:
  1/2 c. yogurt (125 ml) (p. 295)
Serve with sandwiches and fresh fruit.

—Maren Tyedmers, Minden, Germany

Gazpacho (Spain)

Serves 4

(gahth-PAH-choh)

This refreshing chilled soup is consumed in all parts of Spain, particularly during hot summer months. It is also popular in some areas of Latin America. The secret to this soup is to serve it very cold.

Puree in blender or food processor:
  4 medium ripe tomatoes, peeled
  1/4-1/2 green pepper
  1 clove garlic, peeled
  11/2 T. vinegar (20 ml)
  2 T. oil (30 ml)
  11/2 t. salt (7 ml)
  3-4 slices French bread (may be stale) soaked
    in water until saturated
  1/2 cucumber (optional)
Place this concentrated mixture in refrigerator to chill.
Before serving, thin to soup consistency by adding ice water.
Serve cold, garnished with combination of:
  tomato, chopped
  onion, chopped
  green pepper, chopped
  cucumber, chopped
  croutons

—Frances Penner, Madrid, Spain

Creamy Carrot Soup (Germany)

Mohrrübensuppe
(MOH-rooe-ben-ZOO-peh)

Serving coffee and cake between 3:00 and 5:00 p.m. on Saturdays and Sundays is a tradition in many German homes. This replaces supper for some; others prepare a light soup for those still hungry. Creamy Carrot Soup is a favorite.

• *Option:*
Swirl a dab of sour cream or yogurt decoratively on top of each bowl instead of adding it to pot.

ⓣ⒮ 🅼 *Serves 2*

Melt in large saucepan:
3 T. margarine (45 ml)
Add and sauté:
2 medium carrots, sliced
Sprinkle over carrots to glaze:
1 T. sugar (15 ml)
Add:
2 T. flour (30 ml)
1/2 t. curry powder (2 ml) or more to taste
2 c. chicken or beef broth (500 ml)
Bring to a boil while stirring and cook until carrots are tender. Remove from heat and puree in blender until smooth.
Add:
salt to taste
1-2 T. sour cream or yogurt (15-30 ml)
2 T. white wine (30 ml) (optional)
Pour into soup bowls and serve immediately.

• *Microwave:*
In 2-qt. casserole (2-L), combine margarine and carrots, cover, and cook on high 5-7 minutes or until carrots are tender. Stir once at about 3 minutes. Add sugar, flour, and curry powder and stir until smooth. Stir in broth, cover tightly, and cook on high 7-10 minutes or until thickened, stirring once or twice. Puree until smooth and add other ingredients.

—*Maren Tyedmers, Minden, Germany*

Herbed Yogurt Soup (Iran)

Mast
(mahst)

This cold soup is as economical as it is tasty in summer when cucumbers, dill, and mint grow in the garden. Serve it as an appetizer or main dish.

ⓣ⒮ *Serves 6-8*

Mix:
2 qt. yogurt (2 L) (p. 295)
1/2 c. raisins (125 ml)
2/3 c. fresh cucumber, peeled and grated (150 ml)
1 medium onion, finely diced
1 T. fresh dill, bruised (15 ml)
several sprigs fresh mint, bruised
1 t. salt (5 ml)
1/8 t. pepper (.5 ml)
Stir well and refrigerate several hours. Serve with pita bread (p. 51).

—*Lila Paydarfar, Iran; and Naomi E. Fast, Newton, Kansas*

Juliana Soup
(Guatemala)

Serves 6

Sopa de Juliana
(SOH-pah day
who-LYAH-nah)

*Carmen de Marin, a
middle-income Guatemalan
homemaker, created this
recipe in response to the
worsening economic
situation and rising inflation
in her country. Instead of
zucchini, she uses* wiskel
and quicoy, *local squash
varieties.*

• *Option:*
Thicken soup by adding 2 T.
flour (30 ml) mixed with 1/4 c.
cold water (50 ml).

Chop in small pieces and set aside:

1 turnip
4 medium carrots
2 small zucchini or yellow squash
1/4 head cabbage
3 potatoes

Fry in large saucepan in 2 T. oil (30 ml):

1 leek or medium onion, chopped
dash of pepper
pinch of ground turmeric

Add:

chopped vegetables
1 c. corn (250 ml)
1 qt. chicken broth (1 L), or 2 bouillon cubes
and equivalent water
1 c. cooked chicken pieces (250 ml) (optional)

Bring to a boil. Simmer until vegetables are tender.
Season with salt to taste. Serve.

—*Carmen de Marin and Fanny Ellen Yoder, Guatemala City, Guatemala*

Borscht
(Russia)

Serves 10-12

(bohrsht)

*There are many variations of
this popular Russian
cabbage and beet soup. This
recipe originated in the city
of Nizhni Novgorod, where it
is made with homegrown
vegetables, stored through
the winter in root cellars.*

• *Option:*
Instead of stirring in cream
or yogurt, serve as side dish
and add to soup as desired.

In Dutch oven or large pot, cook until tender:

1 lb. beef or soup bone (500 g)
3 qt. water (3 L)

Chop meat or remove from bone and return to broth.
Add:

6 potatoes, chopped
2 carrots, chopped
1 green pepper, chopped
10 oz. cabbage, chopped (300 g)
(3-4 c./750-1000 ml)

Cook until potatoes are almost tender, then add:

1 onion, chopped
1 small red beet, shredded
5 tomatoes, chopped, or 3 c. canned tomatoes,
or tomato juice (750 ml)
dill and parsley to taste
2 t. salt (10 ml) or to taste
1/4 t. pepper (1 ml)
1 bay leaf (optional)

Just before serving, stir in:

1/2 c. heavy cream, sour cream, or yogurt
(125 ml) (p. 295)

—*Edith Moskova, Nizhni Novgorod, Russia; and Susan Froese,
Saskatoon, Sask.*

Belizean Chicken Stew
(Belize)

●●●●●●●●●●●●●●●●●●●●●●●●●●●●●●
-H-
Serves 6-8

Escabeche
(ays-cah-BAY-chay)

Escabeche is a festive meal in Mayan Indian villages of northern Belize. Big stacks of hot, yellow corn tortillas accompany Escabeche and are sometimes used in place of spoons to scoop up the soup. Chicken pieces are eaten by hand. Belizeans would increase the amount of onions called for in this recipe.

• **Option:**
Debone chicken before serving.

In large soup pot, brown in 3 T. oil (45 ml):

2-3 lb. chicken, cut in pieces (1-1.5 kg)

Add:

2 qt. water (2 L)
1-2 cloves garlic, minced
salt and pepper to taste
3 whole cloves
2 t. oregano (10 ml)
1/4 c. vinegar (50 ml)
2-3 whole hot chili peppers (optional) +!

Bring to a boil, then simmer until chicken is tender, about 20-30 minutes.

Meanwhile, cut into rings:

1 lb. onions (500 g) (about 4 medium onions)

Soak in warm water 30 minutes. Drain and add to other ingredients. Cook 2 minutes. Serve with tortillas and/or Belizean Potato Salad (p. 113).

—*Felina Apolonio, Belize City, Belize; and Phyllis Wulliman, Goshen, Indiana*
—*Delsie Cadle, Belize City, Belize; and Dorothy Eby Horst, Gaithersburg, Maryland*
—*Vincenta Magaña de Torres, August Pine Ridge, Belize; and Doris Stauffer, Plain City, Ohio*

Egg Drop Soup
(Korea)

●●●●●●●●●●●●●●●●●●●●●●●●●●●●●●

Makes 6 cups (1.5 L)

Keran Kook
(kay-rahn kook)

A perfect first course for Asian meals.

Combine in saucepan:

5 chicken or beef bouillon cubes
6 c. water (1.5 L)
4 green onions, chopped

Cook until bouillon dissolves and onions are tender.
Beat lightly:

2 eggs

Remove saucepan from heat. Slowly dribble in beaten eggs, stirring gently until eggs are cooked through.

• **Microwave:**
Cook all ingredients except eggs on high 10 minutes or until bouillon cubes dissolve and onions are tender. Add beaten eggs to hot broth, stirring gently until cooked through.

—*Yon Sook Suh, Boston, Massachusetts; and Pat Yoder, Goshen, Indiana*

Bu Yani's Chicken Soup (Indonesia)

Serves 6

Soto Ayam
(soh-toh ah-YAHM)

Boil until tender in 1 1/2 qt. water (1.5 L):
  2-3 lb. chicken, quartered, skinned (1-1.5 kg)
  1 t. salt (5 ml)
Debone chicken and cut in bite-size pieces.
Sauté in 1 T. oil (15 ml):
  2-3 cloves garlic, minced
  1-2 t. ginger root, minced (5-10 ml)
Add:
  broth
  meat
  pepper to taste
  1 t. sugar (5 ml)
Simmer 15-20 minutes to blend flavors.
While soup cooks, sauté until crisp in a little margarine, being careful not to burn:
  1 onion, minced
Set aside.
Place in saucepan in small amount of water:
  1 1/2 c. fresh bean sprouts (375 ml)
Cook 2-3 minutes until crisp-tender. Set aside.
Mince:
  3 T. parsley (45 ml)
Cook:
  1 c. rice (250 ml) (p. 143)
To serve, place 1/3 c. cooked rice (75 ml) in each bowl. Top with soup, onion, sprouts, and parsley.

—Bu Yani, Salatiga, Java, Indonesia; and Lois Deckert, North Newton, Kansas

Bu Yani managed the kitchen, shopping, and meal planning for Lois Deckert the year Lois' husband was a visiting faculty member at Indonesia's Staya Wacana Christian University. "After Bu Yani's first day of work," recalls Lois, "I knew the kitchen was hers, not mine. If I entered, it would be as a guest."

Not ready to relinquish all ties to the kitchen, Lois decided to become an apprentice to Bu Yani to learn Indonesian cooking. "I took the tall kitchen stool and set it just outside the kitchen door where I would be out of the way. With journal in hand, I asked questions and Bu Yani answered. Not always understanding each other, we kept asking, pointing, and explaining as the kitchen became a savory smelling cooking school."

Lois soon filled her journal with notes. Crushing garlic on a grinding stone with salt makes a fine puree. Meat need not be the main course; small amounts flavor a variety of stir-fry dishes. Food must be attractive both in color combinations and in the way it is served.

"The lessons went on and on. I no longer felt like a cook without a kitchen," says Lois.

Chicken Rice Soup
(Philippines)

●●●●●●●●●●●●●●●●●●●●●●●●●●●●●●●

Serves 4

Arroz Caldo
(ah-ROHSS CAHL-doh)

Filipinos make this soup for people who are sick or recently recovered from illness. They also serve it to nursing mothers.

Boil until tender:
  5 c. water (1.3 L)
  1 chicken breast or leg quarter, skinned
Meanwhile brown in 1 T. oil (15 ml):
  3 cloves garlic, minced
Set aside.
Debone chicken. Return meat to broth and add:
  1/2 c. uncooked rice (125 ml)
  1 T. ginger root, crushed (15 ml)
Cook 20 minutes. Add:
  sautéed garlic cloves
  2 green onions, chopped
  1/2 t. salt (2 ml) or to taste
  1/4 t. pepper (1 ml)
  saffron to taste
Serve immediately. If preparing ahead of time, do not add rice until 30 minutes before serving, since rice will absorb broth.

—Helen M. Gaspar, Chicago, Illinois

New Mexican
Hominy Soup
(United States)

●●●●●●●●●●●●●●●●●●●●●●●●●●●●●●●

Serves 6

Posole
(poh-SOH-lay)

Posole is a traditional Mexican feast-day meal, common also among New Mexican people of Hispanic descent. In recent years a number of Anglo churches in the Southwest United States have incorporated Posole suppers into their Christmas tree-decorating festivities. Posole is always made with whole kernels, not hominy grits. This recipe replaces traditional dried hominy with canned or frozen hominy.

Place in saucepan:
  2 lb. pork neck or other bony parts (1 kg)
  3 cloves garlic, peeled
  1 bay leaf
  1 qt. water (1 L) or enough to cover
Bring to a boil and reduce heat. Simmer, covered, until pork is tender. Remove meat from bones and return meat to broth.
Add:
  2 20-oz. cans white hominy, drained (1.2 kg total)
  or 2 lb. frozen hominy (1 kg) (about 5 c./1.3 L)
  1 t. salt (5 ml)
  2 t. chili powder (10 ml) or to taste
Cover and simmer 1 1/2-2 hours. Hominy should be soft but not disintegrating. Serve in bowls with stack of warm flour tortillas. Each person adds seasonings to taste:
  raw onion, minced
  fresh or dried oregano
  lemon or lime slices
  chili powder

—Socorro Avila and Jan Walter, Guadalajara, Mexico
—Daniel Erdman, Lancaster, Pennsylvania

Vegetable Beef Stew (Argentina)

Serves 6-8

Carbonada Criolla
(car-boh-NAH-dah
cree-OH-zhah)

In Argentina, this harvest dish sometimes contains mandioca, a starchy root, instead of potatoes.

Heat in saucepan:
3 T. oil (45 ml)
Brown and discard:
1 clove garlic
Add to oil and sauté:
1 1/2 c. onions, finely chopped (375 ml)
2 tomatoes, chopped
2 green peppers, chopped
Add:
salt and pepper to taste
1 T. fresh parsley, chopped (15 ml)
Remove vegetables from saucepan and set aside.
Add and brown:
1 lb. stew meat, cubed (500 g)
Add:
6 cobs corn, cut in thick, round slices, or 17-oz. can corn, drained (500-g)
1/2 lb. pumpkin or winter squash, peeled and cubed (250 g) (about 2 c./500 ml)
1/2 lb. potatoes, peeled and chopped (250 g) (1-2 medium potatoes)
Add:
sautéed vegetables
meat stock or water to cover
1 T. uncooked rice (15 ml)
Cover, bring to a boil, and simmer 30 minutes, or until vegetables and rice are tender. Add more liquid if necessary. Serve alone as soup or over rice.

—*Graciela Darino and Frieda S. Erb, Buenos Aires, Argentina*

*P ray for us, brothers and sisters in Christ,
that we may not fail in the oil of comfort,
the wine of justice, the involvement of the
patient mule,
and the generosity which, having given,
promises more,
until recovery is complete.*

—*A plea from Hong Kong*[2]

Highland Broth (Guatemala)

Serves 4-5

Caldo
(CAHL-doh)

Caldo (broth) originated in the Mayan Indian communities of Guatemala, where it is still served for special guests and occasions like corn plantings (see story, p. 138) and birthdays. Today it is also popular among Spanish-speaking Guatemalans and is served in fine restaurants. Contributor learned this recipe from K'ekchi' Indian friends in the village of San Pedro Carcha in Alta Verapaz district.

Cook slowly 2-3 hours in large saucepan:

1 chicken, cut into pieces, or 2 lb. stew beef, cubed (1 kg)
3 qt. water (3 L)
3 tomatoes, chopped
1 onion, chopped
4 cloves garlic, minced
1 bunch cilantro or handful of mint leaves
1 t. chili powder (5 ml)
2-3 t. salt (10-15 ml)

Debone chicken and set aside. To serve, fill bowls with hot broth and place a few pieces of chicken or beef in each. Serve with tortillas, cooked rice (which can be added to soup), and a cooked vegetable.

—Pris Garrett, Lancaster, Pennsylvania

During a visit to Guatemala, a friend took me to the home of a K'ekchi' Indian farmer. When we arrived, we found that he had been sick. His illness, however, did not dampen the welcome he gave us. He invited us into his small house and pulled up wooden chairs so we could sit and visit.

Later in the morning when he was feeling stronger, he led us around to the back of his house to show us his animals. While we were there, his wife came and caught a chicken, an indication that we would have lunch before leaving.

An hour or so later, his wife invited us into the kitchen. In the center of the room an open fire burned on the earthen floor. Over this fire she had prepared *caldo*, a spicy chicken soup. Now she used the same fire to cook tortillas.

We sat on a backless bench with soup bowls before us on another bench of equal height. There was no table in this kitchen. Neither were there any utensils for eating. We used steaming hot tortillas to ladle up the soup. The woman did not sit to eat, but continued to quietly pat out tortillas, occasionally adding a chuckle or a quiet word to the subdued conversation.

No prior invitation. No table. No utensils. No dinner music. Broth with only one bony piece of chicken. Hospitality? Indeed. And some of the finest I have ever experienced. The savory flavors of the *caldo* and fresh tortillas satiated my appetite. The gentle rhythmic patting of tortillas soothed my spirit. The warm smiles penetrated our language barrier, making me feel honored and at home.

—jhs

● ●

Hot and Sour Soup (China)

Makes 4 servings

Suanla Tang
(swan-lah tahng)

Hot and Sour Soup, one of China's most delicious and most easily prepared soups, likely originated in Szechwan Province, known for its spicy-hot foods. This version is relatively mild, although you can make it hotter using Szechwan hot bean paste, available in Asian food stores.

• **Options:**
If dried black mushrooms are unavailable or expensive, substitute any fresh mushrooms. Omit soaking.
•
For hotter soup, replace pepper with 3/4 t. Szechwan hot bean paste (3 ml) (or more to taste). +!
•
Add 1/2 c. cubed tofu (125 ml) just before serving.

Soak in warm water 15 minutes:
3 dried black (Chinese) mushrooms
Drain and dry well. Separate and shred stems, and quarter or shred caps. Set aside.
Mix and set aside:
2-3 t. soy sauce (10-15 ml)
1 T. rice wine or lime juice (15 ml)
1 T. vinegar (preferably Chinese red) (15 ml)
1/4-1/2 t. white or black pepper (1-2 ml)
1/2 t. salt (2 ml) (omit if chicken stock is salted)
Bring to a boil in large saucepan:
1 qt. chicken stock (1 L)
Sprinkle in, taking care that chicken pieces don't clump together:
3/4 c. raw chicken breast (175 ml), cut in 2-inch shreds (5-cm)
Cook 2 minutes over medium heat.
Add and cook 2 minutes:
reserved black mushrooms
2 T. canned bamboo shoots (30 ml), cut in 2-inch shreds (5-cm)
Stir in seasoning mixture.
Add:
2-3 T. cornstarch (30-45 ml) mixed with
1/4 c. cold water (50 ml)
Return soup to a boil and cook slowly 1-2 minutes until soup thickens.
Slowly dribble in, while stirring gently:
1 large egg, lightly beaten
Stir until egg is cooked through, remove from heat, and serve immediately.

—*Harriet Burkholder, Goshen, Indiana*

In Haiti neighbors share food, sending it in covered dishes carried by children. At young ages children imitate the customs of their parents, tearing off tiny portions of their two-cent pieces of cassava bread to share with friends.

It is never polite to eat in the presence of others without offering some of your food. An unexpected guest who arrives when someone is eating may ask for some of the food without being considered rude. Haitians believe strongly that *manje kwit pa gen met*—cooked food has no owner.

87

Beef Noodle Soup (Vietnam)

Pho' Bò
(fuh baw)

This tasty soup is eaten in Vietnam and neighboring Laos for breakfast, lunch, or a snack. Use chopsticks to eat the noodles and a large spoon for the broth. Anise stars and fish sauce can be purchased in Asian stores.

• *Options:*
Raw beef slices may be omitted, although they give the soup part of its unusual appeal. For well-done beef slices, precook in a little broth before adding to bowl.
•
Substitute chicken bones or chicken and chicken broth. Use cooked chicken pieces in soup bowl, rather than raw.

Combine in large saucepan:

3 qt. water (3 L)
1/2-11/2 lb. beef or beef soup bones (250-750 g)
2-4 beef bouillon cubes
1 onion, cut in half
1 t. salt (5 ml) (optional)

Cover and simmer 2-3 hours until broth is flavorful. Skim residue so broth is as clear as possible.

1 hour before serving, add:
4 whole anise stars

Continue to simmer.

While broth simmers prepare the following, keeping each separate:

mixture of 1/3 c. each cilantro, chopped, and
green onion, thinly sliced (75 ml)
2 oz. raw beef tenderloin or boneless sirloin,
thinly sliced while partially frozen (50 g)
12 oz. thin rice noodles (375 g)

To prepare rice noodles, place in saucepan of boiling water and cook until soft, about 3 minutes. Do not overcook. Rinse in cold water and drain thoroughly in strainer.

Just before serving, remove bone, cut meat into tiny pieces, and return to broth. Add:

1 T. sugar (15 ml)
2-3 T. fish sauce (30-45 ml)
salt to taste (optional)

Broth should be a bit saltier than you might normally prefer, because rice noodles are bland. To serve, place portions of noodles, cilantro-onion mixture, and raw beef slices in large soup bowls. Cover with very hot broth. The hot broth will cook the meat in the bowls.

Have a plate of bean sprouts, mint leaves, hot chili pepper slices, and lemon slices and a small dish of Seasoned Fish Sauce (p. 282) on the table for people to add as desired.

—*Minh Kauffman, Bangkok, Thailand; and Linda Peachy, Lancaster, Pennsylvania*

*t*hose who are generous are blessed,
for they share their bread with the poor.

—*Proverbs 22:9*

• •

Vietnamese Chicken Soup (Vietnam)

Serves 4

Pho' Gà
(fuh gah)

Boil until tender:

2 lb. chicken or leg quarters (1 kg)
water to cover
1-2 t. salt (5-10 ml)
1 star anise (optional)

Remove chicken, debone, and pull or cut into pieces. Skim broth and keep hot.

Place in each of 4 soup bowls:

2 T. cabbage, thinly sliced (30 ml)
1/2-1 green onion (including stem), finely chopped
2 sprigs cilantro or parsley
2 T. chicken pieces (30 ml)
a little cooked rice or thin noodles (optional)
1/2-1 t. oyster or fish sauce (2-5 ml) (optional)

Cover with boiling chicken broth.

Add:

black and ground red pepper to taste +!

Use remaining chicken pieces in Vietnamese Chicken Salad (p. 112) and serve salad with soup.

—Catherine Baer, Goshen, Indiana

....

I have been learning new lessons about hospitality since coming to work with Vietnamese refugees in the Philippines. Nhan, one of the women I have learned to know, comes to cook with me once a week. I receive much more from our cooking times. She has taught me to stretch food to feed more people, rather than overfeeding myself.

Once we invited 60 refugee camp construction and maintenance workers for lunch. Nhan and two other Vietnamese women worked with me for a day and a half to prepare 500 *cha giò* (spring rolls). Our preparations began with a 6:00 a.m. trip to the open-air market to bargain for meat and vegetables, followed by four hours of washing, chopping, and mixing. The following morning we began filling *lumpia* wrappers at 7:00 a.m. and cooked *cha giò* for two hours.

It didn't matter that I had only 33 inches of counter space; we squatted on the floor to work. It didn't matter that I had no hot water at the sink; Nhan and her friends carried their water from a single faucet used by hundreds of others in the refugee camp. It didn't matter that I only had a two-burner hot plate; they cooked over charcoal.

And it didn't matter that 80 rather than 60 people showed up for lunch. No one went away hungry.

Nhan has taught me to appreciate my less-than-ideal kitchen. I have learned to serve a dozen guests each day without a microwave, dishwasher, freezer, oven, mixer, slow cooker, tin cans, packaged mixes, supermarkets, or take-out restaurants.

Compared to Nhan, I am rich, yet she is a talented and generous cook. She has shown me what I don't need.

—Karen Glass-Hess, Morong, Bataan, Philippines

Navajo Mutton Stew (United States)

••••••••••••••••••••••••••••••••

Serves 8

'Atsi' Hahaázh Beezh
(AT-see ha-HAAZH bayzh)

'Atsi' Hahaázh Beezh (with more meat) is one of four different Navajo terms for mutton stew. This indicates the stew's importance in the Navajo diet. Mutton stew always has mutton and potatoes, and cooks add other vegetables as available.

Combine in large soup pot:

2 lb. mutton neck or bones (1 kg)
2 qt. water (2 L)
2 t. salt (10 ml)
1 t. pepper (5 ml)

Simmer 2-3 hours. Remove bones from broth and set aside. Set soup pot in cold place to harden fat. Remove fat. Return soup pot to heat and add to broth:

2 large onions, chopped
6 large potatoes, diced
1/2 medium cabbage, chopped

Simmer until vegetables are tender. Remove meat from bones and add to soup. Simmer a few minutes longer. Serve with Fry Bread (p. 49).

—*Ernestine Chavez, Rebecca Eldridge, Annabelle Yazzie, and Ethel Bundy, Bloomfield, New Mexico*

Barley Soup (Colombia)

••••••••••••••••••••••••••••••••

Serves 4-6

Sopa de Cebada
(SOH-pah day say-VAH-dah)

Colombians often make this with a cow's tail instead of stewing beef.

• Options:
For wheat soup, substitute ham bone for beef, and 1/4 c. cracked wheat (50 ml) for barley.
•
To make vegetarian stew, omit meat.

Cut in small pieces:

1 lb. stewing beef (500 g)

Boil in 6 c. water (1.5 L) with 1 beef bouillon cube until meat is tender.
Skim fat, then add:

1/4 c. pearl barley (50 ml)
2 large onions, chopped
1 c. peas, fresh or frozen (250 ml)
2 carrots, chopped
1 c. celery, chopped (250 ml)
1 T. vinegar (15 ml)

Cook until barley and vegetables are tender. Add:

salt and pepper to taste

—*Mary Hobe Stucky, Bogotá, Colombia*

*D*onde come uno, comen dos.
Where one eats, two can eat.

—Colombian proverb

Harvest Stew (Chile)

Serves 6

Porotos Granados a la
Chilena
(poh-ROH-tohss
grah-NAH-dohss ah lah
chee-LAY-nah)

*For many Chileans, this
end-of-summer celebration
dish symbolizes the joys of
rural living and producing
one's own food. Most of the
ingredients are homegrown.
The mother prepares the
meal with the help of the
older daughters and does
not eat until everyone else
has finished.*

• *Option:*
Serve with a simple tomato
salad: Combine 2 c. sliced or
chopped tomatoes (500 ml),
and 1 c. sliced or chopped
onions (250 ml); oil and salt
to taste.

In large saucepan, sauté in 3 T. oil (45 ml):
   1 onion, finely chopped
   1 clove garlic, finely chopped
   1 t. chili powder (5 ml)
   2 hot green chili peppers, finely chopped +!
   salt, pepper, oregano to taste
Add:
   **1 1/2 c. fresh or canned tomatoes, chopped
   (375 ml)**
   **2 c. pumpkin or winter squash, peeled and
   cubed (500 ml)**
   2 c. fresh, frozen, or canned corn (500 ml)
Cook until tender.
Add:
   2 c. white beans, cooked (500 ml)
Simmer at least 30 minutes. The soup will be thick and
chunky, with a mild spicy flavor.

• *Option:*
Substitute canned pumpkin for fresh pumpkin. Soup will be
less chunky.

—*Jacquelín Galleguillos, Santa Clara, Chile; and Linda Hines Geiser,
Apple Creek, Ohio*

Country Bean Soup (Serbia)

Serves 4-5

Srpski Grah
(serp-ski grahh)

*A simple, nourishing soup
the contributor enjoyed in
many settings while living in
the former Yugoslavia.*

• *Option:*
To cook in slow cooker, soak
beans in water overnight. In
morning, add bacon, carrots,
and salt. Cook on high 1-2
hours, followed by 8-10
hours on low. Or cook 5-6
hours on high, or 10-12
hours on low. Add flour
mixture 1 hour before
serving.

Soak overnight or by quick method (p. 162):
   2 c. white or pinto beans (500 ml)
   2 qt. water (2 L)
Add:
   8-10 slices bacon or end of ham bone
Bring to a boil, and simmer 45 minutes.
Add:
   1-2 carrots, thickly sliced
   1 1/2 t. salt (7 ml) or to taste
Cook 35-40 minutes until carrots and beans are tender.
In small frypan, melt:
   2 T. margarine (30 ml)
Stir in:
   2 T. flour (30 ml)
   1 T. paprika (15 ml)
Add flour mixture to soup. Cook until thick. Serve with
fresh bread.

—*Nela Williams, Zagreb, Croatia; and Sara Wenger Shenk,
Harrisonburg, Virginia*

Pea Soup with Doughboys (Canada)

Serves 6-8

This recipe comes from Newfoundland, a colorful province with brightly painted homes and unique town names such as Heart's Content, Come By Chance, and Too Good Arm. Newfoundlanders traditionally lived off the sea and land, preserving their fish and meat by salting, pickling, smoking, and sun-curing. The doughboys in this soup are small dumplings.

Soak separately overnight (ham bone need not be soaked):

1 lb. salt meat or ham bone (500 g)
2 c. split peas (500 ml)

Drain. Combine in large saucepan:

meat
split peas
2 qt. water (2 L)
1 onion, chopped

Bring to a boil. Simmer until peas are soft, 2-3 hours.
Remove meat and cut into pieces or remove from bone.
Return to saucepan and add:

1 c. celery, diced (250 ml)
1 c. potatoes, diced (250 ml)
3 carrots, diced

Simmer 30 minutes, until vegetables are nearly tender.
While soup simmers, prepare doughboys (optional):
Mix together:

1 1/2 c. flour (375 ml)
1 T. baking powder (15 ml)
1/2 t. salt (2 ml)

Cut in:

3 T. margarine (45 ml)

Add to make soft dough:

2/3 c. water or milk (150 ml)

Drop by teaspoonfuls into soup. Cover tightly and cook 15 minutes. Thin soup with water, if too thick. Reheat and serve.

—Kathryn Loewen, St. John's, Newfoundland

Different tribes in Kenya have different ways of showing hospitality. Among my Kikuyu tribe, there is a basic assumption that every time you visit a home the host will feed you. Most visits are unannounced. It is impolite not to feed a visitor, and it is impolite for a guest to decline the food that is offered.

A Kikuyu proverb says, *"N'garagu ndi noyaguwo uhoro (hunger is not questioned)."* This means that when people are traveling and become hungry, they may stop at any garden and eat. Most gardens have sweet potatoes, bananas, and sugarcane. If the garden owner comes by while the travelers are eating, there is no problem, as long as they pick only what they can eat at the moment. Carrying food away is considered stealing.

—Loice Robi Byler, Jackson, Mississippi

Garbanzo Lamb Stew (Libya)

●●●●●●●●●●●●●●●●●●●●●●●●●●●●●●
-**H**-

Serves 6-8

Shorba
(SHOHR-bah)

Contributor's aunt learned to make this spicy soup while living in Libya. Easy to double for a larger group. The soup pasta commonly used for this soup is a small oval, about the size of a pea.

In large saucepan, cook 1-2 minutes over high heat:

1/4 c. olive oil (50 ml)
1/2-11/2 t. ground red pepper (2-7 ml) +!
1/2 onion, chopped
3/4 c. tomato paste (175 ml) (6-oz. can/175-g)

Add:

2-4 c. lamb or beef, cubed (.5-1 L)
10 c. water (2.5 L)
1 T. ground turmeric (15 ml)
2 t. salt (10 ml)

Bring to a rapid boil, reduce heat, and cook slowly 11/2-2 hours until tender. Add:

21/2 c. canned or cooked chickpeas, drained (625 ml)
2 bunches parsley, chopped
more water, if stew is too thick

Just before serving, add:

6 T. soup pasta (90 ml)

Cook until pasta is tender. Serve with lemon wedges and bread.

—*Mary F. Beck, Cairo, Egypt*

Mma Sakina's Bean Soup (Botswana)

●●●●●●●●●●●●●●●●●●●●●●●●●●●●●●

Serves 4-6

Sopho ya Dinawa ya Mma Sakina
(SOUP-oh yah dee-NAH-wah yah mah sah-KEE-nah)

Contributor Norma Johnson writes that in a culture where recipes are seldom recorded, Mma Sakina (mother of Sakina) was amazed that anyone would want to write down this simple soup recipe. The authentic recipe calls for removing all bean skins. Busy cooks may rinse away part of the skins or simply leave them in the soup.

Soak overnight or by quick method (p. 162):

2 c. dried lima or butter beans (500 ml)

Cook 15 minutes or until skins are loose. Drain and rinse. Slip off bean skins (optional).
Add to beans:

2 onions, chopped
approx. 1 qt. water (1 L)
2 beef bouillon cubes
pepper to taste

Cook approximately 1 hour or until beans are soft. If skins are removed, beans will break apart, thickening broth. Add:

4 medium tomatoes, peeled and diced
salt to taste (optional)

Simmer until tomatoes are cooked through.

—*Mma Sakina, Lobatse, Botswana; and Norma Johnson, Newton, Kansas*

Bean Soup with Eggs (Nicaragua)

Sopa de Frijoles
(SOH-pah day
free-HOH-layss)

For Nicaraguans, Sopa de Frijoles is the first meal from a pot of freshly cooked beans (p. 162). Remaining beans are reserved and served later with rice. Tester commented, "This really hit the spot."

• Options:
Instead of cooking eggs in soup, chop hard-cooked eggs and sprinkle over soup.
•
Instead of stirring sour cream into soup, add a dab of sour cream or yogurt (p. 295) to each bowl at the table.

Combine in large saucepan or pressure cooker:

1 lb. black or red beans, presoaked (500 g)
2 qt. water (2 L)
1 t. salt (5 ml)
3-4 cloves garlic, peeled

Cook until beans are tender (p. 162).

Remove beans from saucepan or pressure cooker. Return 2-3 c. beans (500-750 ml) to broth along with:

1 T. margarine (15 ml)
1/2 c. onion, chopped (125 ml)
1/4 c. green pepper, chopped (50 ml)
salt to taste
2 T. cilantro leaves, chopped (30 ml) (optional)
1/2 c. milk (125 ml) (optional)
1/4 c. sour cream (50 ml) (optional)

Bring soup to a boil and carefully break in:

4-6 eggs (1 per person)

Cook over medium heat without stirring until eggs are cooked. Dish into soup bowls, placing one egg in each bowl. Serve with tortillas and a salad.

—*José Avalo and Angela Silva, Managua, Nicaragua; and Ann Graber Hershberger, Harrisonburg, Virginia*

Mbodangaaku, the tradition of the Wodaabe, is the way we hold hands with one another. This is the way we feel attached to each other.

Mbodangaaku is the only wealth of the Wodaabe. It is their true wealth. When we go to the villages of the sedentary people, we are hungry and thirsty because no one gives us anything without money. But when we travel in the bush, wherever there is a Wodaabe camp, we are at home.

When someone comes to your camp, it is because of the tradition of *Mbodangaaku* that you welcome him. You take a mat for him to the west of your camp. You take him water to drink. You light a fire for him even if it is not cold. You take him food.

Even if you yourself do not like your guest, when his foot comes to your camp, you go to welcome him as if he were your God. The proverb says: "Your guest is your God!"

—*Bodaado man of the nomadic Wodaabe tribe of Niger*[3]

Jokai Bean Soup (Hungary)

Serves 6

Jokai Bableves
(yoh-kay bop-le-vesh)

Named after popular 19th century Hungarian writer Mór Jókai, this soup is filled with Old World flavor. Hungarians serve it as an appetizer, but it is hearty enough for a festive main-course soup. Serve with warm, freshly baked bread.

• *Options:*
Substitute 2 c. canned kidney beans with (500 ml) liquid for dried beans. Add to soup with vegetables.
•
For additional seasoning, add a bit of tarragon vinegar along with a bit of sugar to offset the vinegar's sour flavor.

Soak overnight or by quick method (p. 162):

1 c. dried kidney beans (250 ml)
3 c. water (750 ml)

Place in soup pot:

1/2-3/4 lb. smoked pork hocks (250-375 g)
6 c. water (1.5 L)

Bring to a boil and simmer, covered, 1 hour. Add soaked beans with soaking water and continue simmering 30 minutes. Remove pork hocks and set aside. Skim fat.
In frypan, brown in 1 T. skimmed fat (15 ml):

3/4 c. carrots, sliced (175 ml)
2/3 c. white turnip, sliced (150 ml)

Add browned vegetables to soup pot along with:

1 c. green pepper, chopped (250 ml)
1 medium tomato, chopped
1 clove garlic, chopped
1 bay leaf
1/2 t. salt (2 ml) or to taste

Return to a boil and simmer 30 minutes, until vegetables and beans are tender.
Brown in frypan:

1/2 lb. smoked sausage, sliced (250 g)

Add to soup pot.
Mix into thick paste:

2 T. sausage drippings, skimmed fat, or margarine, melted (30 ml)
6 T. flour (75 ml)
1 t. paprika (5 ml)
1 t. fresh parsley, chopped (5 ml)
2-3 T. water (30-45 ml)

Stir paste into soup and cook briefly until soup thickens.
Stir in:

1/3-1/2 c. yogurt (p. 295) or sour cream (75-125 ml) (optional)

Remove from heat. Cut meat from reserved hocks and place in soup tureen. Add soup.

—Joseph S. and Julie Miller, Ephrata, Pennsylvania

ℳi casa es tu casa.
My house is your house.

—Latin American saying

Kentucky Soup Beans (United States)

A simmering pot of soup beans is a common sight in eastern Kentucky homes; many churches have soup bean suppers. Pinto beans, introduced with other government commodities during the Depression, gradually replaced homegrown shucky or "leather batch" beans used in earlier days. Because of its few ingredients, Kentucky Soup Beans is accessible to people of all income levels.

In 4-qt. saucepan (4 L) soak overnight or by quick method (p. 162):

2 c. dry pinto beans (500 ml)
6 c. water (1.5 L)

Add:

1/8 lb. salt pork, whole, with slits cut in it (65 g)
1/2 c. onion, chopped (125 ml)
1/2 t. salt (2 ml) or to taste

Bring beans to a boil. Reduce heat and simmer covered until beans are soft, about 1 1/2 hours. Check periodically and add more water if needed. Beans should have consistency of thick soup. Garnish with raw onions, if desired. Serve with Kentucky Cornbread (p. 56).

• **Options:**
Omit salt pork. Flavor with bacon drippings and/or 1-2 t. salt (5-10 ml).
•
Add a bit of cured ham.

• **Option:**
To make in slow cooker, soak beans in water overnight. In morning add other ingredients and cook 5-6 hours on high or 10-12 hours on low.

—*Debbie Beverly, Hindman, Kentucky; and Carol Loeppky, Whitesburg, Kentucky*

Making people feel at home doesn't come automatically. We were more at home in Kentucky than we ever thought possible. But that feeling didn't come by chance. It came because Cathy and Philip Adams had us over for dinner in our first few weeks there. It came because Jane Breeding offered to keep Stephanie while we were at the hospital to have the baby. It came because neighbor Gina invited me to walk up the hollow with her and introduced me to her mom. It came because neighbor

Juanita pushed Lynanne in the swing while I got ready for Bible study group.

These special gestures to us, the foreigners, the strangers, the outsiders, were the reason we left part of our hearts in Kentucky. May we be so gracious in welcoming others who have the same need to feel at home.

—*Kathy and Steve Wiest, Kingsburg, California*

Norm Caudill is a dispatcher in the mines of eastern Kentucky. He is one of about 60 members of the Isom Presbyterian Church. Amidst a group of people with different viewpoints and struggles, Norm quietly lets others know that he cares about them.

Norm once stopped at the pastor's home only to find an empty house and a sink full of dirty dishes. The sink was empty when he left. One Sunday he made lunch for us and left it in our car. Another week when the church prayed for families who had trouble heating their homes, Norm volunteered his two-day wood supply for anyone who might need it.

—*Carol Loeppky, Whitesburg, Kentucky*

Pinto Bean Soup (Mexico)

•••••••••••••••••••••••••••••••••

(ts)   -H-   *Serves 4*

Sopa de Frijol
(SOH-pah day free-HOHL)

*Serve a bright lettuce and
tomato salad to add color to
this tasty Mexican bean soup.*

• *Options:*
Substitute black beans,
common in southern Mexico.
•
To save time, do not sauté
vegetables; simply liquefy
them in blender with beans.
•
Instead of liquefying beans in
blender, mash with masher.

Heat in large saucepan:
   2 T. oil or margarine (30 ml)
Add and fry until browned:
   1 medium tomato, chopped
   1/2 small onion, chopped
   **1-3 fresh green chilies, finely chopped, or
      Tabasco pepper sauce to taste +!**
Liquefy in blender:
   4 c. canned or cooked pinto beans (1 L)
   2 c. liquid in which beans were cooked (500 ml)
Add blended beans to sautéed vegetables along with
enough additional water, 1-1½ c. (250-375 ml), to make
soup of medium-thin consistency.
Season to taste with:
   salt or chicken bouillon powder
   cilantro
Cook 15-20 minutes over low heat to blend flavors.
Garnish with grated cheese, croutons or *totopos* (tortillas
cut in bite-size wedges and browned in oil). Serve with
Mexican Quesadillas (p. 257) or grilled cheese sandwiches.

—*Marie Palafox, Guadalajara, Mexico; and Emily Will, Ciudad
   Guzmán, Jalisco, Mexico*

Red Lentil Soup (Turkey)

•••••••••••••••••••••••••••••••••

Serves 8

Merchimek Chorbasi
(mer-chuh-MEK
CHOR-bah-suh)

*Dried, crushed mint is always
added to Turkish soups,
much like North Americans
add salt and pepper.*

In large soup pot, sauté in 1 T. oil (15 ml):
   2 medium onions, finely chopped
When onions are soft, add:
   1/2 lb. red lentils, rinsed (250 g)
Stir several minutes.
Add:
   2 qt. beef or chicken stock (2 L)
   1 t. paprika (5 ml)
   1 bay leaf
   1 t. salt (5 ml)
   1/8 t. pepper (.5 ml)
   1 t. dried mint, crushed (5 ml)
   1/2 t. dried parsley (2 ml) (optional)
   1-2 T. tomato paste (15-30 ml) (optional)
Bring to a boil. Simmer until lentils are very soft, about 35
minutes. Soup may be pureed, if desired, or served as is.

—*Mualla Cemer, Istanbul, Turkey; and Jewel Showalter, Irwin, Ohio*

Spicy Lentil Pot (Egypt)

Serves 4-6

Shorbet Addis
(show-r'bet AH-diss)

This rich, flavorful soup gains its orange color from orange (red) soup lentils, smaller and sometimes more expensive than brown lentils. Look for orange lentils in Asian or health food stores if they are not available at your grocery store.

Chop in large chunks:
- **2 carrots**
- **1 green pepper**
- **1 onion**
- **2 tomatoes or 1 8-oz. can tomato sauce**

Put vegetables in large soup pot with:
- **5-8 cloves garlic, peeled and left whole**
- **1 1/2 c. orange lentils (375 ml)**
- **5-6 c. water (1.3-1.5 L)**
- **1 chicken bouillon cube (optional)**

Cover and boil 20-30 minutes without stirring. Cool slightly and strain or puree.

Return to pot and add:
- **2 t. ground cumin (10 ml)**
- **1 1/2 t. salt (7 ml)**
- **1/4-1 1/2 t. ground red pepper (1-7 ml) +!**

Simmer 10 minutes, stirring occasionally, to blend flavors. In separate pan, fry 1/2 c. onion, chopped (125 ml), in 1 T. oil (15 ml) until toasty brown. Float onions on top of soup. Serve with wedges of lemon to bring out flavor.

—*Fiza, Mattareyya, Egypt; and Mary F. Beck, Cairo, Egypt*

Up on the high
   mountain, where I
   dwell,
there is no cloud of
   worry.
The spring flows without
   ceasing,
   where I drink to quench
   my thirst.
And there is also manna,
   God has provided.
I don't need to worry,
   for I am entering
Into his kingdom.

—*Thai dinner song, translated*
   by Ravadee Arkkapin,
   Bangkok, Thailand

M. Knawles: Kampuchea

Peanut Soup
(Kenya)

• •

-H-

Serves 4-6

Supu ya Karanga
(SOO-poo yah
kah-RAHN-gah)

*Peanuts, or groundnuts, are
a staple in African soups and
stews. African cooks use
wooden mortars and pestles
to pound raw peanuts into a
fine meal. This recipe omits
the pounding—and some of
the authenticity—by simply
using prepared peanut butter.*

Combine in heavy 2-3 qt. saucepan (2-3 L):

1 qt. chicken or beef stock (1 L)
1 medium onion, chopped
1 large leek, with 2 inches of top (5 cm), chopped
2 medium carrots, sliced

Bring to a boil. Cover and simmer 30 minutes.
Remove from heat and puree until smooth.
Return soup to saucepan and add:

1/4 c. uncooked rice (50 ml)
1-inch piece dried hot red chili (2.5-cm) +!
1/2-1 t. salt (2-5 ml)

Bring to a boil. Simmer, covered, 15-20 minutes until rice
is tender.
In small bowl, mix until blended:

1/2 c. of the soup (125 ml)
1/2 c. creamy peanut butter (125 ml)

Stir peanut mixture into soup along with:

1 t. Tabasco pepper sauce (5 ml) (optional) +!

Cover and simmer 5 minutes. Remove dried chili. Thin with
water if too thick. Add additional salt if needed.

—*Mary Lou Cummings, Quakertown, Pennsylvania*
—*Nav Jiwan International Tea Room, Ephrata, Pennsylvania*

• •

Peanut Vegetable
Soup
(Bolivia)

Serves 8

Sopa de Maní
(SOH-pah day mah-NEE)

*Sopa de Maní is the standard
first-course dish at many
Bolivian celebrations. It is
typically garnished with
French-fried potatoes, made
a bit shorter and thinner than
North American-style fries.*

Grind into very fine pieces:

2 c. skinless raw peanuts (500 ml)

Put in large pot:

peanuts
**2 qt. chicken broth (2 L) or 2 qt. water (2 L) with
2 chicken bouillon cubes**
1 large onion, diced
4 large potatoes, diced
4 carrots, diced

Cook 30 minutes.
Add:

1/4 c. uncooked rice (50 ml)
1 c. peas (250 ml)

Cook 15 minutes.
Serve hot, garnishing top of each bowl of soup with:

fresh parsley, chopped
French-fried potatoes (optional)

—*Glenn Klassen, Akron, Pennsylvania*
—*Ingrid Schultz, Elkhart, Indiana*

During the Civil War in Zaire in 1964, two Zairian church workers and an expatriate colleague were traveling in the war-torn South Kasai district. They came to the village of Tshintshianku, where they intended to spend the night. The village had been beautiful with tree-lined roads, flower-lined paths, and neatly kept houses. But on this day they found the village devastated. Homes were now piles of charred rubble with only blackened sticks marking the corner posts.

The travelers entered the village and wondered if they would find their pastor friend. Few people were in sight. They drove on until they saw the church building. As they stopped and stepped out, they saw that the pastor's house was destroyed and that no people were around.

Then, from under the makeshift thatched roof of a temporary building next to the church, came the pastor. He greeted his friends warmly and found some chunks of log for them to sit on. It was all he had. His wife also greeted them, then turned to start a small fire. They watched as she put something into one small pot to cook over the fire. After a bit she came with a flat-bottomed basket and turned it upside down before them as a table. She brought the little pan which contained three small white sweet potatoes.

The men gave thanks and ate their supper.

That evening around the fire, the pastor and his wife told their guests that they had been burned out and lost their possessions three times. They had just returned from six weeks of hiding in the woods. But in all of their accounting, there was no word of complaint, only thankfulness that God had spared their lives so that they could begin to work and minister again.

—*Eudene Keidel, Clearbrook, British Columbia*

Lord, we know that you'll be coming through the line today,
So Lord, help us to treat you well,
help us to treat you well.

—*Prayer of Mary Glover, an African American helping with the weekly foodline a mile and a half from the U.S. White House*[4]

—*Notes*

1. From *I Lie on My Mat and Pray: Prayers by Young Africans*, ed. Fritz Pawelzik (copyright 1964 by Friendship Press, New York, N.Y.; used with permission).

2. Anglican Diocese of Hong Kong, Bishop R. O. Hall; In *With All God's People: The New Ecumenical Prayer Cycle*, comp. by John Carden (Geneva, Switzerland: WCC Publications, 1989), p. 40.

3. Angelo Miliki, ed., *Belldum: Joy and Suffering Among the Wodaabe* (Mission Catholique, B.P. 10 270, Naimey, Niger).

4. Quoted by Jim Wallis in *Sojourners* (Washington, D.C.; used with permission).

... salads
and vegetables

Jim King: Bangladesh

Years later I still can see old Mulonga standing in the frame of our doorway in Chikankata, Zambia. He would come selling veggies and ask for free "tinnies and newsies," which he would trade for vegetables in outlying villages and return to sell to me.

I had so many different feelings in his presence— amusement over his entrepreneurial skills, irritation when his coming interrupted my dinner preparations, guilt over having so much more than he, and apprehension over how much useful stuff he would find in our garbage can even after I had gleaned it for tin cans and newspapers in anticipation of his visit.

And he always found something. As his sharp eyes spotted a tin I had missed, he would hold it up and with a few well-chosen words and graphic gestures inform me of the value of the item. It could be used for so many things— fashioned into a drinking mug or used to boil water. "You should be more careful next time. Don't throw away this good stuff that I need to make a living," he would admonish.

I remembered old Mulonga on our first visit to a fast-food restaurant after our return to Canada in 1976. All of the valuable containers and items he would salvage to sell in the village were crammed into garbage bags and wasted. I could hardly eat my hamburger.

—Leona Dueck Penner,
  Winnipeg, Manitoba[1]

After returning to Zambia from a visit in the United States, we were delighted by the visits of Zambian friends who came to welcome us back and welcome our new baby. I was especially touched when our good friend Lenty Mutinta came with his wife and youngest child, whom they had named after me.

As we played with each other's babies, I noticed with pain how tiny their little Linda was. At a year, she was only a little heavier than our three-month-old Frieda. I thought of their other children. They once had had four, but two had died from diarrhea.

After a while Lenty signaled to his wife and with a smile she handed me a basket. Looking in I saw a heap of small Irish potatoes and what looked like some plastic trash. I exclaimed with real gratitude about the potatoes, knowing the sacrifice they must have made to find this special treat for their potato-loving white friends.

Lenty leaned forward and picked up the plastic. Holding it out to me with pleasure and dignity, he said, "This is for the baby." My eyes refocused and I saw with a jolt what he was giving her: two little clear plastic glasses and two lovely flat plastic dishes. I thanked him with all the grace I could muster, hoping he had not noticed my lack of composure.

Later, I fought tears as I sat holding those little disposable dishes with "Zambia Airways" inscribed on the bottoms. Why is our world so ordered that people with several sets of dishes constantly discard mountains of containers after a single use? And those who would be pleased to carefully wash and reuse the disposables come upon them so rarely that they treat them as treasures?

—Linda Nafziger-Meiser,
  Elkhart, Indiana

5

● ●

Caring for the Earth . . .
Caring for One Another

I was brought up to respect everything that was on the
earth, "to the smallest grain of sand," my mom used to
say, to those trees there, to the smallest insect, to the big
bears that we have here. My first lesson in life was respect
for those things; to be thankful when I got any food from
the sea, to thank the sea and the fish for giving me life, to
never take for granted anything that I received.

But when logging companies look at trees, they see only
dollar signs. Many of them do clear-cut logging—not one
tree left on top of the mountain. So with the rain we get
here, there is flood after flood, taking all the soil. So what's
left is going to be bare rock.

We were put here as caretakers of this land. Our forefathers
took good care of this land for thousands of years, without
harming it. Now in less than 150 years, there's been so
much irreparable damage that Telanzuin Island will never
be revived. And if there is nothing left on this island,
there's going to be nothing left of us. If you don't have a
land, you don't have a culture and you don't have a people.

—*Diane Brown, Haida Indian*[2]

Land, culture, and people—they are intimately connected. If you respect
one, you will nurture all three. But remove, change, or destroy any
one, and the others will change in like manner.

Grave social problems facing many North American native
communities today stem directly from nation-building activities that
forced native peoples onto reserves, stripped away their traditional
occupations, and restricted their hunting activities and access to
sacred lands. Current consequences of actions a century earlier
provide strong evidence of the ecological, or interrelated, nature of
life.

Despite enormous cultural loss, voices from within the native
communities continue to express the deep philosophical

understanding of their ancestors: The earth is sacred. All living things are interrelated.

In recent years interest in environmental issues has mushroomed on every continent. Members of quiet farm communities in Canada and the United States work to solve the problem of ground water contamination while urban counterparts seek alternatives to overflowing landfills. Citizens in newly autonomous countries in Central Europe want to clean the air and rivers of their industrial cities. Brazilian rubber-tappers are organizing themselves against encroaching development schemes that threaten the life of the rainforests. In Africa, many people are working to slow the growth of the deserts.

To heal the scars of a raped earth, and to permanently restore and protect it, requires that we stop and examine the values and lifestyles that led to the environmental crisis. Why did we abuse creation in the first place?

Wesley Granberg-Michaelson attempts to answer this question in his book, *A Worldly Spirituality*. He quotes from the letter of a friend living on the Lakota Indian reservation in South Dakota:

> **When most Christians talk about being good stewards of the earth, what they have in mind is something like this: We conserve resources so we can use them in the future, and we conserve some wildlife areas so we can admire and enjoy their beauty. I don't think this is biblically sound because both of these ideas are still caught up in human idolatry. . . . The creation exists for the welfare of the human race in this thinking. I don't believe that. I think we all are part of the entire creation, with our own unique roles, and we exist for God.**
>
> **. . . We are all in relationship with one another because we are all in relationship with God. . . . The Lakota people have an elaborate kinship system [including] the earth, who is your grandmother, the sky and eagle, who are your brothers. When you think circular like this you place prime importance on right and proper relationships. You don't abuse or use your relatives, human or otherwise.**[3]

Despite expanded systems of knowledge, communication, and transportation, many individuals and communities run the risk of losing their personal connections to the earth and to their global neighbors. Too busy to garden and too transient to tend an orchard, most of us buy fruits and vegetables from the supermarket. The colorful displays of produce represent various countries and geographical regions, but we have little way of knowing who cultivated and harvested the produce, or what their working and living conditions are.

The stories in this section highlight our important relationships with the earth and with neighbors. We will meet people who suffer because of destructive forces in those relationships. We will find others working to develop more constructive partnerships with the earth, and to reinforce community relationships. They encourage us to redouble our efforts at caring for the earth and caring for one another.

Paul Brallier: Burkina Faso

It is better to sleep with an empty stomach than with a troubled heart.

—Ugandan proverb

K ul a yi'ii wahare baanda wulii, soofnu nde maada.
When you see the beard
of your neighbor burning,
start to put water on your own beard.
(You know that the fire which has taken your friend
will not fail to burn you also. Then you are with him;
then you are together. The death and suffering of
others is also your death and suffering.)

—Wodaabe proverb as related by Bodaado woman of Niger[4]

105

Spicy Cabbage Salad (Korea)

Kim Chi
(kim chee)

Crunchy, tangy-hot Kim Chi is a mainstay of the Korean diet. Like rice, it is eaten at every meal. Korean cooks make Kim Chi in substantial quantities, 10 to 15 times larger than this recipe. The crushed red pepper traditionally used in this recipe resembles red-colored instant coffee granules and is sold at Asian food stores.

● ●

Makes 11/2 qt. (1.5 L)

Remove core and cut in 2-inch pieces (5-cm):
   11/2 medium heads Chinese cabbage (napa) (about 3 qt./3 L)
Place in large bowl. Rinse and drain, then sprinkle with:
   2 T. salt (30 ml)
Mix well and let stand several hours or overnight. Wash thoroughly in cold water and drain.
Mix with cabbage:
   2-3 t. crushed red pepper (10-15 ml) or to taste +!
   3 cloves garlic, crushed or minced
   1/2-1 t. ginger root, crushed or minced (2-5 ml) +!
   3 green onions, including stems, cut in half lengthwise, then in 1-inch lengths (2.5 cm)
   11/2 T. sugar (20 ml)
   1 t. salt (5 ml) or to taste
Cover and let stand 1 day at room temperature. Store in refrigerator. Serve with Korean or other Asian meals.

—Juyoung Chang, Notre Dame, Indiana

Celery and Green Bean Salad (Philippines)

Ensalada ng Kintsay at Sitaw
(ehn-sah-LAH-dah nahng KEEN-tsai aht SEE-tao)

• *Microwave:*
Cook green beans and 2 T. water (30 ml) on high 5-6 minutes, stirring once. Chill and add other ingredients.

● ●

(ts)   M

Serves 4

Boil 5 minutes, until crisp-tender:
   2 c. green beans, cut in halves (500 ml)
Chill and drain.
Add:
   2 T. sweet pickle, chopped (30 ml)
   1 egg, hard-cooked and diced
   1/4 c. celery, chopped (50 ml)
Mix together:
   1 T. lemon juice (15 ml)
   1/4 c. mayonnaise (50 ml)
   1/4 t. salt (1 ml)
Toss gently. Serve on bed of crisp lettuce.

• *Option:*
Use frozen, French-cut green beans.

—Norrie del Fierro and Fanny P. Miray, Nueva Vizcaya, Philippines

● ●

Roasted Sweet Pepper Salad (Bosnia)

Serves 3-4

Pecena Paprika
(PEH-cheh-nah PAH-pri-kah)

This autumn salad is made with thick-walled sweet peppers. Bosnians roast long yellow peppers on a fork over the gas flame or electric element of the kitchen stove. Peppers can also be roasted on an outdoor barbecue or broiled in the oven. Especially attractive with various colors of peppers.

Remove stalk, but leave seeds in 4 large sweet peppers of any variety. Roast or broil until skin cracks. Peppers should be well toasted and can be cooked until skins are almost burned, since the outer skin is removed. Because most peppers are unevenly shaped, some areas will remain unroasted. When well roasted and still hot, carefully peel off skin. Chop or leave whole. (Seeds are left in whole peppers, but not eaten.)

Pour over peppers:

2 T. oil (preferably olive) (30 ml)
2 t. vinegar (10 ml)
1/4 t. garlic, chopped (1 ml), or 1/8 t. garlic powder (.5 ml)
pinch of salt

Serve while still warm. Good with potatoes and a bean salad or meat.

—*Nurka Habibovic, Sarajevo, Bosnia; and Sara Wenger Shenk, Harrisonburg, Virginia*

● ●

Cauliflower Salad (Germany)

Serves 6-8

Blumenkohl Salat
(BLUE-men-kohl zah-LAHT)

Use only fresh herbs. They provide the flavor for this colorful salad.

• Microwave:
Cook cauliflower in covered casserole dish with 1/4 c. water (50 ml) on high 4-7 minutes until crisp-tender. Stir once or twice. Let stand 3 minutes. In separate covered dish, cook beans and carrots in 1/4 c. water (50 ml) on high 2 minutes. Add celery, stir well, and cook another 5-7 minutes on high, stirring once or twice, until crisp-tender. Allow to stand, covered, 3 minutes before cooling.

Cook in a little water and cool:

5 c. cauliflower florets (1.3 L)
1 c. green beans, chopped (250 ml)
1 c. carrots, diced (250 ml)
1 c. celery, chopped (250 ml)

Drain and combine with:

16-oz. can red kidney beans, drained (500 g) (about 2 c./500 ml)
2 tomatoes, chopped

Mix together:

2 T. mayonnaise (30 ml)
3 T. yogurt (45 ml) (p. 295)
3 T. lemon juice (45 ml)
1 T. fresh parsley, chopped (15 ml)
1 T. fresh dill, chopped (15 ml)
1 T. fresh chives, chopped (15 ml)
dashes of salt, pepper, paprika

Pour over vegetables, toss, and let stand at least 30 minutes before serving.

—*Edna Martens, Kandern, Germany*

Festive Vegetable Platter (Brazil)

●●●●●●●●●●●●●●●●●●●●●●●●●●●●●●●●●

Salada de Festa
(sah-LAH-dah day FES-tah)

A colorful salad for a crowd.

Cover large serving platter with layer of leaf lettuce.
Arrange decorative pattern of any or all of the following:
 tomatoes, sliced
 cucumbers, sliced
 green pepper, cut in rings
 carrots, cooked to tender-crisp, cooled, and
  cut in sticks
 eggs, hard-cooked and quartered
 palm hearts, sliced
 black olives
 onions, sliced and separated into rings
 peas, cooked and cooled
Sprinkle with salt and pepper. Drizzle with equal amounts
olive oil and vinegar. Chill.

—*Mert Brubaker, Lancaster, Pennsylvania*

Lentil Salad (Ethiopia)

●●●●●●●●●●●●●●●●●●●●●●●●●●●●●●●●

Serves 6

Miser Salatta
(miss-ehr sah-LAH-tah)

*Prepare this salad a day
ahead to mix flavors. Use
pieces of Ethiopian Flat
Bread (p. 47) to scoop up the
salad, which can be used as
a side or main dish.*

In large saucepan, combine:
 2 c. dried lentils (500 ml)
 5 c. water (1.3 L)
Bring to a boil. Cover and cook on low heat until tender,
but still somewhat firm, about 25 minutes. Drain.
Add:
 3-4 T. lemon juice or vinegar (45-60 ml)
 3 T. oil (45 ml)
 1 t. salt (5 ml)
 1/2 t. pepper (2 ml)
 1/2 c. red shallots or onions (125 ml), cut in thin
  strips, 1/2-inch long (1-cm)
 1-2 hot green chili peppers, cut into thin strips,
  1/2-inch long (1-cm) +!
Marinate at room temperature for 30 minutes. Refrigerate
several hours or overnight before serving.

• *Option:*
**Replace half of the lentils with finely chopped, cooked red
beets.**

—*Sharon Jantzi Kraybill, Lancaster, Pennsylvania*

●●●●●●●●●●●●●●●●●●●●●●●●●●●●●●●●●●

Tomatoes with Oil and Vinegar Dressing (France)

Serves 6-8

Tomates Vinaigrette
(toh-MAHT vi-nay-GREHT)

When summer gardens are producing in rural France, this salad is served each night with fresh boiled potatoes. Add cottage cheese for a light, satisfying meal.

Slice and place in overlapping layers on serving plate:
tomatoes
cucumbers (optional)
Combine in small bowl:
1/2 c. fresh parsley, chopped (125 ml)
2-3 cloves garlic, minced
3 T. oil (preferably olive) (45 ml)
3 T. vinegar (45 ml)
salt and pepper to taste
Spoon dressing over tomatoes and cucumbers. Let stand 1/2-1 hour, spooning dressing over tomatoes several times to blend flavors.

—Mrs. Kauffman, Belfort, France; and Sara Regier, North Newton, Kansas

●●●●●●●●●●●●●●●●●●●●●●●●●●●●●●●●●●

Tomato and Basil Salad (Italy)

ⓣⓢ

Serves 4-6

Pomodori con Basilico
(poh-moh-DOH-ree kohn bah-ZEE-lee-koh)

Italians prefer tomatoes that are still pink, rather than red, for this salad. Serve with mozzarella cheese and fresh Italian bread to dip up the juices.

Cut in thin wedges:
6 tomatoes
Sprinkle with bit of salt and let stand until juice is drawn from wedges. Combine:
6-8 fresh basil leaves, chopped, or 2 t. dried basil (10 ml)
freshly ground pepper to taste
2 T. oil (preferably olive) (30 ml)
1 T. wine vinegar (15 ml)
2 T. onion, finely chopped (30 ml) (optional)
Sprinkle over tomatoes. Let stand 15 minutes before serving.

—Chaira Monti, Florence, Italy; and Naomi Lehman, Lititz, Pennsylvania

***B**efore you finish eating breakfast this morning, you've depended on more than half the world. This is the way our universe is structured. . . . We aren't going to have peace on earth until we recognize this basic fact of the interrelated structure of reality.*

—Martin Luther King, Jr.[5]

Shehzad Noorani: Bangladesh

Robert Maust: Ethiopia

In most less-industrialized countries and in much of Europe, the street market is a symbol of interdependence. Fruit and vegetable producers bring their produce directly to the market, sell it to a vendor, or market it themselves.

The market is home and community for many vendors and shoppers. Babies sleep in small cribs nestled in the corners of vending stalls. Toddlers sit in grain sacks playfully measuring the contents. School-age children run errands for their parents. As they haggle over prices, buyers and sellers share stories of life's joys and hardships, seeking and giving advice.

The market is a center of innovation where entrepreneurs and shoppers with limited resources have created environmentally-sound packaging materials. Central American farmers wrap eggs in corn husks and cheese in banana leaves. Around the world shoppers carry purchases in baskets and bags they reuse for each market trip.

—jhs

Limes still make me smile. On my first visit to a rural Kenyan market I was overwhelmed by the sound of unknown languages and the myriad of bright colors. In a back corner I saw an ancient woman sitting with back erect and legs outstretched beside a pyramid of some 30 withered, scrawny limes. At first I avoided her hopeful eyes, but then I approached her, thinking of what it must be like to spend a long day in the hot sun with so little to sell.

"*Bei gani, Mama?*" I asked, picking up four of the limes. We haggled over the price for a while, neither understanding the other well, but I was surprised when she adamantly held out for 25 cents. Finally I conceded and, bargain concluded, she chuckled out loud as she began loading the limes into my purse, pockets, and skirt. She had sold me not four, but the whole lot!

I had reaped a bonanza, and as I jubilantly walked away, limes bounced behind me like green Ping-Pong balls. The old woman and her friends laughed as they watched me disappear from sight. We all got more than we bargained for that day.

—Mary Lou Cummings,
Quakertown, Pennsylvania

110

Marketplaces

*T*he Rhamu market in northern Kenya was located originally under a big tree. Some years ago Kenyan soldiers ordered the vendors to move to an area covered by a tin roof so they could charge them one shilling per day to rent the space. Not everyone obeyed; some still prefer to sit under the big tree. The vendors in Rhamu are Somali pastoralist women who sit on the ground with their items in front of them. Most sell milk from traditional wooden containers. Since it is the staple food of the Somali people, one can buy sweet and sour milk from cows and camels, all permeated with a characteristic flavor from the smoke used to disinfect the wooden containers between uses.

The remaining vendors sell sugar, tea leaves, rice, flour, tomato paste, onions, eggs, limes, mangoes, and tiny tomatoes. In this subsistence economy, people purchase only what they need for each day. Vendors sell tomato paste by the spoonful, wrapped in pieces of scrap plastic, and cooking oil by the bottle capful.

Women come to the market and linger to chat with friends they meet. They squat in the dust to visit with the sellers. Product variety may be limited in the Rhamu market, but trusted relationships abound.

—Nancy Brubaker, Lancaster, Pennsylvania

*W*hile our family lived in Nairobi, Kenya, my husband, Bob, and our son, Chris, often shopped at a local market. It was a colorful place with heaping tables of bananas, tomatoes, peas, cabbages, papayas, and pineapples. The aisles were strewn with refuse and the air hummed with the sound of bartering, conversation, children playing, and babies cooing and crying.

On one of their first visits, Chris, 14 and very blond, suddenly looked around at the mass of people moving about him and said, "Dad, we're the only white people in this whole place."

Preoccupied with counting out shillings into a vendor's hand, his father murmured, "Well, the way I look at it, all of us are just human."

The market woman evidently understood English, and she met Bob's eyes with a knowing smile. As Bob and Chris walked away, they heard her sharing the anecdote in Swahili with her neighboring vendors. It was a small thing, a glance between strangers, but Chris began to relax and feel that he belonged in the mass of humanity that moved in the crowded market stalls.

—Mary Lou Cummings, Quakertown, Pennsylvania

*d*o not borrow off the earth, for the earth will require its own back with interest.

—Swahili proverb

*P*eople are not palm nuts, self-contained.

—Ugandan proverb

Paul Brubaker: Guatemala

Chicken Salad
(Vietnam)

Gói Gà
(goi gah)

Low-calorie Gói Gà makes a delicious main-dish salad and goes well with Vietnamese Chicken Soup (p. 89).

Cook and debone:
  1 lb. chicken pieces (500 g) (or use leftover chicken from Vietnamese Chicken Soup, p. 89)
Place in serving bowl:
  3-4 c. cabbage, chopped in thin slices (750-1000 ml)
Add:
  1 t. salt (5 ml)
Rub salt in cabbage and let stand a few minutes.
Add:
  1 1/2 T. vinegar (20 ml)
  1 T. sugar (15 ml)
  3 green onions, chopped
  3 sprigs cilantro or fresh parsley, finely chopped
  chicken meat, chopped
  1/2 c. peanuts, coarsely chopped (125 ml) (optional)
  black and ground red pepper to taste
Mix and serve.

—*Catherine Baer, Goshen, Indiana*
—*Cao Thi Nhan and Karen Glass-Hess, Morong, Bataan, Philippines*

Chinese Chicken
Noodle Salad

Jikuai Feng Tiao Liang Cai
(jee-kwie fung tee-ow lee-ung t'sai)

When contributor began collecting Chinese recipes, she had to go to the Chinese sections of cities where she lived to find ingredients such as hot oil, a spicy mixture of sesame oil and chili pepper. Now she often finds these ingredients in international food sections of supermarkets.

Cook until tender and set aside:
  1 chicken breast
Cook until tender:
  1 lb. rice noodles or thin spaghetti (500 g)
In large bowl, combine:
  1/4 c. sesame oil (50 ml)
  1/4 c. soy sauce (50 ml)
  3 T. rice or wine vinegar (45 ml)
  1/2 t. ground ginger (2 ml)
  1 clove garlic, crushed
  1/2 t. hot oil (2 ml) (optional) +!
When noodles are tender, drain in colander and rinse with cold water. Add noodles to seasoning ingredients in bowl and mix.
Add:
  cooked chicken breast, cut in small chunks
  6 scallions, sliced
  1 sweet red pepper, chopped
Toss. Garnish with cilantro (optional). Chill and serve.

—*Melanie Baer, Lancaster, Pennsylvania*

Belizean Potato Salad

M *Serves 6*

This Belizean Sunday lunch specialty is often served with Escabeche (p. 82). Testers found this combination of vegetables a "nice change from our traditional potato salad."

• *Microwave:*
Cook potatoes and 1/4 c. water (50 ml) on high, tightly covered, 7-10 minutes; let stand, covered, 3 minutes. Cook carrots and 2 T. water (30 ml) on high, tightly covered, 2-4 minutes; let stand 3 minutes. Cook peas and 2 T. water (30 ml) on high 2-3 minutes, stirring once.

Cook in salted water, then cool:
2 c. potatoes, peeled and diced (500 ml)
1 c. carrots, diced (250 ml)
1 c. peas (250 ml)
Combine with:
1 c. cabbage, thinly sliced (250 ml)
1 c. onion, diced (250 ml)
1 c. mayonnaise (or slightly less) (250 ml)
salt and pepper to taste
Chill several hours and serve on bed of lettuce garnished with parsley.

• *Variation:*
To make Red Salad, served on Christmas Eve and other special occasions in the Dominican Republic, substitute cooked, diced red beets for cabbage; reduce onion to 1/2 c. (125 ml); add 2 chopped hard-cooked eggs; season dressing with oregano and garlic powder to taste.

—Phyllis Wulliman, Goshen, Indiana
—Patricia Zwier, Santo Domingo, Dominican Republic

Lebanese Potato Salad

Serves 6

Salatit el Bataata (sah-lah-TEET el bah-TAA-tah)

This makes a delicious summer picnic dish—it contains no eggs to spoil in the heat.

Toss together:
4 large potatoes, cooked, peeled, and cubed
1/2 c. fresh parsley, snipped or chopped (125 ml)
1/4 c. green onions, finely chopped (50 ml)
1/4 c. olive oil (50 ml)
1/4 c. lemon juice (50 ml)
1 t. salt (5 ml)
dash of garlic powder or 1 garlic clove, minced
dash of pepper
Chill several hours before serving.

—Alice W. Lapp, Akron, Pennsylvania

Heavenly Parent, as the miry bottom of the pond helps the lotus flower to grow, so may our often unlovely environment encourage growth in us. And as the lotus blossom in all its radiance rises above the mire, so help us to transcend our earthly environment to become heavenly personalities worthy to be called your children. Amen.

—Prayer of a Chinese Christian[6]

Wheat and Parsley Salad (Middle East)

Tabouli
(tah-BOO-lee)

Spellings abound for this popular Middle Eastern salad—Tabouli, Taboolee, Tabbouleh, Taboulleh—typically served as the main dish of a light supper. Middle Eastern cooks devote hours to meticulously chopping and mincing the vegetables and herbs. Tabouli is an economical dish in summer when fresh parsley and mint are readily available. It makes a nice picnic salad.

Soak several hours:

1 c. cracked wheat (bulgur) (250 ml)
3 c. boiling water (750 ml)

Meanwhile mix:

1 1/2 c. fresh parsley, finely chopped (375 ml)
1/2 c. fresh mint, finely chopped (125 ml)
1/2 c. onions (preferably green onions), minced (125 ml)
1 small cucumber, chopped
3 firm tomatoes, chopped
1 1/4 t. salt (6 ml)
1/4 t. pepper (1 ml)
1/4 c. oil (preferably olive) (50 ml)
1/4 c. lemon juice (50 ml)

Drain wheat thoroughly in large sieve. Toss with other ingredients, cover and chill. Serve with romaine lettuce. Traditionally each person breaks the lettuce into small pieces, using them as utensils for eating Tabouli. This salad may be prepared a day in advance and refrigerated, but do not add the lemon juice until just before serving.

—*Nevart Manatzaganian, Jericho, West Bank; and Grace Bergey, Hatfield, Pennsylvania*
—*Khadige Coutney and Edna Hohnstein, Edmonton, Alberta*
—*Alice W. Lapp, Akron, Pennsylvania*

Endive Apple Salad (Netherlands)

(ts)

Andijvie Sla
(ahn-DIE-vee slah)

Curly endive has deep green, narrow, lacy leaves. This salad adds color and zest to any meal, or makes a satisfying main-dish lunch salad served with freshly baked bread.

• Option:
Substitute chopped lettuce or other greens for half the endive.

Combine:

1 head curly endive, finely chopped
2-3 apples, finely chopped
1/4 c. onion, finely chopped (50 ml)
1/2 c. raisins (125 ml)
1/2 c. toasted sunflower seed kernels (125 ml)
3-5 oz. sharp cheese (Gouda or cheddar), cubed (100-150 g)

Mix together:

3 T. vinegar (45 ml)
3 T. oil (45 ml)
1 t. spicy mustard (5 ml)
1/4 t. salt (1 ml)
dash of pepper

Add dressing to salad and toss lightly.

—*Chris Elzinga and Annelies Mencke, Haarlem, Netherlands; and Cynthia Shenk, Nijmegen, Netherlands*

Mixed Salad (Lebanon)

Serves 6-8

Fattoush
(fah-TOOSH)

Lebanese Muslim families often eat Fattoush to break a day of fasting during the holy month of Ramadan. The salad is also a common Lenten meal for Middle East Christians. It is commonly made without lettuce or garlic.

• *Note:*
Purslane (portulaca) is a fleshy annual herb that many consider a troublesome weed. Native to Asia and Africa, it is common in Europe and North America.

Break in small pieces:
   1 pita bread round, toasted or dried (p. 51)
Chop in bite-size chunks and combine with bread in large bowl:
   1 large cucumber
   1 onion
   2 medium tomatoes
   1 medium head lettuce
Chop finely and add to salad:
   3/4 c. parsley (175 ml)
   3/4 c. fresh mint leaves (175 ml)
   3/4 c. purslane (175 ml) (optional)
Crush together:
   2-3 cloves garlic
   1/2 t. salt (2 ml)
Stir in:
   juice of 1 lemon
   1/2 c. olive oil (125 ml)
Add dressing to salad. Toss well and serve.

—*Marlaine Jarrouge Reynolds, Bloomington, Indiana; and Carol McLean, Baaqline, Lebanon*

In Ouagadougou, the capital city of Burkina Faso, it has become fashionable to be seen munching Western-style lettuce salads at streetside tables, amid brightly colored plastic tablecloths, dust, and constant moped traffic. The salad dressing consists of peanut oil, often laced with *lait sucre*, sweetened condensed milk.

A popular story circulates, often in these same cafés, ridiculing this new culinary delight. Lettuce is much more expensive and much less nutritious than local greens, such as the baobab leaf, which is also delicious.

According to the story, a European was disturbed by the crunching of chicken bones as he sat relishing his salad one day. Repeatedly he turned to watch a Burkinabe man enjoying his dinner. Finally, unable to contain his irritation, the foreigner said, "Well, if you eat all the bones, what do you feed your dogs?"

The local man replied, "Salad."

—*Pamela Leach, Toronto, Ontario*

Greek Salad Dressing (Greece)

Lathi kai Xethe
(LAH-thee keh KSEE-thee)

This recipe is popular in the Greek American community.

• Options:
Substitute 1/2-3/4 c. vegetable oil (125-175 ml) for a lighter dressing.
•
Add 1-2 t. dillweed (5-10 ml) for extra flavor.

●●●●●●●●●●●●●●●●●●●●●●●●●●●●●●●●

Makes 2 cups (500 ml)

Combine:
  1/2 c. red wine vinegar (125 ml)
  1 t. salt (5 ml)
  1/4 t. pepper (1 ml)
  1/2 t. sugar (2 ml)
  11/2 t. dry mustard (7 ml)
  11/2 t. oregano (7 ml)
  1/2 t. garlic, minced (2 ml)
  1/2 t. lemon juice (2 ml)
Let stand 15 minutes. Add gradually:
  11/2 c. olive oil (375 ml)
Store in refrigerator.
Make a large tossed salad of leafy lettuce, crumbled feta cheese, chopped tomatoes, sweet onions, fresh black olives, and chopped or sliced cucumber. Add salad dressing to taste, toss, and serve.

—*Suzanne Myers and Deb Laws-Landis, Lancaster, Pennsylvania*

Orange and Peanut Salad (Colombia)

Ensalada de Naranja y Maní
(ayn-sah-LAH-dah day nah-RAHNG-hah ee mah-NEE)

Green and orange colors combine to make an attractive, festive salad—an ideal complement for meat dishes.

●●●●●●●●●●●●●●●●●●●●●●●●●●●●●●●●

Serves 8

Peel, section, and remove membranes from:
  2 seedless oranges
Combine in large salad bowl:
  1 small head Boston lettuce, broken in small pieces
  orange sections
  1/2 medium red onion, sliced and separated
  1/2 c. peanuts, crushed (125 ml)
Combine in blender:
  1 clove garlic, peeled
  1/4 c. orange juice (50 ml)
  11/2 T. wine vinegar (20 ml)
  1 T. lemon juice (15 ml)
  11/2 t. sugar (7 ml)
  1/4 t. prepared mustard (1 ml)
  2 t. orange peel, grated (10 ml)
  2 T. oil (30 ml)
Blend on medium speed until smooth and creamy. Pour dressing over salad and toss.

—*Irene Suderman, Bogotá, Colombia*

• •

Sesame Spinach Salad (Korea)

Serves 2-4

Sigumchi Namul
(see-GOOM-chee nah-mool)

This salad is typical of the way Koreans prepare and season cold vegetables. Tester found this to have a surprisingly wonderful flavor: "I hate spinach and just loved this!"

Steam until just tender and still green:
1 lb. fresh spinach (500 g)
Strain and squeeze out as much water as possible. Cut spinach coarsely.
Place in serving bowl and add:
3 T. soy sauce (45 ml)
2 T. sesame oil (30 ml)
1 T. Toasted Sesame Seeds (15 ml) (p. 290)
1 clove garlic, minced
1 T. sugar (15 ml)
1 T. vinegar (15 ml)
dash of black or ground red pepper, or to taste
Mix, chill, and serve.

—*Pat Yoder, Goshen, Indiana*

Pilot Chiluma grows vegetables for a living on his farm near Lusaka, Zambia. An improviser and inventor, he leads the Young Farmers Club in his village.

Like many Zambian farmers, Chiluma earlier was using a number of imported chemical pesticides such as Dieldrin and DDT. Some of these have been banned in North America and Europe for more than 10 years. Zambian farmers know the danger of consuming pesticides, but most are unaware of the harm from inhaling or absorbing the chemicals through the skin. Men and women often work in the fields with bare arms and feet; some women carry chemical pesticides in baskets on their heads and strap sprayer packs to their backs.

When Chiluma learned of the danger of chemical pesticides, he disposed of the Dieldrin and DDT he had and began reading a book on natural pest control. Then he began searching for a natural alternative to kill the aphids that thrived in his gardens.

From his studies at Zambia's Natural Resources Development College, Chiluma knew that aphids and head lice have similar digestive systems. He knew that women used a small, wild gourd to control head lice, and guessed that the gourd likely was not poisonous since monkeys ate it.

Chiluma prepared a spray by boiling the wild gourds. When he applied it to his tomatoes, okra, and cabbages, the aphids died. His experiment was successful. By combining traditional and modern knowledge, Chiluma found an appropriate, nonlethal way to get rid of insect pests.

—*Gary and Linda Nafziger-Meiser, Elkhart, Indiana*

Cucumber Yogurt Salad (India)

Serves 4

Khira Raita
(KEE-rah RIE-tah)

Yogurt is used frequently in Indian cooking, often added to main-dish curries at the end of the cooking process. Raita combines yogurt with fresh vegetables or fruits to produce cool side dishes for spicy curries.

Mix:
   3/4 c. yogurt (175 ml) (p. 295)
   1 cucumber, thinly sliced
   1 onion, finely chopped
   1 tomato, chopped (optional)
   pinch of salt and pepper
   garlic powder or ground cumin to taste
Sprinkle on top:
   dash of ground red pepper (optional) +!
Chill and serve.

—*Sara Larson Wiegner, Akron, Pennsylvania*

Banana Yogurt Salad (India)

Serves 3-4

Kela Raita
(KAY-lah RIE-tah)

A simple, cool side dish to serve with hot curry meals. Children can help prepare this simple recipe that makes a healthy hot-weather snack or pleasant light meal.

Slice:
   2 bananas
Sprinkle with:
   2 t. lemon juice (10 ml)
Toss with:
   2/3 c. yogurt (150 ml) (p. 295)
Top with:
   2 t. shredded coconut (10 ml) (optional)

• *Option:*
To sweeten, add a bit of sugar.

—*Sara Larson Wiegner, Akron, Pennsylvania*

Yogurt is a common Turkish cooking ingredient, used as a side dish to complement the strong flavor of tomato and peppery foods, and mixed into cakes, pastries, salads, soup, and stew broth. Turkish shoppers buy yogurt by the pailful, returning empty pails for reuse. They avoid the waste of one-serving-size, plastic, throwaway containers common in North America.

Middle East Vegetable Relish

•••••••••••••••••••••••••••••

Serves 6-8

Salata
(sah-LAH-tah)

Middle East cooks prefer slightly green tomatoes in this relish. Serve with Sesame Sauce (p. 259), Hummus (p. 259) and pita bread (p. 51), for a first course or light supper plate. This relish is sometimes mixed with Sesame Sauce.

Finely mince:
   2 small cucumbers
   1 green pepper
   2-3 green onions or 1/4 c. minced onion (50 ml)
   3 medium tomatoes
   4 radishes (optional)
Toss with:
   2 T. olive oil (30 ml)
   3 T. lemon juice (45 ml)
   1 t. salt (5 ml)
Spread on plate and garnish with 1 T. minced parsley (15 ml). Scoop up with small pieces of pita bread.

—Alice W. Lapp, Akron, Pennsylvania

Avocado Egg Salad (Nicaragua)

•••••••••••••••••••••••••••••••

Serves 4-6

Guacamole Nicaragüense
(gwa-kah-MOH-lay
nee-kah-rah-GWAYN-say)

Combine in serving bowl:
   4 eggs, hard-cooked and chopped
   2 large avocados, chopped
Sprinkle with:
   salt and pepper to taste
   2 T. lemon juice (30 ml)
   1/8 t. garlic powder (.5 ml) (optional)
Stir gently. Chill.

—Teresa Palacios and Leslie Book, Managua, Nicaragua

....

La sabana de Bogotá, the plateau where the Colombian capital is located, is productive farmland formerly used to produce wheat, barley, and other agricultural products. In recent years acres and acres of this food-producing land have been turned into nurseries to grow carnations, mums, and other flowers for export.

....

k̶nowledge is like a garden. If it is not cultivated, it cannot be harvested.

—African proverb

119

Red Beets in Vinegar (Guatemala)

Ensalada de Remolacha
(ayn-sah-LAH-dah day
ray-moh-LAH-chah)

This simple salad is the principal way Guatemalan cooks prepare red beets.

• Option:
Substitute 2 T. fresh lemon juice (30 ml) for vinegar.

●●●●●●●●●●●●●●●●●●●●●●●●●●●●●●●

Serves 4

Cook until tender in salted water:
1 large whole red beet or several small ones
Cool, peel, and slice.
Combine with:
**1 small onion, sliced
1/2 c. vinegar (125 ml)
salt and pepper to taste**
Chill.

—Fanny Ellen Yoder, Guatemala City, Guatemala

Oro lives in a medium-size town in a poor rural "homeland" in South Africa. With his mother he moved into a one-room house across the street from us when we were living in Transkei. Like many neighboring children, Oro came to our house each day. But instead of playing, he simply sat or stood to watch the activity. He didn't look ill, but he had little energy. Frequently he whined and ran away when others bumped him. The children tolerated him, but did not welcome him. He wasn't much fun to play with.

Then for a few weeks no one saw Oro. He had gone to the rural village where his extended family had land. When he returned, hardly anyone recognized him. He seemed taller. The watery eyes and whine were gone. He was alert, lively, and talkative. One of the children commented that they liked to play with Oro now.

In the following weeks and months, Oro gradually lost his energy and bright eyes. Each evening his mother returned from work with a bag of potato chips and a slice of bologna for his supper. His mother, a teacher, was well-off—one of the lucky ones with a job. She could afford to buy potato chips and sweets for Oro.

Since she worked all day and didn't have a kitchen or time to look for firewood, she preferred this convenient alternative to the time-consuming traditional meal of cooked dried corn with beans or vegetables. Although Oro wasn't dying of starvation like some children in Africa, he was a quiet victim of "progress."

—Judy Zimmerman Herr,
 Gaborone, Botswana

Edible Greens

The edible, green, leafy vegetable repertoire is truly varied, including both cultivated and wild plants. Foraging for young, tender, wild greens is a social activity for groups of rural women living in many parts of the world. These women also make wise use of the leaves of squash plants and some root vegetables.

In Zaire women tear the leaves from red root (amaranth, what some people refer to as pigweed) stems and pound them in large wooden mortars and pestles before adding them to palm oil sauces. In rural Tanzania women gather leafy vegetables during the rainy season and preserve them for later use by drying them in the sun.

The people of Papua New Guinea sometimes prepare fresh greens by stuffing them into a section of a bamboo tube. They cover the open end with a banana leaf and, with covered end up, place the bamboo shoot over a fire. As the greens steam, more are pushed in. Meat drippings and salt are added before or after the steaming process.

Almost any kind of green, leafy vegetable can be used in recipes calling for spinach, chard, or kale. Gardeners may enjoy experimenting with squash and pumpkin leaves, and find a good use for troublesome red root. A note of caution: Always check with a reputable source to ascertain the safety of eating any unfamiliar wild plant.

—Eva Biswaro, Dar es Salaam, Tanzania
—Ann Wideman, Ukarumpa via Lae, Papua New Guinea

Cooked Spinach (Botswana)

Serves 4

Morogo
(moh-ROH-hoh)

In Botswana women sometimes dry the vegetables for this mixture together and store for later use. Tester calls this "the best way we've ever had spinach." Swiss chard, pumpkin leaves, pigweed, collard greens, and other greens can be substituted for spinach.

Cook in small amount of water, approx. 1/4 c. (50 ml):

3 c. fresh spinach, chopped (750 ml)
1-2 red chili peppers, chopped +!
1 T. oil or margarine (15 ml)
1 onion, chopped
1 potato, chopped
1-2 tomatoes, chopped

When soft, serve with rice or Nshima (p. 151).

• *Microwave:*
Combine 2 T. oil (30 ml), onion, and potatoes in covered casserole. Cook on high 5 minutes. Stir and add tomatoes and chilies. Cover and cook on high 4-6 minutes. Stir, add spinach, and cook on high 1-2 minutes, stirring once. Let stand 1 minute.

—Debbie Meyer and Kay Miller, Gabarone, Botswana

Pumpkin Leaves with Groundnuts (Zambia)

••••••••••••••••••••••••••••

 ⓜ

Serves 5-6

Lupusi Abuntele
(loo-POO-see
ah-voon-TEH-lay)

Choose pumpkin leaves that are young, yet fully developed, or substitute spinach, pigweed, kale, Swiss chard, or other greens. Serve with Cabbage and Tomato Sauce (p. 123) or Stewed Beef (p. 243) and Nshima (p. 151) for a Zambian-style feast. May also serve with rice.

• *Microwave:*
Combine onion, tomato, and peanuts and cook on high 2-4 minutes until onion is tender. Add pumpkin leaves (still damp from rinsing), cover tightly, and cook on high 7-10 minutes. Add margarine and salt.

Rinse well, devein, and chop:
2 lb. pumpkin leaves (1 kg) (about 2 qt./2 L)
Cook in 2 c. water (500 ml) 5 minutes.
Add and simmer 5 minutes:
1 medium onion, chopped
1 medium tomato, chopped
Add:
1-1 1/2 c. peanuts, coarsely ground with pestle or in blender (250-375 ml)
Cook over low-medium heat about 15 minutes, stirring often to avoid sticking. Add more water if necessary.
Just before serving, drain any excess water and add:
1 T. margarine (15 ml) (optional)
1/2 t. salt (2 ml)

• *Options:*
Substitute 3/4 c. chunky peanut butter (175 ml) for ground peanuts.
•
Use frozen greens instead of fresh.

—*Sarah Mwaanga, Mizinga, Zambia; and Esther Spurrier, Dillsburg, Pennsylvania*

African Greens (Kenya)

••••••••••••••••••••••••••••

ⓣⓢ

Serves 4-5

Sukuma Wiki
(soo-KOO-mah WEE-kee)

In Kenya a bunch of Sukuma Wiki (push the week along) costs approximately five cents (U.S.). Eaten with ugali *(grain porridge) it is the cheap, nutritious staple meal of many Kenyans. Kale is the closest substitute in North America.*

In small amount of water, cook until just tender:
leaves from 1 bunch kale, finely chopped
1 green pepper, chopped
salt to taste
Brown in 1 T. oil (15 ml) over medium heat:
1 large onion, thinly sliced
Add and fry until oil separates:
2 T. tomato paste (30 ml)
1 clove garlic, crushed
Add cooked kale and mix thoroughly.
Serve with Nshima (p. 151), rice, or Chapatis (p. 48).

• *Options:*
Substitute Swiss chard or spinach for kale.
•
Cook 2 chopped carrots and small head of chopped cabbage with kale.

—*Loisi Maina, Muranga, Kenya; and Annetta Miller, Nairobi, Kenya*
—*Mary Lou Cummings, Quakertown, Pennsylvania*

Cabbage and Tomato Sauce (Malawi)

● \ ● ● ● ●

(ts) M *Serves 4*

Ndiwo
(en-DEE-woh)

Simple, nutritious, and delicious.

• *Microwave:*
Cook oil and onion on high 3 minutes. Add other ingredients and cook on high 6-10 minutes.

Brown in 1 T. oil (15 ml):
1 onion, chopped
Add:
3 tomatoes, peeled and sliced
Stir. Cover and simmer 3 minutes.
Add:
1/4 medium cabbage, cut in small pieces
Cover and cook on low 5 minutes.
Add:
**salt and pepper to taste
1/2 c. water (125 ml) (optional—for a juicier sauce)**
Cover and cook 10-15 minutes, until cabbage is tender.
Serve with Nshima (p. 151) or rice.

• *Variation:*
To make Zambian Cabbage and Peanut Stew, mix 1/4 c. crunchy peanut butter (50 ml) with the water. Stir into cabbage and cook as directed.

—*Gudrun Mathies, Elmira, Ontario*
—*Tina Muzyamba Munsaka, Ndola, Zambia*

Red Root Sauce (Kenya)

● ●

(ts) *Serves 4*

Mchicha na Mchele
(m'chee-chah nah m'chel-eh)

Cumin and coriander turn red root (see p. 76) into a flavorful topping for rice. Substitute spinach or other greens when red root is not available.

• *Option:*
Add 1/4 lb. ground beef (125 g) when sautéing vegetables.

Chop finely and set aside:
**1 qt. red root leaves (1 L)
1 onion
1 potato
2 tomatoes**
In large saucepan, melt:
2 T. margarine (30 ml)
Add and sauté 3-5 minutes:
**chopped onions, potato, and tomatoes
2 T. cilantro, chopped, (30 ml) or 1 t. ground coriander (5 ml)
2 t. cumin seed, crushed (10 mi)**
Add:
**2/3 c. water (150 ml)
1 t. salt (5 ml)**
Stir in red root. Simmer, covered, until potatoes and greens are tender, about 15-20 minutes. Serve over rice or as a relish for Nshima (p. 151).

—*Marian Yussuf, Suna, Migori, Kenya; and Sylvia L. Hess, Bausman, Pennsylvania*

Red Cabbage and Apples (Netherlands)

●●●●●●●●●●●●●●●●●●●●●●●●●●●●

Serves 6

Rode Kool
(ROH-deh kohl)

Rode Kool is traditionally served with boiled potatoes and meat.

• *Option:*
Substitute 1 T. raisins (15 ml) for sugar.

Combine in saucepan:
1/2 head red cabbage, finely chopped
6-8 whole cloves
1/4 c. vinegar (50 ml)
Cook 20 minutes or until tender.
Add:
1-2 tart apples, peeled and chopped
1 T. margarine (15 ml)
1 T. sugar (15 ml)
Cook 10 minutes.

—Gert Renkema and Cynthia Shenk, Nijmegen, Netherlands

Roasted Cauliflower (India)

●●●●●●●●●●●●●●●●●●●●●●●●●●●●●

M -H-

Serves 4
350°F 180°C
20 min.

Bhapa Phul Gobi
(BAH-pah fool goh-BEE)

A spicy way to enjoy garden cauliflower. Serve with rice, Chapatis (p. 48), or pita bread (p. 51); or alongside a meat or bean curry.

• *Microwave:*
Prepare fried ingredients as directed above. Place cauliflower pieces in 2-qt. casserole (2-L) and cover with fried ingredients. Cover tightly and cook on high 5-7 minutes or until tender. Let stand, covered, 3 minutes.

Grind or blend into paste:
1 c. onions (250 ml)
5-6 cloves garlic
3 T. ginger root, grated (45 ml) +!
a little water
In frypan, heat:
1/4 c. oil (50 ml)
Add onion paste and fry until brown.
Add:
4 medium tomatoes, cut in 8 slices each
3/4 c. peas (175 ml)
1/2 t. ground red pepper (2 ml) +!
1 t. ground turmeric (5 ml)
1 t. sugar (5 ml)
1 t. salt (5 ml)
Sauté briefly until tomatoes are soft. Remove from heat. Place in pressure cooker, roasting pan, or casserole:
1 medium cauliflower, cut in even pieces
Cover with fried ingredients. Rinse frypan with 1/4 c. water (50 ml) and pour over vegetables. Pressure-cook 2-3 minutes with pressure regulator rocking slowly (cool cooker immediately), or bake in covered dish at 350°F (180° C) 20 minutes or until cauliflower is soft.

—Radha Biswas and Cynthia Peacock, Calcutta, India

Creamy Potatoes and Cabbage (Ireland)

Colcannon
(call-can-non)

This dish, reputed to have been the favorite dish of writer Jonathan Swift, is served especially on All Saints Day.

• Microwave:
Place cabbage or kale and 2 T. water (30 ml) in 2-qt. casserole (2-L), cover tightly, and cook on high 8-10 minutes. Drain and liquefy. Cook potatoes and 1/4 c. water (50 ml) in separate dish on high 10-16 minutes, stirring once; let stand, covered, 3 minutes. In glass measuring cup or small dish, cook cream or milk and leeks 1 minute or onions 2-3 minutes. Combine and complete recipe.

• Option:
Substitute ground nutmeg for mace.

Serves 6

Strip green leaves from:
   1 lb. cabbage or kale (500 g)
Shred cabbage or kale, place in saucepan with a little water, and bring to a boil. Reduce heat and simmer until crisp-tender, 5-10 minutes. Drain well. Liquefy in blender (optional).
Boil separately, covered, until tender:
   1 lb. potatoes, peeled and diced (500 g) (about 4 potatoes)
In small saucepan, cook about 10 minutes:
   2 small leeks or onions, or 6 green onions with tops, chopped
   1/2 c. cream or milk (125 ml)
Mash potatoes, then season with:
   1/4 t. salt (1 ml)
   1/8 t. pepper (.5 ml)
   1/8 t. mace (.5 ml)
Mix in onions and milk. Combine potato mixture with cabbage or kale, beating it to pale green fluff over low heat. Pour into deep warmed dish. Dab with butter or margarine. Leftovers can be fried in oil until crisp and brown on both sides.

—Pauline Fisher, Goshen, Indiana

Indian Peas and Cabbage (India)

Mattar Gobi
(MAH-ter goh-BEE)

(ts)

Serves 4

Brown in 1 T. oil (15 ml):
   1 clove garlic, minced
Add:
   1 c. frozen peas (250 ml)
   1/2 t. ground cumin (2 ml)
Stir briefly. Add:
   1/4 c. water (50 ml)
Boil until water evaporates. Add:
   1 lb. cabbage, shredded (500 g) (about 5 c./1.3 L)
   1/4 t. ground turmeric (1 ml)
   1/2 t. salt (2 ml)
   dash of ground red pepper or to taste
Stir and cook over medium heat 10 minutes. Cover during last 2-3 minutes.

—Urmila Patel, India; and Naomi Fast, Newton, Kansas

Potatoes with Creamy Tomato Sauce (Colombia)

Papas Chorreadas
(PAH-pahss choh-ray-AH-dahss)

This rich sauce over potatoes is hearty enough for a main dish.

• *Microwave:*
Cook margarine, onions, and tomatoes on high 3-4 minutes until onions are tender. Add other ingredients, reducing salt to 1/4 t. (1 ml). Cook on medium 3-4 minutes or until cheese melts, stirring twice. To cook potatoes, pierce skins, place in circle on paper towel, and cook on high 15-20 minutes until tender, turning over once. For boiled potatoes, pierce skins, place in casserole in 1/4 c. water (50 ml), cover tightly, and cook on high 8-11 minutes, turning over once; let stand, covered, 5 minutes.

• •

☒ M

Serves 6-8

In frypan, melt:
2 T. margarine (30 ml)
Add and fry:
6 green onions, cut in 1-inch lengths (2.5-cm)
1/2 c. onion, diced (125 ml)
5 tomatoes, peeled and coarsely chopped
Cook, stirring frequently, until soft and transparent, about 5 minutes.
Lower heat and add:
1/2 c. cream (125 ml)
1 t. cilantro, finely chopped (5 ml)
1/4 t. dried oregano (1 ml)
pinch of ground cumin
1/2 t. salt (2 ml)
freshly ground black pepper to taste
Cook over low heat, stirring constantly.
Add:
1 c. mozzarella cheese, grated (250 ml)
Continue stirring and cook until cheese melts.
Pour sauce over:
8 large potatoes, unpeeled and boiled

• *Option:*
Serve sauce over green beans, broccoli, or cauliflower instead of potatoes.

—*Irene Suderman, Bogotá, Colombia*

Curried Mashed Potatoes (India)

Alu Bhartha
(AH-loo BAHR-tah)

This unusual and tasty mashed potato dish is served over rice, alongside a meat curry or Dhal (p. 156). It is a common daily vegetable dish for poorer families in some parts of India. Sometimes it is shaped into balls for easier serving and eating.

• *Option:*
For smoother dish, puree browned onions and peppers before adding to potatoes.

• •

-☒ H-

Serves 4-5

Boil:
4 potatoes, peeled
Cool slightly and mash.
Sauté in 1 T. oil (15 ml):
1 onion, finely chopped
2 chili peppers, minced, or 1/8 t. ground red pepper (.5 ml) +!
Mix with mashed potatoes. Add:
1/2 t. ground turmeric (2 ml)
salt to taste

—*Cynthia Peacock, Calcutta, India*

Indonesian Rijstaffel

Indonesians use a *rijstaffel* (rice table) to celebrate special occasions such as a first birthday or the visit of special guests. Christian families use the *rijstaffel* to celebrate christenings, confirmations, and baptisms.

Steamed rice is the foundation of the meal. A number of different vegetable dishes and a *sambal* (hot sauce) accompany the rice. The number of people eating

and the importance of the occasion determine the actual number of dishes. "It has the qualities of a good potluck," comments Lois Deckert, "except that the guests don't bring anything."

Deckert recommends the *rijstaffel* as a creative menu for celebrating the summer and fall bounty of locally grown produce. As you plan, consider textures, flavors, and colors. Prepare one-half cup of raw, long-grain

rice for each person and several vegetable dishes to accompany the rice.

Additional Indonesian recipes that may be included in a *rijstaffel* include Shish Kabob (p. 249), Shrimp Cakes (p. 184), Soybean Cake with Red Chilies (p. 212), Crisp Potato Balls (p. 215), and Sweet Soy Sauce (p. 281).

Yellow Vegetable Relish (Indonesia)

Acar Kuning
(ah-CHAR koo-NING)

Indonesian cuisine combines the flavors of India, China, Arabia, and Europe.

• **Microwave:**
Combine top half of ingredients, omitting oil and reducing salt to 1/4 t. (1 ml). Cook on high for 1-2 minutes. Add vegetables and coat well with spice mixture. Cook on high 3-4 minutes, stirring once.

Serves 6-8

Heat in wok or large frypan:
   1 T. oil (15 ml)
Add:
   8 almonds, finely crushed
   1 clove garlic, minced
   1/8 t. ground turmeric (.5 ml)
   1/4 c. water (50 ml)
   1 t. ginger root, minced (5 ml)
   1/2 t. salt (2 ml)
   1 T. sugar (15 ml)
   2 T. vinegar (30 ml)
Cook about 3 minutes over medium heat. Add:
   1 1/2 c. fresh broccoli, cut in florets (375 ml)
   1 1/2 c. fresh cauliflower, cut in florets (375 ml)
   1/2 c. fresh pimento or sweet red pepper, thinly sliced (125 ml)
   1/2 c. carrots, cut in julienne strips (125 ml)
Cook over medium-high heat about 3 minutes, mixing and turning constantly. Remove from heat and turn into large bowl. Cover and refrigerate at least 2 hours. Stir before serving.

—*Moelyani, Salatiga, Java, Indonesia; and Lois Deckert, North Newton, Kansas*

Cucumber Salad (Indonesia)

Acar Ketimun
(ah-CHAR keh-tee-MOON)

● ●

Serves 4

Mix together:

2 small cucumbers, cubed
1/2 medium onion, sliced
1/2 c. white vinegar (125 ml)
1 T. oil (15 ml)
1 1/2 t. salt (7 ml)
1 t. pepper (5 ml)
1/2 t. garlic powder (2 ml)
1/2 T. sugar (7 ml)
slices of hot chili pepper to taste (optional) +!

Marinate at least 30 minutes. Chill and serve.

—*Reprinted with permission from* To All My Grandchildren: Lessons in Indonesian Cooking, *by Leonie Samuel-Hool (Berkeley, Calif.: Liplop Press, 1981).*

Sweet Vegetables (Indonesia)

Sayur Manis
(sah-YOOR mah-NEES)

A tasty and unusual squash dish.

● *Microwave:*
Combine all ingredients, uncooked, except salt in 2-qt. casserole (2-L) and cook on high 8-12 minutes, turning twice, until vegetables are tender. Let stand 10 minutes before serving. Add 1 t. salt (5 ml) or less to taste. This is a good dish to make ahead of time, let stand to absorb flavors, and then reheat briefly in microwave.

● ●

M   -H-   *Serves 4-6*

Cook until crisp-tender:

3 c. butternut squash, peeled and cubed (750 ml)

In separate saucepan, bring to a boil:

2 c. coconut milk (500 ml) (p. 280)
3 cloves garlic, minced
1/4 c. onion, sliced (50 ml)
1 t. ginger root, minced (5 ml)
1/2 t. ground turmeric (2 ml)
2 t. salt (10 ml)
2 fresh red pimento or sweet red pepper, thinly sliced
1 red jalapeño, thinly sliced (optional) +!

When boiling, add:

cooked squash

Simmer about 10 minutes, allowing squash to absorb flavors.

● *Options:*
Add cubed squash directly into sauce, without precooking. Simmer until tender.
●
Substitute green beans, cut diagonally, for half the squash.
●
Add 1/2 lb. small shrimp, shelled and deveined (250 g).

—*Lois Deckert, North Newton, Kansas*

128

Assorted Vegetable Sauté (Indonesia)

●●●●●●●●●●●●●●●●●●●●●●●●●●●●●●

-*H*-

Serves 6

Oseng Oseng Sayuran
(o-SENG o-SENG
sah-yoo-RAHN)

This stir-fry is as common in Indonesia as eggs and ham are in parts of North America.

• Option:
Substitute regular soy sauce, 1 T. brown sugar (15 ml), and a dash of ginger (optional) for Sweet Soy Sauce.

Fry 2 minutes in 2 T. peanut or vegetable oil (30 ml) in wok or frypan:

1/4 c. onion, thinly sliced (50 ml)
2 cloves garlic, finely minced

Add and stir-fry 5-7 minutes until crisp-tender:

2 c. cabbage, coarsely shredded (500 ml)
1 c. green beans, chopped (250 ml)
1 c. carrots, sliced thin diagonally (250 ml)
1/2 green pepper, sliced
1 t. dried red chili pepper (5 ml) (optional) +!
1 t. salt (5 ml)
1/2 t. sugar (2 ml)
1 bay leaf

Add:

1-2 T. Sweet Soy Sauce (15-30 ml) (p. 281)

Cook about 2 minutes. Do not overcook. Serve with rice.

—*Reprinted with permission of Atheneum Publishers, an imprint of Macmillan Publishing Company (New York), from* The Indonesian Kitchen, *by Copeland Marks with Mintari Soeharjo (copyright ® 1981 by Copeland Marks and Mintari Soeharjo).*

Moisés Crisóstomo, the program director of a social service agency in the Dominican Republic, lives in a small house with no yard in the city. He plants winter squash in a flowerpot, trains the vines up the side of the house with wires, and harvests the squash off the flat roof of his house.

*Yo te pido Señor:
Que cese la violencia,
El retorno a nuestra tierra,
y poder pedirte agua
para la milpa.
Te pido un pasado
Que no vuelva.*

*Lord, I pray
That the violence will end,
That we will return to our land
And be able to ask for rain
For the corn fields.
I pray that our past
Will never return.*

—*Prayer of Tobías Romero, a young Salvadoran refugee in the Mesa Grande refugee camp, Honduras*

Thai Stir-Fried Vegetables (Thailand)

Serves 4-6

Pad Pak Rooam
(pahd pahk ROO-ahm)

Thai cuisine incorporates an abundance of fresh vegetables, either raw or slightly cooked, but always served crisp. The fish and oyster sauces used to season this dish can be found in Asian food stores and some large supermarkets.

Heat in wok or large frypan over high heat:
   3 T. oil (45 ml)
Stir-fry a few seconds:
   4 cloves garlic, minced
Add:
   2 broccoli stalks, split lengthwise and cut in bite-size pieces
   1 green pepper, chopped in bite-size pieces
   10 fresh baby corns, sliced in half lengthwise
   1 c. green beans (250 ml), sliced in 1-inch lengths (2.5-cm)
   2 c. mushrooms, sliced (500 ml)
Fry about 2 minutes.
Add:
   3 T. water (45 ml)
   1 T. fish sauce (15 ml)
   1 t. soy sauce (5 ml)
   1 T. ketchup (15 ml)
   1 t. sugar (5 ml)
   1 T. oyster sauce (15 ml) (optional)
Stir quickly and cook 1-2 minutes until vegetables are lightly cooked but crisp. Add:
   3 tomatoes, cut in wedges
Stir briefly to heat and serve.

—*Khun Deng and Lily Bérubé, Phanat Nikhom, Thailand*

Solitude is not happiness. Solitude kills. Life together is happiness; it is joy. We Wodaabe like to live with others. At times we accept living alone so that our herd can find their joy in good pastures. But in the rainy season, it is different. . . . No one can live outside the clan.

The months of the rainy season are the best months of the year, . . . especially for us women. In the dry season, we hardly ever see anyone.

We stay in the house, and the camps are far from each other. The men see each other at the wells. But we wait with impatience for the arrival of the first rains. This means that the clan will come together again.

During the drought, our greatest suffering was the dispersion of the clan. That year there was no rainy season and therefore the clan did not come together. But God helped us. After a silence of two years, after the

suffering, joy came again. We were able to meet again in the bush during the rainy season.

Oh that God will let us have many more rainy seasons in the midst of the clan! Oh that God will enable us to live together in joy.

—*Bodaado woman of the nomadic Wodaabe tribe, Niger[7]*

In NaLao, a village in the heart of northeast Thailand, members of a silk group cooperatively plant and tend mulberry trees. They harvest the leaves to feed the silk worms. Later they dye the silk that the worms spin and weave cloth on handmade looms.

At lunchtime, the work group eats together on woven reed mats in the shade of a tamarind tree. Each member contributes to the common spread—baskets of steamed sticky (glutinous) rice, bowls of *bon blah* (spicy fish sauce), steamed greens, banana flowers, boiled bamboo shoots, squash, papaya *pok pok*, fermented fish sauce, and homemade hot sauce. Some dishes are prepared on the spot.

Everyone removes their shoes before sitting on the mats. Using no utensils, they reach with their fingers into the serving dishes, forming balls of sticky rice and dipping it into the sauces. People compliment each other and ask, "Is it good? Is it spicy?"

Obviously germs are shared and fingers become sticky in the course of the meal. To a North American, this seems unsanitary and untidy. We guard against sharing germs even with our immediate families. Nevertheless, the entire silk group shares this meal without reservation. Here in the Thai village virtually everyone *is* family. People address one another as aunt, grandmother, sister, and little brother. They share space, work, child care, food, and germs. Consequently, the entire community takes an interest in the health of each person.

—Carol Rose, Wapipathum, Mahasarakam, Thailand

• •

Vegetable Croquettes (Korea)

Serves 6

Chasoh Juhn
(chah-soh juhn)

Koreans make croquettes with a variety of vegetables, but potatoes are always a main ingredient. Vegetable croquettes make a tasty appetizer or side dish for Asian meals.

Mix together:
   1 c. potatoes, coarsely grated (250 ml)
   3/4 c. carrots, coarsely grated (175 ml)
   1/2 c. onions, chopped (125 ml)
   1 clove garlic, minced

Make batter of:
   3/4 c. flour (175 ml)
   1 t. salt (5 ml)
   1/4 t. pepper (1 ml)
   2 eggs, beaten
   1/4 c. water (50 ml)

Stir into vegetables.

Heat in skillet:
   1/2 c. oil (125 ml)

Drop vegetable mixture into hot oil by teaspoons or tablespoons depending on size desired. Fry until browned on both sides. Drain on paper. Serve hot.

—Pat Yoder, Goshen, Indiana

Greek Green Beans (Greece)

Serves 5-7

Fasoulakia Fresca Yahnista (fah-sou-LAH-kee-ah FRES-kah yah-nees-TAH)

Mint gives the unique Greek flavor to this dish.

• Microwave:
In 2-qt. casserole (2-L), combine oil, garlic, and onion, then cook on high 2 minutes. Add other ingredients except tomato, stir gently, cover, and cook on high 3 minutes. Add tomato, stir, cook on high 5-9 minutes, stirring once, until beans are tender. Let stand, covered, 3 minutes.

Brown in 2 T. olive oil (30 ml):
1 clove garlic, minced
1 onion, chopped
When vegetables are transparent, add:
1 lb. green beans, chopped (500 g) (about 3 c./750 ml)
1-2 t. fresh mint, chopped (5-10 ml)
2 beef bouillon cubes, dissolved in a little water
1 large tomato, peeled and chopped (or equivalent of canned tomato)
2 t. tomato paste (10 ml)
little fresh parsley, chopped (optional)
Stir gently and add enough water to allow beans to simmer. Cover and simmer about 30 minutes. Check periodically and add water as needed to keep beans from sticking.
Add:
salt and pepper to taste

—*Barbara Antonoplos and Marsha Jones, Atlanta, Georgia*

Green Squash Bake (Argentina)

Serves 6-8
350°F 180°C
30 min.

Torta de Zapallitos (TOR-tah day sah-pah-ZHEE-tohss)

Serve as a side dish, or a main dish for a light meal. Eggs and cheese provide plenty of protein.

• Microwave:
Place chopped squash and onion in large pie plate, cover loosely, and cook on high 4-6 minutes or until tender, stirring twice. Combine and pour other ingredients over squash. Cook on medium for 6-8 minutes or until a knife inserted 1 inch (2.5 cm) from center comes out clean and center is almost set. Let stand 5 minutes; center will set during standing time.

Cut in small pieces:
3-4 small green summer squash, such as zucchini (about 1 pound/500 g)
1 onion
1 small hot red pepper +!
Mix with:
3 T. flour (45 ml)
1/2 t. baking powder (2 ml)
salt and pepper to taste
Place in small, greased baking pan and top with:
3 eggs, beaten
1 c. cheese, grated (250 ml)
Bake at 350° F (180° C) until squash is cooked through, about 30 minutes.

—*Nélida de Pandulla and Frieda Schellenberg Erb, Buenos Aires, Argentina*

●●●●●●●●●●●●●●●●●●●●●●●●●●●●●●

Scalloped Corn (Paraguay)

Serves 8

375°F 190°C

30 min.

Chipa Guazú
(CHEE-pah gwah-SOO)

This year-round dish is especially associated with harvest time in Paraguay, since it is best made with fresh, tender corn. It is typically baked in an outdoor, round beehive oven. The name Chipa Guazú comes from Guaraní, the language of one of Paraguay's indigenous populations. Served as a side dish in Paraguay, Scalloped Corn has adequate protein for a main dish.

Sauté in frypan in 2 T. oil and/or bacon drippings (30 ml):
2 onions, chopped
Place onion mixture in 9 x 13-inch lightly greased baking pan (3.5-L).
Add and mix together:
1/4 c. flour (50 ml)
1 c. cornmeal (250 ml)
1 t. salt (5 ml)
21/2 c. mild cheese, grated (625 ml)
11/2 c. milk (375 ml)
2 eggs, beaten
31/2 c. fresh, frozen, or canned sweet corn
kernels (875 ml)
Mixture will be quite moist. Bake at 375°F (190°C) for 30 minutes or until golden brown. Bottom should be brown and crusty.

—*Jonathan and Ruth Beachy, Asunción, Paraguay*
—*Hilde Amstutz, Elkhart, Indiana*
—*Mary Wenger, Versailles, Missouri*

●●●●●●●●●●●●●●●●●●●●●●●●●●●●●●

Zucchini Skillet (Madagascar)

(ts) *Serves 4-6*

Karazam-boatavo
(kah-rah-zahm-boo-ah-TAH-voh)

This easy dish features a blend of garlic, bay leaves, and tomato.

• *Variation:*
Omit parboiling. Place zucchini strips directly into frypan with other ingredients to be sautéd. Sauté until zucchini is brown and softened, then add tomatoes and simmer until all vegetables are tender, about 5 minutes.

Parboil 2 minutes:
4 medium zucchini
Cut zucchini in long strips, 1-inch wide (2.5-cm), and sauté briefly in 2 T. oil (30 ml). When lightly brown, add:
3 tomatoes, chopped
4 bay leaves
8 cloves garlic, crushed
salt and pepper to taste
Cook briefly and stir gently, so zucchini strips do not fall apart. Turn off heat and let rest at least 30 minutes to absorb flavor. Reheat if needed.
Remove bay leaves and garlic cloves and serve with rice.

• *Microwave:*
Parboil zucchini in microwave on high 2-4 minutes.

—*Honorine Kiplagat, Tamatave, Madagascar; and Annetta Miller, Nairobi, Kenya*

133

When José Antonio Filho bought 12 hectares of scrub land near Tacaimbó in northeast Brazil, his neighbors laughed. They thought him foolish to even consider farming the land. The soil was so eroded that rain had literally washed away the previous owner's brick house.

The neighbors are not laughing anymore. Instead, they are coming to learn from Filho, to discover how he managed in a few short years to turn the wasteland into a wonderland of productivity. Filho now produces enough to feed his eight-member family and has surplus to sell.

Filho achieved this success by abandoning several traditional farm practices that were damaging the terrain and climate. He stopped planting up and down hillsides and burning the crop trash. In their place he adopted new techniques such as planting grass barriers, plowing and planting on the contour of his rolling land, and leaving the crop trash in the fields. As one walks through Filho's fields, it is difficult to believe that his healthy rows of corn and beans grow on what were deep gullies not long ago.

–Emily Will, Ciudad Guzmán, Jalisco, Mexico

Some 40 to 50 million trees are cut every year in Haiti, a country that is already 98 percent deforested. As the trees disappear, the soil they held to the mountains washes into the sea. Old folks observe now and then that the hills look like they are getting old. "You can see their bones sticking out," they say.

Most of Haiti's mountains are becoming desolate and bald, spotted only with occasional mango or banana trees. When it rains, the rivers turn brown with earth carried from the burned and hoed hillside gardens. But without the green canopies that used to call the rain down, it now rains less frequently and plentifully than before.

Is it just the Haitian peasants' imagination that the dry season becomes dryer and the earth less productive each year? They say the amount of rice they harvested this year is several measures less than last year, which was less than the year before—not quite enough to get by on.

When a mountainside turns from a subtropical forest of palm and pine trees to a charred slope of stumps, the whole community suffers from the mountain's wound. Unless it is healed and reforested, hunger and poverty will only increase.

—Jennie Smith, Bwardlorens, Haiti

Mike Mullin: Haiti

The central Asian country of Nepal has a serious deforestation problem. Most reports conclude that the problem stems from population growth. But Nepal's land is distributed in a way that forces poorer people onto the steep hills of marginal lands. Since they do not have access to the flatter, fertile lands, they clear land that should not be cleared so they can feed their families. If land and thus wealth were more equally distributed, perhaps poor Nepalis would not need to farm the mountainsides or rely on the forests for fuel.

—June Thomas-son, Fairbanks, Alaska

Indonesian Vegetable Platter

Ⓜ️

Serves 8

••••••••••••••••••••••••••••••••

Gado Gado
(gah-doh gah-doh)

Colorful Gado Gado makes a wonderful late summer meal when garden vegetables are plentiful. Vegetables may be cooked 1-2 hours in advance and need not be kept hot. Indonesians serve this dish at room temperature.

• *Microwave:*
Cook each vegetable separately in 2 T. water (30 ml) 3-5 minutes on high or arrange vegetables around the outside rim of large microwave platter, with cauliflower, broccoli, and beans at outside, then carrots, and placing cabbage and bean sprouts in center. Sprinkle with 2 T. water (30 ml). Cover loosely, leaving opening to vent. Cook on high 5-8 minutes until crisp-tender, rotating once after 3 minutes. Let stand, covered, 1 minute. For peanut sauce, combine 2 T. oil (30 ml), onions, and garlic in uncovered dish. Cook on high 2-4 minutes until onions are tender. Add 2 1/2 c. water or stock (625 ml) and cook on high 2-5 minutes or until it boils. Add a bit more water if sauce is too thick. Stir in other ingredients and cook on high 1 minute.

Vegetables:
Cook or steam each vegetable separately until crisp-tender:
   1/2 **small head cabbage, cut up**
   11/2 **c. fresh green beans, chopped or French-cut (375 ml)**
   1 **small head cauliflower, cut in florets**
   2 **c. fresh or canned bean sprouts (500 ml)**
   4 **carrots, cut in small strips**
Other vegetables may be added or substituted. Drain vegetables, reserving stock for peanut sauce.
Peel and quarter:
   4 **eggs, hard-cooked**
Slice:
   2 cucumbers
   6-10 radishes
Peanut sauce:
Sauté in 3 T. oil (45 ml):
   1/2 **c. onions, finely chopped (125 ml)**
   2 **cloves garlic, minced**
When onions are soft and transparent, reduce heat and add:
   31/2 **c. hot water or vegetable stock (875 ml)**
   11/8 **c. chunky peanut butter (275 ml)**
   2 **t. hot chili peppers, chopped (10 ml) or Tabasco pepper sauce to taste +!**
   2 **bay leaves**
   1 **t. ginger root, finely grated (5 ml)**
   2 **t. lemon juice (10 ml)**
   grated rind of 1 lemon
   1 **t. salt (5 ml)**
   1 **t. Sweet Soy Sauce (p. 281) or brown sugar (5 ml) (optional)**
Simmer 15 minutes. Adjust seasonings to taste.
Group vegetables attractively on large platter(s) with bowl of peanut sauce in center(s). Garnish with eggs, radishes, and cucumbers. Serve with hot rice. To eat, each person takes serving of rice, tops it with vegetables, and ladles peanut sauce over top.

• *Options:*
For a more authentic sauce, substitute coconut milk (p. 280) for part of the water or vegetable stock.
•
Add shrimp (shelled and deveined) or shrimp slices, steamed, to vegetable platter.

—*Adapted from* More-with-Less Cookbook, *by Doris Janzen Longacre (Herald Press, 1976; all rights reserved; used with permission).*

Okras in Yogurt (India)

Dahi Bhendee
(DAH-hee BEN-dee)

This cold side dish accents any curry meal.

• **Microwave:**
Place okra, onion, green chilies, 2 T. water (30 ml), and 1-2 T. vinegar (15-30 ml) in 1-qt. dish (1-L). Cover and cook on high 3-4 minutes or until okra is cooked. Gently stir after 2 minutes. Cool and proceed with recipe.

Combine in frypan:
> **1/2 lb. okra, rinsed and left whole (250 g)**
> **1 onion, chopped**
> **2 hot green chili peppers, slit down middle +!**

Add:
> **1/2 c. water (125 ml)**
> **1/4 c. vinegar (50 ml)**
> **salt to taste**

Cook until okra is done, adding more water if needed. Let cool.

Mix until smooth:
> **1/2 t. ground coriander (2 ml)**
> **1/4 t. ground cumin (1 ml)**
> **1/8 t. chili powder (.5 ml)**
> **1 c. yogurt (250 ml) (p. 295)**

Remove hot green chilies from okras. Place cooked okras in serving dish and pour yogurt mixture over to cover; sprinkle with ground cloves, cinnamon, and cardamom. Serve.

—*Rose Chater and Cynthia Peacock, Calcutta, India*

You are a mighty tree with big branches laden with fruit. When children come to you, they find something to eat.

—*Ashanti prayer, Ghana, Africa*

— Notes

1. Adapted from *Mennonite Reporter* (January 22, 1990), p. 12.
2. From a discussion with Leona Dueck Penner during the January-February 1986 blockade against logging companies on the Queen Charlotte Islands, British Columbia. Adapted from *Mennonite Reporter* (January 22, 1990), p. 12.
3. Wesley Granberg-Michaelson, *A Worldly Spirituality: The Call to Take Care of the Earth* (San Francisco: Harper & Row, Publishers, 1984), p. 28.
4. Angelo Maliki, ed., *Belldum: Joy and Suffering among the Wodaabe* (Mission Catholique, B.P. 10 270, Niamey, Niger).
5. Copyright © Martin Luther King, Jr.; used with permission of Joan Daves.
6. "Prayer of a Chinese Christian," *World at One in Prayer*, ed. by D. J. Fleming (New York: Friendship Press; used with permission).
7. Angelo Maliki, ed., *Belldum: Joy and Suffering Among the Wodaabe* (Mission Catholique, B.P. 10 270, Niamey, Niger).

... grains, dried beans, stews, and main dishes

Judith Dick: West Bank

The fresh, early-morning air in the mountains of north-central Guatemala is charged with a sense of peace and well-being. This is corn-planting day, the day in the K'ekchi' Indian culture around which all other activities center. Corn is the staff of life for the Indians, the basis of their work, celebrations, buying, and selling.

The day culminates weeks of preparation: locating the field, clearing, burning, and then fencing it. After the corn is planted, the work will continue: weeding, bending the cornstalks, harvesting and storing the corn, shelling, and hauling it to the village.

The planting day begins with a meal of beans, coffee, and fresh, thick, steaming tortillas. After eating, Christian families offer a prayer for safety during the planting and for God's blessing on the seeds, and those of traditional Mayan belief offer a ritual of sacrifice to the corn god.

The seed is carefully distributed among the men. They leave for the field with only two objects: a bag of seed slung over their shoulders and a planting stick—a long, slender tree limb with the end sharpened to a fine point. The planters move across the field in a routine pattern—poke hole, drop corn, cover up, move forward, poke hole. . . .

By early afternoon when the field is planted, the women who have stayed behind are ready for the ravenous appetites of the men. They have several dressed turkeys, a huge cauldron of soup, pots of coffee, and a never-ending supply of tortillas. When everyone has eaten, guests wrap leftovers in banana leaves to take home. The hosts express their gratitude and appreciation as they send their relatives and neighbors on their way.

The corn is planted and with it the hope that new life and opportunities will spring forth. An entire year's livelihood depends upon the result of this day's labor.

—Mary Jane Newcomer, Lake Wales, Florida

Sometime in September, if God grants health, good rains, and a successful harvest, the Senufo people of southwestern Burkina Faso celebrate the "seed corn meal." At planting time and until harvest, they carefully save and protect a portion of their seed, their only insurance against crop failure. But once the ears of corn are full on the stalk, they can make a meal of the seed corn.

Normally only one woman from the extended family prepares corn for a meal, but for this special occasion all the women participate. They begin by pounding the bran off the kernels. Every woman in the family, from the oldest grandmother to the youngest girl, takes a turn with the large mortar and pestle. Next they take turns winnowing the corn, dropping it from one basket into another so the wind can carry off the chaff. One by one they kneel at the two grinding stones between which they crush the grains of corn. After the corn is ground and sifted, the women pour it into a pot of boiling water. They use a long wooden paddle to stir it until it becomes a thick mush.

When it is time to eat, the women of the family share one common bowl and the men share another. They dip hand-formed balls of mush into a sauce that may contain a bit of meat that everyone shares at the end of the meal.

We have eaten the seed corn. *Barika!* (Praise to God!) May God grant us another harvest next year!

—Mawa Coulibaly and Kathy Peterson, NDorola, Burkina Faso

6

●●●●●●●●●●●●●●●●●●●●●●●●●●

Honoring the Everyday

Bris Michel's pace is brisk as he walks to his garden. A full day's work awaits him; he must hoe and clean the weeds from his corn rows. But today he will not work alone. He is hosting a *kombit*, and before long several neighbors, friends, and relatives—women and men—arrive to join in the work.

These communal workdays, apparently of African origin, are common in rural Haiti where most farmers are too poor to hire labor during their peak work periods. So Bris and his neighbors share their labor through reciprocal work parties.

The work party's labor in the garden is matched by the labor of Bris' wife, Venans, who remains in the kitchen this day. With the help of an assistant, she prepares the satisfying meal of cornmeal and beans that the workers will enjoy at day's end. Working continuously from early morning until late afternoon when the meal is served, they haul water (five gallons at a time), clean beans (sorting out the stones and any weevil-eaten or moldy ones), pound garlic, wash and sieve the cornmeal, clean and chop cabbage. Combining the ingredients in a large pot, cradled on three stones over an outdoor fire, they stir the mixture as it simmers.

Stan Reedy: Vietnam

The women leave their food preparations only long enough to carry drinking water to the workers in the garden. Then they return and make sure all is in order for serving. Venans carefully dishes up the savory cornmeal and beans, emptying the pot while giving everyone an equal portion. Her expert estimation reflects a common Creole proverb: *"Bon mama kon partagé bien* (good mother can divide well)." In a society where many families cannot afford adequate nourishment, this is an important principle.

—Carla Bluntschli, Bwardlorens, Haiti

Bris and Venans spend long hours planting, harvesting, and preparing food. And because they eat primarily what they produce, their diet changes little from day to day. Even on important days when a crowd gathers to work, the menu remains much the same, except in quantity.

Cornmeal and beans every day, several times a day, may sound mundane for people accustomed to a richer, more varied diet. But such grain and legume combinations—often supplemented with

Earl Martin: Philippines

vegetables and occasionally with meat—are the menu of millions. And there are as many tasty variations of this simple fare as there are cooks who have no choice but to make the same foods palatable for their families day after day.

Such ordinary cuisine is "the poor man's invention out of necessity, but it is light years away from poor cooking," wrote Robert Farrar Capon in *The Supper of the Lamb*. "Every dish . . . provides a double or treble delight: Not only is the body nourished and the palate pleased, the mind is intrigued by the triumph of ingenuity over scarcity—by the making of slight materials into a considerable matter."[1]

People who are intimately involved in food production—but produce little surplus—do not take food for granted. They treasure it as the staff of life, as something sacred. They scrape the pots and plates clean, suck any bones until they are shiny, and carefully use all edible parts of both plants and animals. Even when food is scarce, its sacred nature assures that it is shared, not hoarded. Any meal can accommodate an unexpected guest.

It is ironic that this high regard for food is all but lost in societies where food abounds in quantity and variety, but where few people directly work to produce it. Food is simply another commodity to buy, sell, and consume. Young and old glibly speak of "nuking" food in a microwave oven and thoughtlessly toss leftovers in the garbage. People still give prayerful thanks to God for the "blessings of abundance," but overabundance quickly spoils, becoming a curse of obesity, heart disease, and perpetual dieting schemes.

The recipes in this section, along with many in chapters four and five, represent everyday foods from the world community. They invite us to savor the flavors of simplicity and to appreciate the modest beauty of a bowl of steaming rice or stiff cornmeal mush.

Overall, the recipes contain little or no meat, drawing their flavors from herbs, spices, and innovative ingredient combinations. Many are extremely basic, others more elaborate. Some ingredients that are common and affordable in one part of the world are less available and more expensive elsewhere, and cooking techniques that are routine in one setting may seem complex in another.

May the recipes and stories of food production help us reflect anew on the sacred nature of food and remember those who produce most of the food they eat.

According to a Swahili proverb, "Rice is all one but there are many ways of cooking it." Although rice is a nearly universal food, the following recipes show geographical preferences for type of rice as well as preparation method.

Short- and medium-grain, and glutinous (sticky) rice are common varieties in eastern Asia. Asian cooks rarely add oil or salt to their everyday rice, preferring a bland accompaniment to well-seasoned main dishes.

Long-grain rice is common in much of Latin America. Many cooks fry the rice in oil until it is pearly white, then add water to complete cooking.

Basmati, an aromatic long-grain variety, is used for special occasions in much of India, Bangladesh, and Nepal. It tends to be more expensive than other rice in those regions as well as in North America, where it can be found in Asian food stores. *Basmati* rice should be rinsed well before cooking.

Brown rice is a less-processed form of polished white rice. After the hulling, the kernel is left intact for greater nutrient retention. Brown rice requires about twice the cooking time as white rice.

Rice pilafs, or pilaus, are made by frying raw rice in oil, often with spices or onions, and then cooking it in chicken or beef bouillon or tomato juice. Sautéed chopped onions, peanuts, and raisins may be added as a garnish.

Wild rice was an important part of the traditional diet and economy of native communities in Canada and the United States. Some native communities are today regaining a share of the market, lost to commercial firms which sell wild rice primarily as a gourmet food. Wild rice recipes in this book were developed by the Kagiwiosa Manomin wild rice project of an Ojibway community at Wabigoon, Ontario. Kagiwiosa Manomin is marketed in Canada through the Mennonite Central Committee SELFHELP Crafts program.

Kagiwiosa wild rice needs no presoaking and cooks in 30 minutes, quicker than other commercial wild rice, because it is roasted, following a traditional method, before the husk is removed. Most other brands of wild rice must be presoaked before cooking. For a quick method, wash rice in cold water. Stir 1 c. rice (250 ml) into 3 c. boiling water (750 ml). Boil 5 minutes. Remove from heat, cover, and soak one hour. Drain, rinse, and cook as directed in recipe.

....

*R*emove far from me falsehood and lying;
    give me neither poverty nor riches;
    feed me with the food that I need,
or I shall be full, and deny you,
    and say, "Who is the Lord?"
or I shall be poor, and steal,
    and profane the name of my God.

—*Proverbs 30:8-9*

Basic Steamed Rice

• •

Serves 4-6

Combine in heavy saucepan:
1 1/2 c. rice (375 ml)
1/2 t. salt (2 ml)
just enough water to rise 1 inch above rice
    level (2.5 cm) (Asians measure using index
    finger from tip to middle of first knuckle)

Bring to a boil over high heat. Stir with fork, loosening grains at bottom of saucepan. Reduce heat to simmer, cover with tight-fitting lid, and do not stir or peek for 20 minutes. (If electric burner stays too hot and causes rice to boil over, pull saucepan partially off burner for first 5 minutes of cooking time.) After 20 minutes, turn off heat and let rice stand, covered, until ready to serve. Flake gently while transferring to serving dish. Yields tender but slightly chewy dry rice with no gluey moisture at bottom.

• Options:
Measure 1 2/3 c. water (400 ml) to 1 c. rice (250 ml). Proceed as above, but reduce water when cooking large quantities.
•
Use brown rice; increase cooking time to 45 minutes.
•
Omit salt if serving rice with salty or spicy side dishes.

—*From* More-with-Less Cookbook, *by Doris Janzen Longacre*
  (Herald Press, 1976; all rights reserved; used with permission).

Baked Rice

• •

Serves 3-4

350°F 180°C

45 min.

Preheat oven to 350°F (180°C).
Combine in covered casserole:
2 c. hot water (500 ml)
1 c. rice (250 ml)
1/2 t. salt (2 ml)
1 T. margarine (15 ml)

Cover and bake 45 minutes. Additional baking time is needed for larger quantities.

—*From* More-with-Less Cookbook, *by Doris Janzen Longacre*
  (Herald Press, 1976; all rights reserved; used with permission).

Sticky Rice
(Laos/Thailand)

●●●●●●●●●●●●●●●●●●●●●●●●●●●●●●●●

Serves 4

**Khao Niew
(cow NEE-oh)**

Sticky Rice is the staple food of the people of rural Laos and northwestern Thailand. It is served daily in special, covered baskets, frequently accompanied by fresh, uncooked greens and a vegetable broth eaten from a common bowl. Meat and eggs are a rare treat. The essential chili sauce, Jayo (p. 283), adds spice to the meal. Laotian families sit on the floor to eat around a large rattan-and-bamboo tray elevated about six inches off the floor. They use their fingers to roll Sticky Rice into bite-size balls and dip them into the Jayo. Look for Sticky Rice in Asian food stores. It may also be called sweet or glutinous rice.

Soak in water at least 4 hours, or overnight:

2 c. uncooked rice (do not substitute regular rice)

Drain and rinse in cold water.

Place in steaming basket or vegetable steamer over boiling water. Cover and steam 20-30 minutes. For uniform steaming, flip rice over for last 5-10 minutes. Place in lidded basket or covered dish that is not airtight. Serve with Jayo (p. 283) and Thai Stir-fried Vegetables (p. 130), Grilled Chicken (p. 229) or Cashew Chicken (p. 229).

—*Nonglak Pana and Carol Rose, Wapipathum, Mahasarakam, Thailand*
—*Somphane Thadavong, Vientiane, Laos; and Linda Peachey, Lancaster, Pennsylvania*
—*Martha Zimmerly, Orrville, Ohio*

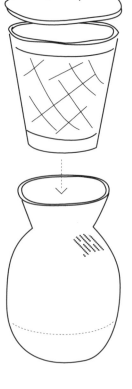

Rice steamer used in Thailand and Laos. Upper basket containing rice rests inside the top of a metal pot of steaming water until rice is tender.

The dream of a farmer in Thailand is to have rice in the field and fish in the water. Thais usually eat rice at each meal. When inviting others to eat, they commonly ask, *"Thaan khao may?* (Would you like to eat rice?)"* Thais refer to the good life as "eating hot rice and sleeping late." To "smash the rice pot" is to destroy one's means of livelihood.

Central American-Style Rice

•••••••••••••••••••••••••••••••

Serves 4

Arroz Blanco
(ah-rohss BLAHN-koh)

Use this rice as a side dish for Latin American meals.

In medium saucepan, sauté in 1 1/2 T. oil (20 ml):
- **1 small onion, minced**
- **1 clove garlic, minced (optional)**
- **1 T. green pepper, minced (15 ml) (optional)**

Stir-fry until onion is clear.
Add:
- **1 c. uncooked rice (250 ml)**

Stir-fry 1-2 minutes, until rice is pearly white.
Add:
- **1/2 t. salt (2 ml)**
- **13/4 c. water (425 ml)**

Bring to a boil. Reduce heat, cover, and simmer 15 minutes over low heat. Turn off heat; keep rice covered 10 minutes more. Flake with fork and serve.

—*Martha Azaguierre, El Hatillo, Honduras; and Dorothy Hood, El Naranjal, Honduras*
—*Beverlee Ludema, San José, Costa Rica*

Mexican Rice Skillet (Mexico)

•••••••••••••••••••••••••••••••

(ts)

Serves 4

Arroz con Elote y Queso
(ah-ROHSS kohn ay-LOH-tay ee KAY-soh)

Mexicans serve this rice with chicken. It can also be a main dish for a light meal.

In large heavy frypan, heat:
- **2 T. oil (30 ml)**

Add:
- **1 c. uncooked rice (250 ml)**

Fry 1-2 minutes, stirring gently.
Add:
- **1 small onion, minced**
- **5 cloves garlic, minced**
- **1/2 c. water (125 ml)**
- **1/2 t. salt (2 ml)**

Cook, stirring constantly, until water is absorbed.
Add:
- **1 c. boiling water or broth (250 ml)**
- **2 medium green peppers, cut in strips**
- **1 c. canned or frozen corn (250 ml)**

Cover and simmer about 20 minutes without stirring until liquid is absorbed. Remove from heat.
Spread over top:
- **8 oz. sour cream (250 ml)**
- **sharp cheese, shredded, to cover**

Cover and let stand 5-10 minutes until cheese melts.

—*Adriana Castillo Adame, Mexico City, Mexico*

Painted Rooster (Nicaragua)

(ts)

Gallo Pinto
(GAH-yoh PEEN-toh)

This simple but tasty dish derives its name from the dark red and white speckled color of the rice and beans mixture, resembling the coloration of the Barred Plymouth Rock rooster. Gallo Pinto is a popular breakfast dish, often served with salty, dry white cheese. A good way to use leftover rice and beans.

Cook:
  1 c. rice (250 ml) (p. 143)
Have ready:
  3/4 c. red or black beans, cooked and drained (175 ml) (p. 162)
In frypan, sauté in small amount of oil:
  2 T. onion (30 ml)
When onions are clear, add:
  beans
  1/2 t. ground cumin or ground coriander (2 ml) (optional)
Sauté until dry. Stir in rice and cook until heated through. Top with grated cheese, sour cream, or yogurt (p. 295). Serve with hot tortillas and fried or scrambled eggs (optional).

—*Teresa Palacios and Leslie Book, Managua, Nicaragua*

Rice and Pigeon Peas (Puerto Rico)

Arroz con Gandules
(ah-ROHSS kohn gahn-DOO-layss)

Rice and beans are a staple food, eaten several times a week, in the Puerto Rican community in New York City. Pigeon peas—gandules verdes—are a favorite bean, but others are used as well. Look for canned pigeon peas in Spanish food stores or large supermarkets.

• *Option:*
Pigeon peas have a special taste worth trying; if unavailable, substitute other beans.

In heavy saucepan, sauté in 1-3 T. oil (15-45 ml):
  1/2 c. ham, sausage, or bacon, chopped (125 ml)
Add:
  3 T. onion, chopped (45 ml)
  2 T. green pepper, chopped (30 ml)
  2 T. cilantro, chopped (30 ml)
  1 small green chili pepper, chopped
  3 T. olives or capers (45 ml)
  1/2 c. tomato sauce (125 ml)
Simmer 5 minutes. Add:
  1 t. dried oregano (5 ml)
  1/2 t. garlic powder (2 ml)
  1 1/2 t. salt (7 ml)
  1/8 t. pepper (.5 ml)
  1-lb. can pigeon peas with juice (500 g)
  2 c. water (500 ml)
  3 c. uncooked rice (500 ml)
Bring to a boil, then turn heat down very low. Cook, covered, until water is absorbed and rice is tender, 30-45 minutes. Peas will all be on top; rice should be dry and fluffy. A brown crust called *pegao*, which forms on the bottom, is a favorite part of the meal for many people.

—*Ana Martinez and Martha Miller, Bronx, New York*

Fried Rice
(Vietnam)

(ts)

Serves 3-4

Com Chien
(guhm JEE-uhn)

*Vietnam Fried Rice turns
leftover rice and vegetables
into an attractive, tasty meal.*

• *Options:*
Replace peas with other
vegetables such as carrots,
green beans, or shredded
cabbage.
•
Omit meat and add extra
vegetables.
•
For additional flavor, sprinkle
on Seasoned Fish Sauce
(p. 282) at table.

Cook:
**1 c. rice (250 ml) or have ready 3 c. leftover rice
(750 ml) (see p. 143)**
Heat in large frypan:
3 T. oil (45 ml)
Add:
**1/4-1/2 lb. cooked or raw meat (any kind), cut in
thin strips (125-250 g)**
3 cloves garlic, minced
1 large onion, coarsely chopped
1/4 t. pepper (1 ml)
1 t. sugar (5 ml)
1 T. soy sauce (15 ml)
1 T. fish sauce (15 ml) (optional)
Stir-fry until meat is tender and hot, 1-2 minutes.
Add:
3 c. rice, cooked (750 ml)
Stir-fry 5 minutes.
Add and stir well:
1 c. leftover peas (250 ml)
Just before serving, add:
2 eggs, beaten.
Over medium heat, stir carefully through rice until eggs
are cooked through. Serve piping hot with a green salad.

—*Tran Thi Trinh, Quang Ngai, Vietnam; and Pat Hostetter Martin,
Ephrata, Pennsylvania*

Meal preparation in
Laos is the task of
women—as is carrying
water for bathing and
cooking, caring for
children, hulling rice for
the day's consumption,
tending vegetable
gardens, washing clothes
in the river or stream, and
helping with chores in the
rice paddies.

In rural Laos where
most homes do not have
refrigerators or other
means to preserve food,
food preparation involves
a daily trip to the market.
To have the best pick of
produce, most women do
their marketing right after
sunrise; latecomers are
disappointed.

Zainab's Pilaf
(Kenya)

Serves 3-4

Mchele ya Zainab
(m'CHE-leh yah ZIE-nahb)

Somali women living in northern Kenya use goat and camel meat sparingly, with only a few pieces in dishes like this rice pilaf.

Brown in frypan in small amount of oil:
  1/4-1/2 lb. beef, goat, or turkey meat, cubed or ground (125-250 g)
Set aside.
In heavy saucepan, sauté in 1-2 T. ghee or oil (15-30 ml):
  1 small onion, finely sliced
Add:
  3-4 cloves garlic, crushed
  1 medium tomato, peeled and cut in chunks
  1/4-1/2 t. curry powder (1-2 ml)
  1/4 t. ground cinnamon (1 ml)
  1/2 t. salt (2 ml)
Fry briefly over medium heat, stirring constantly, until oil appears around edges.
Add:
  browned meat
  1 1/2 c. water (375 ml)
Bring to a boil.
Add:
  1 c. long-grain rice (250 ml)
Cover and cook 20 minutes on lowest heat, or finish cooking according to basket cooking directions (p. 173).

—*Zainab Hajji Ahmed, Rhamu, Kenya; and Nancy Brubaker, Lancaster, Pennsylvania*

Red Rice
(United States)

Serves 4-5

Contributor learned to make this southern U.S. dish while living in an African-American community on Johns Island, South Carolina.

Cook:
  1 1/2 c. rice (375 ml) (p. 143)
In frypan, fry until crisp:
  4 strips bacon
Drain on paper; crumble and reserve.
Drain excess bacon fat from frypan and add:
  1/3 c. onion, chopped (75 ml)
  1 1/2 stalks celery, chopped
  3/4 c. green pepper, chopped (175 ml)
Sauté until onion is transparent.
Add:
  1/2 lb. kielbasa or smoked sausage, split lengthwise, then sliced (250 g)
Fry until sausage is heated through. Mix into cooked rice.

(*more* →)

Stir in:

crumbled bacon
8-oz. can tomato sauce (227 g) (about
3/4 c./175 ml)

Heat through.
Add:

Tabasco pepper sauce to taste +!

—Fred Newswanger, New Holland, Pennsylvania

Spiced Mung Beans and Rice (Bangladesh)

- **- H -**

Serves 6-8

Bhuna Khichuri
(BHOO-nah ki-chu-ree)

Contributor is a self-taught Bengali gourmet cook. He notes, "Traditional Bengali cooking does not follow strict recipes. People learn cooking from experience and experiments. In rural Bangladesh, most women learn to cook from their mother or grandmother. I took up the job as a hobby because I always appreciated good food."

• Option:
If mung beans are unavailable, substitute lentils, which do not need to be presoaked.

Soak overnight or by quick method (p. 162):

1 c. mung beans (250 ml)

In large saucepan, heat:

1/4 c. margarine (50 ml)

Add and fry briefly:

1 1/2 t. ginger root, finely chopped or grated (7 ml)
1 bay leaf

Add:

1 c. mung beans, rinsed and drained (250 ml)
2 c. long-grain or basmati rice, rinsed (500 ml)
2 whole cloves
1/2 t. ground cinnamon (2 ml)
1 t. ground red pepper (5 ml) +! (optional)

Fry 15 minutes, stirring occasionally.
Add:

6 c. boiling water (1.5 L)
1 T. salt (15 ml)

Cover and simmer 25-30 minutes on low heat until beans and rice are tender.
In separate frypan, fry:

1/4 c. onion, chopped (50 ml)

Place beans and rice in serving dish. Garnish with fried onions and slices of 1 hard-cooked egg.

—Richard Sarker, Dhaka, Bangladesh

*d*on't take another mouthful before you have swallowed what is in your mouth.

—African proverb

Cornmeal Porridge

The staple food of much of central, eastern, and southern Africa is a stiff porridge made of white maize (corn) meal or starchy root vegetables. The consistency is much like play dough, easily handled without utensils. To the uninitiated, it is somewhat bland and tasteless. Those who enjoy it every day discriminate between a good and bad preparation. The best maize meal is made with newly harvested corn freshly ground into mealie meal without lumps.

Preparation of this staple food varies from country to country as does its name: *nshima* (Zambia), *tô* (Burkina Faso), *sadza* (Zimbabwe), *posho* (Kenya), *begobep* (Botswana), *papa* (Lesotho), *ugali* (East Africa), *boule* (Chad), and *musa, luku, fufu, bukula,* or *bidia* (Zaire). Various grains (millet, yellow corn meal, soy, wheat), tuberous plants (cassava, yams, potatoes), and fruits (plantains, green bananas) can substitute for the maize.

We offer a recipe for the Zambian *nshima*. The stiff porridge is made most often in a cast-iron, three-legged pot over an open fire. When preparing *nshima* for a feast, several women at a time take turns stirring the porridge with wooden paddles as it thickens in 30-gallon pots.

Nshima is served in a rounded mound on a common plate. Each person shapes the porridge into balls about the size of a walnut, makes an indentation in one side with the thumb, and then scoops up some of the accompanying "relish," a vegetable sauce. Beef, goat, or pork are served with porridge only at a feast. Chicken is occasionally served for a company meal at home, but most families would never eat chicken or meat for an everyday meal.

—*Kikuvu Malenge, Honeybrook, Pennsylvania*
—*Esther Spurrier, Dillsburg, Pennsylvania*

Cornmeal and Bean Porridge (Swaziland)

Sishwala
(see-SHWAH-lah)

In Swaziland this porridge is made with ground maize and served as a main dish or with a stew. Like rice or mashed potatoes, it is somewhat bland. Heap a vegetable or meat stew over it, or serve with a spicy dish.

●●●●●●●●●●●●●●●●●●●●●●●●●●●●●●●●

Serves 4-6

Soak overnight or by quick method (p. 162):
  1 1/2 c. navy beans (375 ml)
  6 c. water (1.5 L)
Cook in soaking water until beans are soft, but not mushy. Add:
  1 t. salt (5 ml)
  1/2 c. cornmeal (preferably white) (125 ml)
  1/2 c. cream of wheat (125 ml)
Simmer 10-15 minutes, stirring regularly, until porridge has consistency of thick cream of wheat or stiff mashed potatoes.

—*Busie Nsibande, Mbabane, Swaziland; and Rose Breneman Stewart, Lancaster, Pennsylvania*

150

African Cornmeal Porridge (Zambia)

Serves 6

• •

Nshima
(en-SHEE-mah)

Zambians make Nshima with mealie-meal, ground, unrefined white field corn. Stone-ground white cornmeal is a close substitute. Africans would not use yellow cornmeal, although North Americans may enjoy experimenting with it. Tester noted: "I couldn't imagine eating this porridge for supper, so I cooked rice too. We were all amazed at how good Nshima tasted!"

Boil in large soup pot:
   6 c. water (1.5 L)
Mix in bowl:
   1 c. white cornmeal (250 ml)
   1 c. water (250 ml)
Stir until smooth, then add to boiling water. Simmer 15-20 minutes, stirring occasionally.
Add, about 1/2 c. (125 ml) at a time:
   2 1/4-2 1/2 c. extra cornmeal (550-625 ml)
   1 t. salt (5 ml) (optional)
After each 1/2 c. of cornmeal (125 ml), stir well with wooden spoon until all dry particles disappear and all lumps are smoothed. Continue stirring vigorously a few more minutes until Nshima is stiff enough to handle easily without dripping off fingers. Remove from heat, cover, and let stand 10 minutes. The longer it sits, the stiffer it becomes. Stir again before serving.
Spoon Nshima into large serving dish, smoothing it into rounded mound with back of wet spoon, or serve on platter in large patties. Soak pot in cold water for easier washing. Serve with vegetable "relishes" such as Morogo (p. 121) and Ndiwo (p. 123), or stews such as Gumbo Stew (p. 177) or Stewed Beef (p. 243). Fry leftovers like cornmeal mush.

—Tina Muzyamba Munsaka, Ndola, Zambia
—Edith Makwembo, Chikankata, Zambia; and Linda Nafziger Meiser, Elkhart, Indiana
—Renee Muleya, Lusaka, Zambia; and Ruth Thiessen, Clearbrook, British Columbia
—Esther Spurrier, Dillsburg, Pennsylvania

....

Sejo senyane ha se fete molomo.
A little bit of food cannot pass the mouth. (It is as good as a feast.)

—Sesotho proverb (Lesotho)

....

*O*ne person is thin porridge; two or three people are a handful of stiff cooked maize meal.

—Tanzanian proverb

Wild Greens with Cornmeal (South Africa)

Serves 4-6

Imifino
(ee-mee-FEE-noh)

Imifino turns any edible greens—red root, sow thistle, lamb's-quarters, pumpkin leaves, chard, or spinach—into a hearty main dish. To increase protein content, serve with baked beans or fried eggs and milk to drink.

Bring to a boil in 2 c. water (500 ml):
  4 c. loosely packed greens, chopped (1 L)
  1 onion, chopped
  2 cloves garlic, minced
Add:
  2 c. cornmeal (500 ml)
Steam 10 minutes without stirring.
Stir in:
  1 1/4 t. salt (6 ml)
  approx. 2 c. hot water (500 ml)
This will be a thick consistency. Cover and cook 15-20 minutes on very low heat. Stir and serve with dabs of margarine. Refrigerate leftovers; slice and fry in bacon grease.

—Nancy Harman, Engcobo, Transkei, South Africa

Enchilada Casserole (Paraguay)

Serves 3-4

350°F 180°C

20 min./5 min.

Locro
(LOH-kroh)

This tasty, easy-to-prepare dish is sure to please at the end of a busy day. Canned hominy gives Locro the flavor of Mexican enchiladas, but without all the work.

Preheat oven to 350°F (180°C).
Fry:
  1/2 lb. ground beef (250 g)
  1/2 c. onion, chopped (125 ml)
  1/3 c. green pepper, chopped (75 ml)
  1/2 t. salt (2 ml)
Skim fat.
Add:
  1 c. tomato sauce (250 ml)
  3 c. canned hominy or whole kernel corn, drained (750 ml)
Mix well and place in small casserole. Bake 20 minutes.
Remove from oven and spread over top:
  1/2 c. cheese, shredded (125 ml)
Return to oven and bake additional 5 minutes.

• **Option:**
Instead of baking, cover frypan and cook over medium heat 5 minutes. Uncover and simmer 10-15 minutes until mixture begins to thicken. Remove from heat, add cheese, cover and let stand 5 minutes until cheese melts.

—Mary Wenger, Versailles, Missouri

Many international main-dish recipes are vegetable and meat stews and sauces that are served over rice or cornmeal porridge, or eaten with pita or other flat breads. We have tried to suggest the authentic accompaniment for stews from various places. You can also mix and match. Ethiopian stews, authentically served with injera, are tasty over rice. Indian stews, meant to be served with rice or chapatis, can be scooped up with pita bread instead. Many stews are good served over potatoes, pasta, or noodles. In most places, people do not smother their rice, bread, or pasta with stew; instead, they use small amounts of stew to flavor the starchy staple.

● ●

Old Indian Stew (Nicaragua)

Serves 6-8

Indio Viejo
(EEN-deeoh veeAY-hoh)

Fresh mint and lemon give this cornmeal-beef stew a unique flavor. Nicaraguans serve Indio Viejo on occasions when a little meat must serve a crowd—at all-night wakes, all-night Protestant church services that are interspersed with food, coffee breaks, and informal visiting, and for Catholic saints' day celebrations. It is often prepared in large clay pots over wood fires and stirred with wooden paddles.

Cook until tender:

3/4 lb. boneless beef or pork (375 g)
3 c. water (750 ml) (or enough to cover meat)
1/2 t. salt (2 ml)

Remove meat and shred or cut in small pieces. Reserve broth. In large heavy saucepan, sauté in 2 T. oil (30 ml):

1 onion, chopped
1/4 c. green pepper, chopped (50 ml)
3 cloves garlic, chopped

Add:

2 tomatoes, chopped, or 1 c. canned tomatoes (250 ml)
cooked meat

Fry until tomatoes are soft.
Add:

reserved broth plus water to make 5 c. (1.3 L)
1-2 beef bouillon cubes (optional)
1/4 c. lemon juice (50 ml)
4 sprigs fresh mint
1 T. paprika (15 ml)
1 c. cornmeal (250 ml) mixed with 1 c. water (250 ml)
1/2 t. salt or to taste (2 ml)

Stir well. Bring to a boil and reduce heat. Cover and simmer, stirring occasionally, until cornmeal thickens, about 20 minutes. When thick add:

2 T. margarine (30 ml) (optional)

Serve with rice and cabbage-tomato salad seasoned with salt and lemon.

—*José Avalo and Angela Silva, Managua, Nicaragua; and Ann Graber Hershberger, Harrisonburg, Virginia*
—*Lois Swartz de Orozco, Managua, Nicaragua*

Food preparation is extremely time-consuming for rural African women, because it involves far more than cooking. Women must first grow and harvest their crops. During the millet harvest in Zaire, women manually cut the heads of grain, pound them with a large wooden mortar and pestle, and then winnow to remove the chaff. For all this work, they return home at the end of a long, hot, dry day carrying one dishpan of grain on their heads.

Muesli
(Netherlands)

•••••••••••••••••••••••••••••••

(ts)

Serves 2

(MYOOS-lee)

This Dutch version of the Swiss oatmeal-yogurt-fruit blend makes a healthy and delicious breakfast, lunch, snack, or dessert. Making your own combinations from scratch is less expensive than buying packaged brands. Contributor suggests using hazelnuts, sunflower seed kernels, raisins, dried apricots, or dried apples.

Place in bowl:
   1 c. yogurt (250 ml) (p. 295)
   1/2 c. milk (125 ml)
   1/4 c. uncooked quick or rolled oats (50 ml)
   approx. 1/2 c. dried fruits and nuts (125 ml)
   fruit syrup, honey, or sugar to taste (optional)

Mix well and allow to stand 30-40 minutes. Will have pudding-like consistency.

—*Cynthia Shenk, Nijmegen, Netherlands*

Cooked Wheat
(Serbia)

•••••••••••••••••••••••••••••••

Serves 4

Koljivo
(KOH-lyee-voh)

Serbian Orthodox Christian families prepare Koljivo on their patron saints' days to offer guests. They make it with whole wheat kernels, shape it in a decorative mold, and serve it topped with whipped cream. We substitute quicker-cooking bulgur, and recommend it as a breakfast cereal or a unique dessert.

Combine in saucepan:
   1 c. bulgur (250 ml)
   1 1/2 c. water (375 ml)
   1/2 t. salt (2 ml)

Bring to a boil, then cover and simmer 15-20 minutes, until liquid is absorbed and bulgur is tender.
Add:
   1/2 c. almonds, hazelnuts, pecans, or walnuts,
      finely chopped (125 ml)
   3-4 T. honey or sugar (45-60 ml)
   1 T. margarine (15 ml) (optional)

Stir and serve with milk as breakfast cereal. For dessert, mold and chill, cut in wedges and top with whipped cream. Exquisite!

—*Nena and Stevan Madarac, Bacuga, former Yugoslavia; and Sara Wenger Shenk, Harrisonburg, Virginia*

....

Olugenda enjala teludda.
A visitor who leaves with an empty stomach because you did not offer food will not easily return.

—*Ugandan proverb*

Groundnut Sauce (Uganda)

••••••••••••••••••••••••••••••

Serves 6

Ennva ze Ebinyeebwa
(en-VAH
z'eh-bee-NYAY-bwah)

*Groundnut (peanut) Sauce
and matooke (plantains
steamed in banana leaves)
are the "mashed potatoes
and gravy" of southern
Uganda. Ugandans also
enjoy boiled sweet potatoes
or rice with this sauce, which
they make by grinding
roasted peanuts in a large
mortar and pestle.*

• Option:
Substitute 2 1/2-3 c. chunky
peanut butter (625-750 ml)
for peanut powder. If peanut
butter contains salt, omit salt.

Roast in saucepan 1 minute:
   1 lb. raw peanuts (500 g)
Pound peanuts with mortar and pestle, grind in blender, or
put through meat grinder several times to make coarse
peanut powder.
Fry in 2 T. oil (30 ml):
   3-4 onions, chopped
   2 tomatoes, chopped
   1 T. curry powder (15 ml)
   1 clove garlic, minced
   1 t. ginger root, grated (5 ml) (optional)
Add peanut powder.
Cook 2-3 minutes. Add slowly to form sauce:
   3 c. water or milk (750 ml)
Cook 15-20 minutes.
Add:
   1 t. salt (5 ml)
Serve over rice.

—*Rose Najjuku and Joyce Maxwell, Kampala, Uganda*

Groundnut Porridge (Zambia)

••••••••••••••••••••••••••••••

(ts)   M

Serves 4

Icele Abuntele
(ee-SEH-lay ah-voon-TEH-lay)

*Cornmeal porridge, made
with white cornmeal and
served without salt, sugar, or
milk, is a common Zambian
milk supplement for babies
and breakfast cereal for
adults. If you like cornmeal
porridge, try this version with
a dab of butter, honey or
brown sugar and milk for a
hot breakfast cereal.*

In medium saucepan, bring to a boil:
   2 1/4 c. water (550 ml)
Combine in bowl to make a smooth paste:
   1 c. water (250 ml)
   1 c. cornmeal (preferably white) (250 ml)
Add to boiling water, stirring constantly to avoid forming
lumps. Simmer 3 minutes.
Add:
   **1/2 c. peanuts, coarsely ground, or chunky
      peanut butter (125 ml)**
Simmer 3-5 more minutes.

• Microwave:
To cook individual serving, stir together 3/4 c. water (175 ml)
and 2 1/2 T. cornmeal (35 ml) in cereal bowl with deep sides (if
too shallow the cereal may bubble over as it cooks). Cook on
high 1 minute. Stir. Cook on high 30 seconds. Stir. Cook an
additional 30 seconds, if needed, until most of water is
absorbed and cereal is thickened. Add 2 T. ground peanuts
or chunky peanut butter (30 ml). Stir. Cook on high 15-20
seconds to re-warm.

—*Tina Muzyamba Munsaka, Ndola, Zambia*

155

Curried Split Peas (Kenya)

Serves 4-6

Dhal
(dahl)

East African cooking has been influenced by contact with India, the neighbor across the Indian Ocean. Full of flavor and simple to make.

Soak overnight or heat to boiling, turn off heat, and let stand 1 hour:

1 c. yellow split peas (250 ml)
3 1/2 c. water (875 ml)

Bring to a boil, then simmer until soft and mushy, about 45 minutes.

In separate frypan, sauté over medium heat in 2 T. oil (30 ml) until brown:

2 medium onions, chopped
4-6 cloves garlic, crushed

Add:

2 T. curry powder (30 ml)
2 t. ground cumin (10 ml)
1 t. salt (5 ml)

Fry 1 minute. Mix with cooked split peas.
Add:

2-4 T. cilantro, chopped (30-60 ml)

(If you aren't acquainted with cilantro, start with 2 T./30 ml. It has a potent flavor).
Simmer briefly to blend flavors. Eat with Chapatis (p. 48) or rice.

—*Annetta Miller, Nairobi, Kenya*

Dhal (India)

Serves 4-6

(dahl)

This everyday dish is commonly made with red lentils, but can be made with any lentil or split pea. Dhal is often mild, eaten with spicier curries. It can also be made fiery hot with ground red pepper or chili peppers.

• *Option:*
For spicier Dhal, add to spice mixture 1-2 minced green chilies or ground red pepper to taste.

Fry in 2 T. oil (30 ml) until golden brown:

1 onion, diced
1-2 cloves garlic, minced
1 t. ground turmeric (5 ml)
1 1/2 t. ground cumin (7 ml)
1 t. ginger root, finely grated (5 ml) (optional)
1/4 t. ground cardamom (1 ml) (optional)

Add:

1 c. dried lentils or split peas (250 ml) (if using split peas, soak overnight or by quick method, p. 162)
3 c. hot water (750 ml)
1 t. salt (5 ml) or to taste

Bring to a boil. Reduce heat, cover, and simmer until lentils are tender, about 45 minutes. Remove cover and simmer over very low heat, stirring frequently, about 20 more minutes, until lentils are mushy and thick, about the consistency of refried beans. Garnish with onions, thinly sliced and browned, or a squeeze of lemon. Serve with rice.

—*Author's recipe*

Curry refers both to a spicy blend of seasonings (cumin, coriander, turmeric, and others) and to the dishes flavored with these seasonings. Curry dishes, native to the subcontinent of central Asia, are also found in parts of eastern and southern Africa influenced by Indian immigrants, and elsewhere.

Authentic curry dishes are typically spicy hot. Individual cooks often grind and blend their spices as they cook, using different blends for different dishes. Curries are served with any combination of rice, Puris (p. 49) or Chapatis (p. 48), plain yogurt (p. 295) or raitas (p. 118), a chutney (p. 276), or other vegetables. The number of accompaniments depends on the wealth of a family and whether the meal is ordinary or festive. Poorer families commonly eat curry meals with either rice or bread—not both.

Red Lentils with Zucchini (India)

Serves 4

Laoo Dhal
(lah-oo DAHL)

In the villages of West Bengal, Indian families prepare Laoo Dhal with red lentils and white pumpkins, which are plentiful and inexpensive. We substitute zucchini for white pumpkin, making this a good end-of-summer dish.

Heat in saucepan:
  2 T. oil (30 ml)
Add:
  1 large onion, chopped
  1/2 t. ground turmeric (2 ml)
  1/2 t. cumin seed (2 ml) or 1/4 t. ground cumin (1 ml)
  1 hot red pepper +!
  1 bay leaf
Fry 1-2 minutes.
Add:
  1 c. red lentils (250 ml)
  3/4 t. salt (3 ml)
  1 t. sugar (5 ml)
  2 c. water (500 ml)
Bring to a boil. Reduce heat, cover, and simmer 15 minutes.
Add:
  2 c. zucchini, cut in small pieces (500 ml)
Stir to mix. Return to a boil. Cook, covered, stirring occasionally, until water is absorbed and lentils and zucchini are tender. Serve hot with Chapatis (p. 48) or rice.

—*Cynthia Peacock, Calcutta, India*

Bangladeshi village women prepare meals in separate bamboo cookhouses that have mud stoves called *chulas* built into the earthen floors. The cookhouse also serves as dining room. Family members sit in a circle on small stools two to three inches high. They use the fingers of their right hand to eat from their plates of rice.

Each morning it is the job of the daughter-in-law to prepare rice and curry for her extended family's lunch. She often makes enough so leftovers can be reheated for supper. Some families cook fresh food for both meals, especially during the hot season.

East Indian Spinach and Lentils (India)

Baji Dhal
(BAH-jee DAHL)

Contributor grew up in India eating rice and dhal (spiced lentils) almost every day. This is a dish she enjoys making for her family—not too hot or spicy. Curry lovers may increase the spices.

• Option:
Substitute other lentils and vegetables.

Serves 6

In large saucepan, brown in 3 T. oil (45 ml) over medium-low heat:
1 large onion, chopped
Add and brown lightly:
4 cloves garlic, minced
2 T. ginger root, finely chopped (30 ml)
Stir in, being careful not to burn:
2 t. whole cumin seed (10 ml)
2 t. curry powder (10 ml)
2 t. salt (10 ml)
1 fresh hot chili pepper, seeded, chopped +!
Stir in, coating with spice mixture:
2 c. red lentils, rinsed (500 ml)
Add:
5 1/2-6 c. water (1.3-1.5 L)
2 large potatoes, peeled and sliced (optional)
1 bunch spinach, chopped (may use frozen)
Bring to a boil. Reduce heat and simmer, partially covered, until lentils and potatoes are tender. Place in serving dish and sprinkle over top:
2 T. cilantro, chopped (30 ml)
Serve with hot rice, tomato and cucumber slices, Puris (p. 49), or Chapatis (p. 48).

—*Kim Warren, Seattle, Washington*

Spicy Main Dish Bean Dip (Sudan)

Ful
(fool)

This Sudanese breakfast dish, eaten with pita bread, has an adaptable ingredient list—make it to suit your taste. Ful provides a balanced meal in one dish with few dishes to wash since you eat it with your hands. Fava beans, commonly used in this dish, are known to cause toxic reactions in a small percentage of people, particularly those of Middle Eastern ancestry.

Serves 2-4

Soak overnight or by quick method (p. 162):
1 c. dried fava, kidney, or pinto beans (250 ml)
4 c. water (1 L)
Add:
1/2 t. salt (2 ml)
Cook until beans are soft.
Drain off excess water, leaving about 1/2 c. water (125 ml) or enough so beans don't stick to bottom if reheated.
Stir in:
2 t. ground cumin (10 ml)
1/2 t. salt (2 ml)
1 T. tahini (sesame seed paste) (15 ml) or 2 T. sesame oil (30 ml)
(more →)

• Options:
Replace dried beans with about 3 c. cooked or canned beans of same kind (750 ml).
•
Combine about 1 t. ground red pepper (5 ml) and 2 T. lemon juice (30 ml) on saucer. Dip pita bread into pepper/lemon juice mixture before dipping into bean dip.
+!

Remove from heat and add any combination of the following:
1-2 eggs, hard-cooked and finely chopped
1/4 c. feta cheese, crumbled (50 ml)
1 tomato, diced
3-4 Falafels, crumbled (p. 166)
1 medium onion, finely chopped
Stir lightly to mix. Put warm bean mixture in serving dish. Break off pieces of pita bread (p. 51) and dip into bean mixture, using bread as utensil.

—*Phyllis Horst Nofziger, Ephrata, Pennsylvania*

Everyday Lentils and Rice (India)

Serves 6

Khichri
(KICH-ree)

Khichri is a popular dish among India's rich and poor, but the ingredients vary according to family resources—families with limited means add few spices or vegetables. Because of the high regard for lentils and rice, Khichri is one of the foods that Hindu people serve to the gods and goddesses during Pujas (prayers). It is also one of the first solid foods offered to babies. The West Bengal Voluntary Health Association recommends Khichri as a low-cost, nutritious lunch or supper.

In large saucepan, heat:
2 T. oil (30 ml)
Add and sauté 2 minutes:
1 large onion, chopped
2 green peppers, sliced
2-inch stick cinnamon (5-cm)
4 cardamom pods or 1/2 t. ground cardamom (2 ml)
4 whole cloves
Add:
1 c. uncooked rice (250 ml)
1/2 c. lentils (125 ml)
Stir-fry about 5 minutes.
Add:
11/2 c. potatoes, cubed (375 ml)
1 c. cauliflower, chopped (250 ml)
1 large tomato, chopped
11/2 t. salt (7 ml)
4 c. water (1 L)
Bring to a boil. Reduce heat, cover, and simmer until rice, lentils, and vegetables are tender, 20-30 minutes. Consistency will be like stew, not dry or fluffy.

• Options:
Use any combination of vegetables, including dark green leafy vegetables.
•
Use brown rice. Soak rice 30 minutes and drain before frying with lentils.

—*Cynthia Peacock, Calcutta, India*

Egyptian Rice and Lentils

Koshary
(KOH-shah-ree)

Koshary is Egypt's street food. Vendors serve this low-cost, nutritious meal in dishes or plastic bags from little kiosks. It is also an important dish for Coptic Orthodox Christians because it is meatless and can be eaten during times of fasting. In Egypt the sauce is made from fresh tomatoes, and the rice and lentils are always served with macaroni.

Sauce:
Combine in saucepan:
  3/4 c. tomato paste (175 ml)
  31/2 c. tomato juice, tomato sauce, or pureed tomatoes (875 ml)
  1 green pepper, chopped
  3 T. celery leaves, chopped (45 ml)
  3 cloves garlic, minced
  1 T. sugar (15 ml)
  1 t. salt (5 ml)
  11/4 t. ground cumin (6 ml)
  1/4 t. ground red pepper (1 ml) or crushed hot chilies to taste +!
Bring to a boil, reduce heat, and simmer 20-30 minutes.

Rice and lentils:
In heavy saucepan or frypan with cover, heat:
  2 T. oil (30 ml)
Add:
  11/4 c. lentils (300 ml)
Brown lentils over medium heat 5 minutes, stirring often.
Carefully add:
  3 c. boiling water or stock (750 ml)
  1 t. salt (5 ml)
  dash of pepper
Cook, uncovered, 10 minutes over medium heat.
Stir in:
  11/2 c. uncooked rice (375 ml)
  1 c. boiling water or stock (250 ml)
Bring to a boil, reduce heat, cover, simmer 25 minutes.

Macaroni:
Cook in salted water according to package directions:
  2 c. macaroni, any variety (500 ml)
Drain macaroni and mix with:
  3 T. of sauce (above) (45 ml)
  1 T. oil (15 ml)

Browned onions:
In large frypan, heat:
  2 T. oil (30 ml)
Fry over medium heat until brown, 10-15 minutes:
  3 onions, sliced
  4 cloves garlic, minced
Serve rice-lentil mixture in one serving dish and macaroni in another. Pile side-by-side on plates, ladle sauce over and top with browned onions. Or pile rice-lentil mixture and macaroni on a large serving platter. Spread tomato sauce over, and top with onions. Individuals may add plain yogurt (p. 295).

—*Fiza, Mattareyya, Egypt; and Mary F. Beck, Cairo, Egypt*

***N**al'a yoma wa, nan dagin a ñima.*
If you are short on flour, adjust the amount of water.

—*Gourmantché proverb, Burkina Faso*

***M**abelle ke ngoetse ea malapa 'ohle.*
Sorghum is the daughter-in-law of every household.

—*Sesotho proverb (Lesotho)*

***B**etter is a dinner of vegetables where love is than a fatted ox and hatred with it.*

—*Proverbs 15:17*

Randy L. Eigsti: Lesotho

Dale Natziger: Nepal

One cup dried beans (250 ml) yields about 2 1/2 cups cooked beans (625 ml). Because beans require long cooking, which uses energy, cook a pound or two at a time for various recipes or freeze for later use. To decrease cooking time, soak beans overnight in three to four cups of water (750-1000 ml) per cup of dry beans (250 ml). Or, for a quick method, bring beans to a boil for two minutes and soak one hour before cooking. Cook beans in soaking water.

Cooking time varies according to size of bean. Smaller beans usually need less than an hour; larger beans 2 to 3 hours. Test for tenderness by tasting.

In a pressure cooker, the appliance of choice in places where cooking fuel is limited and expensive, most presoaked beans require only 10 to 15 minutes of cooking with pressure regulator rocking slowly. Because some beans tend to sputter and foam when cooking, some authorities warn against pressure cooking. Never fill a pressure cooker more than three-fourths full, and never cook soybeans in a pressure cooker without first removing the bean casings.

In a slow cooker, presoaked beans require 1-2 hours on high, followed by 8-10 hours on low; or 5-6 hours on high.

To can beans, soak 4 pounds of beans (2 kg) overnight in plenty of water. In the morning, bring to a boil to remove foam. Place beans in 7 sterilized quart (litre) jars, fill to the neck with water, and add 1 teaspoon salt (5 ml) per jar. Seal and process in pressure canner 1 1/4 hours at 10 pounds pressure.

Refried Beans (Guatemala)

Serves 4-6

Frijoles Volteados
(free-HOH-layss
vohl-tay-AH-dohss)

Refried Beans were traditionally mashed with the back of a spoon, but a smooth puree is now common in homes that have blenders. This makes a hearty breakfast, served with eggs and fried plantains, or a nourishing side dish for any meal. Beans are easiest to puree when freshly cooked and warm.

Puree in blender:

3 c. cooked black, red, or pinto beans with liquid (750 ml)
1/3 c. onion, chopped (75 ml)
1-2 cloves garlic, crushed
1/4 c. green pepper, chopped (50 ml) (optional)

Heat in frypan:

1 T. oil (15 ml)

Add:

pureed beans
salt to taste
1/2 t. ground cumin (2 ml) (optional)

Simmer, uncovered, over low heat, stirring occasionally, until beans thicken, 10-15 minutes. Form into loaf on serving plate.

• *Option:*
Mash beans with potato masher or fork. Sauté onion, green pepper, and garlic in oil. Add mashed beans and seasonings. Cook as directed.

—*Fanny Ellen Yoder, Guatemala City, Guatemala*

Pot of Beans (Central America)

Makes about 7 cups (1.8 L)

Frijoles Cocidos
(free-HOH-layss
koh-SEE-dohss)

Soak overnight or by quick method (p. 162):

1 lb. dried red or black beans (500 g) (about 3 c./750 ml)
2 qt. water (2 L)

Before cooking add:

1 t. salt (5 ml)
3 whole cloves garlic, peeled
1 T. oil (15 ml) (optional, to reduce foaming)
1-2 beef bouillon cubes or several strips bacon, chopped (optional)

Bring beans to a boil and cover. Simmer until tender.

—Author's recipe

"We have rice and beans for breakfast, beans and rice for lunch, and *gallo pinto* for dinner," quipped a Central American friend. Red and black beans are daily fare in the homes of most families in Central America. Families with limited resources eat beans as a main dish three times a day, and wealthier families serve them as a side dish with full-course meals.

Women cook beans by the potful and use them in a variety of dishes, adding various seasonings: cumin, chopped cilantro, chopped onions, green pepper, black or red pepper. Freshly cooked beans are served whole or pureed, sometimes topped with sour cream or finely shredded cheese, and accompanied by rice, salad, eggs, tortillas, or cooked bananas. Savory bean soups (pp. 94, 97) are prepared with some of the beans and excess cooking broth. Cooked beans can be refrigerated for five to seven days and quickly reheated for an easy meal or snack—mixed with rice (Painted Rooster, p. 146) or pureed for Refried Beans (p. 162).

—jhs

Cuban-Style Black Beans (Puerto Rico)

(ts)

Serves 6

Habichuelas al Estilo Cubano
(ah-vee-CHWAY-lahss ah
lays-TEE-loh coo-BAH-noh)

Puerto Ricans credit their Cuban neighbors with this black bean dish, eaten often in Puerto Rico.

In large frypan, sauté in 2 T. olive oil (30 ml) until soft:

1 c. green pepper, chopped (250 ml)
2 cloves garlic, crushed

Add:

2 16-oz. cans black beans (1 kg total) or 4 c. cooked beans with juice (1 L)
1/2 t. dried oregano (2 ml)
3 T. vinegar (45 ml)

Cover and simmer 10 minutes over low heat. Serve over rice.

—Elizabeth Figarella, Waterbury, Connecticut

Legend has it that during the time of slavery in Brazil, when large landholders butchered meat for a festive occasion, they would leave the scrap pieces of the animals (pig snouts, feet, ears, tails) for the slaves to cook with beans. At some point the wealthy people caught a whiff of the savory aroma rising from the slaves' cooking pots and wanted a taste. Impressed with the flavor, they began eating this "scrap" food.

After slavery was abolished, Brazilians continued to eat *feijoada*. Many consider it the national dish. Elegant restaurants that serve it as an expensive entrée add meatier cuts of meat, but retain the authentic scrap pieces— "everything but the squeal." In poor areas of Northeast Brazil, resourceful cooks add less expensive vegetables to stretch the meat and beans.

—*Amalia, Silvia, Suse, and Teodoro Penner, São Paulo, Brazil*

Savory Brazilian Beans

-*H*-

Serves 8

Feijoada
(fay-zhoh-AH-dah)

There are numerous versions of Brazilian Feijoada, many with more meat than this recipe contains. Cooks in southern Brazil use black beans; those in the north use red beans. Beans simmer nicely in a slow cooker. A perfect dish for carry-in dinners.

• *Option:*
Omit pork hock; sauté 1/4-1/2 lb. chopped smoked sausage (125-250 g) with onion and garlic mixture.

Soak overnight or by quick method (p. 162):
   2 c. black, kidney or pinto beans (500 ml)
   6 c. water (1.5 L)
Before cooking add:
   1 t. salt (5 ml)
   1 ham hock or pork hock
Cook about 2 hours or until tender. Cut meat from bones and return to beans.
Add:
   1 t. Worcestershire sauce (5 ml)
   2 t. ground cumin (10 ml)
   1 bay leaf
   1/2 t. dried oregano (2 ml)
   1/2 t. crushed red pepper (2 ml) (optional) +!
   1/2 t. basil (2 ml)
   3 T. lemon juice (45 ml) (optional)
   pepper to taste
Cook uncovered until thick, about 30 minutes.
In separate saucepan, cook about 4 c. of 2-4 of the following vegetables, cut in large pieces (1 L):
   potatoes
   cabbage
   yams
   sweet potatoes
   okra
   carrots
   cauliflower leaves
Cook just until tender. Drain liquid.
In frypan sauté in 2 t. oil (10 ml):
   2 cloves garlic, minced
   1 medium onion, chopped
   1/2 green pepper, chopped (optional)
      (*more* →)

When onion is transparent, add:
1 1/2 c. tomatoes, chopped (375 ml)
Cook until tomatoes are tender.
Add cooked vegetables and sautéed vegetables to beans.
Heat 2 minutes. Serve with rice and slices of orange.

—Goldie Kuhns, Akron, Pennsylvania
—Jeanne Rhodes Smucker, Pittsburgh, Pennsylvania

● ●

Bean and Cabbage Stew (Nigeria)

Serves 6-8

Dafa Duka
(dah-fah doo-kah)

Contributor Martha Adive adapted a traditional Nigerian bean recipe to include cabbage, a crop that grows well in her home area.

● *Option:*
Omit meat. Use meat broth or bouillon to flavor sauce.

Cover with water and soak overnight or by quick method (p. 162):
2 c. black-eyed, navy, or pinto beans (500 ml)
Cook until soft.
In separate saucepan, combine:
1/2-1 lb. chicken or beef, cut in large pieces (250-500 g)
water to cover, at least 2 c. (500 ml)
1 large onion, halved or quartered
salt to taste
Cook, covered, until meat is tender and broth is flavorful.
Discard onion. Reserve broth for sauce.
In separate saucepan, sauté in 2 T. oil (30 ml):
1 large onion, diced
1 sweet red or green pepper, chopped
Add:
3 c. fresh tomatoes, diced (750 ml), or 2 c. tomato sauce (500 ml)
1 t. salt (5 ml)
1 t. curry powder (5 ml)
1/2 t. thyme (2 ml) (optional)
1/4 t. pepper (1 ml) (optional)
reserved broth plus enough water to make 2 c. (500 ml)
Cover and simmer 30 minutes.
Cut in large chunks:
half of small cabbage or 1/3 of large cabbage
Combine:
cooked beans
cooked meat (if chicken, deboned)
cabbage chunks
Pour tomato mixture over all. Cover and cook 20-30 minutes over medium heat until cabbage is tender. Serve alone in soup bowls or over rice.

—Martha Adive and Suzanne Ford, Jos, Nigeria

Falafel
(Middle East)

(fah-LAH-fehl)

This ancient dish is believed to originate in Egypt, where it is made with dried white fava beans. It is a common street food in all Middle East countries. In the Old City of Jerusalem, Falafels are sold on virtually every street corner. They are served in pita bread (p. 51) on top of a layer of french-fried potatoes, and topped with chopped cucumbers, tomatoes, and Sesame Sauce (p. 259). They have no wasteful wrapper to discard and are easy to eat while strolling through the market. This recipe makes enough to stuff six pita sandwiches.

• *Option:*
Instead of processor, use food grinder. Grind beans, garlic, and soaked bulgur together, then add spices and eggs and stir.

Soak 30 minutes in 1/2 c. water (125 ml):
  1/3 c. bulgur (cracked wheat) (75 ml)
Drain excess water.
Combine in food processor or blender:
  drained bulgur
  15-oz. can garbanzo beans, drained (475-g) (about 1 3/4 c./425 ml)
  1 t. baking soda (5 ml)
  2 T. flour or bread crumbs (30 ml)
  6 cloves garlic
  1/2 t. ground red pepper (2 ml) +!
  1 t. ground cumin (5 ml)
  2 t. ground coriander (10 ml) (fresh-ground seeds are best)
  1/2 t. ground turmeric (2 ml)
  1-2 eggs
  1/2 t. salt (2 ml) (optional)
Process into smooth paste. If too thick, add second egg to help Falafel balls hold together when frying. Heat 2 inches oil (5 cm) in heavy saucepan to 350-365°F/180-185°C. Form batter into small balls with 2 teaspoons (like drop cookies) and drop into hot oil. Balls should not be too large, and oil must stay hot. Cook, 4-5 at a time, 4-5 minutes until golden brown. Nuggets should be moist inside, but not wet. Drain on paper. Makes about 30 balls. To serve as an appetizer with Yogurt or Sesame sauces, let cool a bit after cooking, so Falafels hold together better. As a meal, serve hot or at room temperature in pita bread, with cucumbers and tomatoes or lettuce and olives, and sauces.
A ready-made Falafel mix is commonly available in Greek and Asian food stores and can be used to make Falafel at short notice.

—Mary Berkshire Stueben, Seattle, Washington

Yogurt Sauce for
Falafel
(Middle East)

•••••••••••••••••••••••••••••••

Makes 1/2 c. (125 ml)

Laban
(le-bun)

Dip Falafel into this or Sesame Sauce (p. 259).

• *Option:*
Add hot red or green peppers, chopped. +!

Mix:
  1/2 c. yogurt (125 ml) (p. 295)
  1/2 t. ground coriander (2 ml)
  1/4 t. ground cumin (1 ml)
  1/4 t. ground turmeric (1 ml)
Let stand 30 minutes to blend flavors.

—Mary Berkshire Stueben, Seattle, Washington

Garbanzo Stew (Spain)

Serves 6-8

Cocido de Garbanzos
(koh-SEE-doh day
gahr-BAHN-sohss)

Spaniards commonly speak of "earning our garbanzos." They are fond of other beans too, frequently prepared as a first plate in a meal. Spanish bean dishes are seasoned with garlic and an assortment of meats, including pig ears and feet. This recipe contains chorizo, a spicy Spanish sausage found in delicatessens.

• Options:
Substitute unsoaked lentils for garbanzos; omit eggs and spinach.
•
Cook beans, meat, and seasonings a day ahead and refrigerate. Reheat and add spinach, eggs, and oil just before serving.

Soak overnight or by quick method (p. 162):

1 lb. garbanzo beans (500 g)

Discard soaking water.

In large soup pot, pressure cooker, or slow cooker, combine:

**soaked beans
ham bone or hocks
1 lb. sausage (preferably chorizo) (500 g) (optional)
1-2 slices bacon, chopped (optional)
1 onion, chopped
2 carrots, cut in chunks
1 large red sweet pepper, quartered
4 cloves garlic, peeled
1/2 t. paprika (2 ml)
1 t. salt (5 ml) or to taste
1/4 t. pepper (1 ml)
1 bay leaf (optional)
water to cover**

Cook until tender. Skim fat and cut meat into pieces.

Just before serving, add:

**1/2-1 lb. spinach, chopped (250-500 g)
(11/2-3 c./375-750 ml)
3 eggs, hard-cooked and chopped
1 T. oil (preferably olive) (15 ml)
additional salt and pepper if desired**

Avoid overcooking to keep spinach color bright.
Serve with plenty of bread.

—*Connie Bentson Byler, Burgos, Spain*

K olya enkya, kogwa nako.
What you eat in the morning may have to take you throughout the whole day.

—*Ugandan proverb*

Sweet Potato and Bean Loaf (Uganda)

Mugoyo
(moo-GOY-oh)

Since sweet potatoes and beans are inexpensive and store well, Mugoyo is usually prepared during winter months when food is not being harvested and is less available. When Ugandans travel, they often pack food for their journey. Mugoyo is one of their traveling foods.

● ●

Serves 8-10

Soak overnight or by quick method (p. 162):

1 lb. dried white beans (500 g)
2 qt. water (2 L)

Before cooking add:

1-2 t. salt (5-10 ml)

Bring to a boil. Reduce heat, cover, and simmer until tender.

In separate saucepan, cook until tender:

1 lb. sweet potatoes, peeled and cut in chunks (500 g)

While still hot, drain excess water from beans and sweet potatoes. Combine beans and potatoes and mash until smooth. Consistency will be stiff and dry; flavor mild. Form into loaf and slice. Ugandans serve as main dish with cooked greens and beverage.

—*Juliet Male-Busulwa and Joyce Maxwell, Kampala, Uganda*

I thought we were teaching our children to eat responsibly. Our parents had survived famine in the Ukraine, and we, with our children, had seen hunger face to face on a previous service assignment in Africa. We all agreed that wasting food was unacceptable and overeating obscene.

Then we went to Matabudukwane, a village in southern Botswana, and saw ourselves through the eyes of Rose and her seven children.

As part of our orientation to the language and customs of Botswana, Rose graciously hosted us for a week. She made delicious meals with the basic foods we had brought along to supplement her supplies and served them on her best dishes.

On the final day of our stay, Rose made a chicken dinner. Knowing we had not brought chicken, we realized she had sacrificed one of her few laying hens. She smiled at our expressions of thanks, telling us to enjoy the meal. The piles of gnawed bones on our plates testified that we had done that. Or so we thought.

At dishwashing time I realized how vastly my ideas of eating responsibly differed from Rose's. Scattered about the kitchen floor were the bones from our plates. But these were shiny white, cleaned of every vestige of meat, skin, gristle, and juice. The waste from our table had become a banquet for Rose's little ones. Near the open door two of them played together, each still contentedly sucking a bone.

—*Margaret Reimer, Leamington, Ontario*

Milk Beans (Tanzania)

Serves 4

Maharagwe na Maziwa
(mah-hah-RAH-gweh nah
man-ZEE-wah)

*Milk Beans are tasty and
simple to make using leftover
or canned beans.
Seasonings can vary
according to personal
preference.*

• *Option:*
To make with dried beans,
soak and cook 1 c. dried
beans (250 ml) in 4 c. water
(1 L). Drain excess water.
Proceed as directed.

In large saucepan, sauté 2-3 minutes in 1 T. oil (15 ml):
1 c. onions, chopped (250 ml)
**1 c. fresh or canned tomatoes, chopped; or
tomato sauce (250 ml)**
Add:
**2 c. cooked pinto, kidney, or other beans with a
bit of liquid (500 ml)**
**approx. 2/3 c. milk (150 ml), for gravylike
consistency**
1 t. salt (5 ml)
pepper to taste
Add 1 or more of the following spices:
1/2 t. ground cumin (2 ml)
1/2 t. ground coriander (2 ml)
1/2 t. ground turmeric (2 ml)
1 t. curry powder (5 ml)
1 1/2 t. chili powder (7 ml)
Bring to a boil. Reduce heat and simmer 15-20 minutes to
blend flavors. Serve over rice.

—*Ellin Meta Brubaker, Shirati, Tanzania; and Nancy Brubaker,
Lancaster, Pennsylvania*

Chick-Peas in Coconut Milk (Tanzania)

Serves 6

Kunde na Nazi
(KOON-day nah NAH-zee)

*This recipe comes from the
Tanzanian island of Zanzibar,
where coconut is plentiful
and cloves are a major cash
crop. Turmeric gives the dish
a bright, yellow color. Make a
day ahead and reheat for
best flavor.*

• *Option:*
Substitute any other bean
for chick-peas.

Combine in saucepan:
**2 c. cooked or canned chick-peas (garbanzos),
drained (500 ml)**
1 tomato, chopped
4 whole cloves or 1/8 t. ground cloves (.5 ml)
2-3 cloves garlic, minced
1 1/2 c. coconut milk (375 ml) (p. 280)
1 1/2 t. ground turmeric (7 ml)
1/2 t. salt (2 ml)
Bring to a boil. Reduce heat and simmer at least 20
minutes to blend flavors. Serve with rice.

—*Annetta Miller, Nairobi, Kenya*

Haitian Bean Sauce

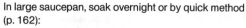

Sòs Pwa
(sohss pwah)

This thick bean gravy is eaten over cornmeal porridge from tin bowls in peasant homes, and over rice in fancy Haitian restaurants. Haitians mash, mix, and strain the beans several times to remove all the hulls for a smooth sauce. When farmers host cooperative work parties, they serve Sòs Pwa and cornmeal to all who come to help.

In large saucepan, soak overnight or by quick method (p. 162):

11/2 c. dried red, black, or white beans, pigeon peas, or a mixture (375 ml)
water to cover

Before cooking add:

3 cloves garlic, diced or mashed
8 whole cloves or 1/2 t. ground cloves (2 ml)
1/2 t. pepper (2 ml)
1/2 c. onion, diced (125 ml)
1 T. oil (15 ml)

Bring to a boil, reduce heat, cover, and simmer until beans are tender. Drain off liquid and reserve. Remove 1/2 c. cooked beans (125 ml) and reserve.

Puree in blender:

cooked bean mixture
2 c. bean broth (500 ml)

Return pureed sauce and reserved whole beans to saucepan.

Add:

1 hot chili pepper, chopped, or 1/4 t. ground red pepper (1 ml) +!
salt to taste
1 T. margarine (15 ml)

Bring to a boil and simmer, uncovered, until thickened to consistency of gravy. Serve over rice or thick cornmeal mush. Haitians use a porridge like Nshima (p. 151), made with yellow cornmeal. Garnish with slices of avocado or lemon.

—*Janèt Pierre-Gille and Heidi Ulrich Gingerich, Bwardlorens, Haiti*

The most indispensable piece of cooking equipment in Africa and parts of the Africa-influenced Caribbean is a mortar and pestle. These range in size from that of a tree trunk to hand-held versions. Rhythmic pounding can be heard almost any time of day as women husk grains and coffee, or smash garlic and other spices.

●●●●●●●●●●●●●●●●●●●●●●●●●●●●●●●●

Chick-Pea Curry (India)

Serves 3-4

Cholé
(choh-LAY)

Cover with water and soak overnight or by quick method (p. 162):

1 c. dried chick-peas (250 ml)

Drain and rinse.

Put in heavy saucepan, slow cooker, or pressure cooker:

soaked chick-peas
just enough water to cover
2 t. salt (10 ml)
2 bay leaves

Cook until just tender.

Heat in separate heavy saucepan:

1 T. oil (15 ml)

Add and fry, stirring frequently, until golden:

1 large onion, finely chopped
3 cloves garlic, chopped
2 t. ginger root, finely chopped (10 ml)

Add:

1/2 t. ground turmeric (2 ml)
1/2 t. ground cardamom (2 ml)
1/4 t. ground coriander (1 ml)
1/2 t. ground cumin (2 ml)

Fry a few seconds.

Add:

2 large tomatoes, peeled and chopped
chick-peas and cooking liquid
1 fresh green chili, seeded and sliced +!
1 T. fresh mint or cilantro, chopped (15 ml) (optional)

Stir well. Cover and simmer 20-30 minutes over low heat, until chick-peas are very tender and tomatoes are well cooked.

Add:

1 T. lemon juice (15 ml) or to taste

Place in serving dish and garnish with fresh mint or cilantro leaves, chopped. Serve with rice, Chapatis (p. 48), or Puris (p. 49).

—*Author's recipe*

....

*E*n todas partes se cuecen habas.
Lima beans are cooked everywhere.
(Mistakes can be made even in the best of families.)

—*Colombian proverb*

White Beans and Vegetables (Iran)

Pilaki
(pih-LAH-kee)

Leftovers from this tasty bean dish can be served as cold salad on lettuce leaves garnished with lemon slices and tomato wedges, or turned into bean soup and served with Kentucky Cornbread (p. 56).

In soup pot, soak overnight or by quick method (p. 162):

> **1 lb. dried white, great northern or navy beans (500 g)**
> **7 c. water (1.8 L)**

Before cooking add:

> **1 1/2 t. salt (7 ml)**

Bring to a boil. Reduce heat, cover, and simmer 1-1 1/2 hours, until nearly tender.

Add:

> **1 1/2 c. potatoes, diced (375 ml)**
> **1 c. carrots, diced (250 ml)**
> **1/2 c. fresh parsley, chopped (125 ml)**
> **2-3 c. fresh or canned tomatoes, chopped (500-750 ml)**
> **1/4 c. olive oil (50 ml)**
> **1 medium onion, chopped**
> **2 cloves garlic, finely minced**
> **1 t. pepper (5 ml)**

Return to a boil. Simmer, covered, 45 minutes, stirring occasionally so it does not stick. Serve with fresh, warm bread.

—*Roohi Gavamhi, Iran; and Naomi E. Fast, Newton, Kansas*

....

The humble bean, often the brunt of gastro-intestinal jokes in North America, is an integral part of the diet in the West African country of Nigeria. People in the village of Kagbu use the *wake* (black-eyed pea) for both ordinary and festive occasions.

For festive meals like Christmas and New Year's, *wake* is boiled whole and served with rice, a spicy tomato and palm oil stew, and a piece of meat for important guests. For everyday use it is ground raw into a smooth paste, seasoned and fried into *kosai* (bean cake) or steamed for *alele* (a soft, spicy bean paste).

These are common breakfast foods and between-meal snacks for students and teachers. Nigerians regard *kosai* as an especially nutritious dish for women who have just given birth and for babies who are learning to walk.

Mariamu Auta lives in Kagbu. When she makes *kosai*, she uses a grinding stone to break the raw beans into small pieces. With rhythmic sweeping motions, Mariamu grinds the beans between an oblong "daughter" stone and the large flat "mother" stone embedded in the floor. She places the broken pieces in water and

scrubs off the skins, discarding skins and adding new water several times.

After Mariamu returns the wet beans to the grinding stone, she works them into a smooth paste, adding chunks of onion. She adds a bit of salt and slips spoonfuls of bean batter into a pan of hot oil heated over a wood fire. During the rainy season when she must make her fire inside, this is a smoky process.

—*Karen Clement, Afton, Iowa*
—*Milcah Terman, Jos, Nigeria*

Basket Cooking

The YWCA in Zambia promotes "basket cooking"—a nonelectric, ecologically sound slow cooking method—as part of its appropriate technology program. Many different containers and insulating materials can be used. Zambian women generally use baskets lined with hay or wild cotton. In Swaziland, refugee students from Mozambique constructed and sold cardboard "wonder boxes" that contained two cushions loosely filled with broken bits of styrofoam.

Basket cooking is ideal for rice, potatoes, stewed meat or chicken, and dried legumes. First bring the food to a boil in a short-handled pot with a tight-fitting lid on a regular stove. Then transfer the boiling pot into the basket or box, nesting it snugly between the cushions, and cover the box. The food will require approximately twice the normal cooking time, but will not use any additional energy. Some foods requiring long cooking need to be brought to a boil a second time and returned to the basket for further slow cooking.

Rice: Bring 1 cup of rice (250 ml) and 3/4 teaspoon salt (3 ml) to a boil in 2 scant cups of water (about 500 ml). Boil 2 minutes. Place in wonder box for 40 minutes.

Potatoes: Cover potatoes with water and boil 2 minutes. Place in wonder box for 1 hour.

Beef: Cube stewing beef and cover with 2-3 inches of water (5-7.5 cm). Boil 2 minutes and place in wonder box. Midway through the cooking process, return beef to the stove and boil a second time, adding additional water if necessary. Return to wonder box to finish cooking.

Chicken: Add just enough water to cover a whole chicken, or if cooking pieces, cover with 2-3 inches of water (5-7.5 ml). Boil 2 minutes and place in wonder box.

Zambian dried beans: Cover beans with twice as much water as beans. Soak overnight. Place in a short-handled pot and add additional water so beans are several inches below the surface. Boil 2 minutes. Place in wonder box to complete cooking. Beans will need to be reboiled at least once, perhaps twice, during the cooking process, depending on the type of bean. When tender add to a mixture of sautéed onions and tomatoes. Flavor with salt and curry powder to taste. Serve over rice or Nshima (p. 151).

—Marian Hostetler, Goshen, Indiana
—Gudrun Mathies, Elmira, Ontario
—Ruth Thiessen, Clearbrook, British Columbia

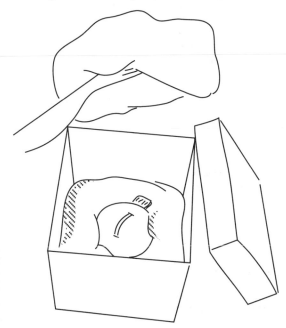

A boiling pot of food, nested between two loosely filled cushions, continues to cook without additional energy inside a "wonder box."

Somali Stew
(Somalia)

Serves 8

Maraq
(MUH-ruhk)

This looks like a North American stew, but the flavor is a pleasant surprise. Many Somalis eat Maraq daily, using camel or beef. A common kitchen sound is the grinding of cumin and garlic with a mortar and pestle.

• *Option:*
Add hot chili peppers or ground red pepper for a spicy stew. +!

In large heavy saucepan, sauté in 1-2 T. oil (15-30 ml):
   1 onion, chopped
Add and brown:
   1 lb. stewing beef, cubed (500 g)
Add:
   2 large tomatoes, chopped
Cook 10 minutes over high heat, stirring occasionally.
Add:
   1 c. squash, cubed (250 ml)
   2-3 okra, sliced
   3 carrots, sliced
   approx. 1/2 c. tomato paste (125 ml)
   1 c. water (250 ml)
Continue to cook on high.
Add:
   1 large potato, sliced or cubed
   1 large green pepper, chopped
   1 T. salt (15 ml)
   1 T. ground cumin (15 ml)
   2-3 cloves garlic, minced
   1/3-1/2 c. cilantro, finely chopped (75-125 ml)
   1 c. water (250 ml) or enough for stew
      consistency
Simmer until meat and vegetables are tender. Somalis serve Maraq over rice or with Injera (p. 47), known as *canjeero* in Somalia.

—*Asha Sharif Mohammed, Mogadishu, Somalia; and Barbara Witmer, Dayton, Ohio*
—*Medino Cali, Mogadishu, Somalia; and Julia Sensenig, Denver, Pennsylvania*

People in Lesotho do not ordinarily invite guests to their home specifically for a meal. But they readily share prepared food with anyone who comes by.

Late one afternoon I stopped to visit a school teacher friend. Another guest also dropped in and the three of us visited around the kitchen table. Then my friend excused herself and began preparing food. I assumed she was preparing supper for her two young sons who were playing in the yard and thought I should leave so they could eat.

But before I could stand up, she brought two plates of food and set them before us. Each plate was filled with *papa* (the thick corn porridge that is a daily staple), pumpkin, a slice of tomato, and a nice piece of chicken. My friend probably had only enough meat for her family, and now she had given two-thirds of it to her unexpected guests. "I've been wanting to do this for a long time," she said to me.

—*Tina W. Bohn, Peka, Lesotho*

Chicken Stew for Couscous (Algeria)

(ts) -🄷- *Serves 6-8*

**Couscous
(kooss-kooss)**

Couscous (ground seminola) is steamed and served with North African stews. Traditionally prepared in special steamers, packaged couscous sold in North American food stores is easily cooked following package directions. Contributor learned to enjoy couscous and stew while living in Algeria.

• *Options:*
Substitute goat or lamb for chicken.

•
Soak and cook 1 c. dried chick-peas (250 ml) to replace canned chick-peas.

Combine in large saucepan:
**3 c. chicken broth (750 ml)
1 chicken bouillon cube
2 c. chicken, cooked and chopped (500 ml)
1 medium onion, chopped
2 c. fresh or frozen green beans, cut (500 ml)
    (1 lb./500 g)
2 carrots, sliced
1 t. ground cumin (5 ml)
1 t. basil (5 ml)
1 clove garlic, minced (optional)
2 bay leaves (optional)
1/2 t. dried parsley (2 ml) (optional)
salt and pepper to taste**
Bring to a boil. Reduce heat and cook, covered, about 8 minutes.
Add and cook briefly:
**2 medium tomatoes, chopped
2 small or 1 medium zucchini, sliced**
Add:
**16-oz. can chick-peas, drained (500-g)
1/4 t. ground red pepper (1 ml) or to taste +!**
Cover and cook until heated through. Serve over steaming bowls of couscous.

—*Marion Keeney Preheim, Newton, Kansas*

Most of the cookware in rural Malawi is handmade. Women make earthenware pots of various shapes and sizes. They use the *nkhali* for cooking *nshima* (corn porridge) or rice, and the *mphika* for cooking *ndiwo* (vegetable and meat sauces). They carry water in the *mtsuko* and use the *mbiya* for storing water and home brew.

Men make wooden spoons, sometimes decorating them with black, burned-in designs. They also make large ladles and food storage containers from gourds. Women decorate the gourds with intricate beadwork.

mbiya

mtsuko

nkhali

mphika

175

Saudi Chicken Stew (Saudi Arabia)

●●●●●●●●●●●●●●●●●●●●●●●●●●●●●●●●●●●

Serves 6

Rus Bukhary
(rooz BOO-khah-ree)

Whole spices give a better flavor and color to this stew than ground spices, although stew is tasty both ways. Remove whole spices just before serving or while eating.

Have ready:

3 c. cooked long-grain rice (750 ml) (about 1 c./250 ml uncooked)

Simmer 25 minutes:

2 1/2-3-lb. chicken, skinned and cut in pieces (1.3-1.5-g)
1 qt. water (1 L)
1 t. salt (5 ml) or to taste
pepper to taste

Remove chicken from broth and set aside. Skim fat, strain broth (optional), and reserve.

Heat in large saucepan with tight-fitting lid:

3 T. margarine (45 ml)

Add and sauté:

2 medium onions, thinly sliced

Push onions to side and sauté on medium heat about 10 minutes until browned:

6-8 carrots, thinly sliced

Mix in bowl:

cooked rice
2-inch stick cinnamon (5-cm) or 1 t. ground cinnamon (5 ml)
1 t. whole cardamom pods (5 ml) or 3/4 t. ground cardamom (3 ml)
6 whole cloves or 1/2 t. ground cloves (2 ml)

Lay pieces of cooked chicken evenly over sautéed vegetables. Cover with rice-and-spice mixture.

Pour over rice:

2 c. tomato juice (500 ml)
2 c. chicken broth (500 ml)

Cover and simmer slowly 1 hour. If contents become too dry, add a little reserved chicken broth.

—*Mrs. Mansoor Alohaly, Saudi Arabia; and Naomi E. Fast, Newton, Kansas*

....

Somali women prepare all their meals with a few essential utensils: a large knife used for everything from cutting meat to peeling garlic, a spoon to stir sauce, an aluminum pot with a flat lid and no handles, a mortar and pestle for grinding spices, and a charcoal stove to cook on.

Green Bean Hash (Costa Rica)

•••••••••••••••••••••••••••••••

Serves 4-5

Picadillo de Vainica
(pee-kah-DEE-yoh day
vie-NEE-kah)

Picadillo uses little meat and little cooking fuel, since the small vegetable pieces cook quickly. Costa Rican cooks make Picadillo from a variety of vegetables. Carrots can be the main vegetable, with potatoes and green beans playing a lesser role. Green plantains also make a delicious Picadillo.

Sauté in 3 T. oil (45 ml):
   1 medium onion, chopped
   2 cloves garlic, minced
   1 sprig fresh parsley, chopped
   2 stalks celery, finely chopped
   1-2 sprigs cilantro, chopped (optional)
Add and brown:
   1/4 lb. ground beef (125 g)
Add:
   2 bouillon cubes or equivalent bouillon powder
   1/8-1/4 t. pepper (.5-1 ml)
   3 c. fresh green beans (750 ml), cut in 1/4-inch pieces (.5-cm)
   3-4 medium carrots, peeled and finely diced
   2-3 medium potatoes, peeled and finely diced
   salt to taste (optional)
Cover and cook over low heat, stirring occasionally, until vegetables are tender, about 20 minutes. Serve over steaming rice with simple cabbage salad.

—*Bitinia Sosa Herrera and Beverlee Ludema, San José, Costa Rica*

Gumbo Stew (Burkina Faso)

•••••••••••••••••••••••••••••••

(ts)   *Serves 6-8*

Sauce Gombo
(sohss gohm-BOH)

Okra, or gombo in several African languages, is a vegetable that serves as a thickening agent. West African cooks use it as the base of many stews, which they usually serve with stiff porridge made of cassava, millet, or maize flour. Tester said, "This was delightfully easy to prepare. . . . The taste and texture make a wonderful treat for the taste buds."

Brown:
   1 lb. hamburger (500 g)
Add and cook until soft:
   1 large onion, chopped
   1 clove garlic, minced
Add:
   4 c. cooked tomatoes or tomato sauce (1 L)
   2 c. fresh or frozen okra, chopped (500 ml)
   1 t. salt (5 ml)
   1 t. crushed red pepper (5 ml) +!
   1 t. chili powder (5 ml)
Simmer 20 minutes.
Add:
   2 c. fresh or frozen spinach, or other dark greens, chopped (500 ml)
Simmer 5 minutes.
Serve hot over rice or with Nshima (p. 151).

—*Martin Zerbo, Ouagadougou, Burkina Faso; and Nancy Heisey, Ephrata, Pennsylvania*

Ethiopian Vegetable Stew

Serves 4-5

Alecha
(ah-LEE-chah)

Alecha is the common name for any mild Ethiopian stew. Alechas are normally served with Ethiopian Flat Bread (p. 47), along with one or more spicy stews.

• *Microwave:*
In large, covered casserole, cook 1 T. margarine (15 ml), garlic, and onion 3 minutes on high. Add potatoes and accompanying ingredients and cook 7 minutes on high, stirring once; reduce salt to 1/4 t. (1 ml). Add cabbage, 1/8 t. salt (.5 ml), and green chili pepper and cook 14-20 minutes on high, stirring once, until all vegetables are tender. Let stand, covered, 3 minutes.

In large saucepan, combine:
> **2 T. margarine or oil (30 ml)**
> **1 clove garlic**
> **1 onion, chopped**

Sauté until onions are soft, but do not brown.
Add:
> **1/2 c. water (125 ml)**
> **3 medium potatoes, chopped in large pieces**
> **2-3 carrots, chopped**
> **1/2 t. salt (2 ml)**
> **1/2 t. ground ginger (2 ml)**
> **1/2 t. ground turmeric (2 ml)**
> **1/4 t. pepper (1 ml)**

Cook about 10 minutes until potatoes and carrots begin to soften. Add:
> **1 lb. cabbage, chopped (1 kg) (about 5 c./1.3 L)**
> **1/2 c. water (125 ml)**
> **1/4 t. salt (1 ml) or to taste**
> **1 green chili pepper, seeded and quartered +!**

Cook until vegetables are tender. Stir gently to combine, taking care not to mash vegetables.

• *Option:*
Serve with rice.

—Charmayne Denlinger Brubaker, Lancaster, Pennsylvania
—Phyllis Horst Nofziger, Ephrata, Pennsylvania

Summer Corn Gravy (United States)

ⓣⓢ

Serves 4

Native Americans in the Southwest make Summer Corn Gravy with fresh corn cut from the cob. Their native variety of corn is smaller than the sweet corn grown in other parts of the country.

In heavy frypan, fry in 2 T. oil (30 ml):
> **4 c. green or yellow summer squash, thinly sliced (1 L)**
> **2 c. fresh or frozen corn (500 ml)**

Cover and simmer 10-15 minutes, until squash is tender. Move corn and squash to side of frypan. Add and brown:
> **1 1/2 T. flour (20 ml)**

Add:
> **3/4 c. water (175 ml)**
> **salt and pepper to taste**

Simmer briefly until thickened. Serve over tortillas, toasted bread, or cooked potatoes.

—Evangeline Hiebert, McPherson, Kansas

178

Vegetable Adobo (Philippines)

●●●●●●●●●●●●●●●●●●●●●●●●●●●●●●●●●●

Serves 6-8

Adobong Gulay
(ah-DOH-bohng GOO-lai)

The flavors of peppercorns, garlic, soy sauce, and vinegar characterize Adobo—considered by many to be the Philippine national dish. Although meat is the primary ingredient in most Adobos (Chicken Adobo, p. 227), contributor Edna Lungan Concepcion created this version for vegetable lovers. Masarap! (Delicious!)

• Options:
Use any combination of vegetables.
•
Omit meat. Add 1-2 chicken or beef bouillon cubes with water.

In soup pot, combine:
  2-3 pieces chicken, beef, or pork
  2 cloves garlic, finely chopped
  3-4 peppercorns, crushed, or 1/4 t. pepper (1 ml)
  2 bay leaves
  1/2 c. soy sauce (125 ml)
  1/2 c. vinegar (125 ml)
  1-1 1/2 c. water (250-375 ml)
Cook together until meat is almost tender. Meanwhile, cut in large pieces:
  2-3 large carrots
  3-4 potatoes
  1-2 green or red sweet peppers
  2-3 medium onions
  1-2 c. string beans (250-500 ml)
If using chicken, remove bones. Layer vegetables on top of meat, starting with longer-cooking vegetables and cooking those a few minutes first. Then add quicker-cooking ones and cover with:
  5-7 large cabbage leaves
Cook, covered, until vegetables are tender-crisp. To thicken broth, stir in 1-2 T. cornstarch (15-30 ml) mixed with a little water to form paste. Serve with rice.

—Edna Lungan Concepcion, Cagayan Valley, Philippines; and Carolyn Schrock-Shenk, Lancaster, Pennsylvania

Before every meal in Japan, people say "*Itadakimasu* (I receive this food with thanks)." This is the traditional way to express thanks to the farmers who work hard to produce rice, and for children to express thanks to their parents who provide their food.

We Christians can say it and think of people who work hard to make food available to us. We think of God's love working in them. We remember people who are starving or in miserable situations.

—Mitsuko Yaguchi, Sapporo, Japan

Vegetable Curry (Nepal)

••••••••••••••••••••••••••••••••••
-H-
Serves 6-8

Alu Gobi Tarkari
(ah-loo goh-bee tahr-kah-ree)

This is a somewhat dry curry with a lovely blend of flavors. In countries where rice, rather than potatoes, is the traditional starchy complement to other foods, potatoes are treated as a vegetable and potato curries and hashes are commonly served over rice.

• *Options:*
Substitute broccoli or cauliflower for cabbage.
•
For more sauce, add 1 c. water (250 ml) when cooking potatoes.

In a large saucepan, sauté in 2 T. oil (30 ml):
   2 onions, thinly sliced
   2 cloves garlic, minced
   1 t. ground coriander (5 ml)
   1 t. ground turmeric (5 ml)
   1/2 t. ground cumin (2 ml)
   1/2 t. ground ginger (2 ml)
   1/4 t. dry mustard (1 ml)
   1 hot pepper or 1/8 t. ground red pepper (.5 ml)
   +!
Add:
   1 T. oil (15 ml)
   5-6 c. potatoes, diced (can be unpeeled)
   (1.3-1.5 L)
Fry, stirring often to coat potatoes with seasonings. When potatoes are almost tender, add:
   4 c. cabbage, chopped (1 L)
   1 t. salt (5 ml) or to taste
   2 tomatoes, chopped
   1-2 T. curry powder (15-30 ml) (optional) +!
Cover and simmer until cabbage is tender. Serve with rice or Puris (p. 49).

—*Selma Unruh, North Newton, Kansas*

Curried Peas and Potatoes (India)

••••••••••••••••••••••••••••••••••
-H-
Serves 4-6

Mattar Alu Kari
(MAH-ter ah-loo KAH-ree)

Forks and spoons are rarely used in Indian and Bangladeshi villages. People eat rice and curry with their fingers, using the right hand only. The rice, curry, dahl, and chutneys are in separate piles on the plate. The eater mixes rice with a bit of stew or salad, a bite at a time. Like most curries, this colorful vegetable dish is excellent when made ahead of time and reheated; leftovers heat well in microwave or on stove top.

In medium saucepan, heat:
   2 T. ghee or oil (30 ml)
Add and sauté:
   2 1/2 t. ginger root, chopped (12 ml)
   2 1/2 t. garlic, chopped (12 ml)
   1/2 c. onion, chopped (125 ml)
   1/4 t. salt (1 ml)
When onions are brown, add:
   1 t. ground cumin (5 ml)
   1/2 t. ground turmeric (2 ml)
   1/8-1/4 t. ground red pepper (.5-1 ml) +!
Stir in:
   3 medium tomatoes, chopped
   1 1/2 T. cilantro, chopped (20 ml) or 1 1/2 t.
   ground coriander (7 ml)
Cook 5 minutes, until liquid evaporates.

(*more* →)

Add:

1 large potato, cubed
3/4 c. water (175 ml)

Stir well. Bring to a boil. Simmer, covered, 10 minutes.
Add:

3 c. frozen peas (750 ml)

Simmer 5 minutes, or until potatoes and peas are tender.
Garnish with 1 T. cilantro, chopped (15 ml), and 1/2 t.
garam masala (2 ml) (p. 289) (optional). Serve over rice as
main dish, or as side dish with curry meal.

• Option:
Substitute 2 c. canned tomatoes (500 ml) for fresh tomatoes.
Reduce or omit water when cooking potatoes and peas.

—*Nancy Kinsinger Halder, Parnell, Iowa*

Potato Curry
(Bangladesh)

Serves 4-6

Alu Torkari
(AH-loo TOHR-kah-ree)

Potato Curry is especially
wonderful when made with
tiny whole new garden
potatoes. This recipe comes
from the Punjab, a traditional
potato-growing region of
India.

In heavy frypan sauté in 1 T. oil (15 ml) until brown and
crisp:

1-2 large onions, finely sliced

Remove onions and reserve for garnish.
Add and fry in 1 T. oil (15 ml) until soft, but not brown:

1 medium onion, chopped
2-4 cloves garlic, crushed

Add:

2 large tomatoes, chopped
3/4 t. garam masala (3 ml) (p. 289)
3/4 t. ground turmeric (3 ml)
1/2 t. salt (2 ml)
2 fresh green chilies, chopped, or 1/4 t. ground
red pepper (1 ml) +!
2 T. fresh parsley, chopped (30 ml)

Stir-fry 2-3 minutes, until tomatoes are very soft and oil
appears around edges of sauce.
Add:

1 T. lemon juice (15 ml)
4 potatoes, cubed (about 1 lb./500 g)
a few tablespoons water

Cover loosely and simmer slowly, stirring occasionally,
until sauce is thick and potatoes are tender. Add a bit more
water if necessary during cooking. Garnish with browned
onions and serve with rice or Chapatis (p. 48) and Dhal
(p. 156) or another more juicy curry dish.

—*Nancy Brubaker, Lancaster, Pennsylvania*
—*Katie Myers, Akron, Pennsylvania*

Spinach in Cottage Cheese (India)

Palak Paneer
(pah-lahk pah-neer)

This combination of fresh greens and creamy cottage cheese is served with rice or Chapatis (p. 48). A common and nutritious everyday dish in North India.

Serves 4

Heat in saucepan:
   2 T. oil (30 ml)
Add:
   1 large onion, chopped
   1-inch piece ginger root, grated (2.5 cm),
      or 1/2 t. ground ginger (2 ml)
Fry until golden brown.
Add:
   1 lb. spinach, chopped (500 g) (4-5 c./1-1.3 L)
   1/8 t. ground red pepper (.5 ml) or to taste +!
   3 cloves garlic, minced
   salt to taste
   1-inch cinnamon stick (2.5-cm)
Cook about 10 minutes.
Add:
   1 tomato, chopped
   1 c. cottage cheese (250 ml)
   1/4 c. water (50 ml)
Cook about 10 minutes or until most of liquid is absorbed.
Place in serving dish. Sprinkle with:
   1/2 t. ground cumin (2 ml)

—Cynthia Peacock, Calcutta, India

Vegetable Stir-fry (Philippines)

Pritong Gulay
(PREE-tohng GOO-lai)

Stir-fry dishes offer attractive, tasty vegetables for a reasonable amount of money and time. Chop any assortment of seasonal vegetables in advance (green beans, carrots, squash, or cabbage), refrigerate in a tightly covered container, and this meal is almost ready.

• *Option:*
If fish sauce is not available, add a bouillon cube for additional flavor.

Serves 5-6

In large frypan, brown in 2 T. oil (30 ml):
   2-3 cloves garlic, minced
   1 large onion, finely chopped
Add and brown:
   1/4-1/2 lb. pork, cut in small cubes (125-250 g)
Add:
   2-3 medium tomatoes, diced
   1 c. water (250 ml)
Bring to a boil; reduce heat, cover, and cook 5 minutes.
Add:
   4 c. assorted vegetables, chopped (1 L)
Cook, stirring frequently, until tender-crisp.
Add:
   1 small green pepper, finely chopped
   2 T. fish sauce (30 ml)
   salt or soy sauce to taste
Stir-fry 1-2 minutes. Serve over rice or noodles.

—Dan and Esther Epp-Tiessen, Kitchener, Ontario

● ●

Stir-fry with Marinade (China)

Serves 4

Yan Rou
(yahn roh)

Marinade:
Mix:

2 cloves garlic, minced
1-inch ginger root, thinly sliced (2.5-cm)
1 1/2 T. soy sauce (20 ml)
1/4 t. salt (1 ml)
1/4 t. pepper (1 ml)
1 t. sugar (5 ml)
1 T. cooking sherry (15 ml) (optional)

Add:

1/2 lb. beef tenderloin or sirloin, pork, or chicken, cut in thin strips (250 g)

Marinate at least 1 hour, up to 24 hours.
After marinating, add to meat:

1 T. cornstarch (15 ml)
1 T. oil (15 ml)
dash of water, if too dry

Set aside.

Stir-fry:
In wok or frypan, heat a little oil and fry:

1 clove garlic, minced

Add variety of chopped vegetables, totaling 5-6 c. (1.3-1.5 L):

green peppers
carrots
celery
onions
bamboo shoots
cauliflower
broccoli

Add:

salt and soy sauce to taste

Stir-fry vegetables until just tender; do not overcook.
Remove from pan. Place marinated meat in frypan with a
little oil. Fry until tender, 3-5 minutes. Return vegetables to
pan and heat through. Serve over rice or noodles.

—*Helen Lo, Hong Kong; and Nancy Kinsinger Halder, Parnell, Iowa*

....

t **hanks for the food we have,**
for beautiful flowers,
for sun and for rain,
and for saving us from danger,
and for happiness.
We give thee thanks. Amen.

—*Thai dinner prayer, translated by Ravadee Arkkapin, Bangkok,
  Thailand*

Curly Kale with Smoked Sausage (Netherlands)

●●●●●●●●●●●●●●●●●●●●●●●●●●●●●

M

Serves 4-6

Boerenkool met Rookworst
(boo-ren-KOHL met
ROHK-vohrst)

The Dutch have a special fondness for kale, a hearty fall crop that tastes best after frost. This dish, also called Farmer Dinner, includes the characteristic nutmeg the Dutch use to flavor greens.

• **Microwave:**
Pierce sausage with fork and place around outside edges of 2-qt. casserole (2-L). Pile kale on top of sausage and in center, cover tightly, and cook on high 5-8 minutes, stirring once. In separate covered casserole, cook potatoes with 1/4 c. water (50 ml) on high 9-12 minutes. Let stand, covered, 3 minutes. Mash potatoes and combine with kale and sausage.

Combine in saucepan:

1 lb. curly kale, stripped from stems and finely chopped (500 g), or 10-oz. pkg. frozen chopped kale (300 g)
1 lb. smoked sausage (500 g)
a little water

Simmer, covered, until kale is tender.

In separate saucepan, cook until tender in salted water:

6-7 potatoes, peeled and chopped (about 2 lb./1 kg)

Mash potatoes with:

1 T. margarine (15 ml)
dash of pepper
1/2-1 c. milk (125-250 ml)

When well mashed, add cooked kale and mix well. Mound potato-kale mixture on platter, sprinkle with ground nutmeg (optional), and arrange sausages around sides of plate. Serve with leftover broth or gravy (optional) and spicy mustard for sausage.

• **Option:**
For meatless dish, omit sausage. Top with grated sharp cheese.

—*Rie Eterman, Driebergen, Netherlands; and Betsy Beyler, Fairfax, Virginia*
—*Cynthia Shenk, Nijmegen, Netherlands*

Shrimp Cakes (Indonesia)

●●●●●●●●●●●●●●●●●●●●●●●●●●●●●●●

Serves 3

Rempeyek Udang
(rehm-peh-yehk oo-dahng)

Indonesians eat these shrimp fritters with rice and hot green chili peppers. See Indonesian rijstaffel (p. 127) for other dishes to accompany Shrimp Cakes.

Mix:

1 c. flour (250 ml)
1 egg, beaten
1/2 c. bean sprouts (125 ml)
1/4 c. celery, finely chopped (50 ml)
1/4 c. onion, minced (50 ml)
1 clove garlic, crushed
1/2 t. salt (2 ml)
1/4 c. water (50 ml)
1/2 c. small shrimp, shelled and deveined (125 ml)
1 T. lemon or lime juice (15 ml)
1/8 t. ground red pepper (.5 ml) (optional) +!

In deep pan, heat 1 1/2 inches oil (3.5 cm). Drop mixture by spoonfuls into hot oil. Fry until golden on both sides.

—*Ibu Djojodihardjo, Pati, Java, Indonesia; and Anne Warkentin Dyck, Swift Current, Saskatchewan*

● ●

Mashed Potato and Meat Pie (Brazil)

Nhoques de Forno
(NYOH-kees day FOHR-noh)

A tasty one-dish meal. Since eggs, milk, and cheese in the mashed potatoes add extra protein, keep ham and cheese slices thin.

• **Option:**
Reserve 1 c. potato water (250 ml) and mix with 1/3 c. dry milk powder (75 ml) for milk.

Serves 6

300°F 150°C

30 min./10 min.

Peel and cook until soft:

8 medium potatoes (about 4 c./1 L mashed)

Drain and mash.
Add:

1 c. warm milk (250 ml)
2 T. margarine (30 ml)
2 eggs
1/2 c. mild cheese, grated (125 ml)
3 T. cornstarch (45 ml)
3 T. flour (45 ml)
1/2 t. salt (2 ml)
2 t. baking powder (10 ml)

Mix until smooth. Spread half of potato mixture in a greased 9 x 13-inch cake pan (3.5-L). Cover with:

thin slices of ham
thin slices of mild cheese such as mozzarella

Spread remaining potatoes over top and bake 30 minutes at 300°F (150°C). Remove from oven, pour sauce (below) over top, and continue baking 5-10 minutes.

Sauce:

In saucepan, brown in 1 t. oil (5 ml):

2 T. onions, finely chopped (30 ml)
1/2 lb. ground beef or turkey (250 g) (optional)

Drain any excess fat.
Add and simmer about 10 minutes:

1 c. tomato sauce (250 ml)
pinch of salt
dash of pepper
1/4 t. garlic powder (1 ml) (optional)

—*Vanilda V.S. Rodrigues, Goiás, Brazil; and Lois Musselman, Pará, Brazil*

Measuring utensils, like language, vary greatly from country to country. The most basic and universal utensil is the hand. Dry ingredients such as flour are measured by the handful; salt by a pinch between the thumb and index finger. North Americans rely primarily on volume measures and equip their kitchens with one or more sets of standardized measuring cups. Bolivian cooks find that tuna cans make fine measuring cups, and West Africans use cigarette tins. In many areas, including Europe, homemakers measure ingredients by weight rather than volume. Nicaraguan market vendors make simple hand-held scales with wooden weights on knotted strings to weigh the products they sell.

White Pizza
(Italy)

Pizza Bianco
(PEET-zah bee-AHN-koh)

Pizza Bianco (white), without tomato sauce, is popular in Italian American communities. Many versions feature cheese toppings. This classic rendering with a seasoned egg topping has been handed down in the contributor's family. Like regular pizza, the toppings may vary. Parmesan cheese is a must and black olives are common. One can also use pepperoni and other meats. This pizza is often eaten at room temperature, an hour or more after it comes out of the oven, making it a good party or potluck food.

• •

Serves 4

375°F 190°C

20-25 min.

Make your favorite pizza dough recipe for 1 pizza, but add 1 egg to dough before kneading.

Spread dough on pan. Build up small rim around edges so egg topping won't run off sides. Spread small amount of oil over dough and rub gently into top:

2 t. dried oregano (10 ml) or to taste
1 t. garlic powder (5 ml)

Beat and pour over dough:

3 eggs

Top with some of following:

grated Parmesan cheese (sprinkle liberally)
black olives, sliced
green peppers, diced
mushrooms, sliced
onions, chopped
tomatoes, thinly sliced
mozzarella cheese, grated or sliced

Bake at 375°F (190 C°) 20-25 minutes, until dough is crusty and eggs are set (or follow baking directions for your pizza crust recipe).

• Option:
To replace egg topping with feta cheese topping, spread dough in pan and brush it with a little olive oil. Sprinkle on a little garlic powder (optional). Top with black olives, mushrooms, sautéed peppers (or other toppings of your choice), and lots of crumbled feta cheese. Bake until dough is crusty.

—*Josephine Gullo Burnett, Batavia, New York*

Instant Potato
Pizza
(Japan)

Add your favorite pizza toppings to this simple dish.

• •

(ts)

Serves 2-3

Mix in bowl:

3 medium potatoes, finely sliced or grated
2 T. flour (30 ml)
1/4 t. salt (1 ml)

Add:

1 egg

Stir. Heat in nonstick frypan:

1 T. oil (15 ml)

Add potato mixture. Bake both sides in skillet until light brown and crusty. Add to top of potato crust:

ham, sliced
green pepper, sliced or chopped
onion, sliced or chopped
mushrooms, sliced

(*more* →)

Cover with a little tomato sauce mixed with salt and pepper, or ketchup.
Sprinkle with:

cheese, shredded

Cover and simmer 5-7 minutes.

—Hiroko Sakabe, Obihiro, Japan

● ●

Cheesy Tortilla Skillet (Mexico)

Serves 3-4

Chilaquiles
(chee-lah-KEE-layss)

Mexicans serve Chilaquiles for a substantial breakfast or for supper, using day-old corn tortillas. Mexican cooks are inventive and there are probably as many variations of this recipe as there are cooks.

• *Options:*
Add leftover vegetables and bits of cooked meat to eggs and tomato sauce.
•
Instead of frying tortilla pieces, sauté with onion and garlic in 4-6 T. oil (60-90 ml). Proceed as directed. Texture of tortillas will be less crisp.

Tear in 1-inch strips (2.5-cm), then tear each strip in bite-size triangular or square pieces:

12 5-inch corn tortillas (12.5-cm)

In large frypan, heat 1/2 c. oil (125 ml). Fry small batches of tortilla pieces until golden brown, 3-5 minutes. Drain on paper. Remove excess oil from frypan and sauté briefly:

1 clove garlic, minced
1/4 c. onion, chopped (50 ml)

Add:

fried tortilla pieces

Pour over:

2 eggs, beaten
spicy tomato sauce (recipe below)

Cook over low heat 10-15 minutes, stirring as little as possible, until liquid is absorbed and mixture appears fairly dry. Sprinkle over top:

1 c. mild cheddar or Monterey Jack cheese, grated (250 ml)

Remove from heat and cover until cheese melts.
Serve with fresh fruit or green salad.

Spicy tomato sauce:
Whirl together in blender until smooth:

2 medium tomatoes or 1 c. canned tomatoes (250 ml)
1-2 fresh green chilies or several drops Tabasco pepper sauce or 1/2 t. chili powder (2 ml) +!
1 t. salt (5 ml)

—Marie Palafox, Guadalajara, Mexico; and Emily Will, Ciudad Guzmán, Jalisco, Mexico

Visitors to the Mesa Grande camp for Salvadoran refugees in Honduras were often surprised by the plates used to serve them the traditional noon meal of rice, beans, and tortillas. The refugees so highly valued their rare occasions to host visitors that they diverted a donation of frisbees for children's play to use as spare dinnerware for guests.

—Nelson Weber, Reading, Pennsylvania

Tico Tortilla Skillet
(Costa Rica)

Chirrasquiles
(chee-rahss-KEE-layss)

Chirrasquiles are an everyday meal for Costa Ricans and other Central Americans. Fillings vary, and often include plantain, carrots, green beans, or other vegetables. The tortillas need not be strictly fresh; the tomato sauce softens them. Serve alone for a satisfying lunch or with Central American-Style Rice (p. 145) and a salad for a complete meal.

• *Options:*
Omit dipping tortilla in egg and frying. Simply pour sauce over filled tortillas, heat, and serve.
•
If tortillas are too dry and brittle to fold, soften by passing briefly through running water before filling.

Sauce:
In saucepan, sauté in 2 T. oil (30 ml):
1/2 c. onion, minced (125 ml)
2 cloves garlic, minced
1/3 c. green pepper, chopped (75 ml)
1 T. fresh parsley, chopped (15 ml)
1 T. cilantro (15 ml) (optional)
Add:
6-oz. can tomato paste (175-g) (about 2/3 c./ 150 ml), mixed with
1 1/2 c. water (375 ml)
1 beef bouillon cube
1/4 t. pepper (1 ml) or to taste
1/2 t. chili powder (2 ml) (optional)
1/4 t. dried oregano (1 ml) (optional)
Bring mixture to a boil. Cook until bouillon cube is dissolved, then simmer 10-15 minutes to enhance flavor.

Filling:
Sauté until onions are clear in 1 T. oil (15 ml):
1 c. onions, chopped (250 ml)
1/2 c. green pepper, chopped (125 ml)
4 cloves garlic, minced
1 T. fresh parsley, chopped (15 ml)
1 T. cilantro, chopped (15 ml) (optional)
Add and brown:
1/2-3/4 lb. ground beef or turkey (250-375 g)
Add:
1 beef bouillon cube
1 medium potato, diced
Stir until bouillon cube dissolves and potatoes are soft. Cool slightly.

Tortilla preparation:
Separate 2 eggs. Beat whites until soft peaks form. Stir in yolks with a fork.
Have ready 8-10 6-inch corn tortillas (15-cm).
Heat in frypan:
1/4 c. oil (50 ml)
Place about 1/3 c. filling (75 ml) in each tortilla. Fold tortilla over and dip in egg mixture. Place in hot oil and fry on both sides, turning carefully, until golden brown. Remove and place in separate large frypan. When all tortillas are fried, pour tomato sauce over and heat until bubbly. Top each serving with a bit of sour cream (optional).

—*Bitinia Sosa Herrera and Beverlee Ludema, San José, Costa Rica*

Spanish Potato Tortilla (Spain)

Serves 4-5

Tortilla de Patatas
(tohr-TEE-yah day
pah-TAH-tahss)

This potato omelet is probably the most typical dish prepared throughout Spain. It is a popular midmorning snack, a common supper in many homes, and a wonderful picnic meal served with salad. Spaniards enjoy Tortilla de Patatas hot or cold.

• *Option:*
For additional flavor and texture, add pimento strips, fried mushrooms, bacon, or sausage pieces.

Fry until tender in enough hot oil (preferably olive) to cover:
   4 medium potatoes, peeled, thinly sliced or cut as if for French fries
Drain.
Meanwhile, in separate frypan, sauté slowly until golden and tender:
   1 large onion, chopped
In large bowl, beat:
   8 eggs
Add and mix well:
   fried potatoes
   sautéed onions
   salt and pepper to taste
In medium nonstick frypan, heat 1 T. oil (15 ml). Pour in half egg-potato mixture and cook slowly until sides and bottom are light golden color, and filling is not too liquid. To turn, place similar-sized plate over top and quickly turn tortilla over onto it. Add a few drops of oil to frypan and slide tortilla back into it, letting liquid fall first. When both sides are browned and egg is set, turn onto another plate as before. Cover to keep warm while frying remaining mixture. Serve with bread or toast.

—*Connie Bentson Byler, Burgos, Spain*
—*Frances Penner, Madrid, Spain*

Tomato Poached Eggs (Mexico)

(ts)   *Serves 4*

Huevos Ahogados
(WAY-vohss
ah-oh-GAH-dohss)

Huevos Ahogados (drowned eggs) is a zesty, colorful, aromatic dish. Children will enjoy breaking the eggs into the tomato sauce and watching them cook. Although Mexicans serve this with rice, it is also tasty over cooked noodles.

In frypan, sauté in 1-2 T. oil (15-30 ml):
   1 onion, chopped
   1 clove garlic, minced
   1 t. dried oregano (5 ml)
   2 t. dried parsley (10 ml)
   salt and pepper to taste
   1 t. chili powder (5 ml) or to taste
When onion is transparent, add and sauté 3-5 minutes:
   2 medium green peppers, chopped
   1 1/2 c. canned tomatoes (375 ml) (drain and reserve juice)
   3 hot green chili peppers, chopped (optional) +!
Add juice from tomatoes; bring to a boil. Gently drop in:
   4 eggs
Cook until eggs are ready to serve. Serve over rice with a few drops:
   Tabasco pepper sauce (optional) +!

—*Velia Velazques, Mexico; and Nancy Kinsinger Halder, Parnell, Iowa*

Tuna Omelet (Brazil)

Serves 4-6

Mal Assado
(mahl ah-SAH-doh)

Homemakers in Northeast Brazil use this dish to stretch eggs and tuna or sardines to serve more people. They serve Mal Assado along with rice and beans.

Beat until stiff:
   3 egg whites
Add:
   3 egg yolks, beaten
Mix well.
Fold in:
   1 tomato, chopped
   2 T. green pepper, chopped (30 ml)
   2 T. onion, chopped (30 ml)
   6 1/2-oz. can tuna or sardines, drained (185-g)
   salt and pepper to taste
Heat in nonstick frypan:
   1-2 T. oil (15-30 ml)
Pour in egg mixture. Fry over medium heat until bottom is golden brown. Turn and cook other side. Turning is tricky; use wide spatula. Serve with rice and green salad.

—*Nena da Silva, Belo Jardim, Brazil; and Crissie A. Graber, Colmeia, Brazil*

Egg Curry (India)

(ts)   *M*

Serves 4

Anda Kari
(ahn-DAH KAH-ree)

Contributor received this recipe from a friend she met at the London Mennonite Centre in England. "Prior to going to England, the art of cooking held no fascination for me. But the wonderful smells emanating from the kitchens of other residents—from Mexico, Burma, Zambia, Hong Kong, Malaysia, India, and Great Britain—tantalized me. I had to learn to duplicate the delightful aromas and beautiful dishes."

• *Microwave:*
Combine onions, garlic, and 1 T. oil (15 ml); cook on high 3 minutes. Add spices and tomatoes; cook on high 6-8 minutes. Add eggs; cook on high 3-5 minutes.

In frypan, sauté in 2 T. oil (30 ml):
   2 large onions, chopped
   2 cloves garlic, minced
When onions are transparent, add:
   1 t. ground turmeric (5 ml)
   1 t. ground ginger (5 ml)
   1 t. ground cumin (5 ml)
   1 t. paprika (5 ml)
   1 1/2 t. ground coriander (7 ml)
   1/2 t. salt (2 ml)
   1/4 t. ground red pepper (1 ml) (optional) +!
   1 t. garam masala (5 ml) (p. 289) (optional)
Fry 1-2 minutes.
Add:
   1 1/2 c. tomatoes, fresh or canned (375 ml)
Cover and simmer until thick, about 20 minutes.
Add:
   4-6 eggs, hard-cooked and cut in half
Simmer 5 minutes. Serve over rice with chutney on side.

—*Nancy Kinsinger Halder, Parnell, Iowa*

Brazilian Quiche

● ●

Serves 6-10

350°F 180°C

30-40 min.

Torta Salgada
(tor-tah sahl-GAH-dah)

*This versatile recipe can turn
leftover vegetables and meat
into an attractive and tasty
main dish or snack food.
Brazilians serve Torta
Salgada hot or cold, as an
afternoon snack, finger food
at parties, or for picnics. This
crustless quiche has a more
dense and sturdy texture
than French quiche.*

In bowl, combine any of following to make 2 c. "salad"
mixture (500 ml):

**onion, chopped
tomato, chopped
fresh parsley or cilantro, chopped
mixed vegetables, diced and cooked (peas,
    beans, carrots)
hot dogs, thinly sliced, or other cooked meat
    chunks**

Add:

**1/2 t. salt (2 ml)
1/4 t. pepper (1 ml)**

Mix well and set aside.

In separate bowl or blender, mix:

**3 eggs
1/2 c. oil (125 ml)
2 c. flour (500 ml)
1/2 c. sharp cheese, grated (125 ml)
1 t. salt (5 ml)
1 T. baking powder (15 ml)
2 c. milk (500 ml)**

Preheat oven to 350°F (180°C). Pour half of batter in
greased 9 x 13 baking pan (3.5-L). Spread salad mixture
over batter. Pour remaining batter over top. Arrange sliced
olives on top as garnish. Bake 30-40 minutes, or until
batter is set. Batter will rise as it bakes, and fall when
removed from oven.

—*Dona Vitalina, Jundiaí, São Paulo, Brazil; and Lois Musselman,
    Pará, Brazil*
—*Crissie A. Graber, Colmeia, Brazil*
—*Betty Hochstetler, Curitiba, Brazil; and Esther Falb, Orrville, Ohio*

....

**In 1987-89, people in
developed countries
consumed nearly three
times as much grain per
capita as people in
less-developed
countries. In the
developed countries,
people ate 63 percent of
the grain indirectly via
meat, while people in
less-developed countries
ate 81 percent of the
grain directly. On
average, Canadians
receive 129 percent of
the calorie requirements
in comparison to people
in Ghana who, on
average, receive only 76
percent of the calories
they need.[2]**

191

Iraqi Baked Dinner

Serves 6-8

350°F 180°C

1 hour

Moussaka
(moo-SAH-kah)

This medley of flavors,
colors, and textures will
please when garden
vegetables are still plentiful
in early fall, but it is cool
enough to use the oven.

Cut in 1/2-inch slices (1-cm):
   1 medium eggplant
Cut slices in half and spread on waxed paper or cookie
sheet. Sprinkle with salt and set aside.
Cook in saucepan 6 minutes:
   3 medium potatoes, peeled, cut in 12 1/2-inch
      slices (1-cm)
Meanwhile, mix:
   1 lb. lean ground beef (500 g)
   2 cloves garlic, minced
   1 t. salt (5 ml)
   1/4 t. pepper (1 ml)
   1/4 t. allspice (1 ml)
Shape into 12 2-inch patties (5-cm).
Prepare:
   3 medium tomatoes, cut in 12 thick slices
   2 onions, cut in 12 thin slices
Rinse eggplant. In deep 3-4 qt. casserole (3-4 L), arrange
eggplant, potatoes (drained), tomatoes, meat patties, and
onions alternately in rows, standing on end.
Mix:
   15-oz. can tomato puree or tomato sauce
      (425 g)
   1/2 can water
   3/4 t. salt (3 ml)
   1/4 t. pepper (1 ml)
Pour over casserole. Bake in 350°F (180°C) oven 1 hour,
or until potatoes and eggplant are cooked through. Serve
with warm, freshly baked bread.

—*Uum Zaki, Busrah, Iraq; and Hilda Staal, Hudsonville, Michigan*

....

*g*ood millet is known at the harvest.
—*African proverb*

....

North Americans tend
to label as food anything
remotely edible,
regardless of its
nutritional content. In
contrast, people in the
East African country of
Uganda use the word
food only in reference to
their staple food, not for
snacks.

••••••••••••••••••••••••••••••••••

Spaghetti Sauce With Meatballs (Italy)

Serves 4-6

Salsa di Pomodoro
(SAHL-sah dee
POH-moh-DOH-roh)

The recipe for this mild sauce comes from the Sicilian American community. Simmer on low heat or in slow cooker for several hours for full flavor. A simple company dish.

• *Options:*
Substitute ground turkey for beef.
•
To make simple meat sauce, sauté 1/2 lb. ground beef or turkey (250 g) with garlic and onions, instead of making meatballs.
•
Omit meat for a tasty vegetarian sauce.

Tomato sauce:
Sauté in 1 T. olive oil (15 ml):

- **1/4 c. onions, chopped (50 ml), or 1 T. onion powder (15 ml)**
- **1 clove garlic, minced, or 1/4 t. garlic powder (1 ml) or more to taste**

Add:

- **18 oz. tomato paste (575 g)**
- **4-5 c. water (1-1.3 L)**
- **2 t. salt (10 ml)**
- **1/4-1/2 t. pepper (1-2 ml)**
- **1 t. dried oregano (5 ml)**
- **1 t. dried basil (5 ml)**
- **1 bay leaf**
- **2 t. sugar (10 ml)**
- **3 T. dry red wine (45 ml) (optional)**

Meatballs:
Mix well:

- **3/4 lb. ground beef (375 g)**
- **3 T. bread crumbs (45 ml)**
- **3 T. Romano cheese (45 ml)**
- **2 dashes of salt and pepper or to taste**
- **1 T. onion, minced, or onion flakes (15 ml)**
- **1 t. dried basil (5 ml)**
- **2 eggs, lightly beaten**
- **dash of Tabasco pepper sauce or to taste (optional)**

Roll into 1-inch diameter balls (2.5-cm) and fry, or broil in oven, or bake at 350°F (180°C) until cooked through. Add to sauce.

Bring sauce to a boil. Simmer 2-3 hours to mix flavors (can simmer all day on low in slow cooker).

Cook spaghetti according to directions on package. Drain. Add a little sauce and dash of olive oil to keep spaghetti from sticking. Serve cooked spaghetti on individual plates; pour generous amount of sauce over top and sprinkle with grated Parmesan or Romano cheese.

—*Josephine Gullo Burnett, Batavia, New York; and Tom Burnett, Akron, Pennsylvania*

....

When you reap the harvest of your land,
 you shall not reap to the very edges of your field,
 or gather the gleanings of your harvest;
you shall leave them for the poor and for the alien:
 I am the Lord your God.

—*Leviticus 23:22*

Eggplant Sauce for Spaghetti (Italy)

Salsa di Melanzane per Spahetti
(SAHL-sah dee meh-lahn-ZAH-nay pair spah-GEH-tee)

This thick sauce is a good way to introduce eggplant to skeptics.

• *Microwave:*
In a 2-qt. casserole (2-L) combine eggplant, onion, garlic, parsley, and 2 T. oil or water (30 ml). Cook on high 5 minutes. Stir and cook 2 more minutes. Add other ingredients, cover, and cook on high 4-6 minutes until eggplant and tomatoes are heated through.

M

Serves 6

In saucepan, sauté in 1 T. oil (preferably olive) (15 ml) until onion is tender:

1 medium onion, finely chopped
1 clove garlic, crushed
2 t. dried parsley (10 ml) or 1/4 c. fresh parsley, snipped (50 ml)

Add:

1/4 c. water (50 ml)
2 large eggplants, cut in 1/2-inch cubes (1 cm)

Bring to a boil, reduce heat, and simmer 5 minutes.
Add:

28-oz. can whole tomatoes (875-g) or 8-10 fresh Italian tomatoes, chopped
2 of 6-oz. cans tomato paste (375 g total) (about 1 1/2 c./375 ml)
2 t. dried oregano (10 ml)
1 t. salt (5 ml)
1 t. sugar (5 ml)
dash of pepper

Heat to boiling; reduce heat. Cover and simmer 15 minutes, stirring occasionally. Serve over hot spaghetti; sprinkle with Parmesan cheese.

• *Options:*
Add fresh or canned mushrooms.
•
Substitute zucchini squash for 1 eggplant.

—*Sherry Holland, Caracas, Venezuela*

---

*A*lmighty God, Lord of heaven and earth,
  we humbly pray that your gracious care may give
    and preserve the seeds which we plant in our
    farms that they may bring forth fruit in good
    measure;
that we who constantly receive from your goodness
    may always give thanks to you,
    the giver of all good things;
through Jesus Christ, your Son our Lord.

—*Prayer used during planting season in the Cameroon*[3]

Baked Eggplant Rollatini (Italy)

Rollatini di Melanzane
(roh-lah-TEE-nee dee meh-lahn-ZAHN-ay)

Contributor discovered this "zesty way of serving eggplant and cutting meat costs" from Italian friends in her community. Since this dish freezes well, prepare several recipes when vegetables are in season and freeze for busy-day meals.

●●●●●●●●●●●●●●●●●●●●●●●●●●●●●●●●

Serves 6-8

Broil 5-7 min.

350°F 180°C (30 min.)

Preheat oven to broil.
With sharp knife, slice lengthwise in 1/8-inch slices (.5-cm):

1 1/4 lb. eggplant (625 g)

Mix in pie plate:

1 egg
1/4 c. milk (50 ml)

Place on piece of waxed paper:

1 c. dried bread crumbs (250 ml)

Dip eggplant slices into egg mixture, then coat with crumbs. Arrange slices in 1 layer in well-greased 15 1/2 x 10 1/2-inch pan (40 x 25 x 2 cm). Broil 5-7 minutes, until tender and lightly browned. Repeat with remaining slices. Reset oven at 350°F (180°C).
Mix in bowl:

15-oz. can tomato sauce (475-g)
2 t. sugar (10 ml)
1/4 t. pepper (1 ml)
1 c. water (250 ml)
1/4 t. ground oregano (1 ml)

Set aside.
Shred:

1/2 lb. Colby, mozzarella, or Monterey Jack cheese (250 g) (about 2 c./500 ml)

Mix in bowl:

1 c. ricotta cheese (250 ml)
1/4 t. dried oregano (1 ml)
1/4 t. salt (1 ml)
all but 2 T. of shredded cheese (30 ml)

Spoon about 2 T. cheese mixture (30 ml) in 1/2-inch strip (1-cm) on each eggplant slice. Roll, starting at narrow end. Spoon some tomato sauce mixture into bottom of 2-qt. baking dish (2-L). Place eggplant rolls, seam side down, in sauce in baking dish; top with remaining sauce. Bake at 350°F (180°C) 30 minutes, or until heated through. Sprinkle rolls with remaining shredded cheese and return to oven until cheese melts.

—*Margaret Dyck, St. Catharines, Ontario*

Addingana amawolu yagagyako omukuto.
Don't throw away leftover food. Keep serving it and you will be satisfied.

—*Ugandan proverb*

Garden Vegetable Bake (Turkey)

Guvetch
(goo-VETCH)

Serve this all-vegetable dish with pita bread (p. 51), a tossed salad, and cheese for a satisfying meal.

• **Microwave:**
In 3-quart casserole (3-L) place eggplant, carrots, potatoes, and zucchini in layers. Top with tomatoes, salt, and pepper. In another container, cook olive oil, celery, onion, and parsley 2 minutes on high. Add to vegetable casserole and cover tightly. Cook 8-15 minutes on high, or until vegetables are tender-crisp, rotating dish after 5 minutes. Let stand, covered, 5 minutes. Zucchini and eggplant will be a bit softer, since they cook faster than potatoes and carrots.

●●●●●●●●●●●●●●●●●●●●●●●●●●●●●●●●●

Ⓜ

Serves 4-6

Broil 5-7 min.

325°F 160°C (2 hr.)

Peel and slice:
   1 eggplant
Salt and let stand in colander while preparing other vegetables.
Slice:
   3 carrots
   2 stalks celery
   2 large or 3 medium potatoes
   1 large or 2 small zucchini
   1 large onion
Pat slices of eggplant dry, brush with olive oil, and broil until golden, 5-7 minutes. Reset oven to 325°F (160°C).
Layer all vegetables in large casserole along with:
   4 cloves garlic, crushed
   salt and pepper to taste
Top with:
   1/2 c. fresh parsley, chopped (125 ml)
   2 T. olive oil (30 ml)
   3 tomatoes, peeled and chopped, or 1/2 c. tomato sauce (125 ml)
Cover tightly and bake 2 hours at 325°F (160°C). Occasionally check and add tomato juice or water if vegetables are too dry. When almost done, cover with crumbled feta cheese and let melt (optional).

—*Mukkader Akpinar, Turkey and Greece; and Naomi E. Fast, Newton, Kansas*

Noodles with Broccoli and Meat (Cambodia)

Kuy Tew Cha
(goi dieu chah)

Contributor Chanlyda Seasrin Lang brought this recipe to the United States when she came as a refugee. Noodles with Broccoli and Meat represents frugal, but tasty, everyday food in which a little meat flavors a large amount of noodles.

• **Option:**
Substitute 1 c. thinly sliced beef (250 ml) for pork and shrimp.

●●●●●●●●●●●●●●●●●●●●●●●●●●●●●●●●●●

ⓣⓢ

Serves 4

Cook according to package directions:
   8 oz. Chinese noodles or thin spaghetti (250 g)
Drain. Add 1 T. oil (15 ml) to keep noodles from sticking together, cover, and set aside.
In separate saucepan, cook or steam until tender-crisp:
   1 1/2 c. broccoli, cut in pieces (375 ml)
Meanwhile, in separate frypan sauté 8-10 minutes in 1-2 T. oil (15-30 ml):
   2 cloves garlic, minced
   1/2 c. pork, cut in small pieces (125 ml)
   6-8 shrimp, shelled and deveined
Add broccoli to meat along with:
   1-2 T. soy sauce (15-30 ml)
   1 t. sugar (5 ml)
   1/2 t. salt (2 ml) (optional)
Toss with noodles and serve with additional soy sauce as desired.

—*Chanlyda Seasrin Lang and Cathy Godshall, Elkhart, Indiana*

Rice Noodles with Vegetables (Philippines)

Serves 4-5

Pancit Bihon
(PAHN-sit BEE-hohn)

This is a favorite Philippine dish for marienda *(afternoon snack) or parties. It makes a lovely main dish for family or guests.*

• **Options:**
Substitute pork for part of chicken pieces.
•
Substitute regular thin noodles for rice noodles.
•
Substitute other vegetables; increase amount of vegetables.

Sauté in large saucepan:
  2 T. cooking oil (30 ml)
  2 cloves garlic, minced
  1 large onion, finely chopped
Add:
  1 c. cooked chicken, cut in small pieces (250 ml)
  2-3 t. fish sauce (10-15 ml)
  2 c. chicken broth (500 ml)
  1/2 t. salt (2 ml)
  1/4 t. pepper (1 ml)
Simmer 10 minutes. Stir in:
  1 carrot, finely diced (about 1 c./250 ml)
  1 c. string beans, finely diced (250 ml)
  1 c. cabbage, coarsely shredded (250 ml)
  1/2-1 c. small shrimp, shelled, deveined, and cut in half (125-250 ml) (optional)
Bring to a boil, then reduce heat. Add:
  8 oz. rice noodles (250 g)
  1/4 t. salt (1 ml) or to taste
  1/4 t. pepper (1 ml)
Stir and cook until noodles are tender, 5-8 minutes. Add several tablespoons broth or water if mixture is too dry.
Serve on large platter, garnished with:
  2 eggs, hard-cooked and chopped
  2 green onions, diced
  lemon slices, arranged around sides
Each person squeezes lemon over serving as desired. Pass dish of Seasoned Fish Sauce (p. 282) for extra flavoring.

—Carolyn Schrock-Shenk, Lancaster, Pennsylvania

The Yagaw Hanunóo, an indigenous group living in the mountainous forests of Mindoro Island in the Philippines, manage one of the most complex and sophisticated farming systems in the world. Following the ancient system of "shifting" agriculture, they clear parcels of land and for several years plant a deliberately ordered succession of different crops before allowing the natural jungle growth to return. In addition to their primary crop of rice, they grow maize, leguminous crops, sweet potatoes, sugar cane, and fruit trees.

Largely isolated from the rest of Philippine society, the Hanunóo use no tractors, no imported fertilizers, and no chemical pesticides. None of their members have a degree in agriculture. Yet they have names and know uses for some 3,000 plants in their ecosystem. In their play young children imitate the agricultural activities of their parents, and by age eight they begin to assume responsibility for a plot of land.[4]

Thai Fried Noodles

Serves 4

Pad Thai
(pahd tie)

Thai Fried Noodles is a favorite treat among Thais and foreigners visiting Thailand. It is a popular midday snack or lunch. Testers commented that preparation is somewhat long and involved, but the result is worth it.

• Option:
Substitute chicken for pork, or omit meat.

Soak in warm water at least 15 minutes:
   6 oz. rice noodles (175 g)
Heat in wok or large frypan:
   2-3 T. oil (30-45 ml)
Add and fry until golden:
   2 cloves garlic, minced
Add and fry until cooked through:
   1/4 lb. pork, cut in bite-size, thin slices (125 g)
Add and stir-fry 2-3 minutes:
   8 large shrimp, shelled and deveined
   1 T. dried shrimp (15 ml) (optional)
Gently stir in:
   2 oz. tofu, cubed (50 g) (optional)
Reduce heat and add:
   3 T. lemon juice (45 ml)
   2-3 T. fish sauce (30-45 ml)
   1 T. sugar (15 ml)
Stir gently until sugar dissolves.
Add:
   soaked noodles, well drained
Stir briefly, then push to one side of wok or frypan.
Add a little oil to free side, if necessary, and add:
   2 eggs, beaten
Stir and fry until firm.
Place on noodles:
   scrambled eggs
   2 oz. bean sprouts (50 g)
   3 T. roasted peanuts, crushed (45 ml)
   3 T. green onions, chopped (45 ml)
   2 T. cilantro, chopped (30 ml)
Stir gently through noodles. Serve on plate garnished with cilantro or parsley leaves, and lemon wedges.

—*Khun Deng and Lily Bérubé, Phanat Nikhom, Thailand*

— Notes
1. Robert Farrar Capon, *The Supper of the Lamb: A Culinary Reflection* (Garden City, N.Y.: Doubleday & Company, Inc., 1969), p. 25.
2. USDA, Foreign Agricultural Service—production, supply, and disappearance computer database (Michael Trueblood, March 1990); and James P. Grant, *The State of the World's Children 1990* (New York: Oxford University Press, 1989), pp. 78-79.
3. Presbyterian Church in Cameroon; in *With All God's People: The New Ecumenical Prayer Cycle*, comp. by John Carden (Geneva, Switzerland: WCC Publications, 1989), p. 287.
4. From a presentation by Hugh Popenoe, director of the University of Florida's Center for Tropical Agriculture, at the Transcultural Seminar, Goshen College, Goshen, Indiana, June 1990.

Erica Thiessen: Burkina Faso

The most memorable celebrations in which I have participated are those we have shared with people who have very little. In Winnipeg, Cambodian refugee families sponsored by members of our church have taught us much about thankfulness and celebration by putting on lavish thank-you feasts for our congregation. Buckets of Kentucky Fried Chicken, piles of egg rolls and egg foo young, elaborate birthday cakes, rice dishes, and soft drinks, all given so freely, have made us, the "rich" ones who usually are the "givers," feel quite indebted. And this is as it should be since true celebration equalizes, removing cultural and economic barriers between people and making us truly one body in Christ.

When we visited the Christian Council of Mozambique for the last time before leaving Africa in 1985, the council workers provided a lavish farewell feast. Despite our protests, these Mozambicans who live in one of the poorest countries on earth insisted on giving us a proper celebration. Staff members spent most of a day looking for food—a chicken from a market across town, vegetables from someone's struggling garden, rice, and Coca-Cola from an expensive foreign currency shop.

At last the feast was ready, the opening speeches given, and the meal served. Our friends piled our plates high with food, urging us to eat more and more until our stomachs were fit to burst. All the while, we knew that some of the people at our table would probably go hungry the next day.

It was one of the most painful, precious, and joyful moments of our lives. We, who had come to serve (and who mostly took our food for granted), were being served by those who materially had nothing compared to us, but who could celebrate with lavish abandon because they knew how to love. They knew from experience that true celebration is necessary for survival. It nourishes and strengthens both the givers and the receivers and helps to lighten the crosses in our daily lives.

—Leona Dueck Penner,
Winnipeg, Manitoba

7

Flavors of the Feast

All societies and cultures have ways to celebrate special events and days. Festive celebrations, in many shapes and forms, allow people to break out of their regular routine, to bring their "joy and love of life into public view, and share them with the larger community."[1]

The public nature of celebration and the contrast between routine and festive days are probably most vivid in less affluent parts of the world where limited resources regularly restrict the variety of leisure activities and the consumption of certain foods. Meat, for example, is an important, often preferred, component in the diet of many people in many places. Yet most people in the world can afford to savor its juices only on rare and special occasions.

Even when animal husbandry is an important aspect of the economy, people in nonindustrial village societies without supermarkets, home pantries, refrigerators, and freezers, manage this perishable food item in a unique way. Unable to preserve large quantities of food, they reserve meat almost exclusively for occasions that draw together enough people to consume an entire animal. In South African Xhosa society, the exclusive tie between eating meat and festive celebrations is so strong that people refer to these occasions as times when they "eat meat."

These occasions, known as feasts, highlight the important milestones in the lives of individuals, families, and communities. People plan feasts to dedicate a house, to bid farewell to someone leaving the village, to welcome a visitor or returning family member, to celebrate a child's first birthday or a marriage, to mourn the death of an elder, or to simply share in someone's good fortune.

In many places the feast is a community event with no exclusive guest list. According to tradition in Lesotho, everyone in the village—even a stranger passing by on the road—is welcomed to the feast as long as the food lasts. The cooks take care to reserve a portion of meat for herdsboys who are away tending animals. When the feasting is finished, festivities continue with spirited song, dance, drink, and conversation.

We thank you, Lord,
That was such a good
   meal.
The soup was good.
The meat was good.
The hot pepper and the
   yam were good.
O Lord, our stomachs are
   full.
Our bodies have what
   they need.
This is a new miracle
   every day.
We thank you for it
   and also for the good
   taste
that lingers on our
   tongues.
How refreshing your
   water was!
With this meal you gave
   us
the strength required for
   the day.
Add to it your Spirit
so that we might use your
   strength rightly.
Give us, besides food for
   our bodies,
your heavenly food
for our whole life.
Praised be you, merciful
   God. Amen.

—Prayer of a young Ghanaian
   Christian[2]

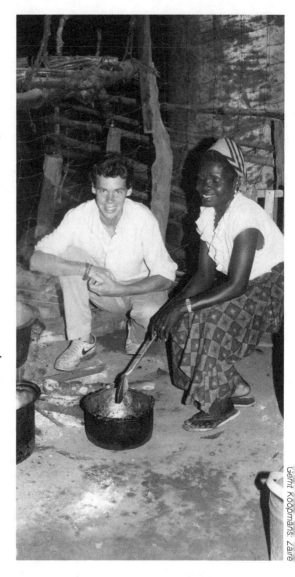

Gerrit Koopmans: Zaire

This pattern of eating meat only at the feast developed and continues in what some would consider impoverished situations, yet it results in a wealth not measured by most economic indicators. Heart disease is less prevalent among people who regard meat as a celebration food. Feasting in community reinforces the bonds of group welfare and identity.

When affluence allows people to feast too frequently and independently of others, feasting loses much of its joy and integrity. It results in ill health and dulls our sensitivity to the needs of others.

Reclaiming the feast may require learning to fast. Regularly abstaining from meat and other rich foods can be a spiritual act of solidarity. Reserving for special events foods we might easily afford, but that are luxury items in the world economy, unites us with those who have less. Robert Farrar Capon wrote:

> **We should be careful about allowing abundance to con us out of hunger. It is not only the best sauce; it is also the choicest daily reminder that the agony of the world is by no means over. As long as the passion goes on, we are called to share it as we can—especially if, by the mere luck of the draw, we have escaped the worst pains of it. . . . Fast, therefore, until His Passion brings the world home free. He works through any crosses He can find. In a time of affluence, fasting may well be the simplest one of all.**[3]

As we learn to fast with the poor, let us also learn their patterns of feasting and celebration. Let us be content with ordinary food on ordinary days. But when there is cause for true celebration, let us break our fast of solidarity and enter into that occasional, lavish abandon of those whom we have remembered.

The recipes in this section represent foods that the majority of the world's people would eat with great pleasure, but at great sacrifice. For North Americans, the sacrificial ingredients will vary. For some, it will be the costly first purchase of new spices. For others, the meat or seafood. For many, it will be a time-consuming preparation.

These are not for every Hallmark holiday, not necessarily for every time we entertain guests. But to mark the truly important personal and community milestones, the recipes invite us to occasionally indulge in the luxury of an afternoon in the kitchen, cooking, eating, and celebrating with others, that we might nourish and draw closer to one another. The stories of celebrations that sustain the poor through the hardest of times may be a new source of energy to those resisting the excesses of affluence.

Pilaf
(India/Bangladesh)

Serves 6

Pilau
(pih-LAO)

This dressed-up rice is common to India, Bangladesh, and Nepal, and is served with Chicken Korma (p. 224) and other meat curries. It is eaten by families of all income levels, but socioeconomic status determines the type of fat used in the preparation. Wealthy families use ghee (clarified butter), middle-class families use shortening, and poor families with access to coconut trees use coconut milk.

• Option:
After browning rice and spices, bake in covered dish at 350°F (180°C) until rice is tender and water is absorbed, about 1 hour.

In large saucepan, fry until crisp and brown in 1/4 c. ghee or oil (50 ml) (see note on coconut milk, below):

2 onions, thinly sliced

Remove onions from oil and reserve for garnish.

Add to oil:

2 1/2 c. long-grain rice (preferably basmati, rinsed) (625 ml)
2 cinnamon sticks
2-3 whole cardamom pods
2 bay leaves
4 whole cloves
1/2 t. ground turmeric (2 ml)
3/4 t. salt (3 ml)
7 thin slices ginger root

Sauté 5 minutes.

Add so that liquid level reaches 1 inch (2.5 cm) above rice level:

water or coconut milk (p. 280) (if using coconut milk, reduce oil above to 2 T./30 ml)
1/4 c. raisins (50 ml) (optional)

Bring to a boil, reduce heat, cover, and simmer until rice is cooked, about 20 minutes.

Serve with crisply fried onion slices and sliced hard-cooked eggs or almond slivers. Remove whole spices while eating.

—Beronica Mendez, Sonapur, Bangladesh; and Gwen Heyerly Peachey, Maijdi, Bangladesh
—Genevieve Friesen, Goshen, Indiana

Coconut Rice
(Indonesia)

Serves 4-6

Nasi Kuning
(nah-SEE koo-NING)

Indonesians serve Coconut Rice at festive occasions. It is delicious with Indonesian vegetable or meat dishes or Asian curries.

• Option:
Use 1/4 t. saffron or ground turmeric (1 ml) instead of yellow food coloring.

In heavy saucepan, bring to a boil:

1 1/2 c. long-grain rice (375 ml)
2 1/2 c. coconut milk (625 ml) (p. 280)
1/2 t. salt (2 ml)
1-2 drops yellow food coloring (optional)
2 bay leaves (optional)

Lower heat and simmer, covered, 20 minutes. Remove from heat and let stand, covered, until ready to serve.

—Lisa Christano, Jateng, Indonesia
—Anne Warkentin Dyck, Swift Current, Saskatchewan

● ●

Blueberry Wild Rice (Canada)

Serves 4-6

The Ojibway name for this side dish is an entire sentence, describing the method of preparing blueberries (miinan) and wild rice (manomin). See p. 142 for information about wild rice.

Combine in saucepan:
   1 c. wild rice (250 ml)
   3/4 c. blueberries, fresh or frozen (175 ml)
   3 c. water (750 ml)
   2 T. sugar (30 ml) (optional)
   dash of cinnamon
Cook 30 minutes, or until rice is tender. Serve hot as side dish, or cool and serve as dessert with whipped cream.

—*May Pitchenese, and James and Kate Kroeker, Dinorwic, Ontario*

● ●

Wild Rice Poultry Stuffing (Canada)

Makes enough for one bird and a small casserole dish on the side.

Cook according to package directions (or see Rice, p. 142):
   2 c. wild rice (500 ml)
   6 c. water (1.5 L)
Drain. Add:
   1-lb. can whole cranberries (500-g)
   1/4 c. vinegar (50 ml)
   1 t. salt (5 ml)
   1 1/2 t. poultry seasoning (7 ml)
Stuff turkey or chicken.

—*May Pitchenese, and James and Kate Kroeker, Dinorwic, Ontario*

My grandmother told me all the stories her grandfather told her a long time ago. One of her grandfathers was there when it happened. They were at Rice Lake. They never knew [rice] was growing in there. One day an old man paddling there saw someone on the shore. The man—or spirit—on the shore said to the Indian, "Come over here. You know what that is, that field?" The Indian said, "No." The man said, "That's *manomin* (rice). If you pull me around in your canoe, I'll show you how to do it."

So the old Indian went to the shore and picked up the man, who instructed him to paddle around the lake without looking back. After making a silent round of the lake and returning to the shore, the man climbed out and disappeared into the bush. The old man looked back and saw that his canoe was full of rice.

Later the man on the shore returned and said, "I'll meet you at the landing where we'll cook the rice." He showed them how to clean it, to cook it, and use it in many different ways. *Manomin* is not only for eating; it is supposed to be medicine too. So they did it the way the spirit told them to.

—*May Pitchenese, elder of the Wabigoon Lake Ojibway Nation, Dinorwic, Ontario*

Upside-Down Company Platter (Jordan/West Bank)

Makhlubbi
(makh-LOO-bee)

Although time-consuming, Makhlubbi or Ma'lubeh (Arabic for upside-down*) isn't difficult to make, and the result is a lovely company dish. Authentically prepared with lamb, beef can also be substituted.*

• Option:
Instead of frying eggplant, lay slices on baking sheet. Preheat oven to broil. Brush slices with olive oil and broil until golden, 5-7 minutes. Proceed with recipe.

Serves 6

In large heavy saucepan or Dutch oven, heat:
   1-2 T. oil (preferably olive) (15-30 ml)
Add and fry until golden brown:
   1 medium head cauliflower, broken into pieces; or 1 eggplant, peeled and sliced 1/2-inch thick (1-cm); or 6 medium carrots, sliced 1/4-inch thick (3/4-cm) (or a combination of 2 of these)
Remove and set aside.
In same oil, brown:
   11/2-2 lb. lamb or beef, cubed (750-1000 g)
   1/2 c. onion, finely diced (125 ml)
   1-2 cloves garlic, minced
Add:
   2 t. salt (10 ml)
   1/2 t. pepper (2 ml)
   1/4 t. ground allspice (1 ml)
   1/4 t. ground nutmeg (1 ml)
   dash of ground cinnamon
   11/2 c. water (375 ml)
Bring to a boil, reduce heat, and simmer, covered, until meat is tender, about 30 minutes for lamb; 45-60 minutes for beef.
Meanwhile in separate medium saucepan, boil:
   3 c. water (750 ml)
Remove from heat and add:
   2 c. long-grain rice (500 ml)
   1/2-1 t. saffron (2-5 ml) or 1/4-1/2 t. ground turmeric (1-2 ml) (optional)
Cover and soak 10 minutes. Drain and set rice aside. When meat is tender, drain and reserve broth. Place browned vegetables over meat in saucepan. If using eggplant, slightly overlap slices in an attractive circle. Top with soaked rice, carefully leveling it off. Add enough water to reserved broth to make 3 c. (750 ml). Slowly pour broth over rice. Do not stir. Bring to a boil, then simmer, covered, until water is absorbed, about 15 minutes. Turn off heat and let stand, covered, 15 minutes. Invert saucepan on a large platter, 1-2 inches in diameter (2.5-5 cm) larger than saucepan. Let stand 10 minutes more while preparing:
   2 fresh tomatoes, cut in wedges
   2 lemons, cut in wedges
   sprigs of fresh mint or parsley
Carefully remove pan so rice does not lose shape of pan. Sprinkle with 1/4 c. browned almonds or pine nuts (50 ml). Lay tomato and lemon wedges and mint and parsley

(more →)

sprigs around edges for garnish. Pass a bowl of yogurt (p. 295) to spoon over top. Squeeze lemon over Makhlubbi as desired to brighten flavors. Serve with Middle East Chutney (p. 277) and pita bread (p. 51).

—Madelaine Aprahamian, Jordan; and Naomi E. Fast, Newton, Kansas
—Issa Zahran, Hebron, West Bank; and Lorraine J. Kaufman, Moundridge, Kansas
—Agatha Esau, Linden, Alberta
—Alice W. Lapp, Akron, Pennsylvania

During special meals in Palestinian homes, the host frequently stands over the guests and keeps filling their plates—if they have plates—or piling the choice pieces of meat in front of them. The only way to stop this generosity is to simply stop eating, amid protests of too much food and compliments of how good everything tastes. Food left on the plate means one has had enough. A clean plate indicates one is still hungry.

Wild Rice Casserole (Canada)

Wild rice production is an important economic activity for some Native Canadian groups. The price is a bit higher than regular rice, but the flavor and texture cannot be duplicated.

● ●

Serves 4 as main dish, 6 as side dish

350°F 180°C

1 hour

Cook until nearly tender, using package directions (or see Rice, p. 142):
  1 c. wild rice (250 ml)
  1/4 t. salt (1 ml)
  3 c. water (750 m)
Drain any remaining water.
Melt in frypan:
  1/4 c. margarine (50 ml)
Add and sauté 5 minutes:
  1/2 lb. mushrooms, sliced (250 g) (about 3 c./750 ml)
  1/2 c. onion, chopped (125 ml)
Toss rice with:
  1 c. cheddar cheese, grated (250 ml)
  2 c. tomatoes, fresh or canned, chopped (500 ml)
  1 t. salt (5 ml)
  dash of pepper
  sautéed ingredients

Place in buttered 2-qt casserole (2-L). Cover and bake 1 hour at 350°F (180°C). If mixture appears too moist, uncover last 10 minutes.

—Menno Wiebe, Winnipeg, Manitoba

Brown Rice with Vermicelli (Middle East)

Serves 4-6

**Ruz Mufalfal
(rooz moo-FAHL-fehl)**

This delicious rice variation is served with barbecued chicken, Skewered Ground Meat (p. 249), or other meat dishes.

Melt in saucepan:
  3 T. margarine or butter (45 ml):
Add and brown, stirring constantly:
  1 c. uncooked brown rice (250 ml)
  1 small onion, chopped
  1/4 c. vermicelli noodles, finely broken into pieces 1/2 inch (1 cm) or less in length (50 ml)
Add:
  2 c. broth or water (500 ml)
Bring to a boil, reduce heat, and simmer gently, tightly covered, until tender, about 25 minutes.
Brown in margarine or butter:
  1/4 c. almonds or pine nuts (50 ml)
Put rice in serving dish and top with browned nuts.

—*Alice W. Lapp, Akron, Pennsylvania*

Rice and Peas (Jamaica)

Serves 6-8

Some refer to this dish as the Jamaican Coat of Arms. The "peas" are actually beans—usually pigeon peas or red kidney beans, but others can be used. The distinctive flavor of Rice and Peas comes from simmering rice and beans in coconut milk, an ingredient North Americans should reserve for festive occasions because of its fat content.

In large saucepan, soak overnight or by quick method (p. 162):
  1 c. dried pigeon peas or kidney beans (250 ml)
  4 c. water (1 L)
Using same water, bring beans to a boil, reduce heat, cover, and simmer until tender. Beans should remain whole.
Add:
  3 c. coconut milk (750 ml) (p. 280)
  2 t. dried thyme (10 ml)
  2 green onions, finely chopped
  1 hot chili pepper, deseeded and chopped +!
  2 cloves garlic, minced, or 1/2 t. garlic powder (2 ml)
  1/2 t. salt (2 ml)
  1 T. margarine (15 ml) (optional)
Boil 5 minutes.
Add:
  2 1/2 c. rice (625 ml)
Stir, cover, and simmer 15-20 minutes, until rice is cooked and liquid is absorbed. Serve with green salad and fried plantain. On special occasions, serve with barbecued or spiced chicken.

—*Pauline Cousins, St. Mary, Jamaica*
—*Hilda Whyte, Kingston, Jamaica; and Betsy Beyler, Fairfax, Virginia*
—*Ginny and Karl Birky, Albany, Oregon*

Stuffed Peppers (Croatia/Serbia)

M

Serves 6-8

Punjena Paprika
(POON-yeh-nah PAH-pri-kah)

This is a traditional fall meal in Croatia and Serbia when sweet yellow, orange, and red peppers flood the outdoor markets. The same peppers are pickled for a popular winter salad.

• **Microwave:**
In 2-qt. rectangular dish (2-L), place peppers, cut side down. Sprinkle with 2 T. water (30 ml). Cover tightly and cook on high 4-8 minutes or until tender-crisp. Remove from dish, drain, and set aside while preparing filling.
In same dish combine ground beef, chopped onion, and garlic. Cook, uncovered, on high 5-8 minutes. Drain meat and stir in egg and spices. Spoon mixture into peppers, place back in dish, cover with sauce, and cook, covered, on medium 20-30 minutes until peppers are tender. Let stand, covered, 3 minutes.

Cook:
1/2 c. rice (125 ml) (p. 143)
This will yield about 11/2 c. cooked rice (375 ml). Rice can be somewhat undercooked; it will simmer later in pepper mixture. While rice is cooking, prepare other ingredients.

Sauce:
Mix:
1/2 c. tomato paste (125 ml)
21/2 c. water (625 ml) or enough to cover peppers
1 t. salt (5 ml)
1 T. sugar (15 ml)
3 T. olive oil or margarine, melted (45 ml)
2 T. flour (30 ml) or enough to slightly thicken
2 T. paprika (30 ml)
Reserve 1/4 c. (50 ml) for stuffing, and pour remainder in large, heavy saucepan or frypan.

Stuffing:
Mix together:
1 lb. ground beef (500 g) or mixture of ground beef and pork
1 onion, chopped
1 egg
cooked rice
2 cloves garlic, minced
several sprigs fresh parsley, chopped
1/2 t. salt (2 ml)
1/8 t. pepper (.5 ml) or to taste
1/4 c. reserved sauce (50 ml)
Stuff into:
8-10 sweet peppers, seeds removed
Fill peppers 2/3 full with rice mixture. Place stuffed peppers in sauce and simmer over low heat 2 hours.
Serve with mashed potatoes or bread.

—*Nela Horak Williams, Zagreb, Croatia; and Sara Wenger Shenk, Harrisonburg, Virginia*

f ood for one person is enough for two, that for two is enough for four, that for four is enough for eight.

—*Islamic saying*

A conciliation commission worked for several years to forge a peace agreement between the Nicaraguan Sandinista government and YATAMA, the armed opposition group representing the indigenous peoples of the eastern coastal area of Nicaragua. Some of the most memorable moments of the reconciliation process came around the meals that were shared by former enemies—fighters from the rebelling indigenous groups and Sandinista officials.

On one occasion Commander Lumberto Campbell, a key leader in the Sandinista government, invited the entire YATAMA delegation to his home for a meal. He had a specially prepared meal of turtle, the most sought-after and cherished meat, particularly among the Miskitu.

But turtle was scarce at that time and there was only enough for one plate. Lumberto shared that plate with Brooklyn Rivera, the head YATAMA leader. Under the large mango trees and in the stifling heat and humidity of the back patio, two native *Costeños* (coastal people), on opposite sides of a war, sat together and ate the dish of their ancestors.

—*John Paul Lederach,
Harrisonburg, Virginia*

Chicken with Rice (Colombia)

•••••••••••••••••••••••••••••••

Serves 6

Arroz con Pollo
(ah-ROHSS kohn POH-yoh)

Arroz con Pollo is a common celebration meal across Latin America. The chicken is traditionally seasoned with sour orange juice instead of lemon.

Season with salt, pepper, and lemon juice:
   3-lb. chicken, skinned and cut in serving pieces (1.5 kg)
In large saucepan, fry in 1/4 c. hot oil (preferably olive) (50 ml), until browned. Remove chicken and set aside. Drain excess oil from saucepan and add:
   1 onion, chopped
   1 c. green peppers, chopped (250 ml)
   3 cloves garlic, mashed
   1/2 c. celery, chopped (125 ml)
Sauté until onion is transparent.
Add:
   1/4 c. tomato paste (50 ml)
   1/2 t. ground cumin (2 ml)
   1/4 t. dried oregano (1 ml)
   1/4 t. pepper (1 ml)
Stir briefly and add:
   browned chicken
   2 c. uncooked rice (500 ml)
Stir a few minutes, then add:
   21/2 c. chicken broth (625 ml)
   1 t. salt (5 ml)
   2 drops yellow food coloring or 1/4 t. ground turmeric (1 ml) or bit of saffron (optional)
Cover and bring to a boil. Reduce heat and simmer until rice is tender and chicken is cooked through, 20-25 minutes.
Before serving, mix in:
   1 c. cooked peas (250 ml)

   (more →)

1 c. carrots, diced and cooked (250 ml)
(optional)

Garnish with:

1 small can mild red peppers, finely chopped,
or 1/4 c. fresh red peppers, sautéed (50 ml)

Heat through and serve.

—Irene Suderman, Bogotá, Colombia

• •

Valencia Rice
(Nicaragua)

Serves 8-10

Arroz a la Valenciana
(ah-ROHSS ah lah
vah-layn-SEEAH-nah)

Valencia Rice bears a modest resemblance to paella, *the sumptuous chicken, seafood, and rice platter native to the Spanish province of Valencia. Nicaraguans serve Valencia Rice at many festive occasions—a day at the beach, a birthday party, or a wedding.*

• Option:
Have Tabasco pepper sauce or Mexican Salsa (p. 284) on table for guests to add to taste.

Cook until tender in large saucepan:

2-3 lb. chicken (1-1.5 kg)
water to cover (about 5 c./1.3 L)
1/8 t. pepper (.5 ml)
1 t. salt (5 ml)

Remove chicken and reserve. Skim foam and fat from broth. Add to broth:

1 carrot, diced
2 potatoes, diced
1/2 c. fresh or frozen peas (125 ml)

Cook until just tender, 8-10 minutes. Remove vegetables from broth and reserve broth and vegetables separately. In large saucepan, sauté in 2-3 T. oil (30-45 ml):

1 medium onion, chopped
1/2 c. green pepper, chopped (125 ml)
1 stalk celery, chopped
2 cloves garlic, minced
2 c. uncooked rice (500 ml)

When rice becomes pearly white, add:

3 c. reserved broth (750 ml)
1 t. salt (5 ml)
dash of pepper
several sprigs fresh mint or cilantro (optional)

Bring to a boil, cover, and simmer 20 minutes. When rice is almost ready, combine in separate saucepan:

reserved vegetables
reserved chicken, deboned
1/2 c. tomato sauce (125 ml)
2 T. cooking wine or vinegar (30 ml)
1 T. Worcestershire sauce (15 ml)
1 t. prepared mustard (5 ml)
1 c. cooked shrimp, shelled and deveined, or
ham, cubed (250 ml)
1/2 c. raisins (125 ml) (optional)
1/2 c. green olives (125 ml) (optional)

Heat through. Stir into cooked rice. Remove from heat and cover. Let stand 10-20 minutes before serving to blend flavors. Serve hot with warm tortillas, a simple salad, or Refried Beans (p. 162).

—José Avalo and Angela Silva, Managua, Nicaragua; and Ann Graber Hershberger, Harrisonburg, Virginia

Soybean Cake with Red Chilies (Indonesia)

Sambel Goreng Kering
Tempeh
(sahm-BAHL goh-reng k'ring
tem-peh)

*Serve with vegetables from
the Indonesian* rijstaffel
*(p. 127). and Coconut Rice
(p. 204).*

• Option:
Substitute tofu for tempeh.

Cut in 1/2 x 1 x 1/2-inch pieces (1 x 3 x 1-cm):

**4 x 8-inch piece tempeh (soybean cake)
(10 x 20-cm)**

Put enough oil in frypan to just cover bottom. Fry soybean
cake in oil until light brown. Remove and set aside.
Fry in 3 T. oil (45 ml):

**1 T. hot red chilies, diced (15 ml) (optional) +!
2 small onions, thinly sliced
2-4 cloves garlic, sliced
1/4 c. brown sugar (50 ml)
1/4 t. salt (1 ml)
2 bay leaves
dash of ground ginger
1 T. lemon juice (15 ml)
1 thin slice laos (galangal) (optional)**

Add:

3 T. water (45 ml)

Add soybean cake, mix thoroughly, simmer 1-2 minutes.

• Option:
**Beat 3 eggs with a bit of salt and pepper. Fry like thin omelet
in large frypan. Cut in small squares or thin strips and serve
as garnish over Soybean Cake with Red Chilies and rice.**

—Lisa Christano, Jateng, Indonesia

....

Muslims are expected to "eat for survival, to maintain good health, and not to live for eating. In Islam, eating is considered to be a matter of worship of God like prayers, fasting, and other religious practices."

Islamic dietary regulations call for a full month of fasting each year. "During Ramadan, the ninth month of the Islamic lunar calendar, a Muslim fasts completely between dawn and sunset. He eats twice during the 24-hour day, ... once before dawn and again just after sunset." During this time of fasting, Muslims devote themselves to additional prayers and devotional exercises. Before the feast of fast-breaking at the end of Ramadan, "each adult member of the family donates the value of one meal to a needy person."

Islamic teaching advises Muslims to routinely "eat not more than two-thirds of their normal capacity" and to share food with others. It also admonishes people to eat together and not to throw away, waste, or treat with contempt this provision from God. Muslims traditionally send a dish of food to a neighbor whenever they prepare something good.[4]

Quick Spicy Tofu (Japan)

Serves 4-6

Mabo Tofu
(mah-boh doh-foo)

This wonderful way to serve tofu is a Japanese version of a hot dish from Szechwan, China. Szechwan food is traditionally very hot. Quick Spicy Tofu is also good with less red pepper. The red miso used in this recipe is a fermented soybean paste available in many Asian food stores. An instant Mabo Tofu seasoning mix is available in Asian food stores—you prepare the tofu, add the mix, simmer, and serve.

Cut in 1/2-1-inch cubes (1-2.5-cm):

2 1-lb. blocks firm tofu (1 kg total)

Dip cubes in boiling water, drain.
Prepare and set aside:

2 t. ginger root, grated (10 ml)
1 clove garlic, minced
2 green onions, finely chopped
1 small hot dried pepper, minced, or 1/4 t. ground red pepper (1 ml) +!

Mix together:

1/3 c. hot water (75 ml)
2 T. soy sauce (30 ml)
1 T. sugar (15 ml)
1 T. red miso (15 ml)
1/4 t. salt (1 ml)
2 t. sesame oil (10 ml)

Heat in frypan:

2 T. oil (30 ml)

Add ginger, garlic, onions, and red pepper and fry 1-2 minutes.
Add:

1/4 lb. ground pork (125 g)

Fry until pork is just cooked through.
Add hot water mixture, then tofu. Simmer gently 10 minutes, trying not to break up tofu.
Add:

2 t. cornstarch (10 ml) mixed with a little cold water

Cook until thickened.
Serve with rice.

—Mrs. Kazuko Kandori and Alice Ruth Ramseyer, Hiroshima, Japan

*ay our sons in their youth
be like plants full grown,
our daughters like corner pillars,
cut for the building of a palace.
May our barns be filled,
with produce of every kind;
may our sheep increase by thousands,
by tens of thousands in our fields,
and may our cattle be heavy with young.
May there be no breach in the walls, no exile,
and no cry of distress in our streets.
Happy are the people to whom such blessings fall;
happy are the people whose God is the Lord.*

—Psalm 144:12-15

Korean Mixed Vegetables with Beef

Chop Chae
(chop cheh)

Serve this Korean company dish with hot tea. Vary vegetable combinations to use seasonal vegetables.

• *Option:*
Substitute chopped spinach for Chinese cabbage.

Combine and set aside:
- **1 c. beef tenderloin or boneless sirloin, cut in bite-size pieces or thin strips (250 ml)**
- **2 T. soy sauce (30 ml)**
- **2 green onions, chopped**
- **1 T. Toasted Sesame Seeds (15 ml) (p. 290)**
- **2 cloves garlic, minced**

Prepare all or 2-3 of following vegetables and set aside, keeping separate:
- **1 c. celery, sliced diagonally in thin slices (250 ml)**
- **2 carrots, sliced diagonally in thin slices**
- **1/2-1 c. fresh or canned mushrooms, sliced (125-250 ml)**
- **1 c. fresh or canned bean sprouts (250 ml)**
- **8-oz. can bamboo shoots (or less as desired) (250-g)**
- **2 c. Chinese cabbage, chopped (500 ml)**

Soften in boiling water 5-10 minutes:
- **4-6 oz. bean thread vermicelli (125-175 g)**

Drain, cover, and keep warm.

Sauté beef and seasonings in frypan in small amount of oil. Place in warm, covered dish. In same frypan, stir-fry carrots and celery. When just tender, add to beef. Stir-fry rest of vegetables and add to beef.

Stir softened vermicelli noodles into meat and vegetables and add:
- **3 T. soy sauce (45 ml)**
- **2 green onions, chopped**
- **1 T. Toasted Sesame Seeds (15 ml) (p. 290)**
- **2 T. sugar (30 ml)**
- **black pepper to taste**

Decorate dish with shredded, fried egg (optional).

To prepare egg:
Beat:
- **2 eggs**

Fry in thin layer in oiled frypan. When firm, turn and cook lightly on other side. Roll, jelly roll fashion, and slice crosswise in thin strips.

—Pat Yoder, Goshen, Indiana

As you can not go to
  heaven alone,
Food is to be shared.
Food is heaven.
As you share the sight of
  heavenly stars,

So food is something
  which must be shared,
Food is heaven.
When food passes your
  throat,
You accent heaven in
  your body.

Food is heaven.
Ah! Food is something
  that must be shared.

—Kim Chi Ha, Korean poet[5]

Jiggs Dinner (Canada)

Serves 6-8

Jiggs Dinner is a common dish at Newfoundlanders' "scoffs"—events that bring family and friends together to eat, sing, dance, and spin a few yarns. This is often served with another meat dish such as chicken. Leftovers make delicious fried hash the following day.

Soak in cold water overnight (6-8 hours):

2 lb. salt beef, salt spare ribs, corned brisket in brine, or corned beef (1 kg)

(If you choose corned beef or brisket, omit soaking it; soak only the salted meats.) Drain meat and place in large pot. Tie in cloth bag, leaving room for expansion:

1 c. split peas, preferably yellow (250 ml)

Place bag in pot with meat. Cover meat and peas with water. Heat to a boil, reduce heat, and simmer 2 hours. Add:

6-8 medium potatoes or larger potatoes cut in half
6 carrots, cut in half if large
1 medium turnip or rutabaga, peeled and cut in chunks

Cook 15 minutes. Add:

1 medium cabbage, cut in wedges

Cook until all vegetables are just tender. Remove excess water so vegetables do not mash and form soup.
Remove peas from bag and place in bowl with:

2 T. margarine (30 ml)
1/8 t. pepper (.5 ml) or to taste

Mash to form "peas pudding."
Arrange meat and vegetables on platter. Serve peas pudding in separate bowl.

—Kathryn Loewen, St. John's, Newfoundland

Crisp Potato Balls (Indonesia)

Serves 6

Perkedel
(per-kuh-DEL)

These potatoes are served with other dishes at Indonesian celebrations. They are traditionally deep-fat fried instead of boiled before mashing. Contributor learned to make Perkedel from her mother, who learned to make it from hers. Serve with vegetables from the Indonesian rijstaffel (p. 127).

Boil:

4 potatoes, peeled and cut in quarters

When cooked through, mash immediately.
Brown in a little oil:

1/2 lb. ground beef (250 g)
2 T. onions, chopped (30 ml)

Add:

mashed potatoes
2 T. leeks, thinly sliced (30 ml)
salt and pepper to taste
2 eggs, beaten

Mix well and form into small balls.
Deep-fat fry until light brown.

—Lisa Christano, Jateng, Indonesia

Annie-Ruth Reddick, a resident of the Atlanta, Georgia, Grant Park neighborhood, likes to cook and entertain guests. One Thanksgiving she made a huge dinner for as many people as she could find to invite. She spent days preparing for it, cooking up 15 to 20 pounds of chitlins, fried pork intestines that are a favorite in the U.S. South. She also made corn bread, greens, cornmeal dressing, and sweet potato pie to accompany the traditional turkey.

When asked how she makes chitlins (or chitterlings), Annie-Ruth replied:

Buy nice clean chitlins, if you can. Then pick the fat off them—but not too much—you want to leave a little on. Just use your fingers to scrape. Put an onion cut in half and a peeled white potato—this cuts the smell a bit—in a big pot with the chitlins and cover it. There's lots of water already in them so just cook them like that—don't add water—for 30 minutes or so.

Then take the lid off and stir them. Add some black pepper, red pepper, and a little salt for flavor and see if you need a little more water to cook them up, you know, not too much—don't cover them, just enough to cook them. Then cover the pot again and cook for four hours. Stir them every once in a while. When they're done, take them out of the pot and cut them up nice and bite-sized and fry them in a pan with a little fat until they're browned slightly. Then they're ready to eat.

—Marsha Jones, Atlanta, Georgia

Hunters' Stew (Poland)

● ●

Serves 4-6

Bigos
(BEE-gohss)

When Poles sit down to eat, they say, "Smacznego! (smahch-NAY-goh: Good appetite!)" The ingredients of this well-known Polish favorite vary with each preparation. A Christmas Eve version contains no meat, but extra mushrooms. Serve with freshly baked bread or boiled potatoes. Make a day or two before serving, as flavor improves with age.

In large saucepan brown in 1 T. oil (15 ml):
   1-2 onions, chopped
   1/2 lb. stew beef, cubed (250 g)
Add:
   1 1/2 c. water (375 ml)
Simmer 15 minutes.
Add and cook 20 minutes:
   1 lb. sauerkraut with liquid (500 g)
   1/2 lb. kielbasa (Polish sausage links), halved and sliced (250 g)
   1/2 lb. fresh mushrooms, sliced (250 g) (optional)
In separate saucepan, cook 10 minutes:
   3 c. fresh cabbage, chopped as for coleslaw (750 ml)
   2 c. water (500 ml)
Drain water from cabbage, reserving liquid. Add cabbage to beef and sauerkraut mixture.
Add:
   2 whole cloves
   1 bay leaf
   1/2 t. pepper (2 ml)
   1/2 t. paprika (2 ml)
      (more →)

2 T. Worcestershire sauce (30 ml) or 1 T. soy
sauce (15 ml)

3 T. tomato paste (45 ml) (optional)

Simmer covered at least 1 hour, stirring every 10-15 minutes. Add a bit of reserved cabbage liquid if mixture becomes dry. Bigos should be a thick stew.

—Krystyna Król, and Eileen and Merlin Becker-Hoover, Warsaw, Poland

Cabbage Rolls (Poland)

Serves 6-8

350°F 180°C

1 1/2 hr.

Golabki
(guh-WOHMP-kee)

This dish is a favorite in Poland and in Polish American communities. Serve with mashed potatoes and green beans.

• Microwave:
Microwave cooking time reduces conventional cooking time by more than half. Start by removing core from cabbage head. Cover tightly with plastic wrap and cook on high 12-14 minutes to blanch leaves. Plunge head into cold water. Detach 20 large leaves and set aside. In large, shallow baking pan or casserole, cook chopped onion and ground beef on high 4-5 minutes, until meat is no longer pink. Drain off meat juice and add other filling ingredients to meat and onion. Stuff leaves, and place in same dish, positioning larger rolls around outside and smaller ones in center. Mix sauce ingredients in separate bowl, reducing tomatoes in sauce to 2 c. (500 ml). Pour over cabbage rolls. Cover tightly and cook on high 12-15 minutes until rolls are tender. Turn pan 1 or 2 times for even cooking. Let stand covered 10 minutes before serving. Testers say flavor is delicious!

Remove 2-inch core (5-cm) from:
1 medium head cabbage

Immerse in boiling water to cover. Bring to a boil and simmer 15-20 minutes. Drain, separate individual leaves, and set aside.

Filling:
Sauté:
2 lb. ground beef (1 kg)
1 large onion, chopped

Remove from heat. Add:
2 c. rice, cooked (500 ml)
2 eggs, beaten
1/4 t. pepper (1 ml)
1/2 t. dried marjoram or oregano (2 ml)
1 t. poultry seasoning (5 ml) (optional)
2 t. salt (10 ml) (optional)

Place about 1/3 c. hamburger mixture (75 ml) at stem end of each cabbage leaf. Roll leaf around mixture, tucking in sides. Place cabbage rolls in 9 x 13-inch pan (3.5-L).

Sauce:
Mix together:
3 c. tomatoes, chopped, or tomato puree (750 ml)
1/2 c. meat broth or bouillon (125 ml)
1 T. brown sugar (15 ml)
1 T. cider vinegar (15 ml)
1/4 t. pepper (1 ml)

Pour sauce over rolls. Cover and bake 1 1/2 hours in preheated 350°F oven (180°C).

• *Option:*
Substitute 10-oz. can tomato soup (300 g) and 1 can water for tomatoes in sauce.

—Adja Tucholska, Warsaw, Poland; and Phyllis Krabill, Philadelphia, Pennsylvania
—Catherine and Rita Lajewski, Elkhart, Indiana

Spinach Pie
(Greece)

● ●

Serves 4-6

350°F 180°C

30-35 min.

Spanokopita
(spah-noh-KOH-pee-tah)

This flaky, mouth-watering combination of spinach, cheese, and phyllo pastry is an International Tea Room favorite. Allow extra time for preparation if you haven't worked with phyllo pastry before. Well worth the effort for special occasions. Serve as a main dish pie.

• Options:
Add 1/2 c. sliced or chopped mushrooms (125 ml) to spinach mixture.
•
Spanokopita can be made up to a day ahead and stored in refrigerator until time to bake. If storing for more than one day, freeze; thaw and bake when ready to eat.

Cook in a little water until tender, about 3 minutes:
   6 c. fresh spinach, chopped (1.5 L), or 10-oz. package frozen spinach (300 g)
Drain.
Mix with:
   1 c. feta, Gruyère, or cheddar cheese, crumbled or shredded (250 ml)
   1 c. cottage cheese (250 ml)
   3 eggs, beaten
   1 onion, minced
   2 T. fresh parsley, chopped (30 ml), or 2 t. dried parsley (10 ml)
   1 t. dried dill (5 ml)
   1/2 t. dried oregano (2 ml)
   1/2 t. salt (2 ml)
   dash of ground nutmeg (optional)
Melt:
   1/2 c. margarine or butter (125 ml)
Brush bottom of shallow oblong pan, about 12 x 7-inch (30 x 12-cm), with a little melted margarine or butter. Reserve rest for phyllo dough.
Take:
   12 phyllo sheets, thawed (about an 8-oz./250-g package of frozen phyllo dough)
Cut sheets in half. Gently separate a half-sheet and place it in bottom of pan, folding edges over to fit bottom. Brush lightly with melted margarine. Repeat with 11 more half-sheets. (Cover unused sheets of phyllo with damp towel while working, so they don't dry out.)
Spread spinach mixture over phyllo dough in pan. Place other 12 half-sheets of phyllo over mixture, spreading each sheet with margarine and tucking in sides around edges to make a neat cover over the filling. Leftover phyllo sheets can be refrozen. Bake, covered, 25 minutes at 350°F (180°C). Uncover and bake 5-10 minutes until golden brown. Let stand 10 minutes. Cut into squares to serve.

• Option:
To make individual Spanokopita, roll up spinach filling like an egg roll in individual sheets of phyllo. Or cut phyllo in 3-inch strips (7-cm), place teaspoon of filling at one end of strip, and fold corner over to make triangle; continue folding strip from side to side in shape of triangle. Freeze. Thaw a few at a time as needed.

—*Nav Jiwan International Tea Room, Ephrata, Pennsylvania*

Lasagna
(Italy)

•••••••••••••••••••••••••••••••••

Serves 6-8

375°F 190°C

40-45 min.

(lah-SAHN-yah)

A rich traditional Lasagna from Italy. Authentic Lasagna is made with ricotta rather than cottage cheese. Ricotta is creamier, without curds and readily available in most communities. Use fresh grated Romano for true flavor. Serve with green salad.

• *Options:*
Add mushrooms, zucchini, or spinach to each layer.
•
Use only 3 layers of lasagna noodles with 2 layers of ricotta cheese mixture between them.
•
Store unused ricotta cheese in the freezer for future use. Lasagna also freezes well, either before or after baking.

Prepare Spaghetti Sauce (p. 193), either the simple meat sauce or vegetarian version.
Cook 12 lasagna noodles (about 2/3 lb./375 g) until just tender. Do not overcook. Drain.
Grate:

8 oz. mozzarella cheese (250 g)

Mix:

1 1/2 lb. ricotta cheese (750 g)
about 2/3 of grated mozzarella cheese
1/2 c. Romano cheese, grated (125 ml)
1 t. parsley (5 ml)
1/2 t. dried oregano (2 ml)
1/2 t. salt (2 ml) or to taste
pepper to taste
3 eggs, beaten
dash of garlic powder (optional)

Pour a little warm sauce on bottom of 9 x 13-inch pan (3.5-L) to prevent sticking. Put down layer of noodles. (With standard pan, 3 noodles side by side will just cover bottom. If pan is odd size, cut noodles to size and arrange to cover entire surface). Add 1/3 of cheese mixture, and drizzle with a little sauce, about 1/4 c. (50 ml). Alternate 2 more layers of noodles, cheese mixture, and sauce. Cover with fourth layer of noodles. Top with 3/4 c. sauce (175 ml) and the remaining mozzarella. You will use up all the cheese mixture in the layers, but not all the sauce. This is a dry, firm Lasagna; a good amount of sauce is left to ladle over top as it is served.

Cover pan and bake 40-45 minutes in preheated 375°F oven (190°C). Remove from oven, loosen or remove cover, and let stand 20 minutes to firm up before serving. Cut in squares and serve. Pour additional warm sauce over top and sprinkle with grated Romano or Parmesan cheese.

—Josephine Gullo Burnett, Batavia, New York; and Tom Burnett, Akron, Pennsylvania
—Joe Garofalo, New York, New York; and Sally Jo Milne, Goshen, Indiana

The man who always takes food is a man who has taken a sword to his neck.

—Somali proverb

Chicken and Sausage Jambalaya (United States)

This classic Cajun dish from Louisiana was originally designed to use up leftovers. Over the years it has become a festive dish made with a variety of meats. Contributor, who learned to make Jambalaya while living in Louisiana, recommends it as a great dish for potluck dinners.

• Option:
To make ahead and freeze, prepare as directed, but do not add rice. When ready to use, thaw, add rice, and cook as directed in the final step.

●●●●●●●●●●●●●●●●●●●●●●●●●●●●●●●●●●●●●

Serves 8

Combine in large saucepan:
   1 large onion, chopped
   4 ribs celery, chopped
   1 1/2 T. salt (20 ml)
   1/4 t. Tabasco pepper sauce (1 ml) +!
   2 qt. water (2 L)
Boil rapidly 10 minutes.
Add:
   2 1/2-3 lb. chicken (1.3-1.5 kg)
Cook until chicken is tender. Skin and debone chicken. Strain and reserve the stock, discarding fat. Reserve cooked onion and celery with chicken. Combine and sauté in heavy 5-qt. pot (5-L):
   1 c. onion, minced (250 ml)
   1/2 c. green pepper, minced (125 ml)
   1 clove garlic, minced
   1 lb. spicy, smoked sausage, sliced in 1/2-inch pieces (1-cm) (500 g)
Skim excess fat. Add reserved chicken, onion, and celery. Mix well.
Add:
   1-lb can tomatoes (500-g) (2 c. tomatoes/ 500 ml)
   2 c. uncooked rice (500 ml)
   3 c. reserved chicken stock (750 ml)
   1 t. salt (5 ml)
   1/4 t. pepper (1 ml)
   1/4 t. ground red pepper (1 ml) +!
   1 T. sugar (15 ml)
   1 1/2 T. Worcestershire sauce (20 ml)
   1/2 t. crushed thyme (2 ml)
Mix well. Heat slowly to a boil, reduce heat, and simmer 20-30 minutes.

—Dave Cronkhite, Lethbridge, Alberta

....

In Lesotho a *mokete* (feast) must have meat, so people plan and host feasts at times when that is possible. Funeral feasts come unexpectedly, however, sometimes when a family cannot afford meat. If they serve a meatless funeral meal, they later host another feast when they are able to kill an animal and share it with others.

Chicken Wat
(Ethiopia)

-⊞-

Serves 4

Doro Wat
(doh-roh wahtt)

Ethiopia is famous for its spicy stews, called wats. This favorite feature in Ethiopian restaurants is an easy and impressive dish to make at home. Serve with Injera (p. 47).

• *Notes:*
This stew is very spicy hot. The uninitiated may want to use one-half or less the amount of Berbere in the stew and add a corresponding amount of paprika. That way the wat will still look red, but won't be as peppery.
•
This is always eaten with Injera in Ethiopia, but is also tasty with rice.

Remove skin from:
   2 1/2-3 lb. chicken pieces (1.3-1.5 kg)
Sprinkle with:
   2 T. lemon juice (30 ml)
   1 t. salt (5 ml)
Let stand while preparing other ingredients.
In large saucepan, melt:
   2 T. margarine (30 ml)
Add, cover, and cook on low heat until onions are soft, but not browned:
   2 c. onions, finely chopped or whirled in blender (500 ml)
   1 T. garlic, minced (15 ml)
   1 t. ginger root, grated (5 ml), or 1/2 t. ground ginger (2 ml)
Add:
   1/4 t. fenugreek, crushed (1 ml)
   1/4 t. ground cardamom (1 ml)
   1/8 t. ground nutmeg (.5 ml)
Stir well and add:
   1/4 c. Berbere (50 ml) (p. 288) +!
   2 T. paprika (30 ml)
Stir over low heat 2-3 minutes.
Pour in:
   1/2 c. water (125 ml)
Bring to a boil over high heat, stirring continuously.
Add chicken to sauce, turning pieces until all are coated. Reduce heat to medium low, cover, and simmer until chicken is tender, about 45 minutes, turning once or twice to coat chicken evenly. If it becomes too dry, add a little water. Sauce should be consistency of heavy cream.
Prepare:
   1 egg, hard-cooked, for each person
Cut shallow slits in eggs to allow color and flavor of sauce to permeate. Add eggs to sauce and simmer 10 minutes. Stew can be made a day ahead of time and refrigerated. Add eggs when reheating.

—*Charmayne Denlinger Brubaker, Lancaster, Pennsylvania*
—*Phyllis Horst Nofziger, Ephrata, Pennsylvania*

Whenever special guests arrive in a Zairian home, it is important for the hosts to kill something or serve "meat with blood." Traditionally, when they kill a chicken, they serve the entire chicken to the visitor. The visitor may ask for any leftovers to take home or leave them for the host family to eat.

Brazilian Chicken

● ●

Serves 4-6

Galinha a Nordestina
(gah-LEEN-yah ah
nor-desh-TEE-nah)

*This is the typical way to
prepare chicken or any kind
of meat in northeast Brazil.
Cumin, coriander, and
colorau, a red powder that
adds color, are essential
seasonings in northeastern
kitchens. Paprika replaces
colorau in this recipe.*

• *Option:*
Instead of frying chicken,
place on pan, brush lightly
with oil (optional), and broil
in oven.

Cut in serving pieces:
   2₁/₂-lb. chicken (1.3-kg)
Sprinkle over or rub into chicken pieces:
   1 onion, chopped
   2 cloves garlic, crushed
   salt and pepper to taste
Refrigerate several hours or overnight to flavor chicken.
Brown chicken in large frypan in a little oil. Set aside.
Sauté in oil:
   1-2 tomatoes, chopped
   2 T. green pepper, chopped (30 ml)
Add:
   browned chicken pieces
   3 potatoes, cut in large pieces
   2-3 carrots, cut in large pieces
Season with:
   1-2 T. ground cumin (15-30 ml)
   1 T. cilantro, chopped (15 ml)
   2 t. paprika (10 ml)
   1/4 c. green onion, chopped (50 ml)
   salt and pepper to taste
Add:
   water, enough to cook, but not to cover
Bring to a boil. Cook on low until chicken and vegetables
are tender.
Serve with rice or spaghetti.

—*María Janete Rocha dos Santos, Belo Jardim, Brazil; and Crissie
   A. Graber, Colmeia, Brazil*

....

Residents of the
Bolivian community of
Barrio Lindo organized a
fiesta to celebrate the
eleventh anniversary of
their soccer field.
Everyone agreed to
contribute a kilogram of
rice and an armful of
firewood. Together they
purchased a heifer to
butcher and barbecue.

A few days before the
big event, 50 men
gathered to cut the grass
at the soccer field. It had
grown tall during the
rainy season. Armed with
sharp machetes, they
sang, joked, and talked
as they rhythmically
sheared the grass.

The people of Barrio
Lindo awoke in a festive
mood on the anniversary
day. During the morning
several men butchered
the cow and dug the
cooking pits. Women
cleaned and sorted rice
and peeled potatoes and
yucca, a tuberous root.

● ●

Creole Chicken (Dominican Republic)

Serves 6

Pollo Guisado
(POH-yoh gee-SAH-doh)

Pollo Guisado is the most typical Dominican dish—the first that every young cook learns to prepare. The same sauce is used with beef, pork, goat, and fish. Contributor writes that one chicken—neck and feet included—served with rice and beans, will feed up to 18 Dominicans.

Mix:
> **3 1/2 lb. chicken pieces (1.8 kg)**
> **2 cloves garlic, crushed**
> **1 1/2 t. dried oregano (7 ml)**
> **1 t. salt (5 ml)**
> **2 t. lemon juice or vinegar (10 ml)**
> **1/2 t. pepper (2 ml)**
> **2 t. Worcestershire sauce (10 ml)**
> **1 bay leaf**
> **1 green pepper, cut in strips**
> **1-2 medium onions, sliced**
> **2 T. fresh parsley, chopped (30 ml) (optional)**
> **1 T. cilantro, chopped (15 ml) (optional)**
> **2 whole allspice (optional)**

Marinate 1 hour or longer.
In saucepan, heat 2 T. oil (30 ml).
Add:
> **1 t. brown sugar (5 ml)**

Remove chicken pieces from spice mixture and brown in oil.
Add:
> **spice mixture**
> **1/4 c. tomato paste (50 ml)**
> **1 c. water (250 ml)**

Cover and cook until soft, adding water if necessary. Serve with rice and spoon sauce over rice. Garnish with capers and/or olives (optional).

—*Patricia Ebersole Zwier, Santo Domingo, Dominican Republic*

Girls chopped armfuls of green onions. Children carried gallons of water from the well.

By late afternoon, with most of the preparations completed, activity waned. Mothers took their children home to bathe and dress them. At dusk everyone gathered for the feast.

The soccer team served plate after plate of barbecued meat, rice, yucca, and salad. As diners finished their meals, women rinsed the dishes for the next seating. When the adults had eaten, the children lined up outside the kitchen hut to receive meat and yucca on large banana leaves.

After the meal men and women gathered to talk in separate small circles. Children played marbles and amused younger brothers and sisters. As the night wore on and small tired children gradually fell asleep in their mothers' arms, the crowd slowly dispersed. All were reluctant to leave, but tomorrow would dawn early with its many tasks.

—*Elena Linda Polsson, Port Simpson, British Columbia*

Sweet Chicken Curry with Yogurt (Bangladesh)

Murgir Korma
(moor-geer kohr-mah)

Yogurt, usually a side dish with curries, is included in the sauce of this tasty sweet curry served at weddings, birthdays, religious celebrations, and for special guests. For fuller flavor, marinate the chicken in the yogurt, garlic, and turmeric several hours before cooking, or prepare a day ahead and reheat before serving. Pilaf (p. 204) accompanies this dish.

• Options:
Substitute 21/2 t. curry powder for ground coriander, ground cumin, and ground red pepper (12 ml).
•
For additional flavor, add 2 t. ground turmeric (10 ml) and 1 T. lemon juice (15 ml) to yogurt.

In heavy pan, fry in 2 T. oil (30 ml) until soft and lightly brown:

3 medium onions, chopped
3 cloves garlic, minced

Add:

1/2 t. ground ginger (2 ml) or 4 slices ginger root, grated
5-6 whole cloves
5-6 whole cardamom pods or 1/2 t. ground cardamom (2 ml)
1-2 cinnamon sticks or 1 t. ground cinnamon (5 ml)
1 t. ground coriander (5 ml)
1 t. ground cumin (5 ml)
1/4-1/2 t. ground red pepper (1-2 ml) +!
1 t. salt (5 ml)

Fry 2-3 minutes, stirring constantly.
Add:

3-lb. chicken, skinned and cut in pieces (1.5 kg)

Brown on all sides. Mix and add:

1 c. yogurt (250 ml) (p. 295)
2 T. shredded coconut (30 ml)
2 T. raisins (30 ml) (optional)
1 c. water (250 ml) (optional, for more sauce)

Cover with tight-fitting lid and simmer 35-45 minutes, until chicken is tender. Serve hot with rice.

—Beronica Mendez and Gwen Heyerly Peachey, Sonapur, Bangladesh
—Ilene Bergen, London, Ontario
—Joanne Dirks, Akron, Pennsylvania

Shaadh (desire) is a Hindu celebration to honor a woman who is going to give birth to her first child. To mark the fifth, seventh, and ninth months of her pregnancy, and to satisfy her cravings for spicy and acidic foods, the mother-in-law invites married female friends and relatives to a meal.

At the fifth month, she prepares five different dishes; at the seventh month, seven different dishes; and at the ninth month, nine different dishes. The pregnant woman may eat whatever she desires. Guests bring gifts of clothing and jewelry, and red coloring to put in the part of her hair.

This celebration is widespread, even in the poorest villages. According to traditional Hindu belief, it is important to satisfy the mother's desires so that if she should die in childbirth, her soul will rest in peace. The practice also helps nourish the mother so she will give birth to a healthy child who will bring joy and laughter to the family.

—Ruma Ghosh, Howrah Women Association, Howrah, India

Asians serve curry dishes with spicy or sweet side salads or chutneys. Consider the following for curry meals: Sweet Tomato Chutney (p. 276), Tomato Chutney (p. 276), Peach Chutney (p. 277), Banana Yogurt and Cucumber Yogurt Salads (p. 118). End the meal with Spiced Tea (p. 31). (See p. 157 for a fuller description of curry dishes.)

Curried Chicken and Onions (India)

● ●

-*H*-

Serves 6

Murghi Dopiaza
(mur-gee doh-p'YAH-zah)

Murghi Dopiaza (double the onions) is a chicken and onion stew, rich with spices, a feast food in India and Bangladesh. Can be made a day ahead and reheated.

● *Options:*
Use equivalent amount of chicken thighs or drumsticks instead of whole chicken.
●
Use a little ground red pepper instead of green chili peppers.

Puree in blender:

3 medium onions, chopped
2-3 cloves garlic
1 T. ginger root, grated (15 ml)
1-3 fresh green chili peppers, seeded (optional) +!

Mix in:

1 T. ground coriander (15 ml)
1 T. ground cumin (15 ml)
2 t. ground turmeric (10 ml)
1 t. ground cinnamon (5 ml)
1 t. ground cardamom (5 ml)
1/4 t. ground cloves (1 ml)

Combine in large saucepan:

3-4 T. ghee or oil (45-60 ml)
3 onions, thinly sliced

Fry onions, stirring frequently, until golden brown. Remove onions and set aside. Add pureed mixture to oil remaining in pan. Stir and fry until color darkens.
Add:

3 chopped tomatoes, fresh or canned

Stir and cook until liquid from tomatoes is almost evaporated.
Add:

3-lb. chicken, cut in pieces (1.5-kg)

Stir well.
Add:

1 c. water (250 ml)
1 T. salt (15 ml)

Cover and cook 45 minutes or until chicken is tender. Top with fried onions and serve with rice or Chapatis (p. 48). Asians would serve chicken on bone, but it can be deboned if desired.

—*Charmayne Denlinger Brubaker, Lancaster, Pennsylvania*

Chicken and Snow Peas (Japan)

Toriniku to Sayaendo no
Itame
(toh-ree-nee-koo toh
sah-yah-en-doh noh
ee-tah-meh)

Fresh ginger root and sesame oil give this recipe its unique flavor. Tester wrote, "These ingredients are a bit higher priced, but the recipe was so special, it was worth it."

● Note:
Soy sauces vary greatly in quality. To find a quality soy sauce, ask someone experienced in Chinese cooking, or inquire at a local Asian food store about which brand names are most authentic.

Cut in 1-inch pieces (2.5-cm):
1/2 lb. chicken (250 g)
Sprinkle with:
1 t. ginger root, grated (5 ml)
Toss chicken and ginger root in mixture of:
2 T. cornstarch (30 ml)
1/4 c. water (50 ml)
Set aside.
Mix together:
3 T. broth or water (45 ml)
1 T. soy sauce (15 ml)
1 T. sugar (15 ml)
1/2 t. salt (2 ml)
1 t. sesame oil (5 ml)
pepper to taste
1 t. ginger root, grated (5 ml) (or more to taste)
In heated wok or frypan place:
3 T. oil (45 ml)
chicken pieces
Fry chicken, keeping pieces separate.
Add and fry briefly:
2 or more shiitake mushrooms, sliced thin (if dried, soak before slicing)
1/2 carrot, cut in 1 x 1/4-inch, thinly sliced rectangles (2.5 x .5-cm)
Add:
1/2 lb. snow peas (250 g)
Heat through. Add broth mixture and turn several times until broth is heated through. Serve immediately with rice.

—*Alice Ruth Ramseyer, Hiroshima, Japan*

T he Chinese cleaver, a large knife with a broad, heavy, razor-sharp blade, is a perfect tool for slicing, shredding, chopping, and mincing. It is strong enough to cut through chicken bones, and its sharp edge allows absolute precision in cutting vegetables into uniform pieces. In only a few seconds the cleaver can reduce onions and garlic to finely minced pieces. The broad side of the blade and the wooden handle are both ideal for crushing garlic or ginger root. Purchase at Asian stores. Use with a wooden chopping block.

Chicken Rendang (Malaysia)

● ●
-H-

Serves 4-5

Rendang Ayam (ren-DAHNG ah-yuhm)

Contributor says the spicy foods of Malaysia are among the best in the world! Rendang—meat with spices, coconut milk, and lemon grass—is a special dish served at religious celebrations and New Year's feasts. The final product is melt-in-your-mouth tender, fairly spicy-hot with definite coconut and lemon grass flavors.

● **Options:**
Malaysians use double the amount of hot chili peppers listed. Add or reduce chili peppers to taste.
●
Substitute stewing beef or lamb. You may want to increase spice amounts for stronger tasting meats.

Fry in 3 T. oil (45 ml):
   6 shallots or 1 large onion, chopped
   2 hot red chili peppers, cut lengthwise, or 1 t. dried hot red pepper (5 ml) +!
   3 t. ginger root, grated (15 ml)
   6 cloves garlic, crushed
When golden brown, add:
   2 lb. chicken breasts, skin removed, cut in medium pieces (1 kg)
   3 stalks fresh lemon grass, ends crushed, or 2 t. dried lemon grass (10 ml)
   2 c. water (500 ml)
   1 1/2 c. coconut milk (375 ml) (p. 280)
Bring to a boil. When chicken is almost cooked, add:
   1 t. sugar (5 ml)
   1 1/2 c. coconut milk (375 ml)
Return to a boil. Lower heat and allow chicken to simmer until very tender, about 1 1/2 hours. When done, chicken will begin to flake apart easily when stirred and much of liquid will be evaporated.
Add:
   salt to taste
Serve with rice and cucumbers sliced diagonally.

—*Barbara Yoder Beachy, Wakkanai, Japan*

Chicken Adobo (Philippines)

● ●

Serves 6

Adobong Manok (ah-DOH-bohng mah-NUK)

Tester calls this the best chicken he ever ate. Easy to prepare.

● **Option:**
Remove chicken pieces from broth when tender. Place on baking sheet and broil in oven until well browned. Return to sauce to serve.

Bring to a boil:
   3-lb. chicken, cut in serving pieces (1.5-kg)
   1/2 c. soy sauce (125 ml)
   2/3 c. vinegar (150 ml)
   1-2 cloves garlic, crushed
   2 bay leaves
   1 t. peppercorns or coarsely ground black pepper (5 ml)
Simmer about 50 minutes until chicken is tender and sauce is reduced by about half.
Add:
   salt to taste (optional)
Serve hot with rice.

—*Norrie del Fierro and Fannie P. Miray, Nueva Vizcaya, Philippines*
—*Carla Kaye Jones, Hampton, Virginia*
—*Lilian Occeña, East Lansing, Michigan*

Braised Chicken in Red Sauce (Thailand)

Gy Nam Daeng
(guy NAHM dang)

Thai food is traditionally spicy hot. You may vary amount of pepper sauce to taste. Serve with rice. Tasty with Coconut Rice (p. 204).

Serves 4-6

Cut in serving pieces:

3-lb. chicken (1.5-kg)

Rub with salt and pepper. Sauté in frypan in a little oil. Remove chicken from pan.

Sauté:

2 T. onion, chopped (30 ml)

Add:

1 T. ketchup (15 ml)
1 T. soy sauce (15 ml)
1 T. Worcestershire sauce (15 ml)
1-2 T. Tabasco pepper sauce (15-30 ml) +!
1 T. sugar (15 ml)
1 c. water (250 ml)

Mix well. Add chicken and braise, covered, over low heat about 1 hour or until tender. Add water if needed.

—*Thavee Sooksamwong, Bangkok, Thailand; and Janet Reedy, Hanoi, Vietnam*

Bang Bang Chicken (China)

Bang Bang Ji
(bahng bahng jee)

In China this dish is sold by street vendors who traditionally summoned customers by banging two sticks together; hence, the name.

Serves 4

In wok or frypan stir-fry briefly in 1-2 T. oil (preferably peanut) (15-30 ml), until chicken is cooked through:

1 whole chicken breast, cut in strips
1 clove garlic, minced
2 t. ginger root, grated (10 ml), or 1/8 t. ground ginger (.5 ml)
1 scallion, chopped in 1-inch pieces (2.5-cm)

Add:

1/4 c. water (50 ml)
2 T. soy sauce (30 ml)
2 T. peanut butter (30 ml)
1 T. red wine vinegar (15 ml)

Simmer 5 minutes. Add:

2 c. broccoli florets (500 ml)
1 cucumber, sliced

Cook until vegetables are crisp tender, about 7 minutes. Serve over rice.

—*Nav Jiwan International Tea Room, Ephrata, Pennsylvania*

Cashew Chicken (Thailand)

(ts)   -冊-   *Serves 4*

Gy Pad Met Mamuang
(guy pahd met
mah-MOO-ang)

Many variations of this quick and easy, tasty stir-fry abound in Thailand. Cashews are often costly; prepare for a special treat.

• *Option:*
Add 1-2 c. raw vegetables (broccoli, carrots, green peppers) (250-500 ml) along with onions.

Sauté 2-3 minutes in 2 T. oil (30 ml):
  1-1 1/2 lb. chicken cut in bite-size pieces (500-750 g)
Add:
  1 large onion, cut in 1/2-inch wedges (1-cm) or 8-10 green onions, cut in 1-inch lengths (2.5-cm)
  1-2 cloves garlic, minced or crushed
  2 t. ginger root, minced (10 ml), or 1/2 t. ground ginger (2 ml)
Fry until onions are tender-crisp and chicken is cooked through, about 3 minutes.
Add:
  1/8-1/2 t. ground red pepper (.5-2 ml) +!
  1/2 t. ground coriander (2 ml)
  4 t. soy sauce (20 ml)
  2-3 t. fish or oyster sauce (10-15 ml)
  3-4 T. water (45-60 ml)
  1 T. lemon juice (15 ml)
  1/2 t. ground cumin (2 ml) (optional)
Fry 1 minute longer to blend flavors.
Add:
  1/2-1 c. unsalted cashews, roasted or fried (125-250 ml)
Mix well. Serve immediately with rice.

—*Khun Deng and Lily Bérubé, Phanat Nikhom, Chonburi, Thailand*

Grilled Chicken (Laos)

Serves 4-6

Ping Gai
(bing gai)

This barbecued chicken is served with Sticky Rice (p. 144) and Jayo sauce (p. 283).

Mix sauce:
  3 cloves garlic, minced
  1/4 t. ground ginger or ginger root, grated (1 ml)
  1/2 t. pepper (2 ml)
  2 t. sugar (10 ml)
  2 T. soy sauce (30 ml)
  1 t. curry powder (5 ml)
  1/2 t. salt (2 ml)
  1 T. fish sauce (15 ml) (optional)
Marinate in sauce 30 minutes or longer:
  2 1/2 lb. chicken, cut up, or chicken pieces (1.3 kg)
Barbecue over charcoal fire or broil in oven, turning and basting until tender. Or bake on baking sheet (with sauce poured over) 10 minutes at 400°F (200°C), then at 350°F (180°C) 45 minutes or until tender.

—*Sompham Thadavong and Lois Foehringer, Vientiane, Laos*
—*Linda Peachey, Lancaster, Pennsylvania*

Onion Chicken (China)

Yang Cong Ji
(yahng tsong djee)

The chicken in this recipe is traditionally cut into chunks with the bone in, using a large meat cleaver. For example, a leg would be cut in two or three chunks. The amount of onions may bring some tears during cutting, but won't overpower the dish.

• *Option:*
Tester recommends using fryer wing drummettes for the small chicken pieces called for in this recipe.

Fry in large saucepan in 1/4 c. oil (50 ml) until transparent:
   3 lb. onions, sliced (1.5 kg) (about 8 c./2 L)
Remove onions and set aside.
Sauté, adding oil if needed:
   2-3 cloves garlic, chopped
   1-inch piece ginger root, chopped (2.5-cm), or
      1-2 t. ground ginger (5-10 ml)
Add:
   3-lb. chicken, cut in pieces (1.5-kg)
Fry until cooked through.
Add, stirring constantly:
   3 T. soy sauce (45 ml)
   salt and pepper to taste
   1/4 c. cooking sherry (50 ml) (optional)
Return onions to pan and cook until browned. Add:
   1 c. water (250 ml)
Turn heat to low, cover, and simmer 30-45 minutes, stirring occasionally.
After simmering, add:
   2 T. sugar (30 ml)
If gravy is too thin, add:
   2 T. cornstarch (30 ml), mixed with
   1/4 c. cold water (50 ml)
Heat through and serve over rice.

—Helen Lo, Hong Kong; and Nancy Kinsinger Halder, Parnell, Iowa

Chicken with Garlic and Ginger (Madagascar)

M

Akoho misy Sakamalao
(ah-KOO-hoo mee-see sha-kah-mah-LAH-oh)

Malagasy cooking is deliciously spiced with abundant garlic and fresh ginger. Use liberally when cooking a Malagasy meal. The original recipe called for crushing "plenty" of fresh ginger and garlic. Vary amounts to taste.

• *Option:*
Cover chicken and bake 50 minutes at 325°F (160°C). Uncover and bake another 10 minutes, or until tender.

Cut in serving pieces:
   3-lb. chicken (1.5-kg)
Remove chicken skin (optional).
Prepare:
   2-inch piece ginger root, grated or crushed (5-cm)
   6 cloves garlic, finely minced or crushed
Rub ginger and garlic into chicken. Sprinkle with a little salt. Place small amount of oil in large frypan, and gently cook chicken on low heat until done, about 40 minutes. Serve with rice.

• *Microwave:*
Marinate chicken in refrigerator 3 or more hours. Place chicken in round dish, with thick parts along edge of dish. Cover loosely and cook on high for 6-8 minutes or until tender. Turn after 4 minutes. Let stand, covered, 2-3 minutes.

—Annetta Miller, Nairobi, Kenya

Chicken with Peanut Sauce (Zaire)

●●●●●●●●●●●●●●●●●●●●●●●●●●●●●●●●

Serves 6

Nsoso ya Muamba
(n'SOH-soh yah
m'WAHM-bah)

Zairians serve Nsoso ya Muamba for special occasions—weddings, births, baptisms, welcomings. The traditional preparation is a lot of work: the peanuts are roasted, then hulled, then pounded into a coarse meal, then finally ground into a paste by hand.

• Option:
Instead of frying chicken, cook other ingredients in large saucepan, add uncooked chicken and sautéed ingredients, and simmer, covered, 40 minutes or until tender, then 10 more minutes, uncovered, to thicken.

Heat in large saucepan:
   2 T. oil (30 ml)
Fry until cooked through:
   3-lb. chicken, cut up, or chicken pieces (1.5-kg)
Add additional oil if needed to keep chicken from sticking. Set chicken aside.
Fry in remaining oil:
   1 large onion, sliced
   1-2 cloves garlic (optional)
Add:
   1 c. tomatoes, fresh or canned (250 ml)
   1/4 c. tomato paste (50 ml)
   1/2 c. peanuts, ground in blender, or chunky peanut butter (125 ml)
Add gradually and stir to make smooth sauce:
   1 c. water (250 ml)
Add:
   1 bay leaf
   2 T. celery or celery leaves, chopped (30 ml)
   1 t. salt (5 ml)
Cook a few minutes, stirring constantly. Return chicken to sauce. Stir to coat pieces well. Cover and cook over medium heat about 15 minutes. If too thick, add a little water. Serve over rice.

—*Berthe Mutchaila and Gloria Good, Kinshasa, Zaire*

Y ou visit the earth and water it,
   you greatly enrich it;
the river of God is full of water;
   you provide the people with grain,
   for so you have prepared it.
You water its furrows abundantly,
   settling its ridges,
softening it with showers,
   and blessing its growth.
You crown the year with your bounty;
   your wagon tracks overflow with richness.
The pastures of the wilderness overflow,
   the hills gird themselves with joy,
the meadows clothe themselves with flocks,
   the valleys deck themselves with grain,
   they shout and sing together for joy.

—*Psalm 65:9-13*

Chicken or Fish with Garlic and Lime Juice (Guadeloupe)

Poulet ou Poisson à L'ail
(poo-LAY oo pwah-SOHN ah LIE)

Contributor's son learned this recipe while studying in Guadeloupe.

• Option:
Reduce number of garlic cloves to taste.

Serves 2-4

Place in frypan:
   4 chicken pieces, skinned, or fish fillets
Rub with:
   7 cloves garlic, crushed
Squeeze over chicken or fish:
   juice of 3 limes
Add:
   1/2 t. ground red pepper (2 ml) or to taste +!
   1/2 t. salt (2 ml) or to taste
Add:
   approx. 1/2 c. water (125 ml)
Cook until dry. Add a little more water and cook until tender.
Serve with rice or potatoes, and salad or brightly colored vegetables.

—Annetta Miller, Nairobi, Kenya

Boiled Cod (Norway)

Kokt Torsk
(kohkt tohsk)

Cod is plentiful and inexpensive in Norway. When contributor Gerd Doroshuk was growing up there, her mother, Dagny Taranger, made this moist and tender dish weekly.

• Option:
Sprinkle chopped parsley over fish, omitting melted margarine.

(ts)

Serves 6

Bring to a boil:
   2-4 c. water (500-1000 ml)
   1-2 T. salt (15-30 ml)
   1 t. vinegar (5 ml)
   1/2 t. basil (2 ml) (optional)
Place in boiling water:
   3 lb. cod (1.5 kg)
Reduce heat; keep water just below boiling point to prevent fish from falling apart. Simmer 8 minutes. Remove fish from water and place on serving platter. Top with chopped parsley in melted margarine, or hollandaise sauce. Serve with boiled potatoes and carrots.

—Dagny Taranger, Frekhaug, Norway; and Gerd Doroshuk,
   Dauphin, Manitoba

Shrimp Curry (Bangladesh)

Chingri Mash Torkari
(cheen-gree mahsh
TOHR-kah-ree)

A favorite recipe from Bangladesh, where shrimp is readily available.

• Option:
Replace lemon grass with 3 T. lemon or lime juice (45 ml) or 1 t. grated lemon peel (5 ml).

Sauté in a small amount of oil until cooked through:
2 lb. shrimp, shelled and deveined (1 kg)
Set aside.
Sauté lightly in 2 T. oil (30 ml):
3 small onions, finely chopped
5 cloves garlic, finely chopped
2 stalks lemon grass, chopped
Add:
1/2 t. ground turmeric (2 ml)
1/2 t. ground cumin (2 ml)
1/4 t. ground ginger (1 ml)
1/8 t. pepper (.5 ml)
2 dried red chilies, finely cut (optional) +!
2 bay leaves
1/2 t. ground cinnamon (2 ml)
1/2 t. sugar (2 ml)
1 t. salt (5 ml)
Cook 5-10 minutes.
Add:
5 tomatoes, finely chopped
Cook 10 minutes.
Add:
2-3 c. coconut milk (500-750 ml) (p. 280)
Cook until mixture takes on curdled appearance, about 10 minutes.
Add shrimp and cook 10 minutes. Serve with rice.

—*Kimole Mankin, Haluaghat, Bangladesh; and Judy Nord, Dhaka, Bangladesh*

Meals in Bangladesh begin with handwashing since the right hand is used to scoop food into one's mouth. Because no other eating utensils are used, meat and vegetables are cut and cooked in small pieces. The left hand may be used to pick up a water glass or to handle a serving spoon. Hosts often choose to serve rather than eat with their guests. They place food on the plates, since it can be awkward for individuals to serve themselves with their left hand. Meals end as they begin, with handwashing.

Festive Shrimp with Coconut Sauce (Brazil)

Camarão com Molho de Coco (kah-mah-RAOWN kohn MOH-yoh deh KOH-koo)

This dish is especially popular during the Easter season in Brazil, when everything, including beans, is made with coconut milk. Serve with Festive Vegetable Platter (p. 108).

• Option:
Use any fish instead of shrimp. Coconut milk makes strong fish more mild and tasty.

●●●●●●●●●●●●●●●●●●●●●●●●●●●●●●

Serves 4-6

Heat in large frypan:
 1/4 c. oil (preferably olive) (50 ml)
Sauté:
 1 green pepper, chopped
 1 small onion, minced
 1 large tomato, chopped
 1 clove garlic, minced
Add:
 1 1/2 t. ground cumin (7 ml)
 1/3 c. cilantro, chopped (75 ml)
 1 1/2 lb. fresh or frozen shrimp, shelled and deveined (750 g)
Sauté a few minutes until cooked through.
Add:
 1 T. flour (15 ml) (optional, for thicker sauce)
Cook 1 minute. Add:
 approx. 2 c. coconut milk (500 ml) (p. 280)
Cook over low heat until thickened.
Add:
 salt and pepper to taste
Serve over rice and garnish with:
 3-4 chopped scallions

—Mert Brubaker, Lancaster, Pennsylvania

Quechua-speaking Indians in the Peruvian Andes use centuries-old communal forms of working the land and distributing the harvest so that the entire community is nourished. During years when some families do not harvest enough to eat, the community organizes an ancient feast called *kausay huñuy*, which means "collecting food to promote life."

The feast takes place at the home of the needy family. The family appoints one member, usually a woman, to serve as the *aqakamoyoq* (host). The *aqakamoyoq* prepares *chicha*, a strong corn drink, and provides a basket for measuring out the products donated during the feast. She spreads out a huge poncho or shawl in the family's patio where the food will be collected.

As neighbors come to contribute something, the *aqakamoyoq* offers them a glass of *chicha*. After visitors place their gift in the basket, the *aqakamoyoq* awards each basketful with another two glasses of *chicha*. Word spreads quickly that this family is serving good *chicha*, encouraging others to come and share.

When the poncho is full, the *aqakamoyoq* calls the family to collect and store the provisions. First they gather around the poncho, bless the crops, and give thanks to the Lord for such generosity. *Kausay huñuy* embodies the solidarity expressed in a common saying, "Today, this is for you: tomorrow it may be for me."[6]

Fish with Mango (Kenya)

•••••••••••••••••••••••••••••••

Serves 6

**Samaki na Embe
(sah-MAH-kee nah EHM-beh)**

Fish with Mango has a delightful tropical taste. Serve with rice. Good with Coconut Rice (p. 204).

• Option:
Substitute peaches for mangoes.

Combine in frypan:

**2 lb. white fish steaks, cut in large pieces (1 kg)
approx. 3/4 c. water (175 ml)
1 onion, thinly sliced or chopped
2 tomatoes, peeled and chopped
2 mangoes, peeled and chopped
1-2 chili peppers, seeded and chopped +!
1/2-1 t. salt (2-5 ml)**

Cover and simmer gently 20 minutes, or until cooked through.

• *Microwave:*
Thinly slice onion and place around outside edges of large round microwave-proof serving plate. Place fish steaks around edges on and next to onions. In center of plate put tomatoes, mangoes, and chili peppers in attractive pattern. Add quick sprinkle of salt over fish. Cover tightly and cook 8-12 minutes or until fish flakes easily.

—*Annetta Miller, Nairobi, Kenya*

Escoveitched Fish (Jamaica)

⒯ Ⓜ

•••••••••••••••••••••••••••••••

Serves 3-4

This Jamaican favorite is an example of Spanish influence in Jamaican cuisine. It is prepared with white fish and often served cold with dumplings and lemonade. Prepare a day ahead for an easy summer meal.

• *Microwave:*
Sprinkle fish with salt and pepper, as directed above. Cover tightly and cook on high 6-12 minutes, until it flakes easily. Place in serving dish and add marinade. Testers reported that both microwave and fried versions were excellent, although there was a slight preference for the taste of the crisp, fried version. Microwave version has no oil.

Prepare:

1 1/2 lb. fish (750 g)

If large fish are used, cut in 1/4-lb. slices (125-g).
Sprinkle fish with:

**1 t. pepper (5 ml)
1/2 t. salt (2 ml)**

Set aside.
Heat in frypan:

1/4 c. oil (50 ml)

Place fish in smoking hot oil and fry until both sides are crisp. Remove from oil, drain, place in serving dish, and set aside.

Marinade:

Drain excess oil from frypan and add ingredients:

**1/3 c. vinegar (75 ml)
2 medium onions, sliced
1 green or red sweet pepper, sliced
1/2 t. whole allspice (2 ml)
1/2 t. peppercorns (2 ml)
1 bay leaf (optional)
1/2 t. salt (2 ml) (optional)**

Bring to a boil. Simmer a few minutes until onion becomes tender. When cool, pour over fish and leave to steep at least 1 hour, preferably several hours. Serve either hot or cold. This will keep up to 3 days in the refrigerator.

—*Pauline Cousins, St. Mary, Jamaica*
—*Ulet (Shirley) Brown-Phillip, Bronx, New York*

Baked Fish with Wild Rice (Canada)

A delicious and elegant way to serve fish. Native Canadians traditionally roasted whole fish, most often walleye, over an open fire.

• *Option:*
Use equivalent amount of fish fillets and bake with stuffing.

● ●

Serves 4
350°F 180°C
30-35 min.

Scale and clean:

large walleye, northern pike, muskie, salmon, lake trout, or white fish (about 1 1/2 lb/750 g)

Remove head, tail, and fins. Wash thoroughly inside and out, and dry. Rub fish inside and out with:

juice of 3 lemons

Sprinkle lightly with salt. Cover and refrigerate 2 or more hours.

Stuffing:

Cook according to package directions, or see Rice (p. 142):

1 c. wild rice (250 ml)
3 c. water (750 ml)

Sauté in a little oil:

1 c. celery, chopped (250 ml)
1 large onion, chopped

Combine celery and onion with cooked wild rice and season with salt and pepper to taste.

Pour over rice mixture:

1/4 c. butter or margarine, melted (50 ml)
1/2 c. hot water (125 ml)

Stir well. Place fish on sheet of foil in roaster. Stuff fish loosely. Bring foil up halfway around fish to hold in stuffing.

Baste fish with:

1/4 c. melted butter mixed with a bit of lemon juice (50 ml)

Bake in 350°F oven (180°C) until meat flakes easily, 30-35 minutes. Baste occasionally. Carefully move fish to serving platter and heap rice around it. Serve with salad and fresh, crusty bread or Bannock (p. 54).

—*Marguerite E. Bright, and James and Kate Kroeker, Dinorwic, Ontario*

Contreras Fish Casserole (Mexico)

Cacerola de Pescado
(kah-say-ROH-lah day
payss-KAH-doh)

Green pepper and tomato team up with ground red pepper—as little or as much as you like—to give this fish casserole a Mexican flair. "One of my sons asked for seconds," reported one tester, "which he almost never does."

● ●

Ⓜ ┤H├

Serves 4-5
350°F 180°C
25-30 min.

Have ready:

2 c. brown rice, cooked (500 ml), or cook 2/3 c. brown rice (150 ml) in scant 1 1/3 c. water (325 ml) 40-45 minutes.

Bake 30 minutes at 350°F (180°C) (allow more time if fish is still frozen), or steam in vegetable steamer until it flakes easily:

1 lb. fresh or frozen fish (500 g)

Set aside.

(*more* →)

• *Microwave:*
Cook fish in ungreased, covered, 1 1/2-qt. casserole (1.5-L) on high 6-8 minutes, or until fish flakes easily with fork. Set aside. To make white sauce, cook margarine on high 45 seconds, or until melted, in 4-c. glass measuring cup (1-L). Stir in flour, salt, and pepper to form a smooth paste. Add milk and blend with wire whisk. Cook on high 4-5 minutes, stirring every 2 minutes, until bubbling and thickened. Add all ingredients to fish in casserole, as directed above. Cover casserole and microwave 10 minutes.

Melt in saucepan:

3 T. margarine (45 ml)

Add:

1 t. salt (5 ml)
dash-1 t. ground red pepper (5 ml) +!
3 T. flour (45 ml)

Stir in gradually:

1 1/2 c. milk (375 ml)

Cook over medium heat, stirring constantly, until mixture thickens. Set aside.

Layer in greased 1 1/2-qt. casserole (1 1/2-L) beginning and ending with rice:

cooked brown rice
cooked fish, flaked
1 green pepper, diced
1 tomato, diced

Pour white sauce over top and dot with:

1 T. margarine (15 ml)

Bake 25-30 minutes at 350°F (180°C).

—*Ernesto Contreras R., Tijuana, Mexico; and Carla Kaye Jones and George Switzer, Hampton, Virginia*

Fish with Parsley Sauce (Mexico)

• •
ⓣⓢ

Serves 6

Pescado al Perejil
(payss-KAH-doh ahl
pay-ray-HEEL)

• *Option:*
For stronger-flavored sauce, replace half the fresh parsley with 1/2 c. cilantro (125 ml).

Whirl in blender:

1 c. fresh parsley (250 ml)
1/2 c. water (125 ml)
2 T. lemon juice (30 ml)
2 cloves garlic, crushed

Wash and dry:

6 fish fillets

Lightly sprinkle fish with salt and pepper.
Heat in frypan:

1 T. margarine or oil (15 ml)

Add and fry until onion is transparent:

1/2 small onion, finely chopped
2 T. celery, chopped (30 ml)
1 bay leaf

Fry fish fillets on both sides about 10 minutes over low or medium heat.
Pour parsley sauce over fish and simmer 10 minutes.

—*Celine Vatterott Woznica, Oaxaca, Mexico*

Shredded Beef (Venezuela)

●●●●●●●●●●●●●●●●●●●●●●●●●●●●●●●●●●●

Serves 6

Carne Esmechada (CAR-nay ays-may-CHAH-dah)

Shredded Beef, served with rice, black beans, and fried plantains, is a popular Venezuelan meal. The beef, typically seasoned with ají dulce, a small flavorful sweet pepper, tenderizes with long, slow simmering. Can be prepared a day in advance and reheated.

Simmer until tender:
  2 lb. stewing beef or inexpensive cut of beef, cut in small pieces (1 kg)
Cool and pull into fine shreds. Set aside.
Sauté in 1-2 T. oil (15-30 ml):
  1 onion, minced
Add:
  1 t. garlic powder (5 ml)
  1/2 c. green peppers, chopped (125 ml)
  3-4 tomatoes, chopped
Cook until juice is nearly cooked away. Add meat, stir, cover, and continue cooking over low heat until meat has absorbed flavor of seasonings.

—*Vivian de Morales and Thata R. Book, Cagua, Venezuela*

Curried Goat (Jamaica)

●●●●●●●●●●●●●●●●●●●●●●●●●●●●●●●●●
-*H*-

Serves 4-6

This is almost a national dish in Jamaica, where it is served with rice or green bananas or both.

• Option:
Substitute lamb or beef for goat mutton.

Cut into 1-inch cubes (2.5-ml):
  2 lb. goat mutton (1 kg)
Season with:
  1 t. salt (5 ml)
  1/2 t. pepper (2 ml)
  1 large onion, chopped
  1 small red chili pepper, chopped and seeds removed +!
Rub in:
  1-2 T. curry powder (15-30 ml) +!
Allow to stand about 30 minutes.
Brown meat cubes briefly in:
  2 T. oil (30 ml) (optional).
Add:
  2 c. water (500 ml)
Cover tightly and simmer slowly until meat is tender.
Add:
  2 potatoes, diced
Cook until gravy becomes somewhat thick.

—*Pauline Cousins, St. Mary, Jamaica*

Stir-Fried Beef and Vegetables (China)

•••••••••••••••••••••••••••••••••••

(ts)　　　　　-H-　　　　　*Serves 3-4*

Xihongshi Niurou
(shee-hong-see new-roh)

In China a little meat or vegetable sauce is a topping for a lot of rice. The Chinese words for food and for rice are the same; anything that is put over the rice is just embellishment. Curry spice used in this recipe is the same curry used in Indian cooking; it is common in Szechwan Chinese cuisine.

Mix sauce together and set aside:
1 T. soy sauce (15 ml)
1 T. Worcestershire sauce (15 ml)
3 T. ketchup (45 ml)
2 t. curry powder (10 ml) or to taste +!
1/4 t. crushed red pepper (1 ml) or to taste +!
1/4 c. water (50 ml)

In separate bowl, mix:
1/2-3/4 lb. beef tenderloin or boneless sirloin
(250-375 g), cut into thin slices about
1/8-inch wide (1/4-cm) and 11/2-2 inches long
(3-5 cm)

(It is easiest to cut beef into thin slices when it is partially frozen.)
2 t. cornstarch (10 ml)
2 t. soy sauce (10 ml)
11/2 t. oil (7 ml)

Heat 2 T. oil (preferably peanut) (30 ml) in wok or frypan. Add:
1 t. ginger root, minced (5 ml)
1 clove garlic, minced

Cook a minute. Add beef mixture and stir-fry until meat is brown, about 2 minutes. Remove meat with slotted spoon and set aside.
Add:
2 large stalks celery, cut in diagonal (slanting)
1/4-inch slices (.5-cm)
1 large onion, cut in wedges and separated
additional oil, if needed
Stir-fry 1-2 minutes. Add:
1 green pepper, cut in 1-inch squares (2.5-cm)

Stir-fry another minute. Add a few drops of water, cover, and steam vegetables until crisp-tender.
Add:
1-2 tomatoes, cut in wedges

Return meat to wok and add sauce. Stir and heat through until bubbling hot. Serve over rice.

—*Agnes Hubert, Winnipeg, Manitoba*

....

*T*he end of an ox is beef, and the end of a lie is grief.

—*African proverb*

African Meatballs (Chad)

Kanda
(KAHN-dah)

The flavor of seeds adds a special touch to this meatball and sauce recipe.

• Options:
Substitute pumpkin or squash seeds for melon seeds.
•
Adjust amount of water for thicker or thinner sauce.

Meatballs:
Grind in meat grinder, food processor, or blender:
   1/4 c. green onions, chopped (50 ml)
   1/4 c. celery, chopped (50 ml)
   2 T. fresh parsley, chopped (30 ml)
   3 cloves garlic, chopped
   1 lb. ground beef (500 g)
Put through food processor or whirl in blender:
   1 c. sesame seeds (250 ml)
   11/2 c. melon seeds (375 ml)
Add a bit of water if needed to make blending possible.
Combine meat and seed mixtures.
Add:
   1-11/4 t. salt (5-6 ml)
   1/4 t. pepper (1 ml)
Form into small meatballs.
Heat a little oil in frypan and cook:
   meatballs
   1 onion, chopped
Brown and simmer 5 minutes.
Remove from frypan and prepare sauce in same pan.
Sauce:
Sauté in 1/4 c. oil (50 ml):
   1 onion, chopped
   1/4 c. tomato paste (50 ml)
   1/2 t. salt (2 ml)
   1 bouillon cube
Add and bring to a boil:
   2 c. water (500 ml)
Place meatballs in sauce and cook 10 minutes. Serve alone or over rice.

—Thamar Nelimta Oumar, Bitkine, Chad; and Anita Hostetler, N'Djamena, Chad

....

A hand-washing ceremony precedes formal meals in Botswana. Two women, sometimes younger girls, move from guest to guest. One carries a pitcher of water and the other carries a basin and a towel. They pour water over each guest's hands into the basin and offer the towel for drying. When all hands are washed, a senior member of the group prays and the people sit down to be served, usually by the younger women.

Beef Wat
(Ethiopia)

-🔳-

Serves 6

Siga Wat
(si-gah wahtt)

*For an Ethiopian feast, serve
with Chicken Wat (p. 221),
Ethiopian Vegetable Stew
(p. 178) or Lentil Salad
(p. 108), and Injera (p. 47).
Yogurt or a yogurt salad will
help cut the heat. This can
easily be made ahead of time
and reheated.*

• Options:
Substitute stewing beef and
cook until tender.
•
This is very spicy hot. Begin
with 1 t. (5 ml) ground red
pepper and substitute
paprika for the rest.
•
This is always eaten with
Injera in Ethiopia, but is also
tasty with rice.

Heat on low in heavy saucepan:
  1/4 c. margarine or oil (50 ml)
  2 large onions, finely chopped
  2 cloves garlic, minced
Cook gently until onions are soft, but do not brown.
Add:
  3 T. ground red pepper (45 ml) +!
  3/4 t. pepper (3 ml)
  3/8 t. ground ginger (1.5 ml)
  3/8 t. ground cloves (1.5 ml)
  3/4 t. ground cinnamon (3 ml)
Simmer 1-2 minutes.
Add:
  **2 lb. beef tenderloin or boneless sirloin (1 kg),
     chopped in approx. 1/2-inch squares (1-cm)**
  1/2 t. salt (2 ml)
Simmer about 30 minutes until meat is tender and flavors
are well absorbed.

—*Charmayne Denlinger Brubaker, Lancaster, Pennsylvania*

*D*isznotar, a ritual
pig-killing feast, is an
important autumn event
in Hungarian peasant
households. Invited
guests and relatives
arrive early in the morning
to drink coffee before the
butchering begins. They
gather around the
warmth of crackling wood
fires, which are heating
water in huge metal
cauldrons.

The pig, the main
attraction of the day, lies
in his sty oblivious to his
coming fate. When every-
thing is ready, several men
bring the kicking and
screaming hog to the barn-
yard. Two men hold the
struggling animal down
while a third plunges a knife
into the pig's throat.
Suddenly all is silent.

It is an unsettling
experience to witness a
living creature being put

to death. Even peasant
men and women who live
intimately with the knowledge that there is a time
to plant and a time to
harvest, a season to kill
and a season to heal, are
appropriately solemn.
There is no joy in such a
task—only the grim
realization that it has to
be done.

When the killing is
finished, a woman brings
a glass of *palinka*, a plum
brandy. In an old Hungar-
ian custom, the three men
share the glass of strong
spirits as they stand over
the dead animal.

Only when the slaugh-
tering is completed does
the mood become festive.
After burning away the
pig's hair with a large
propane torch, knives
come out again to scrape
the hide. Before long
people start to sample

the scorched skin and
nibble at the ears and tail.

The pig is turned on its
back to be carved.Hams
and shoulders are
removed, and then the
innards. Here the women
join the work. They thor-
oughly clean and wash
the stomach and intes-
tines, which they will use
as casings for sausage.

Everyone present
enjoys two huge meals
during the day. Before
the evening meal, the
grandfather of the farm
household calls everyone
together for a heartfelt
prayer of thanksgiving.
When the guests leave
the farm late in the evening, the hosts load them
with sausage, stuffed
cabbage, and bottles of
homemade wine.

—*Joseph Miller, Ephrata,
  Pennsylvania*

Meat Loaf
(South Africa)

•••••••••••••••••••••••••••••••

Serves 4-6

350°F 180°C

45-50 min.

Bobotie
(boh-BOH-tee)

*This glorified meatloaf
flavored with curry is a
favorite South African dish.
The soybean version comes
from Cape Town.*

Soak 1 large slice bread in:
3/4 c. milk (175 ml)
In frypan, melt:
1 T. margarine (15 ml)
Add and fry until golden:
1/2 c. onion, chopped (125 ml)
Add:
1 T. curry powder (15 ml) +!
1/2 t. sugar (2 ml)
1 t. ground turmeric (5 ml) (optional)
1/4 t. salt (1 ml)
dash of pepper
1 T. lemon juice or vinegar (15 ml)
In mixing bowl, combine:
soaked bread (squeeze out milk and reserve)
fried onions and seasonings
1 egg
1 lb. ground beef or turkey (500 g)
Mix well.
Put into well-greased casserole or loaf pan.
Whisk together and pour over meat:
1 egg
reserved milk
dash of salt and pepper
Bake at 350° (180°C) 45-50 minutes, or until egg mixture
is set. Serve with rice or potatoes, and chutney.

• *Variation:*
**For Soybean Bobotie, substitute 2 c. cooked, mashed
soybeans (500 ml) for ground beef. Use 2 slices of bread
instead of 1 slice; 11/4 c. onions (300 ml); add 2 T. raisins
(30 ml) and 1 T. tomato sauce or ketchup (15 ml). After
placing in casserole, insert 3 bay leaves in upright position.**

—*Olga Reimer, Natal, South Africa*
—*Gudrun Mathies, Elmira, Ontario*

One day while living in the village of Rhamu in far northeast Kenya, we went to help our Somali friends Barre and Maryan build a mud-brick oven. While we worked, their children and ours chased and played with the loose goat in their compound.

At some point during the day the goat disappeared, only to reappear again in Maryan's kitchen in the form of curry and fried meat. As we ate the savory preparation, Barre explained that it was customary to kill a goat to serve one's guests and family for a special occasion. Later we observed another custom. Barre and Maryan served the leftovers to poor people who came by the compound, knowing that a special occasion was in progress. Such expressions of hospitality and concern for the poor were common in Rhamu.

—*Nancy Brubaker, Lancaster, Pennsylvania*

Stewed Beef
(Malawi)

Serves 4-6

Ndiwo za Nyama
(en-DEE-woh zah
en-YAH-mah)

*Many Malawians can afford to
eat only two meals each day:
one at midmorning after
working in the garden, the
other at midafternoon.
Stewed beef would be eaten
only on special occasions,
and each person would eat
only one or two pieces of
meat. They would fill up on
cornmeal porridge and a
vegetable sauce.*

• *Option:*
Substitute 2-3 lb. cut-up
chicken (1-1.5 g) for the
beef. Omit flour. Increase
tomatoes to 3. In some areas
of Malawi, a whole cooked
egg yolk added to chicken
stew is considered a
specialty.

Cut in 1-inch cubes (2.5-cm):
1 lb. round steak, chuck, or stewing beef (500 g)
Sprinkle beef with:
2 T. flour (30 ml) (optional)
In heavy saucepan, brown beef in 1 T. cooking oil (15 ml).
Add and sauté:
1 medium onion, sliced
1 clove garlic, crushed (optional)
Add and stir-fry lightly:
2 medium ripe tomatoes, peeled and sliced
Add:
2 c. water (500 ml)
1 t. salt (5 ml) or to taste
1/2 t. pepper (2 ml) or to taste
Bring to a boil. Reduce heat, cover, and simmer 30-45
minutes, or until meat is tender. Serve with Nshima
(p. 151) or rice, and Cabbage and Tomato Sauce (p. 123).

• *Option:*
Add 1/2 c. dried beans (125 ml), presoaked and drained.
Increase simmering time to 1 hour, or until beans are tender.
Add more water if needed.

—*Dorcas Chilimapunga, Malawi; and Gudrun Mathies, Elmira, Ontario*

Gingery Meat Stew
(Malaysia)

Serves 4

Masak Merah
(mah-sahk mair-ah)

Melt in frypan:
1 T. margarine (15 ml)
Add and sauté:
1 small onion, minced
1/2 inch ginger root, grated (1 cm)
dash of ground coriander
dash of ground turmeric
Add:
15-oz. can tomato sauce (475 g)
1 large onion, sliced
1 t. chili powder (5 ml)
Bring to a boil. Reduce heat, cover, and simmer 10 minutes.
Add:
1/4 t. salt (1 ml)
1 t. sugar (5 ml)
1 lb. beef, cubed, or chicken, cut in pieces (500 g)
Return to a boil. Simmer covered until meat is tender,
50-60 minutes. Serve with rice.

—*Jenny Wong, Malaysia; and Carla Kaye Jones and George
Switzer, Hampton, Virginia*

Groundnut Stew (Ghana)

Nketia Fla
(en-KEH-tee-ah flaw)

This West African favorite—a flavorful blend of beef, tomatoes, peanuts, ginger, and red pepper—is sure to surprise and please.

• *Option:*
Use chicken pieces instead of beef.

In heavy frypan or saucepan, brown in 1 T. oil (15 ml):

1 lb. round steak, chuck, or stewing beef, cubed (500 g)

When browned, add 1 T. oil (15 ml) and sauté:

2 c. onions, chopped (500 ml)
1 clove garlic, minced

Add:

ground red pepper to taste +!
1/2 t. ground ginger (2 ml) or 1 T. ginger root, minced (15 ml)
2 c. stewed tomatoes (500 ml) or 2 large fresh tomatoes, mashed
1 beef bouillon cube
1 t. salt (5 ml)
2 c. water (500 ml)
reserved beef

Cover and simmer 30 minutes, or until meat is tender.
In small bowl, mix:

1/2 c. peanut butter (125 ml)
1/4 c. liquid from stew (50 ml)

Slowly stir peanut butter mixture into stew. Cover and simmer, stirring frequently, another 30 minutes. Add more water to thin, if necessary. Add more ground red pepper and salt to taste. Serve with rice.

—Kwali, Amasaman, Ghana; and Erma Grove, Goshen, Indiana

The people of Papua New Guinea celebrate occasions such as weddings, funerals, and dances, with a *mumu*. A *mumu* is both a celebration and a cooking method. Men dig a pit in the ground, place firewood and rocks in it, then build a fire under the rocks to heat them. Women clean and prepare sweet potatoes, yams, corn, tapioca and taro (starchy roots), and a variety of greens.

When the rocks are hot, bamboo tubes are placed among them. Banana leaves are spread over the rocks and food is layered on top, beginning with root vegetables, meat (pork is preferred), and then leaf vegetables. Another layer of banana leaves covers the food, protecting it from the dirt that is piled on top. After water is poured down the bamboo tubes, the tubes are removed and the holes plugged. The food is left to steam in this underground cooker.

The *mumu* requires about three hours to cook, leaving time to relax and socialize after the hard work of preparation. When the food is ready, the dirt is carefully removed and the food is dished into large serving containers. Individuals receive generous portions on banana leaves, and eat with their fingers. Guests return home with leftovers for the following day.[7]

—Anne Wideman, Ukarumpa via Lae, Papua New Guinea

Pot of Beef (Costa Rica)

Serves 10-12

Olla de Carne
(OH-yah day CAHR-nay)

This traditional Sunday meal is usually prepared by the mother of a large, grown-up family for her children and grandchildren who come to visit. Sundays are often farmers' market days, so the vegetables used are extra fresh. In addition to the vegetables listed below, Costa Ricans add yucca, a starchy root, and chayote, a small squash.

• *Variation:*
Argentines make a similar dish called *puchero* with beef or chicken, and without cilantro. After removing cooked meat and vegetables from broth, they add soup pasta instead of rice to make a first-course soup. They accent the meat and vegetables with Chimichurri, Argentine Meat Sauce (p. 287).

Combine in large soup pot:
   6 qt. water (1.5 L)
   4-6 beef bouillon cubes
   2 lb. round steak, brisket, or inexpensive cut of beef, cut in chunks (1 kg)
   pepper to taste
   1 large onion
   3 large celery stalks
   1 large sprig fresh parsley
   1 large sprig cilantro (optional)
   2 medium tomatoes, peeled (optional)
   2 bay leaves (optional)
Bring to a boil and simmer at least 1 hour.
Meanwhile, choose several (at least 5) of the following vegetables and cut in large chunks:
   corn on the cob
   sweet potatoes, peeled
   potatoes, peeled
   squash
   cauliflower
   cabbage
   zucchini
   carrots, peeled
   plantain, peeled
When broth is flavorful, remove onion, celery, parsley, cilantro, and bay leaves. Add salt to taste. Add vegetables to broth, adding harder ones first and cooking a while before adding quicker-cooking vegetables, so all cook evenly.
Place vegetables and meat on serving platter. Ladle broth into individual bowls. Serve with rice, lemon quarters, and avocado slices (optional) for each person to add to broth as desired. Meat and vegetables are eaten on side dish or added to broth. Costa Ricans cook squash with peel; people remove peel as they eat.

—*Bitinia Sosa Herrera and Beverlee Ludema, San José, Costa Rica*

A Catholic priest serving a poor community in the Philippines, where few could afford to eat meat on a regular basis, noticed that meat was always less expensive on Friday. Since the majority Catholic population traditionally abstains from meat on that day, there was less demand and thus a lower price. Convinced that the well-being of his parishioners was more important than tradition, the priest named another day of the week as the fast day for his parish. That way the poor of his congregation could still fast, but also afford to buy meat at least once a week.

—*Elizabeth Dominguez, Manila, Philippines*

Meat and Potato Curry (India)

●●●●●●●●●●●●●●●●●●●●●●●●●●●●

Serves 6

Gosht Alu Tarkari
(gohsht AH-loo
tahr-KAHR-ee)

Serve this flavorful curry with rice, Puris (p. 49), and Spiced Tea (p. 31). Remove the whole spices before serving or while eating. Since the flavors improve with sitting, make a day in advance, refrigerate, and reheat for a company meal.

• Option:
Use 2 1/2 lb. chicken pieces (1.25 kg) instead of beef. Reduce first cooking time from 1 hour to 30-35 minutes.

Melt in saucepan:
   1/4 c. margarine (50 ml)
Add and brown:
   2 lb. beef roast, cubed (1 kg)
Add and brown:
   1 large onion, chopped
   1/2 t. caraway seed (2 ml)
   1/2 t. peppercorns (2 ml)
   1 large bay leaf, crushed
   1/2 t. ground ginger (2 ml)
   1/2 t. ground turmeric (2 ml)
   1/2 t. ground coriander (2 ml)
   1 clove garlic, chopped
   1/4 t. ground cloves (1 ml) or 2-3 whole cloves
   1 cinnamon stick
   salt to taste
   2 cardamom pods (optional)
Add:
   3-4 c. tomatoes, chopped, or tomato juice (750-1000 ml)
Simmer 1 hour. Then add:
   2-3 potatoes, cubed
   1-2 T. curry powder (15-30 ml) +!
   salt to taste
Cook until meat and potatoes are tender. Add a little water if needed.

—*Selma Unruh, North Newton, Kansas*

Ground Beef Curry (Kenya)

●●●●●●●●●●●●●●●●●●●●●●●●●●●●●

(ts)

Serves 4-6

Kima Curry
(KEE-mah KUR-ree)

Contributor Omar Yusuf runs a small restaurant in the heart of Nairobi, Kenya's capital, and serves Swahili dishes from the coast of East Africa.

In frypan sauté in 2 T. oil (30 ml) until browned:
   1 c. onions, sliced (250 ml)
   1 lb. lean ground beef (500 g)
Skim fat.
Add:
   1 1/2 t. curry powder (7 ml)
   5 cloves garlic, crushed
   1 T. ginger root, crushed (15 ml) or 1 t. ground ginger (5 ml)
   3 medium tomatoes, sliced
Fry briefly and add:
   1 T. tomato paste (15 ml)
   (*more* →)

1/2 t. ground cinnamon (2 ml)
1 T. cilantro, chopped (15 ml)

Stir and add:

1/2 c. water (125 ml)
salt to taste

Cook 20 minutes over medium heat to blend flavors. Serve over rice or with Chapatis (p. 48).

—Omar Yusuf and Annetta Miller, Nairobi, Kenya

● ●

Simple Beef Curry (India)

-**H**-

Serves 4

Gosht Kari
(gohsht KAH-ree)

In India this curry is sometimes made with goat meat. Unlike beef and pork, which are prohibited in some religious dietary codes, goat meat is acceptable to Hindus, Muslims, Jews, and Christians.

• *Options:*
Substitute 4 dried red chili peppers for green chili peppers.
•
Substitute 1 1/2 t. ground coriander (7 ml) for the cilantro (fresh coriander).

Brown in 2 T. heated oil (30 ml):

1/2 c. onion, chopped (125 ml)
1 clove garlic, minced
3/4 t. ground ginger (3 ml) or 1 1/2 t. ginger root, minced (7 ml)
2-3 green chili peppers, seeded and minced, or 1/4-1/2 t. ground red pepper (1-2 ml) +!

Add:

3/4 t. ground turmeric (3 ml)
1 T. water (15 ml)
1/2 t. ground cumin (2 ml)

Stir uncovered until all or most liquid evaporates.
Add:

1 lb. round steak or chuck roast, cubed (500 g)
1/2 t. salt (2 ml) or to taste
3 c. tomatoes, chopped (750 ml)
3 bay leaves (optional)

Simmer until meat is tender.
Just before serving, add:

1/4 c. cilantro, finely chopped (50 ml)

Serve with rice or Chapatis (p. 48). Can be made a day ahead of time and reheated.

—Rose Chater and Cynthia Peacock, Calcutta, India
—Junus, Chandwa, India; and Sue Neufeld, Herschel, Saskatchewan

The most important part of eating in Bangladesh that we have retained is the ratio of meat or lentils to rice. In Bangladesh one takes two to three large scoops of rice and one smaller spoon of meat or lentil curry. We continue to balance our foods in that way and have found it healthful. It just feels good! With the current recommendation from nutritionists that 50 percent of our calories come from carbohydrates, we realize the wisdom of this eating pattern.

—Ilene Bergen, London, Ontario

Venison and Wild Rice Stew (Canada)

Serves 6-8

A simple stew with the special flavor of wild game and wild rice. For the story of the origin of wild rice, see p. 205.

• *Options:*
Substitute beef for venison.
•
Add a little oregano or basil.
•
Add more chopped vegetables, such as carrots or zucchini.

Place in large heavy saucepan:
   3 1/2 lb. shoulder of venison, cut in large cubes (1.8 kg)
   2 qt. water (2 L)
   2 onions, quartered
   2 stalks celery, chopped
   1 clove garlic, minced
Simmer 3 hours or until venison is tender.
Add:
   2 t. salt (10 ml)
   1/8 t. pepper (.5 ml)
   1 1/2 c. wild rice, washed in cold water (375 ml)
Cover and simmer 25 minutes. Stir, then simmer, uncovered, another 15 minutes or until rice is completely tender and most of liquid is absorbed.

—*Menno Wiebe, Winnipeg, Manitoba*

Sesame Grilled Beef (Korea)

(ts)

Serves 5-6

Pul Goki
(bool goh-KEE)

Serve Pul Goki (fire meat) with Korean Mixed Vegetables (p. 214) or Kim Chi (p. 106) and rice. Korean desserts are typically fresh fruit. Try Simple Watermelon Dessert (p. 299).

Thinly slice:
   1 1/2 lb. boneless beef (sirloin, top round, or chuck) (750 g)
Mix and add to meat:
   1 T. Toasted Sesame Seeds (15 ml) (p. 290)
   1/4 c. soy sauce (50 ml)
   2 T. sesame oil (30 ml)
   2 T. sugar (30 ml)
   1 green onion, finely chopped
   2 cloves garlic, minced
   dash of pepper
Refrigerate and marinate 1-2 hours. To cook, barbecue over charcoal, broil in oven, bake in oven at 375°F (190°C), or stir-fry in wok. Stir frequently and cook just until both sides are browned. Serve immediately.

—*Yon Sook Suh, Seoul, Korea; and Pat Yoder, Goshen, Indiana*
—*Catherine Baer, Goshen, Indiana*

A festive Korean meal includes a variety of dishes, perhaps as many as 20. Nevertheless, the hostess will apologize for the inadequacy of her offerings, saying, "There is nothing here, but eat much!"

Shish Kebab with Peanut Sauce (Indonesia)

● ●

(ts)

Serves 4-6

Sate Ayam
(sah-tay ah-YAHM)

These tasty kebabs were a favorite with recipe testers.

• *Options:*
Double marinade and use for whole cut-up chicken.
•
Replace Sweet Soy Sauce with regular soy sauce plus 1 T. brown sugar.

In deep bowl, combine:

> **1 t. garlic, finely chopped (5 ml), or 1/2 t. garlic powder (2 ml)**
> **2 T. Sweet Soy Sauce (30 ml) (p. 281)**
> **2 t. lemon juice or vinegar (10 ml)**

Add:

> **3 c. chicken or quality cut of beef, cut in 1-inch cubes (2.5-cm) (750 ml)**

Toss well. Marinate at least 30 minutes. Thread meat on skewers. Brush lightly with oil. Barbecue or broil until crisp and brown. Dip in Hot Peanut Sauce (p. 282). Serve with rice.

—Anne Warkentin Dyck, Swift Current, Saskatchewan
—Mary Wenger, Versailles, Missouri

Skewered Ground Meat (Iraq)

● ●

Serves 4

Kafta
(KAHF-tah)

Variations of this dish are common throughout the Middle East. This recipe comes from the contributor's home community, Kirkuk, Iraq.

• *Options:*
Use ground turkey.
•
While preparing meatballs, marinate large chunks of tomatoes, onions, green peppers, or eggplant in sauce made of equal parts of olive oil and lemon juice, with a dash of salt and pepper. Thread vegetables on skewers and grill alongside meat.

Combine:

> **1 lb. ground beef or lamb (500 g)**
> **1 onion, finely minced or grated**
> **1 egg, beaten**
> **1/4 c. bread crumbs (50 ml)**
> **1/4 c. parsley leaves, finely minced (50 ml)**
> **1/2 t. salt (2 ml) or to taste**
> **pepper to taste**
> **1/2 t. cinnamon (2 ml) (optional)**

Wet hands in water and knead mixture thoroughly. Cover and refrigerate 2 hours. Divide mixture into 6 parts. Dampen hands and pat mixture around 6 skewers into long, flattened patties, about 1 1/2 inches wide (3.5 cm) and 4-5 inches long (10-12.5 cm). Grill or broil in oven until browned and cooked through, about 10-12 minutes. Serve with pita bread (p. 51) or Brown Rice with Vermiceilli (p. 208).

• *Variation:*
For Shish Kebab, marinate 1 lb. lamb or beef cubes (500 g) in mixture of 1 1/2 T. vinegar (20 ml), 1 1/2 T. olive or other oil (20 ml), 1 coarsely chopped onion, 1/2 t. salt (2 ml), and 1/4 t. pepper (1 ml) at least 2 hours. Grill or broil 7-10 minutes until browned and cooked medium rare or well done, as preferred.

—Betty Joseph, Lancaster, Pennsylvania

Shanghai Ham (China)

••••••••••••••••••••••••••••••••

Serves 6-8

Hongshao Zhurou
(hong-shaow djoo-roh)

This fresh pork roast is rich with the flavors of soy, ginger, and anise. A holiday dish, served hot or cold.

Place in large saucepan, Dutch oven, or pressure cooker:
> **4 lb. fresh pork ham, butt, or shoulder (2 kg)**
> **3/4 c. soy sauce (175 ml)**
> **1/4 c. sugar (50 ml)**
> **2 T. lime juice (or dry sherry, optional) (30 ml)**
> **1-inch ginger root, sliced (2.5-cm)**
> **2 cloves garlic, whole or cut in quarters**
> **2-3 anise stars**
> **2 c. water (500 ml)**

Bring to a boil, cover, and simmer until very tender, about 3 hours. Turn pork occasionally to absorb sauce evenly. Remove cover, increase heat and cook about 15-20 minutes, basting occasionally, until only about 1 c. liquid (250 ml) remains. Skim off fat and serve ham hot or cold.

—*Ruth Yu Hsiao, Cambridge, Massachusetts; and Harriet Burkholder, Goshen, Indiana*

Pork Vindaloo (India)

•••••••••••••••••••••••••••••••
-🔳-

Serves 4

Shikar Vindaloo
(SHEE-kahr vin-DAH-loo)

A rich and spicy dish. To serve more people, double amount of pork, and keep the same amount of sauce.

• Option:
This is a hot and fiery dish in India, where chili powder mixtures are much hotter than North American versions. For more spice, substitute ground red pepper for part of chili powder.

Grind or blend in blender, into paste:
> **1 T. cumin seed (15 ml)**
> **1 T. mustard seed (15 ml)**
> **1 T. coriander seed (15 ml)**
> **10 cloves garlic**
> **1-inch piece ginger root (2.5-cm)**

Cut in small pieces and set aside:
> **1 lb. pork (500 g)**

Heat in 2 T. oil (30 ml):
> **1 onion, sliced**

Add and cook another minute:
> **spice paste**
> **1 T. chili powder (15 ml) +!**
> **1 T. ground turmeric (15 ml)**

Add:
> **pork pieces**
> **1 t. salt (5 ml) or to taste**

Fry until pork is browned.
Add:
> **1/2 c. vinegar (125 ml)**

Cook 3 minutes.
Add:
> **1 c. water (250 ml)**

Continue cooking until meat is tender, about 40 minutes. Serve with rice.

—*Lizzy Thomas, Madras, India; and Cynthia Peacock, Calcutta, India*

Diced Pork with Peanuts (China)

●●●●●●●●●●●●●●●●●●●●●●●●●●●●●●●
-H-

Serves 3

Huasheng Rouding
(hwah-shuhng roh-ding)

Szechwan cooking is famous for hot, spicy dishes like this one, commonly served alongside a stir-fried vegetable dish.

• *Options:*
Substitute chicken breast for pork.
•
Replace Chinese hot oil with 1/8-1/2 t. ground red pepper (.5-2 ml) and 1 t. sesame oil (5 ml). +!
•
Add chopped sugar peas or Chinese cabbage when adding hot chili peppers.

Cut in 1/2-inch cubes (1-cm):
1 lb. pork tenderloin (500 g)
Add to mixture of:
1 T. soy sauce (15 ml)
1 1/2 T. cornstarch (20 ml)
1 1/2 T. cold water (20 ml)
Marinate about 20 minutes.
In small bowl, combine and set aside:
1 T. lime juice (15 ml)
1 1/2 T. soy sauce (20 ml)
1 T. sugar (15 ml)
1 t. vinegar (5 ml)
1 t. cornstarch (5 ml)
1 t. sesame oil (5 ml)
1/2 t. salt (2 ml) (optional)
In frypan, sauté in 1 T. oil (15 ml):
1 t. ginger root, chopped (5 ml)
marinated pork
2 hot chili peppers, chopped (optional) +!
Stir-fry 5-7 minutes until pork is tender and browned. Pour in seasoning sauce. Simmer and mix thoroughly until thickened, 5-7 minutes.
Sprinkle in:
1/2-2 t. Chinese hot oil (2-10 ml) +!
Add:
1/2 c. unsalted roasted peanuts (125 ml)
Mix well. Serve immediately with rice.

—Harriet Burkholder, Goshen, Indiana

....

In China, a fair-weather friend is known as a *jiu-rou pengyou*—a wine-and-pig friend.

Weddings are an occasion to eat meat in South Africa's Xhosa society. While we were living in Transkei, some close friends invited us to their traditional village wedding. We arrived at the groom's home the afternoon before the wedding. After introductions one of the women led us to see the wedding preparations. *Iquosho* (beans and corn), cabbage, and potatoes boiled in large, three-legged cast-iron pots over outdoor fires. Huge round loaves of bread baked in smaller cast-iron Dutch ovens buried in coals. In a small storage house, people were cutting up meat—three oxen and seven sheep—for the cooking pots.

As they showed us to our room late that night, our hosts gave us roasted meat, potatoes, and cabbage to put us to sleep. Next morning our breakfast also included large plates of roasted meat along with the traditional porridge. Midmorning, during the gift-giving ceremony in the living room of the groom's mother, more roasted meat and fresh bread were served with tea.

The wedding ceremonies began with the groom going to the bride's family to "steal" her away. After the customary stepping across the courtyard, the groom's elder male relatives instructed the bride about how to be a good wife, and gave her a new, married name.

Because we were expecting guests, we needed to leave before the wedding feast began. As we departed, the groom's mother came running with a parcel. "You must not go without some meat," she said, "or you will say we didn't feed you." We returned home that afternoon with a leg of mutton.

Our hosts did not eat meat often. But when they celebrated, they certainly did eat meat!

—Judy Zimmerman Herr, Gabarone, Botswana

— *Notes*

1. Betty Nickerson, *Celebrate the Sun* (Philadelphia/New York: J.B. Lippincott Company, 1969), p. xiv.

2. From *I Lie on My Mat and Pray: Prayers by Young Africans*, ed. by Fritz Pawelzik (copyright 1964 by Friendship Press, New York, N.Y.; used with permission).

3. Robert Farrar Capon, *The Supper of the Lamb: A Culinary Reflection* (Garden City, N.Y.: Doubleday & Company, Inc., 1969), p. 145.

4. Adapted from Ahmad H. Sakr, "Dietary Regulations and Food Habits of Muslims," *Journal of the American Dietetic Association* (vol. 58, February 1971), pp. 123-126.

5. This poem is part of the "Declaration of Conscience" which Kim Chi Ha, one of Korea's best-known poets, wrote while in prison. He was detained on charges of subversion, for raising issues of justice in the minds of his fellow citizens. He was placed in solitary confinement for smuggling his "Declaration" out of prison.

6. Adapted from Eusebio Huamaní Rodriguez, "Kausāy Hunuy: The Leveling Feast," *Andenes* (Lima, Peru: August-September 1986).

7. To prepare a *mumu* in a nontropical setting, cover the hot rocks with a five-inch layer of corn husks, long grasses, then sheets of aluminum foil. Corn covered with some husk should be placed with the lower layer of root vegetables. Meat and husked corn is placed in the upper layer of leafy vegetables. Cover the food with a layer of heavy aluminum foil, then corn husks, long grass, and a wet burlap bag (optional).

Plastic tubes can replace bamboo shoots. Insert them carefully, only as far as the lower layer of food, so they do not melt on the rocks. Add approximately one gallon of water for every 20 people being served. Remove the tubes and plug holes with corn husks so steam does not escape. Cover with dirt.

After the cooking time, carefully remove the dirt and protective coverings. Scoop food into large serving bowls. The rocks will still be very hot. Serve with cold drinks and salt and pepper.

... appetizers, snacks, and condiments

Earl Martin: Philippines

White man, I doubt that you can stomach our African pepper soup," a fellow guest teased me as we reached into a communal mound of cooked sorghum porridge. We were eating with a cluster of friends in the home of Tijani, a devout Muslim and esteemed Koran teacher.

As we formed the porridge into balls and dipped them into a spicy sauce of fish and greens, he continued, "Not only does the pepper burn you, but you are not accustomed to the way we sit on the ground and eat with our fingers as brothers from one bowl."

But Tijani cheered as I cleaned the food bowl. "Mr. Robert, you are eating food which gives you strength for a whole day of farm work. Tomorrow, you will harvest beans from sunrise to afternoon prayers without tiring. This African porridge fills your stomach and sits there for hours. It's not like European food that is too sweet and has no strength."

Then with a laugh Tijani asked which food I preferred. I immediately thought of prime barbecued Alberta beef served with baked beans, a fresh garden salad, and potatoes smothered in sour cream. But such rich proteins consumed in one meal in Canada were more than most Nigerians living in the drought-ridden, debt-strapped Sahel consumed in a week.

I responded by lauding the balanced and resourceful diet of the farmers, fishermen, and businessmen with whom I was eating. They added variety to their bland daily staple of cooked grains by creating nutritious spicy sauces of products they foraged and cultivated: spinach and sour sorrel leaves, tangy ginger root, hot peppers, okra, beans, locust beans and leaves, fish, goat, sheep, and bush meat—squirrels, lizards, rabbits, and wild birds.

I thought of the watermelon, cucumbers, pumpkins, and peppers which they tossed into salads, and the home-made anise-flavored coffee and tamarind tea that warmed me on chilly mornings. My Nigerian friends were tuned to the land and knew its secrets for their survival. I agreed with Tijani that his African food was better suited than mine to his culture, climate, and economy. He and his guests heartily approved, and we departed, exchanging handshakes and invoking God's blessings for one another.

—*Robert G. Proudfoot, Jos, Nigeria*

Larry Hills was lying in a whites-only hospital ward in East London, South Africa, recovering from cancer-related surgery. One evening as he lay in bed with his eyes closed, he heard voices praying in Xhosa, the language of the people he worked with in Transkei. "Since it was unlikely that black people would be in the ward at that time of night, I assumed that the pain-killing drugs were causing hallucinations," recalls Hills, "and I kept my eyes closed."

When the prayers continued, Hills finally opened his eyes and found two black African men kneeling at the foot of his bed. Seeing that he was awake, they came and stood next to him. "They spoke softly with me; they touched me; they prayed for me."

The two men were members of an African Independent Church that Hills worked with in Transkei. They had traveled four hours to reach the hospital, where they successfully convinced the staff to let them visit their friend.

The men had come from a large church meeting convened to pray for Hills' recovery. The leaders were not satisfied to pray from a distance, however, and decided to send two members to pray with him in person. "This is the most powerful memory I have about that anxious period in my life," he says.[1]

8

Nourished by Diversity

The people of Uganda quote a proverb that says, "The one who has not traveled widely thinks his mother is the only cook." Human nature seems to push us toward uniformity. We like the familiar, the tried and true, and shy away from what is different. We are often skeptical of new ideas and unusual combinations, convinced that what works for us should surely work for others as well.

But to remain at the same table our entire life, never venturing beyond the safe and familiar aromas of our family's cooking pot, would rob us of much of the richness and many of the surprises of life. In our world of nearly 5 billion citizens, there are infinite ways of producing and preparing food to eat, of being family, of expressing love, of resolving conflict. The differences that exist are legitimate preferences because cultural patterns develop and take shape within particular and diverse environments.

In our haste to solve problems, we sometimes ignore this diversity, overlooking the unique characteristics of a specific situation or location. Many modern international agriculture programs, for example, quickly introduced Western monoculture farming methods with hybrid crops in tropical settings. Researchers failed to notice or examine the wisdom of traditional agriculture systems in those regions that used a complex variety of edible leafy vegetable species, fruits and seeds, roots and tubers that were well adapted to delicate tropical soils and weather patterns.

Just as appetizers, snacks, and condiments add a distinctive and satisfying touch to a meal or social occasion, stories of life lived in other cultures can add new flavor to our lives. The stories in this chapter remind us of the endless variety of things to eat, of ways to think, and methods of doing.

"Few joys exceed the joy of discovery," wrote Betty Nickerson. "No one of any age, place, or nation has learned all there is to know. It will be a richer and more exciting world when we can look upon our [international neighbors] as people who also love life and honor certain values that are as important and real to them as ours are to us."[2]

Some of the flavors and stories that follow may neither appeal to us nor be appropriate for our setting; every culture has its strengths and its weaknesses. But if we allow them to, some of the traditional ways of others may foster new ideas and practices to enhance our lives. Extending the table of ideas and embracing the diversity of others will strengthen and nourish us.

Ron Braun: Bangladesh

Jim King: Bangladesh

●●●●●●●●●●●●●●●●●●●●●●●●●●●●●●●●●

Tostadas (Mexico)

(ts)

(tohss-TAH-dahss)

*Serve as a snack or meal.
Each person builds their own.*

Fry day-old tortillas in a little hot oil or heat on ungreased frypan. Drain on paper, if needed.
Spread each tortilla with:
   **approx. 2 T. Refried Beans, hot or cold (30 ml)
   (p. 162)**
Top with:
   **lettuce, shredded
   tomatoes, chopped
   cheese, shredded
   sour cream
   strips of cooked chicken or beef (optional)**
Sprinkle on Tabasco pepper sauce or Mexican Salsa (p. 284). +!

—*Cathy Godshall, Elkhart, Indiana*

●●●●●●●●●●●●●●●●●●●●●●●●●●●●●●●●●

Quesadillas (Mexico)

(ts)

(kay-sah-DEE-yahss)

*Serve Mexican Quesadillas
as a snack or side dish, or
with a green salad for a quick
meal. They are simple, tasty,
and nourishing.*

Soften corn or flour tortillas in frypan over low heat. Use little or no oil. If tortillas are dry, sprinkle frypan and tortillas with a few drops of water as they heat. When tortillas are pliable, put thick slice of mild cheddar or Monterey Jack cheese on half of each one and fold the other half over. Allow cheese to melt, turning as necessary. Serve as is or with green taco sauce or Mexican Salsa (p. 284).

• Options:
**Add small amounts of Refried Beans (p. 162), mashed beans,
or vegetables, such as fresh spinach leaves.**
•
Heat in oven on baking sheet.

—*Emily Will, Cuidad Guzmán, Jalisco, Mexico*

shipment of macaroni that the Italian government donated to Salvadoran refugees living in a Honduran refugee camp presented a problem for the refugees. How would they prepare it? They had no tomato paste or margarine to cook with it.
   With a little experimentation they soon discovered ways to use macaroni that had never occurred to the best Italian chefs. They found that deep-fat-fried macaroni makes a nutty flavored snack. Toasted, pulverized macaroni mixed with a bit of cinnamon, plenty of sugar, and water makes a nourishing, refreshing drink. And ground into flour, macaroni can be baked into bread.

Guacamole
(Mexico)

Serves 4-5

(gwah-kah-MOH-lay)

*Serve as a topping for tacos,
Quesadillas (p. 257),
Tostadas (p. 257), or as dip
for tortilla chips or raw
vegetables.*

In bowl, chop or mash:
   1 avocado, peeled

Stir in:
   1 small tomato, finely chopped
   1-2 T. onion, minced (15-30 ml)
   1 T. lemon juice (15 ml)
   1 clove garlic, minced or crushed
   salt to taste
   cilantro, chopped (optional)
   **1/2 fresh green chili pepper, minced (optional)
      +!**

• *Options:*
Substitute a dash of Tabasco pepper sauce or a bit of
coarsely ground black pepper for green chili pepper.
•
Add 2 T. sour cream (30 ml).

—*Marie Palafox, Guadalajara, Mexico; and Emily Will, Cuidad
   Guzmán, Jalisco, Mexico*

Jim King: Bangladesh

Sesame Sauce (Middle East)

• •

(ts)

Serves 6-8

Taratour
(tah-rah-TOUR)

This all-purpose sauce is served as salad dressing, a topping for Falafel (p. 166) or as a dip. The sesame-seed paste used in this recipe is ground sesame seeds, sometimes marketed as tahini.

Mix in deep bowl, stirring constantly with wooden spoon:
   1 1/2 c. sesame seed paste (375 ml)
   1 c. water (250 ml)
Add:
   1/2 c. fresh lemon juice (125 ml)
   3-4 cloves garlic, minced (optional)
Stir until mixture is consistency of mayonnaise.
Add:
   1/2 t. paprika (2 ml)
   1/4 t. pepper, freshly ground (1 ml)
To serve as first-course dip, place several large spoonfuls on flat dish. Spread around with back of spoon and sprinkle with paprika. Garnish with parsley.

   • *Options:*
   Add 1 T. fresh parsley, finely chopped (15 ml).
   •
   Add hot peppers, minced, to taste.
   •
   Puree ingredients in blender instead of beating with wooden spoon.

—*Alice W. Lapp, Akron, Pennsylvania*

Chick-Pea Dip (Turkey)

• •

(ts)

Serves 4-6

Hummus
(HOO-moose)

Use as a dip with pita bread (p. 51). People also make a meal of Hummus by covering it with fresh, chopped vegetables such as lettuce, parsley, tomatoes, and green peppers and scooping it up with pieces of bread.

Drain, reserving liquid, and place in blender or food processor:
   6 c. canned or cooked chick-peas (1.5 ml)
Puree.
Add alternately and continue pureeing:
   1/2 c. sesame butter (125 ml)
   1/2-1 c. lemon juice (125-250 ml)
Add and blend until smooth:
   4-5 cloves garlic
   1 1/2 t. salt (7 ml)
Sauce should be thick and smooth. If too thick, thin with some of the chick-pea liquid. Place on small serving platter and garnish with parsley; black olives; drizzle of olive oil; dried, crushed mint; or red pepper to taste.

—*Jewel Wenger Showalter, Irwin, Ohio*

Chin Chin
(Nigeria)

(chin chin)

These pastries are one of many deep-fat-fried goodies made by African women who do not have ovens in which to make baked goods. They are sold at roadside stands for traveling snacks, and made in huge quantities for festive occasions. Some varieties of Chin Chin turn hard after they cool, like German peppernuts. This is a softer variation.

Mix until smooth:

1 c. margarine, room temperature (250 ml)
1 c. warm water (250 ml)
2 eggs

Add:

1/2 c. sugar (125 ml)
4 1/2 c. flour (1.1 L)
1/2 t. baking powder (2 ml)
1/2 t. ground nutmeg (2 ml)
1 T. orange rind, grated (15 ml) (optional)

Knead until smooth, adding more flour if needed until dough is no longer sticky. Roll dough to about 1/4-inch thick (.5-cm) and cut into small pieces, about 1/2 x 1 inches (1 x 2.5 cm). Use pizza cutter for fast cutting. In heavy saucepan, heat 1-2 inches oil (2.5-5 cm) to medium heat. Fry Chin Chin, stirring frequently to turn, until golden brown. Cool on paper. Store in covered container.

—*Kathleen Fast, Gabarone, Botswana*
—*Verna Olfert, Akron, Pennsylvania*

Nigerian weddings are large affairs, often attended by more than 1,000 people. To feed such a crowd, the host family kills a cow or several goats. After boiling the meat, they cut it into small cubes for deep-fat frying. A group of women prepare *chin chin* to accompany the meat. They work outside, rolling out the dough with various tools, such as tin cans and glass soda bottles. Other women bring charcoal burners to deep-fat fry the *chin chin*.

On the wedding day, young women and girls move through the crowd of guests with large trays of meat and *chin chin*. No one leaves with an empty stomach.

Stuffed Plantain
Patties
(Guatemala)

Plátanos Rellenos
(PLAH-tah-nohss
ray-YAY-nohss)

A favorite food in Guatemala, these are sold by street vendors or in church fundraisers. Red or pinto beans can be substituted for black beans.

Boil until very soft:

3 large, slightly ripe plantains, unpeeled
1 cinnamon stick

Peel and mash plantains.

Mash:

1 1/2 c. black beans, cooked and drained (375 ml) (Cooking Beans, p. 162)

Form plantain dough into patties and put scoop of mashed bean in center of each. Fold up patties and fry in hot oil. Roll in a little sugar and serve hot.

—*Leonor de Danila and Fanny Ellen Yoder, Guatemala City, Guatemala*

Plantain Chips (Colombia)

● ●

Serves 2-3

Patacones
(pah-tah-KOH-nayss)

Peel:
1 large green plantain
Cut into 3-4 pieces. Fry in shallow layer of hot oil. When golden, remove from oil and pound flat. Return to oil and refry a few minutes.
Remove and drain on paper.
Sprinkle with:
salt to taste
Serve hot or cold.

• Variation:
Slice in 1/4-inch rounds, diagonals, or horizontal slices (1-cm). Fry in oil until golden, drain, and sprinkle with salt.

—Irene Suderman, Bogota, Colombia

Green Soybean Snack (Japan)

● ●

Serves 3-4

Edamame
(eh-dah-mah-meh)

This popular snack food, the Japanese equivalent of popcorn, is colorful, nutritious, and easy to prepare. Just pop the beans straight from the pod into your mouth. Frozen green soybeans in the pod can be purchased in Asian food stores. Fresh soybeans are available seasonally in many areas.

Bring to a boil:
1 qt. water (1 L)
Add:
1 lb. fresh or frozen green soybeans in pods (500 g)
1/2 t. salt (2 ml)
Return to a boil and cook 5 minutes. If you use fresh soybeans that are not young and tender, you may need to cook 8-10 minutes. Drain, sprinkle with salt while hot if desired, and serve either hot or cold.

• Microwave:
Place 2 T. water, broth, or margarine (30 ml), and soybeans in small casserole or pie plate. Cover tightly. Cook on high 4-12 minutes, stirring once.

—Ken Johnson Shenk, Elkhart, Indiana

....

K **indness does not go rotten.**

—Swahili proverb

Onion Lentil Snack
(Bangladesh)

-🗓-

Piaju
(pee-AH-joo)

The name for these spicy treats comes from peaj, *meaning onion in Bengali. They are crisp on the outside and soft inside. Double this recipe for a large group. Serve as a snack with Nepali Spiced Tea (p. 31) or as a side dish with a curry meal.*

• *Option:*
Substitute brown lentils if red lentils are not available.

Soak in cold water 1 hour:
   1 lb. red lentils (500 g)
Drain. Grind or blend in blender, 1-2 c. at a time (250-500 ml).
Add:
   2 onions, finely chopped
   1 t. salt (5 ml)
   1/4 t. pepper (1 ml)
   1-2 green chili peppers, finely chopped +!
   **1 T. cilantro, finely cut (15 ml), or 1 t. ground
      coriander (5 ml)**
Mix all ingredients. Drop by spoonfuls into heated oil. Fry until golden brown. Serve warm.

• *Variation:*
For a Soybean Piaju, replace lentils with 11/2 c. soybeans (375 ml). Cook soybeans 20 minutes. Drain water and reserve. In blender, grind soybeans, 1-2 c. at a time (250-500 ml), with 4 cloves garlic and enough reserve water to make thick paste. Mix in 3/4 c. whole wheat flour (175 ml). To spices listed above, add 2 t. ground turmeric (10 ml), 2 t. ground cumin (10 ml), 4 t. ginger root, minced (20 ml), or 1 t. ground ginger (5 ml). Proceed as directed.

—*Gita Mankin, Kimole Mankin; and Judy Nord, Dhaka, Bangladesh*
—*Ilene Bergen, London, Ontario*

Tempeh Crisps
(Indonesia)

Tempe Goreng
(tem-pay goh-reng)

Tempeh, a fermented soybean product, is a common source of protein in Indonesia. It is available in Asian and specialty food stores.

• *Options:*
Substitute 11/4 t. curry powder (6 ml) for ground coriander.
•
Cut tempeh in small cubes and fry as above. When crunchy and hot, these are excellent croutons for soups, casseroles, or rice. Cool them for salads.

Combine in bowl, mixing well:
   1/2 c. water (125 ml)
   2 t. salt (10 ml)
   1/2 t. ground coriander (2 ml)
   1 clove garlic, minced
Slice in thin strips:
   6 oz. tempeh (190 g)
Dip slices in salt water and drain briefly or pat dry with cloth. Heat oil in wok, frypan, or deep-fat fryer to 350°F (180°C). Slide in tempeh and deep-fat fry or fry in shallow oil 3-4 minutes until crisp and golden brown. Deep-fat frying makes crisper product. Drain briefly on paper and serve immediately. Excellent dipped in Hot Peanut Sauce (p. 282).

—*Joanne Koopmans, Tentena, Sulawesi, Indonesia*

●●●●●●●●●●●●●●●●●●●●●●●●●●●●●●●●●

Cheese Pastry (Bolivia)

Makes 24 pieces

350°F 180°C

30 min.

Rollos
(ROH-yohs)

This is a delicious and simple adaptation of Bolivian cheese rolls, a snack food often sold at bus stops to people who are traveling. Contributor often makes it the night before a trip for an easy breakfast on the road.

Sift:
   4 c. flour (1 L)
   4 t. baking powder (20 ml)
   1 t. salt (5 ml)
   2 T. sugar (30 ml)
Add:
   1/2 c. margarine (125 ml)
   1 c. warm milk (250 ml)
   4 egg yolks (reserve whites)
Mix well. Divide dough in half. Pat out half in greased 13 x 9-inch pan (3.5-L).
In separate bowl, beat until foamy:
   4 egg whites
Add:
   1/2 - 1 lb. Monterey Jack or similar cheese, grated (250-500 g)
Mix. Spread half of cheese mixture on dough in pan. Pat out rest of dough on cheese layer and spread remaining cheese mixture on top. Bake at 350°F (180°C) about 30 minutes until golden brown. Cut in squares to serve.

—*Sherry Holland, Caracas, Venezuela*

....

When an Indonesian family is ready to build a new house, the old house is moved to the back where it becomes a kitchen. The new house rises where the old used to stand. House moving requires major effort and is an impressive example of cooperative labor, akin to North American Amish barn raising.

It takes 40 to 50 people working together to move a house, depending on its size. Each person finds a place along one of the walls. Most position themselves along the outside walls, but several also bear up the inside walls.

When everyone is in place the appointed leader yells out the count of three. In one not entirely smooth motion, the house comes up to waist level. With great shouts of encouragement from the audience of bystanders, the movers walk the house to the back. Slowly, with a stumble or two, they move the house into position, carefully setting it on the foundation of stones prepared to receive it.

A well-coordinated, enthusiastic house moving is a joy to behold. Some things we can do on our own. Other things, like moving a house, go much easier and better in the strength of community.

—*Ted Koopmans, Sulteng, Indonesia*

Vietnamese Spring Rolls

Cha Giò
(cha yaw)

Cha Giò is a popular Vietnamese snack or appetizer. Rice paper, bean thread, and fish sauce may sound unfamiliar, but are readily available at Asian food stores. These delightful rolls are fun to make with a small group of people.

• *Options:*
Wrap spring rolls in lettuce leaves with a little fresh mint, parsley, or cucumber before dipping.
•
If large rice paper isn't available, use smaller size and cut sheets in halves instead of quarters.
•
Substitute sheets of Chinese spring roll wrappers or phyllo dough if rice paper is not available.

Mix together:

1-2 oz. cellophane noodles (bean thread), soaked in warm water until soft, then cut with scissors or knife into short pieces (30-60 g)
1/2 lb. ground pork (250 g)
1 t. fish sauce (5 ml)
1/4 t. pepper (1 ml)
2 green onions, chopped
1 carrot, shredded (optional)
1 small can crab or shrimp (optional)
1/4 c. dried fungus, soaked for 20 minutes and finely chopped (50 ml) (optional) (see Mushrooms, p. 15)

Have on hand:

package of large rice paper

Sheets should be about 12 inches diameter (30 cm). Use 8-9 sheets. Quickly dip rice paper, one sheet at a time, into shallow dish filled with water and 1 t. white or brown sugar (5 ml). Cut rice paper circles into quarters. (Rice paper will dry out quickly; beginners, work with one sheet at a time.) Place rice paper quarters on table with point away from self. Put heaping tablespoon of filling mixture in center. Fold corners in and roll toward point. Set aside and continue until meat mixture is used up.

Fry rolls, half submerged, in hot oil over medium heat until rice paper turns yellowish and meat inside is cooked, 6-8 minutes. Use chopsticks to turn frequently while frying. Drain on paper.

Serve with individual tiny dishes of Peanut Dip (p. 265) and Seasoned Fish Sauce (p. 282). Serve 2-4 rolls—or more—per person as an appetizer; the rolls are much smaller and lighter than Chinese egg rolls.

—*Chi Vai, Quang Ngai, Vietnam; and Sue Neufeld, Herschel, Saskatchewan*

O Jesus,
Be the canoe that holds me up in the sea of life;
Be the rudder that keeps me in the straight road;
Be the outrigger that supports me in times of temptation.
Let your Spirit be my sail that carries me through each day.
Keep my body strong, so I can paddle steadfastly on in the voyage of life. Amen.

—*An islander's prayer from Melanesia*[3]

Peanut Dip for Spring Rolls (Vietnam)

••••••••••••••••••••••••••••••••

Makes 2 cups (500 ml)

Tu'o'ng dâu an Vo'i Cha Giò
(do-ung dow ahn vuh-ee
chah yaw)

• *Option:*
Substitute chunky peanut
butter for crushed peanuts.

In saucepan, brown slightly in 1 T. oil (15 ml):
  1 medium onion, finely minced
  **1/2 red chili pepper (or less), finely minced
  (optional) +!**
Add:
  1 1/2 T. fish sauce (20 ml)
  1-2 tomatoes, finely diced
  3/4 c. water (175 ml)
  2 T. brown sugar (30 ml)
  1 1/2 T. soy sauce (20 ml)
  salt and pepper to taste
  1 T. lime juice (15 ml) (optional)
Mix together and add to mixture:
  1 T. flour (15 ml)
  **7 T. peanuts, crushed with pestle or in blender
  (100 ml)**
Simmer mixture, stirring continually, approximately 5
minutes or until desired consistency is reached. Serve
warm or at room temperature. Leftover dip is delicious with
vegetable sticks.

—*Chi Vai, Quang Ngai, Vietnam; and Sue Neufeld, Herschel,
Saskatchewan*

One reality of life in Laos is lack of privacy. Material hardship seems to foster more interaction among people. People need each other more; more must be shared.

Since the climate is warm, Lao people spend much of their time outdoors. Their houses tend to be small and simple, with doors and windows that are almost always open. People are accessible to each other, and contacts between neighbors are frequent and natural.

Initially, it was disconcerting as we traveled through the country to find that our bedroom was not a sacred sanctuary as in the West. Guesthouse personnel sometimes entered at 5:30 a.m. to refill our thermos with freshly boiled water. Lao colleagues would poke their heads in the window to bid us a good morning or good night.

With time we learned to enjoy this closeness and informal sharing. It was an advantage to know who had the pair of

scissors, the heartburn medicine, or the extra soap powder. It was also easy to pick up a game of cards, or engage in a friendly chat over a bowl of roasted sunflower seeds.

Living with less privacy opened our eyes to what wealth and independence have done in the West: separated people into richly furnished but self-contained rooms that offer little opportunity for frequent human contact.

—*Linda Gehman Peachey,
Lancaster, Pennsylvania*

With patience, you can even cook stones.

—*Hausa proverb*

East Asian Egg Rolls (Indonesia/ Philippines)

Lumpia
(LOOM-pyah)

Homemade egg rolls are a lot of work, but very delicious. Invite someone who has made them to assist the first time. Using prepared egg roll skins, sold in Asian food stores and supermarkets, will simplify the process. Lumpia can be frozen and reheated in the microwave. Serve 1 egg roll per person as an appetizer; 2-3 as a main dish with rice.

• *Options:*
Replace cabbage with 3 large grated carrots. Or combine cabbage and carrots.
•
Add 1/4 lb. shrimp, minced, to chicken or pork.
•
Roll sautéed filling in lettuce leaves instead of egg roll crepes. Serve without further cooking.
•
Instead of deep-fat frying, place filled crepes in buttered frypan or electric skillet. Cover and brown 1 side a few minutes. Turn and brown other side. Outer crepe will be soft instead of crisp.

Filling:
In large, nonstick saucepan, sauté 10 minutes in 2 T. oil (30 ml):
   1/2 **medium onion, minced**
   1 **stalk celery, minced**
   2 **cloves garlic, minced**
   2 **chicken bouillon cubes**
   1/4 **t. pepper (1 ml)**
   1 **small tomato, cut in thin strips (optional)**
Add:
   1 1/2 **c. cooked chicken, deboned and finely chopped (375 ml), or 3/4 lb. ground pork (375 g)**
Do not add water. Cook 5 minutes, or if using pork, until cooked through. Drain excess fat. Add:
   1/4 **t. salt (1 ml)**
   6 **large fresh mushrooms, sliced**
   1 **c. fresh or frozen French-cut green beans (250 ml)**
Sauté 5 minutes. Add:
   1/2 **small cabbage, shredded**
Stir well and sauté 1 minute. Set aside to cool.

Outer crepe:
Beat together in bowl with wire whisk:
   5 **eggs**
   1/4 **c. margarine, melted, or oil (50 ml)**
   1/4 **t. salt (1 ml)**
In separate bowl mix:
   1 **c. cornstarch (250 ml)**
   2 1/2 **c. water (625 ml)**
   little flour (optional)
Add egg mixture and beat well with whisk. Mixture will be thin.

Lightly coat 8-10-inch nonstick frypan (20-25-cm) with oil. Heat to medium-high. For each thin crepe pour 1/4 c. batter (50 ml) into frypan and swirl around. Cook until set. Flip over and cook lightly. Stack on a plate.

Fill crepes individually. Put about 1/2 c. filling (125 ml) in rectangular mound in center of each crepe. Fold bottom edge of wrapper up over filling (*see* next page). Fold in two sides. Moisten top edge with water or egg white, fold over to form roll and seal. Fry egg rolls in several inches of oil heated to 375° (190°C) 4-5 minutes until golden brown. Drain on paper. Serve warm with Lumpia sauces.

—*Lien Kidjo and Pauline Beachy, Paramaribo, Suriname*
—*Violeta Ganal-Maust, La Verne, California*
—*Lilian Occeña, East Lansing, Michigan*

Red Egg Roll Sauce (Indonesia)

**Kuah Lumpia
(kwah LOOM-pyah)**

*This topping for Lumpia
comes from the Indonesian
community in Suriname.*

●●●●●●●●●●●●●●●●●●●●●●●●●●●●●●●●

Makes 2/3 cups (150 ml)

Mix together:
   **1/2 c. ketchup (125 ml)
   1 clove garlic, minced
   1 T. soy sauce (15 ml)
   1 T. sugar (15 ml)
   dash of Tabasco pepper sauce +!**

—Lien Kidjo and Pauline Beachy, Paramaribo, Suriname

Sweet Brown Sauce (Philippines)

**Lumpia Sauce
(LOOM-pyah sauce)**

● *Option:*
For sweet sour sauce, add
2 t. vinegar (10 ml).

●●●●●●●●●●●●●●●●●●●●●●●●●●●●●●●●

Makes about 1 cup (250 ml)

Mix together:
   **1 c. broth or water (250 ml)
   2 T. sugar (30 ml)
   1/4 t. salt (1 ml)
   11/2-2 t. soy sauce (7-10 ml) or to taste**
Boil about 2 minutes.
Add:
   **1 T. cornstarch (15 ml) dissolved in
   2 T. water (30 ml)**
Cook over low heat, stirring continuously, until thickened.
Serve warm or at room temperature.

—Lilian Occeña, East Lansing, Michigan

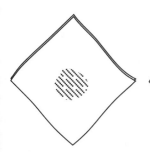
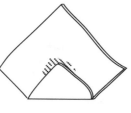

*Moisten edges before
sealing*

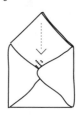

Pork Filled Dumplings (China)

Jiaozi
(JOW-dsuh)

Chinese families gather with relatives and friends to make these tasty dumplings. They are also a common snack food, sold at streetside restaurants. Invite friends to spend an evening making and eating Jiaozi. The homemade skins take time, but are not difficult to make. To simplify the process, buy ready-made dumpling dough or wonton skins at an Asian food store. Dumplings can be an appetizer, but more often are served alone or with fruit as a main dish. For main dish, this recipe will serve 5-6 people (12-15 dumplings each). Serve a larger group with soup on the side.

• *Options:*
Substitute minced chicken or ground turkey for part or all of pork and beef.
•
Instead of boiling, steam in covered bamboo or metal steamer 15-20 minutes. Line steamer with cabbage leaves or damp cloth for easy cleaning.
•
For fried Jiaozi, put 11/2 t. oil (7 ml) in frypan, lay dumplings side by side, just touching. Fry until golden, about 3 minutes. Add mixture of 1 T. flour (15 ml) and 1/2 c. water (125 ml) and pour over dumplings. Cook at medium heat until water is gone.

Dough for dumpling skins:
Stir with chopsticks or wooden spoon 3 minutes:

2 c. cold water (500 ml)
6 c. flour (1.5 L)

Dough will initially be dry and crumbly; knead about 5 minutes until smooth. Cover with damp cloth and let rest 15-30 minutes. Roll into long rope about 1-inch diameter (2.5-cm). Cut into 1-inch lengths (2.5-cm) and shape into balls. Flatten with fingers and roll out on board into very thin disks, about 31/2 inches in diameter (8 cm). If dough sticks, sprinkle board with flour. Lay disks on lightly floured board or table, not overlapping (they stick together easily). If several people are working together, one can immediately begin stuffing and cooking skins, while another continues shaping and rolling dough.

Filling:

11/2 lb. ground pork or beef, or a combination (750 g), mixed with
11/2 T. onion or green onion, minced (20 ml)
1/2-1 t. ginger root, minced (2-5 ml), or 1/8 t. ground ginger (.5 ml)
1-2 cloves garlic, minced

Add:

1-2 T. soy sauce (15-30 ml)
2 T. sesame oil (30 ml)
1 egg (optional)
dash of pepper

Finely shred, to consistency of coleslaw:

1-11/4 large heads Chinese cabbage (sometimes called napa)

After shredding, squeeze out all excess water. Add cabbage to meat mixture and beat until mixture is pasty. (Filling can be made ahead of time and refrigerated).

Stuffing skins:
To stuff skins, place 1 heaping teaspoon filling on each disk. Use fingertips to dampen edges of skin with a little water. Fold disk firmly over filling and press and roll edges together to form half moon. Set on lightly floured or oiled board or plate until ready to cook; Jiaozi should not touch each other, so they do not stick.

Cooking:
Fill large saucepan or soup pot half full of water. Bring to a boil. Add dumplings, 10-15 at a time. Bring to a boil. Add 3/4 c. cool water (175 ml). Bring to a boil. Add 3/4 c. water (175 ml). Bring to a boil. Add a third 3/4 c. water (175 ml). Bring to a boil. Scoop out Jiaozi with slotted spoon.

(*more* →)

Dumplings will be firm and creamy white, and are best if served while still piping hot. Often one person continues cooking while the group begins to eat. If not eaten immediately, keep cooked Jiaozi warm in covered dish, overlapping as little as possible to keep from sticking together. Serve Jiaozi in bowls, with small dishes of Jiaozi Sauce or Simple Jiaozi Dip. Slices of fresh fruit or vegetables complete the meal.

—Li Anchuan, Chongqing, Szechwan, China; and Grace Bergey, Hatfield, Pennsylvania
—Jules Chun, Taiwan; and Marcia Lewandowski, Santa Cruz, Bolivia
—Jen Wu, Hualien, Taiwan; and Dianna Eshleman, Hualien, Taiwan
—Carol Shenk Bornman, Goshen, Indiana
—Lois Keeney, Akron, Pennsylvania
—Christine Weaver, Goshen, Indiana

Jiaozi Sauce
(China)

• •

-**H**- *Makes about 1 cup (250 ml)*

Jiaozi Jer
(JOW-dsuh jer)

Place a small bowl of sauce at each plate. For an extra touch, place small dishes of soy sauce, hot peppers, minced ginger root, and chopped green onion on the table, to add to sauce as desired.

Mix:
1 c. soy sauce (250 ml)
1/4-1 t. Tabasco pepper sauce (1-5 ml) +!
3 cloves garlic, minced
2 t. sugar (10 ml)
4 t. vinegar (20 ml)
2 T. sesame oil (30 ml)
1/4 c. Toasted Sesame Seeds (50 ml) (p. 290)

—Christine Weaver, Goshen, Indiana

Simple Jiaozi Dip
(Taiwan)

• •

Makes about 1 cup (250 ml)

Jiaozi Jer
(JOW-dsuh jer)

Mix:
2/3 c. soy sauce (150 ml)
3 T. vinegar (45 ml)
2 T. sesame oil (30 ml)

—Lois Keeney, Akron, Pennsylvania

A *hasty person misses the sweet things.*

—Swahili proverb

Samosas
(Kenya)

(sah-MOH-sahss)

These spicy meat- or bean-filled pastry triangles originated in India, and are common across East Africa. Also called zamboozies, *they are a favorite snack, served with sweet tea. Each of the fillings listed is sufficient for one dough recipe.*

• *Options:*
Substitute lentils for mung beans. Lentils do not need to be soaked before cooking.
•
For smaller Samosas, divide dough into more pieces and reduce filling in each.
•
To simplify process, use prepared egg-roll skins from Asian food stores or supermarkets. Cut skins in half and fold into rectangles or triangles.

Pastry:
2 c. flour (500 ml)
1/2 t. salt (2 ml)
2/3 c. water (150 ml)
1 T. oil (15 ml)

Aim for slightly moist dough. Knead until smooth, 3-5 minutes. Cover with damp cloth and set aside.

Meat filling:
Sauté in a little oil:
2 onions, finely chopped
1 lb. lean ground beef (500 g)
Add:
1/2 t. salt (2 ml)
1/4 t. pepper (1 ml)
1/4 t. garlic powder (1 ml)
1 t. ground ginger (5 ml)
1/2 t. ground coriander (2 ml)
1 t. ground cumin (5 ml)
1 t. curry powder (5 ml)
1 medium potato, finely chopped or grated
1 c. water (250 ml)
1/2 t. ground cardamom (2 ml) (optional)
2 T. raisins (30 ml) (optional)
ground red pepper or chopped chili peppers to taste (optional) +!

Simmer about 10 minutes until vegetables are cooked through and flavors are blended. Drain thoroughly.

Bean filling:
Soak overnight or by quick method and cook until tender (p. 162):
11/4 c. mung beans (300 ml)
1 t. salt (5 ml)
Drain beans thoroughly.
Fry in 2 T. oil (30 ml):
11/4 c. onions, minced (300 ml)
11/2 t. ground cumin (7 ml)
3/4 t. ground coriander (3 ml) or 1 T. cilantro, minced (15 ml)
21/2 T. curry powder (35 ml) +!
1/2 t. salt (2 ml) (optional)

Stir in mung beans. Mix well. Cool before filling pastry. When filling is ready, divide dough into 2 sections. Keep sections covered until you are ready to work with them. Divide each section into 7 balls. Roll each ball into thin circle, about 5 inches in diameter (12 cm). Cut each circle in half. Place 1 heaping tablespoon filling on each half circle. Moisten edges of pastry with water or milk, fold

(*more* →)

pastry over filling to form triangle, and press edges firmly to seal (*see* below). Repeat with remaining pastry.

Cooking:

To cook, heat about 2 inches oil (5 cm) in heavy saucepan to about 360°F (185°C). Fry pastries a few at a time until golden brown and crisp on each side, 3-4 minutes, turning 2-3 times. Drain on paper. Keep warm in low oven (uncovered or loosely covered) until ready to serve. Serve 4-5 Samosas per person if used as main dish, or 1-2 each if served as appetizer.

To save part of the batch, freeze in tight container before cooking. When ready to use, thaw and fry Samosas. To reheat leftovers, heat uncovered in oven (if covered, they will become soggy).

—Asha Mohamed, Mogadishu, Somalia; and Gloria Shelly, Akron, Pennsylvania
—Mary Lou Cummings, Quakertown, Pennsylvania
—Sylvia L. Hess, Bausman, Pennsylvania

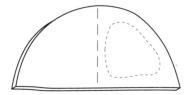

While living in rural Honduras, I was graced to learn to know and work with Catelina Viegas. Between sewing and nutrition classes, we would quickly light a fire and make lunch. As we sat down to eat, Catelina would stop and look at the pile of tortillas we had patted out. Then with her eyes open to the world around her, she addressed God in a most intimate way.

"God be with my children, may they always have enough food.

Maribel's oldest child is sick; please lend your healing hand. Be with Marixa away in high school. May the people where she is staying treat her well and, God, bless her as she grows up. Please help Francis and Angela listen to their teachers and learn well today. . . ." She prayed in this way for each of her own children and for many of the sewing students and people in her community. Then to close she said, "Gracious God, there are many hungry people, many children who cannot eat this lunch with us. God,

please give them food to eat and bless us with this food. Thank you. Amen."

When Catelina was finished, the tortillas were never as hot as they had been when they were set on the table, but meals with Catelina were truly blessed.

—Carol Rose, Wapipathum, Mahasarakam, Thailand

Spinach Pastries (West Bank)

Makes 20 pastries

350°F 180°C

15 min.

Sabanekh ib Kubez
(sah-BAH-neekh ib
KHOH-bez)

*Tester says these
spinach-filled triangles are
delicious. The leftovers
disappeared rapidly.*

• **Option:**
These freeze well. Make a
double recipe and freeze half
before baking.

Dough:
In 3/4 c. warm water (175 ml) dissolve:
1 t. active dry yeast (5 ml)
1 t. sugar (5 ml)
Mix:
3 c. flour (750 ml)
1/4 c. oil (50 ml)
1/2 t. salt (2 ml)
yeast mixture
Knead on floured board until dough is soft and elastic,
adding a little more flour if needed. Let rise 1 hour.

Filling:
Mix:
4 c. spinach, chopped and packed (1 L)
1/4 t. salt (1 ml)
3/4 c. onions, finely chopped (175 ml)
1/4 t. pepper (1 ml)
3/4 t. ground cumin (3 ml)
2 T. olive oil or shortening, melted (30 ml)
Mix well.
Divide dough into 20 small balls. Roll very thin. Put a
heaping 1/4 c. spinach mixture (about 70 ml) in center of
dough. Fold 3 edges in, making triangular shape, and
pinch together at center (see below). Bake at 350°F
(180°C) in greased pan 15 minutes or until golden brown.

—*Bishara and Selwa Awad family, Bethlehem, West Bank*

Pinch edges to seal

Ignorant of what the day held for me, I happily ventured off with a group of young Zairian women to hunt *masenda*, the fat, white grubs added to spicy hot palm-oil sauces. Women called out to me, "Ah, *Mwoyo*, Denisa. So today you go *masenda* hunting. Lots of work! Go well."

Fifteen minutes into the adventure, we reached the river and filled gourds with water for the excursion. Then we continued at a brisk pace until we reached a vast clearing, where we met a few isolated figures hunched over the soil. We stopped, greeted them, and began our work.

I rubbed my hands together in anticipation as I reminisced about past clam digging in the mud flats of California. My 13-year-old guide took her basket down from her head, handed me my hoe, and said, "It's like this, Denisa." She sliced her hoe into a clump of soil, flaking off the top layer and turning it over. Her hands searched the overturned soil, stopping every so often to pluck a white round blob out of the dirt.

When it was my turn, I closed my eyes and grabbed the white squishy form lying before me. I squealed as it wriggled between my fingers, throwing it fast in the direction of the bucket.

When the little bucket was filled, my guide said, "Now we clean them out, Denisa. Hold the head, snap the tail, and out come the guts. Slide your finger from the neck down to make sure all the gunk gets out." Grimacing, I swallowed my pride, my stomach, and my fears, and set to work.

An hour later I was exhausted and plopped down in the dirt to rest. My companions continued tirelessly. Finally, two hours past noon, we headed back, I with my proud collection of 200 or so *masenda*, and my comrades with double the number. At the river we clambered into the icy water to wash the *masenda* and our dirty bodies.

With gourds refilled, we shuffled home. While I went home to bed, my companions went to their cooking pots. That night they would eat well.

—*Denise Feil, Highland Ranch, Colorado*

If you are planning ahead for a year, sow rice;
for ten years, plant trees;
for a hundred years, educate the people.

—*Chinese proverb*

Lower your head modestly while passing,
and you will harvest bananas.

—*African proverb*

Empanadas
(Latin America)

(em-pah-NAH-dahss)

These tasty pastries, with a variety of fillings, are a hit at any party, coffee break, or snack time. Serve with a hot or cold drink.

Shells:
Combine:
4 c. flour (1 L)
1 t. salt (5 ml)
1 t. baking powder (5 ml)
Cut in:
1/2 c. margarine (125 ml)
Add:
1 1/8 c. milk (280 ml)
1 1/2 t. sugar (7 ml)
1 egg
Divide dough into walnut-size balls and roll into 4-inch circles (10 cm). Fill half of circle with 1 large spoonful of 1 of following fillings. Fold other half over and seal into half-moon shape with fork or by pinching with fingers into braid. Deep-fat fry until brown.

Fillings:
1) Chicken and vegetable filling
Boil:
1/3 chicken (about 1 lb./500 g)
1 onion, diced
pinch of salt
Debone chicken.
Boil until tender, but still firm:
3 potatoes, peeled and diced
2/3 c. peas (150 ml)
Fry:
1 medium onion, diced
2 1/2 T. shortening (35 ml)
1 t. ground cumin (5 ml)
1 1/2 t. pepper (7 ml)
Add chicken, potatoes, peas and salt to taste.
Cut in 1/2-inch cubes (1-cm):
2 eggs, hard-cooked
Place chicken-vegetable filling on dough circles, add a little egg and 1 green olive to each, before closing.
This filling is common in Bolivia.

2) Ground beef filling
Fry:
1/2 lb. ground beef (250 g)
1 onion
pinch of salt
1 1/2 t. pepper (7 ml)
1 t. ground cumin (5 ml)
Mixture should be a bit juicy.

(*more* →)

Add:

4 eggs, hard-cooked and diced

This filling is popular in Paraguay and Argentina.

3) Cheese filling

**1 1/2 lb. cheese, grated (750 g) (Monterey Jack
or cheese curd are similar to Bolivian
cheese)
a little chopped onion (optional)**

—*Raquel Flores, Santa Cruz, Bolivia; and Ingrid Schultz, Elkhart,
Indiana*
—*Rosario (Kitty) Guaristi-Bender, Santa Cruz, Bolivia*
—*Doris Friesen, Asunción, Paraguay*
—*Mary Wenger, Versailles, Missouri*

Jim King: India

D. Michael Hostetler: Brazil

Sweet Tomato Chutney (Lesotho)

Chateni ea Tomato
(cha-ta-NEE ya toh-MAH-toh)

In Lesotho this sweet but spicy chutney is served on special occasions as a side dish with cornmeal porridge and vegetable or meat dishes. Serve with any African stew or with Asian curries.

● ●

Makes about 3 cups (750 ml)

Combine in saucepan:
  1 onion, chopped
  3 large tomatoes, chopped
  1/2 c. raisins (125 ml)
  1 T. ground ginger (15 ml)
  2 t. salt (10 ml)
  1/4 c. brown sugar, packed (50 ml)
  1/4 c. vinegar (50 ml)
  1/8 t. ground red pepper (.5 ml) +!
Bring to a boil. Simmer about 1 hour until well blended and onions turn brown. Pour into sterilized 1-c. jelly jars (250 ml), leaving 1/2 inch space (1 cm). Seal with lid and rings, then process in boiling water bath 5 minutes to seal.

—*Maphakiso Masilo, Sehong-hong, Lesotho; and Nicki Petrone, Cleveland, Ohio*

Tomato Chutney (Madagascar)

Lasary
(lah-shah-ree)

Contributor says no Malagasy meal is complete without this chutney, which can be made in advance and refrigerated. An excellent relish to accompany African and Asian curries.

● ●
(ts)

Serves 4-5

Combine:
  3 c. tomatoes, finely chopped (750 ml)
  3 or 4 green onions, diced
  3 T. lemon juice (45 ml)
  dash of salt
  1 hot chili pepper, chopped, or dash of Tabasco
    pepper sauce (optional) +!

—*Annetta Miller, Nairobi, Kenya*

Food is respected in the Buganda region of Uganda. You are not supposed to eat or even drink water while standing or walking. One must take the time to sit down to eat or drink. You are not supposed to eat badly or put a lot of food in the mouth or even sing while eating. Food is always to be shared; even strangers passing by are invited to a meal and should eat their fill.

—*Monica Musomba and Joyce Maxwell, Kampala, Uganda*

Middle East Chutney (West Bank)

●●●●●●●●●●●●●●●●●●●●●●●●●●●●●●●●

Serves 4

Salata Bandura
(SAH-lah-tah bon-DOO-rah)

This juicy tomato relish is a good accompaniment for Makhlubbi (p. 206) and other Middle Eastern dishes.

Blend in blender until parsley is finely chopped:
   juice of 1 lemon
   several sprigs fresh parsley
Combine:
   3-4 ripe tomatoes, peeled and chopped
   1 medium cucumber, peeled and diced
   1-2 t. onion, grated (5-10 ml)
   1 T. olive oil (15 ml)
   salt to taste
Add lemon and parsley. Chill several hours in covered container to blend flavors.

—Issa Zahran, Hebron, West Bank; and Lorraine J. Kaufman, Moundridge, Kansas

Peach Chutney (Botswana)

●●●●●●●●●●●●●●●●●●●●●●●●●●●●●●●●

-🔒-

Makes 4 cups (1 L)

This sweet and spicy side dish is a delight with Nshima (p. 151) and stew, or with curry dishes.

Combine in heavy saucepan:
   1 onion, grated
   1 small apple, grated
   1 hot chili pepper, minced +!
   2 lb. peaches, peeled and finely chopped (1 kg)
      (approx. 6 medium peaches)
   3/4 c. sugar (175 ml)
   3/4 c. raisins (175 ml)
   3/4 c. vinegar (175 ml)
   1 t. salt (5 ml)
   1 t. curry powder (5 ml)
Bring to a boil and simmer 2 hours, stirring frequently to prevent burning, and to enjoy the aroma. Pour in 1-c. or 1-pt. sterilized canning jars (250-or 500-ml), leaving 1/4 inch space at top (.5 cm). Seal with lids and rings, then process in boiling water bath 5 minutes.

—Martha Mphuthing and Kay Miller, Gabarone, Botswana

A bird which does not fly will not find the ripe millet.

—Ugandan proverb

Watermelon Jam (Botswana)

Lekatane Jam
(lay-kah-TAH-nee jam)

Brightly colored Watermelon Jam has a unique, pleasing flavor. Invite children to help remove the seeds.

●●●●●●●●●●●●●●●●●●●●●●●●●●●●●●●●

Makes 3 pts. (1.5 L)

Have ready 3 pint-size jars (500 ml) and flat lids, sterilized by boiling them in water 10 minutes.

Combine in large saucepan:

4 c. watermelon (including juice), seeded and mashed (1 L) (about 4 lb./2 kg before rind is removed)
1/4 c. lemon juice (50 ml)
1/4 t. ground ginger (1 ml)
1 package dry fruit pectin

Bring to a full rolling boil over high heat, stirring constantly. Quickly add:

5 1/2 c. sugar (1.4 L)

Return to a full rolling boil, stirring constantly, and boil 1 minute. Fill sterilized jars immediately to 1/8 inch from top (.3 ml). Wipe jar rims and threads. Cover quickly with lids. Screw threaded bands tightly. Invert jars for 5 minutes, then turn upright. Leave undisturbed until lids seal, about 1 hour.

—*Kay Miller, Gaborone, Botswana*

Tomato Jam (Malawi)

This bright red jam, likely of British origin, is made across southern Africa. Make in fall when tomatoes are plentiful.

● *Option:*
Blend tomatoes in blender instead of peeling.

● *Microwave:*
Place chopped tomatoes, lemon rind, and juice and sugar in 2-qt. casserole (2-L). Mix well and cook uncovered on high 5 minutes. Add fruit pectin. Cook on high 4-6 minutes or until boiling and tomatoes are somewhat cooked down. Stir well to dissolve sugar. Add ginger, stir, and proceed with recipe.

●●●●●●●●●●●●●●●●●●●●●●●●●●●●●●

M

Makes 6 cups (1.5 L)

Peel, chop, and place in large saucepan:

3 c. fully ripe tomatoes (750 ml)

Add:

1 1/2 t. lemon rind, grated (7 ml)
1/4 c. lemon juice (50 ml) (about 2 lemons)

Bring to a boil and simmer 10 minutes. Strain out seeds (optional).

Add:

6 c. sugar (1.5 L)
1 package dry fruit pectin

Mix well.

Over high heat, bring to a rolling boil and boil 1 minute, stirring constantly. Remove from heat.

Stir in:

dash of ground ginger

Skim off foam with metal spoon. Ladle into sterilized 1-c. or 1-pt. canning jars (250- or 500-ml). Seal with lids and rings, and process in boiling water bath 5 minutes.

—*Gudrun Mathies, Elmira, Ontario*

A wedding in Botswana is a family affair. In many ways it is not only the bride and groom, but also their families, who are joined together.

The marriage occurs over a period of one to two months, usually with two major celebrations. The first, called *Patlho*, means "we are looking for *segametsi*, the one who will bring us water." It occurs after two families agree that their son and daughter should be married.

Patlho begins early in the morning. Between four and six in the morning, the groom's aunts and uncles walk to the bride's home. The aunts carry gifts on their heads and chant, *"Re batla segametsi"* (we need the one who will bring us water). They bring the bed, sheets, blankets, and clothes for the bride, but not shoes—so that she does not run away from her husband.

The bride's female relatives receive the gifts at the door, passing each gift from head to head down the line. Meanwhile, male relatives gather to give and receive the bride price, usually cattle or money.

After the gift giving, the bride's family serves food to the wedding party. Relatives sit in a circle and an aunt brings in the bride, who enters on her knees. She carries a mug of water and offers each relative a drink. Then she and the aunt go to the middle of the circle to receive the law of marriage from her family.

The groom is not present during this ceremony. He does not join the bride until after dark. The newly married couple spends the night together, but the groom disappears before dawn. He secretly arrives and departs until the second half of the wedding celebration.

Three weeks before the public wedding ceremony, the families register the couple's names, to allow time for community people to express any disapproval. On the third week the couple goes with their families and witnesses to the *kgotla* (the traditional court of law), the magistrate, and the church to hear the law of marriage.

These final acts seal the marriage. After the church ceremony, the families kill a cow and prepare *seswaa*, a special meat dish reserved for festive occasions.

—Kay Miller, Gaborone, Botswana

Throughout much of Africa, termites are an important component in the diet. Eaten raw or fried, they have high protein and fat content, which makes them an important source of nutrition during certain times of the year. Termites are also important in aerating and circulating soil, and in elevating soil fertility by increasing the organic matter. In some parts of Africa farmers purposely plant crops on termite mounds to increase yields. However, the mounds pose obstacles to cultivation, and the termites feed off the crops.

Africans use various methods of collecting termites. In one common method, people place buckets of water under street lights. The lights attract the termites as they leave their mounds after the rain. Upon landing, they twitch their bodies, discard their wings, and fall into the buckets.

In another creative method, people saturate termite mounds with buckets of water and beat drums to simulate thunder. This brings the termites out.

—Gudrun Mathies, Elmira, Ontario

In regions where coconut palms grow plentifully, coconut milk is often the liquid of choice for cooking rice, beans, stews, and curry dishes. It is also the base for many desserts. Although flavorful, coconut milk is high in saturated fat. We therefore recommend its use only in occasional celebration foods.

Coconut milk is not the clear liquid in the center of a coconut; it is made by adding boiling water to freshly grated coconut and then straining the liquid. The process, which begins in North America by selecting a coconut in a grocery store, can intimidate those who have never opened these hard-shelled fruits. But with practice and plenty of time, opening a coconut, removing the meat, and extracting the milk can be an enjoyable task, one in which children are quick to participate.

When choosing a coconut, listen for the sloshing of liquid inside, which indicates freshness. Before opening the coconut, drain the liquid by hammering a nail or ice pick into the small round spots at one end. Children may enjoy tasting and drinking this "water."

There are two common methods for opening the shell and removing the meat. Place the coconut on a hard surface and tap the coconut on all sides with a hammer. Then give the coconut a swift pound. Or place the coconut on a tray and bake at 300°F (150°C) for 45-60 minutes, until the shell begins to crack. If the shell does not come off cleanly, carefully pry the meat loose with a knife. The brown skin on the meat can be removed with a vegetable peeler if desired.

Coconut Milk

• •

Makes 3 cups (750 ml)

Coconut milk is a common ingredient in international cuisine. Here are several ways to make your own, based on recipes from Indonesia and Brazil. You can also purchase canned coconut milk, not to be confused with coconut cream or cream of coconut, a more expensive, sweet liquid used primarily in desserts.

Combine in blender:
**meat from one coconut, cut in chunks
3 c. boiling water (750 ml)**
Blend 2-3 minutes. Let stand 20 minutes. Strain, squeezing all milk from coconut pulp. Use immediately or store in refrigerator up to 4 days. Freeze for longer storage. Use coconut pulp in baking.

• Options:
Grate coconut and pour boiling water over. Let stand 20 minutes before straining.
•
To make coconut milk from packaged coconut, heat, but do not boil, 11/2 c. milk (375 ml) and 1 1/2 c. water (375 ml). Pour over 11/2 c. grated coconut (375 ml). Let stand in cool place 2 hours. Strain and use.

—*Rose Waltner Graber, Recife, Brazil*
—*Lois Deckert, North Newton, Kansas*
—*Anne Warkentin Dyck, Swift Current, Saskatchewan*

●●●●●●●●●●●●●●●●●●●●●●●●●●●●●●●●

Sweet Soy Sauce (Indonesia)

Makes 23/4 cups (675 ml)

Kecap Manis
(ke-CHOP mah-NEESS)

Sweet Soy Sauce is the most important sauce in the Indonesian repertoire and is used in a great variety of dishes. It can be purchased in some Asian and specialty food stores, but is also easy to make.

• *Option:*
Children may enjoy a little
Sweet Soy Sauce drizzled
over plain rice.

Mix together and set aside:
  23/4 c. Chinese dark soy sauce (675 ml)
  3 cloves garlic, crushed
  1/2 t. star anise pods (2 ml)
  1 bay leaf
  1/2 t. galangal (laos) (2 ml)
  1/2 c. water (125 ml)
Carmelize:
  21/2 c. sugar (625 ml)
To carmelize, heat sugar in heavy saucepan over low heat. Stir constantly until melted into golden brown syrup. When melted, add soy sauce mixture very slowly, stirring constantly. After all is blended, bring to a boil and stir until sugar has dissolved completely. Cook over low heat 10 minutes.
Allow this somewhat thickened syrup to cool, and pour into bottles. Sweet Soy Sauce keeps for several months in the refrigerator.

—Reprinted with permission of Atheneum Publishers, an imprint of Macmillan Publishing Company (New York), from The Indonesian Kitchen, by Copeland Marks with Mintari Soeharjo (copyright © 1981 by Copeland Marks and Mintari Soeharjo).

....

One day while living in Jamaica I was sick, vomiting, feeling depressed, and craving a fizzy soft drink to settle my stomach. Fortunately, an expatriate friend came by and cheered me with two bottles of Coca-Cola.

A few hours later two Jamaican co-workers stopped by. When they saw that I was sick, they immediately rushed out and bought a couple of large husk coconuts. Readily available from vendors lining the streets, these inexpensive coconuts are filled with a natural rehydration liquid. Suitable for adults and children, coconut water is especially important for children who can quickly die from dehydration resulting from vomiting and diarrhea.

—Janet Panning, Lansdale, Pennsylvania

Hot Peanut Sauce (Indonesia)

•••••••••••••••••••••••••••••••••
 Makes about 3/4 cup (175 ml)

Sambal Kacang
(sahm-bahl kah-chahng)

• *Option:*
Instead of Sweet Soy Sauce, substitute regular soy sauce plus 1 1/2 T. brown sugar (22 ml) and dash of garlic.

Stir to make paste:
   4 T. chunky peanut butter (60 ml)
   4 T. milk or water (60 ml)
Add:
   2 T. Sweet Soy Sauce (30 ml) (p. 281)
   1/4 t. ground red pepper (1 ml) or to taste +!
   1 1/2 t. lemon juice (7 ml)
   1 bay leaf

Mix and let stand several hours to blend flavors. Remove bay leaf before serving.
Serve with Indonesian Shish Kebab (p. 249) or Tempeh Crisps (p. 262).

—*Mary Wenger, Versailles, Missouri*
—*Anne Warkentin Dyck, Swift Current, Saskatchewan*

Seasoned Fish Sauce (Vietnam)

•••••••••••••••••••••••••••••••••
 Makes about 1 cup (250 ml)

Nuoc Mam
(nook mom)

Asian food stores sell bottled fish sauce, a common ingredient in Southeast Asia cooking. Asians also dilute the sauce and add seasonings in mixtures like this one, which are sprinkled over foods much like soy sauce is added to Chinese dishes. Fish sauce has an unusual flavor that quickly becomes a favorite; try a little at a time to get started.

Stir together:
   3-4 T. sugar (45-60 ml)
   1 T. lime or lemon juice (15 ml)
   1-2 cloves garlic, minced
   3/4 c. hot water (175 ml)
When sugar is dissolved, add:
   1/4 t. crushed red pepper (1 ml) or to taste +!
   2-3 T. fish sauce (30-45 ml)

Bottle and store in refrigerator. Keeps 2-3 months. To add color, grate a bit of carrot into sauce just before serving.

—*Tran Thi Trinh, Quang Ngai, Vietnam; and Pat Hostetter Martin, Ephrata, Pennsylvania*

● ●

Lao Hot Sauce (Laos)

[M] -[H]-

Serves 4-6

Jayo
(JAY-oh)

This is a spicy Laotian dip for Sticky Rice (p. 144).

• *Option:*
Substitute 3/4 c. thick tomato juice (175 ml) for cooked tomato.

• *Microwave:*
Quarter tomato, cover lightly, and cook on high for 2-3 minutes instead of baking.

Wrap in aluminum foil and broil (or warm in hot oven):
  1 large tomato
When soft, place in mixing bowl and pound gently with pestle or potato masher.
Mix in:
  1-2 cloves garlic, minced
  dash of pepper
  1 t. sugar (5 ml)
  1/4 t. salt (1 ml)
  2-3 t. fish sauce (10-15 ml)
  1-2 t. cilantro, chopped (5-10 ml)
  1-2 hot chili peppers, chopped, or Tabasco
    pepper sauce, to taste +!

—*Somphane Thadavong, Vientiane, Laos; and Linda Peachey, Lancaster, Pennsylvania*

Sulak Sivaraksa, a Thai Buddhist writer and social activist, is critical of the materialism which Thailand is embracing along with its economic expansion. He observes that Western development efforts often promote economic change, but overlook human and personal values. We asked him whether Western Christians inadvertently contribute to what he deplores since we are shaped, often unconsciously, by the materialistic, technological society from which we come.

"You need to find a good friend," Sivaraksa replied. "As you listen and learn from your Thai friends, you will begin to understand their aspirations, their values, their pain, and their joy. As you listen carefully, you will begin to see through their eyes, and will modify your behavior accordingly."

In his book, *A Socially Engaged Buddhism*, Sivaraksa explains that the concept of a good friend is important in Buddhism. "One must indeed find good friends beyond one's national boundary and one's religious affiliation. . . . I feel that we should really get our grassroots (or riceroots) together— using our friendship through our different religious and cultural traditions—yet with common bonds for peace and justice."[4]

International friendships can develop despite unjust economic relations between countries. "There are people from the exploiting countries who recognize that exploitation. It is these people who really are our good friends, and if good friends are together, we can perhaps do something meaningful for our mutual problems. . . ."

—*Janet and Stan Reedy, Bangkok, Thailand*

Mexican Salsa

-🔳- *Makes 2-3 cups (500-750 ml)*

Salsa Picante
(SAHL-sah pee-KAHN-tay)

Use Mexican Salsa as a dip with tortilla chips or a topping for Mexican foods. How hot it will be depends on the number and spiciness of the peppers used. Vary quantities of peppers and seasonings to taste. Cilantro is a favorite seasoning in Mexico.

Mix together:
   3 tomatoes, chopped
   1 onion, finely chopped
   2 cloves garlic, minced
   4 jalapeño peppers, finely chopped +!
   salt and pepper to taste
   2-4 T. cilantro, chopped (30-60 ml) (optional)
   2 T. oil (preferably olive) (30 ml) (optional)
Store in refrigerator.

—Celine Vatterott Woznica, Oaxaca, Mexico
—Melanie Baer, Lancaster, Pennsylvania

Mild Tomato Sauce (Guatemala)

Makes 2-3 cups (500-750 ml)

Chirmol
(cheer-MOHL)

Small clay dishes of Chirmol are a familiar sight on tables in Guatemalan homes and restaurants. This sauce is used over meat and egg dishes. Ingredient amounts can be adapted according to taste.

Sauté 3-5 minutes in 1 T. oil (15 ml):
   3 c. tomatoes (preferably plum), diced (750 ml)
   3/4 c. onion, minced (175 ml)
   1/2 c. green pepper, minced (125 ml)
   2 cloves garlic, minced
Add and sauté briefly:
   1/2-1 t. dried oregano (2-5 ml)
   1-2 T. fresh mint leaves, chopped (15-30 ml)
   2 T. cilantro or fresh parsley, chopped (30 ml)
Remove from heat and add:
   2 T. lemon juice (30 ml)
   salt to taste
Thin with broth or water, if desired. Store in glass jar in refrigerator. Serve at room temperature.

—Fanny Ellen Yoder, Guatemala City, Guatemala

*O**ne trap can make you starve.*

—African proverb

Super Hot Sauce

● ●

-H- *Makes 3-4 cups (750-1000 ml)*

If you like fire in your menu, try this sauce on bean, vegetable, or meat dishes. The pungency of the sauce depends on the size, strength, and number of peppers used. This recipe is not native to Papua New Guinea, but was developed there by the contributors using local chili peppers, a common cash crop.

• *Variation:*
For hot relish, chop all ingredients instead of blending.

Whirl in blender:
   36 small red chili peppers, about 2 c. chopped (500 ml) +!
   1/2 c. oil (125 ml)
   1/2 c. vinegar (125 ml)
Add and blend well:
   2 t. garlic powder (10 ml)
   1/2 t. ground coriander (2 ml)
   1/2 t. oregano (2 ml)
   1 t. salt (5 ml)
   1 medium onion, chopped
   approx. 2 c. tomato sauce, tomato puree, or chopped tomatoes (500 ml)

Put mixture in saucepan, bring to a boil, and simmer until onion is cooked and flavors are well blended. If it sticks to pan, add a little water. Pour into jar and store in refrigerator or freezer.

Always handle chili peppers with care—you may want to wear plastic gloves while washing and chopping peppers. Do not rub eyes with fingers while working with peppers.

—*Allan and Anne Wideman, Papua New Guinea*

S omalis living in northeast Kenya prepare *nyeri-nyeri*, a snack made of goat or camel meat. After drying the meat for several hours, they cut it into small cubes and brown them in shortening. The entire pan of meat and shortening is transferred into a covered container, where it can be safely stored at room temperature—often 100° F (38° C)—for long periods of time.

Women store *nyeri-nyeri* in out-of-the-way places, like under a bed. They bring it out to serve guests, particularly when visitors arrive unexpectedly and no other food is prepared. Wealthier women regularly serve *nyeri-nyeri* with spiced tea to visiting neighbors.

Every society offers age-old folk remedies for treating ailments. Many treatments use herbs and plants that are available locally. There is growing recognition within the nutritional and medical professions that some plants contain chemical substances that produce the physiological effects people attribute to them. In fact, many synthetic medicines contain substances extracted from plants.

More and more, community-based health care workers around the world are promoting the continued use of traditional herbal medicine for specific conditions. Often herbal treatments are less expensive and less harmful than synthetic drugs.

Using traditional medicine helps unite local communities. "If one of us has a plant," said a woman attending a health workshop in a shanty town in northeast Brazil, "we share it with our neighbors." Interest in plants is a healing process in itself, believes Jacob Schiere, who assisted a technology-for-health program in Guatemala. "People who know plants also know their bodies."

Examples of plants which people use medicinally:

Cayenne. The fruit of this African red pepper is a pure and potent stimulant. Unlike black pepper which is an irritant, red pepper can help to heal stomach and intestinal ulcers. Practiced herbalists recommend it for circulatory problems, arthritis, and asthma.

Garlic. This ancient medicinal plant has been used for just about everything, including regulating blood pressure. Jamaican pharmacologist and herbal authority Diane Robertson calls it a "natural antibiotic" in its raw form. During World War I, the British apparently saved thousands of lives by treating wounds with diluted garlic juice. Many international workers find that swallowing one garlic clove each day decreases their susceptibility to discomfort from intestinal parasites, specifically amoebas.

Ginger. Ginger root is a stimulant that functions as an expectorant, helping to loosen mucus in the throat and bronchial tubes. It also helps rid the stomach and intestines of gas. Ginger tea can be made by mixing one teaspoon of ground ginger (5 ml) in one cup of boiling water (250 ml) and sweetening it with honey or sugar. (For additional ginger drinks, see Beverages, chapter 2.)

Aloe vera. The gelatinous juice found in the succulent leaves of this plant is good for treating minor burns, sunburn, minor cuts, and skin irritations. It keeps burns from blistering, infecting, and scarring. Some herbal practitioners prepare a juice from the gel to use as an eyewash and to draw out infection.

Herbal medicines should be taken in proper amounts and with the same care as synthetic medicines.

—*Leland Miller, Lititz, Pennsylvania; Mary Miller, Ankeny, Iowa; and Nancy Loewen, Providence, Rhode Island, worked with medicinal plants during service assignments in Bolivia, Brazil, and Jamaica, respectively.*

When we left Germany for Canada in 1951, Uncle C. F. Klassen boarded the boat in Bremerhaven to wish us farewell. He told my brother and me, "Boys, if you get to Canada, don't forget two things: the first one—don't lose your sense of family. And another thing—when you first come to Canada, you will think that they do everything wrong. Be quiet for five years."

—*Siegfried Bartel, Agassiz, British Columbia*

Frankfurt Green Herb Sauce (Germany)

• •

Makes about 2 cups (500 ml)

Frankfurter Grüne Kraüter
Sosse
(FRAHNK-fur-tehr
GROOE-nah kroy-tehr
ZOH-sah)

*Serve over whole potatoes
boiled in their skins, meat,
fish, or hard-cooked or
poached eggs.*

• *Option:*
Substitute 1 t. dried herbs
(5 ml) for 1 or more of the
fresh herbs.

In medium bowl, mix:
   **3 eggs, hard-cooked and chopped, minus 2 T.
      for garnish (30 ml)**
   1/2 c. oil (125 ml)
   3-5 T. lemon juice (45-75 ml)
   pinch of sugar
   1/2 t. prepared mustard (2 ml)
Stir in:
   1/3 c. sour cream or whipping cream (75 ml)
   1 small onion, minced
Pour into blender.
Add approx. 1 T. each of any of the following fresh herbs,
chopped (15 ml):
   **basil, borage, chives, cress, parsley, chervil,
      sorrel, winter savory, anise, dill, tarragon,
      summer savory, oregano, sweet fennel
      stalks or fennel seeds**
Blend until smooth. The greater the variety, the better the
sauce.
Add:
   salt and pepper to taste
Let stand 1 hour before serving.
Garnish with:
   chopped egg
   minced fresh herbs

—*Christoph Leser, Berlin, Germany; and Carla Kaye Jones,
   Hampton, Virginia*

Meat Sauce (Argentina)

• •
-⚙-

Makes 2 cups (500 ml)

Chimichurri
(chee-mee-CHOO-ree)

*This mild, herbed vinegar
sauce stores well in the
refrigerator and can be
sprinkled on Latin American
meat or vegetable dishes.*

In glass bottle, combine:
   2/3 c. vinegar (150 ml)
   1 1/3 c. water (325 ml)
   1 t. crushed red peppers (5 ml) +!
   **1 t. fresh oregano (5 ml) or 1/2 t. dried oregano
      (2 ml)**
   1-2 cloves garlic, minced
   2 T. fresh parsley, minced (30 ml)
   1 t. salt (5 ml)
Refrigerate 24 hours before using.

—*Inez de Silva, Catamarca, Argentina; and Sara Larson Wiegner,
   Akron, Pennsylvania*

Hot Pepper Seasoning (Ethiopia)

Berbere
(behr-behr-ee)

This version of the basic seasoning mix used in Ethiopian stews is spicy hot, but milder than the Berbere Ethiopians commonly use. Gathering the spices and making this mixture is a little time-consuming, but those who love spicy food will find the effort worthwhile the first time they make Doro Wat (p. 221).

• Option:
Roast spices in heavy frypan on stove top, stirring frequently.

• •
-H-

Makes 1 cup (250 ml)

300°F 150°C

20 min.

Preheat oven to 300°F (150°C).
Combine:
1/4 **c. ground red pepper (50 ml) +!**
1/3 **c. paprika (75 ml)**
1 **t. seasoned salt (5 ml)**
1 **t. poultry seasoning (5 ml)**
1/2 **t. ground ginger (2 ml)**
1/2 **t. garlic powder (2 ml)**
1/2 **t. ground cardamom (2 ml)**
1/2 **t. fenugreek, crushed (2 ml)**
1/4 **t. ground nutmeg (1 ml)**
1/8 **t. ground cinnamon (.5 ml)**
1/8 **t. ground cloves (.5 ml)**
1/8 **t. ground allspice (.5 ml)**

Mix well. Put in small cake pan and roast in oven 20 minutes. Stir every 5 minutes. Watch carefully and stir more often during last 10 minutes. If not watched, Berbere can grow too dark and take on a burnt flavor. Cool and store in tightly sealed container in refrigerator or freezer.

—Mary Jane Wehibe, Elizabethtown, Pennsylvania

Simple Berbere (Ethiopia)

This quick substitute for authentic Berbere can be used for individual dishes when you don't have a supply of Berbere on hand.

• •

Makes about 1/4 cup (50 ml)

Combine:
1 **t. ground ginger (5 ml)**
3 **T. ground red pepper (45 ml) +!**
1/4 **t. ground cloves (1 ml)**
1/2 **t. ground cinnamon (2 ml)**

—From Africa News Cookbook: African Cooking for Western Kitchens *(copyright Africa News Service, Inc., 1985; all rights reserved; used with permission).*

Somalia is a country with more camels than people. No other animal is as well adapted to semiarid land as the camel. It can go long periods of time without water and withstand high temperatures. Its habits protect the environment; it walks softly, browsing rather than grazing.

Camel milk has sustained millions of people in time of drought. Its production has been

Garam Masala (India)

Makes 1/3 cup (75 ml)

450°F 230°C

12 min.

(gah-RAHM mah-SAH-lah)

There are many versions of this special spice powder, commonly used in Indian cooking. Garam Masala is available in many spice and Asian food stores, but it is easy to grind your own, and the aroma is wonderful.

Preheat oven to 450°F (230°C).
Measure:

1 1/2 t. cardamom pods (7 ml) (about 20 pods)

Remove seeds from pods.
Place in small cake pan:

cardamom seeds
5 t. coriander seeds (25 ml)
1 t. cumin seeds (5 ml)
1 1/2 t. whole cloves (7 ml)
2 T. black peppercorns (30 ml)

Bake 12 minutes, stirring once or twice. Cool. Grind to fine powder with mortar and pestle or in coffee mill or blender.

• *Option:*
Instead of baking in oven, toast mixture in heavy frypan on stove top, stirring occasionally.

—Joanne Dirks, Akron, Pennsylvania

During the two years we lived in Jamaica, we hired a domestic worker named Rosetta. Although barely literate, she taught us lessons we will never forget.

Rosetta was the sole provider for her three children and her mother. She owned but one pair of shoes. To make them last as long as possible, she carried them and walked barefoot over the one and a half miles to our house each day. When we returned to the United States, we thought of Rosetta when we heard people complaining because they didn't have a pair of shoes to match each of their purses. We never heard Rosetta complain about her one pair of shoes.

Rosetta was flexible and adjusted to unexpected circumstances. Once when we had a guest, I came home from my teaching job, anticipating a nice Jamaican lunch. Rosetta casually told me the gas tank had emptied and she was unable to use the stove. Seeing my look of disappointment, she quickly assured me that she had built an outdoor fire and lunch was ready.

—Ginny Birky, Albany, Oregon

known to increase as water supplies diminished. The milk does not spoil as quickly as other types of milk. After souring, it can be preserved for several weeks, unrefrigerated and in the heat. A Somali proverb says, "A mouthful of camel's milk keeps you going for half a day."

—Julia A. Sensenig, Denver, Pennsylvania

Toasted Sesame Seeds (Korea)

Ga Soh Kum
(geh soh koom)

These toasted seeds are used to garnish many Korean dishes.

Makes 3/4 cup (175 ml)

Place in heavy frypan:
   1 c. sesame seeds (250 ml)
Brown slowly over medium-low heat, stirring constantly. When seeds are golden brown, about 10 minutes, remove from heat.
Add:
   1 t. salt (5 ml)
Crush seeds with mortar and pestle, in blender, or place in strong bag and crush with rolling pin.

—*Yon Sook Suh and Faith Kim, Seoul, Korea; and Pat Yoder, Goshen, Indiana*
—*Catherine Baer, Goshen, Indiana*

Aymara Indian women from Peruvian highland villages near Juli gather once a week to talk and work. They have formed an artisans' association that enables them to increase their earnings by directly marketing their own products. Two women sit side by side embroidering a large wall hanging. Others spin thread and work on smaller projects.

The same cooperative spirit that fills the air as they work prevails at lunch. Each woman takes out a cloth filled with something she brought for the noon meal and places her contribution on a large colorful cloth known as an *aguayo*. Then the women seat themselves on the ground in a circle around the cloth and share the food: *chuño* (freeze-dried potatoes), puffed corn, and patties made from *quinua*, a high-protein grain.

The women discuss events in their villages as they eat. Not long ago a food aid program offering milk powder, flour, and oil began in their region. Some women have stopped coming to the cooperative gatherings so they can attend the day-long meetings that are required to receive the food aid.

The women gathered around the *aguayo* spread with traditional foods lament the absence of these women and quickly agree they do not want these new foods. "We're happy with the food we and our ancestors have always eaten," comments one. "We do not want aid," concludes another. "All we want are markets in which to sell our embroidery so we can keep growing our own food."

—*Linda Shelly, La Esperanza, Honduras*

— *Notes*
   1. Adapted from an article by Carla Reimer, General Conference Mennonite Church News Service, February 16, 1990.
   2. Betty Nickerson, *Celebrate the Sun* (Philadelphia/New York: J. B. Lippincott Company, 1969), p. xv.
   3. *With All God's People: The New Ecumenical Prayer Cycle*, comp. by John Carden (Geneva, Switzerland: WCC Publications, 1989), p. 231.
   4. Sulak Sivaraksa, *A Socially Engaged Buddhism* (Bangkok: Thai Inter-Religious Commission for Development, 1988), pp. 46-47.

... desserts

Jim King· India

The New Year in Laos is time to delight in the cleansing, life-giving power of water. To the uninitiated, it can be rather startling to watch a whole society go for a drenching, three-day romp in the street, clutching buckets, dippers, and bamboo water guns.

The tradition of wishing each other well by pouring water on New Year's Day arose from a tale in Laotian mythology. According to legend, seven daughters of a beheaded angel needed to pour water on the angel's head once a year to prevent fire, drought, or pestilence on the earth. Incorporated into religious ceremony, the pouring of water on the Buddha, or on one another in a ritualistic style, signifies forgiveness and the washing away of sins.

People living in Luang Prabang, situated on the Mekong River, celebrate New Year's Day by forming teams to build sand castles on an island in the river. Armed with buckets, shovels, and slender bamboo shoots, they ride to the island in long narrow boats.

The celebration begins the moment people step into the boat. People use the oars to slap water at each other. A waiting group on the island welcomes each team by cupping their hands and splashing them liberally with water.

When friend meets friend in the throng of people, the result is always the same. After some good-natured joking and backslapping, one seizes the other, dashes down the bank, and flings his wide-eyed friend into the Mekong. Few escape or particularly care to.

Water blessings also occur in formal settings. One evening in a Luang Prabang hotel, local Communist party officials were hosting a reception for a Vietnamese military delegation. When the reception reached a high point of frivolity, the general secretary of the party left and entered an adjoining dining room, where hotel guests were enjoying dinner.

A portly old gentleman, he had a grin on his face, a look of mischief in his eyes, and a teapot in his hand. He and several cohorts, also with shiny teapots, calmly marched to the long dining table and took up positions at each end. With all due dignity and decorum, they moved down the line, placed the slender spout of their teapot down the collar of each guest, and poured. There were guffaws and chuckles, but always thanks for this generous outpouring of New Year's blessing.

—*Titus Peachey, Lancaster, Pennsylvania*

9

A Season for Sweets

For everything there is a season,
and a time for every matter under heaven:
a time to be born, and a time to die;
a time to plant,
and a time to pluck up what is planted . . .
a time to weep, and a time to laugh;
a time to mourn, and a time to dance . . .
a time to embrace,
and a time to refrain from embracing;
a time to seek, and a time to lose;
a time to keep, and a time to throw away. . . .

—Ecclesiastes 3:1-2, 4, 5b-6

Life in agricultural societies flows with the rhythm of nature. Each year is a cycle of clearing, planting, tending, harvesting, and storing. The changing seasons provide structure for life and, in an intimate yet unpredictable manner, influence the outcome of human labor.

When producing food is a primary concern, it is also the basis of seasonal festivals and holidays. Communities celebrate the promise of plenty at planting time, and the promise fulfilled at harvest. A festive day honors the importance of productive work and provides a much-deserved respite from the burden of that work.

A festive day also entails sacrifice. In subsistence economies the "day of rest is not just a neutral interval inserted as a link in the chain of workaday life";[1] it is not the leisure of modern, industrial society. When people celebrate a holiday, they are giving up the vitally important yield of a day's labor.

Yet the festive quality of their celebrations is unmatched. "Our experience in Lesotho taught us that having to work very hard and being poor didn't keep people from celebrating," commented Brenda and Rich Hostetler Meyer. "Life is hard in Lesotho, but never too hard to celebrate in dance. Women sing the stories of their lives, their praises for work well done, their worship of God. Always there is dance. Without dance, keeping in step with the rhythms of life is difficult, maybe impossible."[2]

In this context desserts and sweets, like meat, resemble a festive dance used to embellish a celebration. In communities where resources are limited, people seldom eat desserts on a daily or even weekly basis. They use them to mark the truly special moments in the life of the fields, the family, and the community.

Technology and machinery have largely muted nature's rhythms in modern society. Our eating patterns bear greater resemblance to the invariable factory production line than to the ebb and flow of nature's seasons, of work and festival. With abundant resources at our disposal, we eat as though each day were a festival, with fresh fruits and vegetables year-round and desserts every day. But our eating lacks the mirth of a long-awaited, well-deserved holiday. When we serve and eat desserts too often, we miss the sheer delight of a rare moment of pleasure.

While living in Germany, Edgar Stoesz observed that Germans ate ice cream cones differently than do North Americans. "The cone is much smaller and the Germans speak of 'enjoying' it rather than 'eating' it. Ice cream is something you eat to savor the taste. You lick it slowly."

Many of the recipes that follow were sent with comments such as, "This, of course, wouldn't be eaten every day, but only for special occasions. It is not customary here to have dessert every day." Let this be our guide. Let us celebrate according to nature's seasons and the authentic events in our family and community life. Let sweetness once again surprise and delight us.

Mvumiliuu hula mbivu.
He who patiently perseveres eats ripe fruit. He enjoys food at its maximum.

—Swahili proverb

Homemade Yogurt

Makes 2 qt. (2 L)

This inexpensive, lowfat yogurt recipe requires less than five minutes of active preparation. Incubate in a yogurt maker, the oven, or an ice chest.

• *Option:*
Put yogurt in glass jars in small ice chest. Fill chest with hot tap water to almost cover jars. Close tightly and leave undisturbed until set, about 6 hours.

Combine in bowl:
4 c. dry milk powder (1 L)
7 1/2 c. warm water (1.8 L)
Stir with whisk.
Combine separately:
1-2 c. of milk from bowl (250-500 ml)
1/2 c. plain yogurt (125 ml)
Stir thoroughly with whisk and return to remaining milk. Stir again and pour into yogurt-maker containers or clean jars. Incubate about 8 hours until set.
To incubate in electric oven without a light, preheat oven to 200°F (100°C). Turn off oven, insert jars wrapped in towels, and leave 6-8 hours. (May need to reheat oven after several hours; remove yogurt and return when oven is warmed.) In oven with light, place unwrapped jars in oven and leave light on. Ideal temperature for incubating yogurt is 110°-120°F (61°-66°C). Store in refrigerator.

• *Note:*
Contributor uses purchased plain yogurt for starter. Yogurt made with starter from homemade yogurt will gradually become more tart in succeeding batches.

—*Marilyn Langeman, Akron, Pennsylvania*

Bananas in Coconut Sauce (Thailand)

Serves 4-6

Glooay Booat Chee
(gloo-eh bow-AHT chee)

Thai cuisine features many sweets, but they are typically served to guests as between-meal snacks, rather than after a meal. The usual finale to a meal is a platter of fresh fruit, skillfully carved and artistically arranged.

Heat in saucepan:
3/4 c. coconut milk (175 ml) (p. 280)
Add:
2 t. sugar (10 ml)
pinch of salt
Bring to a boil and simmer 2 minutes, stirring constantly. Remove from heat.
Stir in:
3 large bananas, peeled and cut in 1/2-inch diagonal slices (1-cm)
Return to a boil for 10 seconds. Serve alone or as topping for ice cream or Sweetened Sticky Rice (p. 300). Best if served immediately so bananas do not discolor.

• *Option:*
Replace coconut milk with regular milk and 2 T. shredded coconut (30 ml).

—*Khun Sureeporn and Lily Bérubé, Phanat Nikhom, Thailand*

Fresh fruit is a favorite dessert in such diverse locations as Kinshasa, Zaire, Jerusalem, and Bangkok, Thailand. A masterpiece of colors, shapes, and textures, it is appropriate at any time or occasion—at a formal dining table or at a picnic in the park. Serve it in a basket or bowl, on a platter or tray. Eat it whole or in slices, polished or peeled. Save the seeds and help the children plan and plant for tomorrow's world.

—Jan Siemens, Bangkok, Thailand

Fruit Mortar (Israel)

Horoset
(hah-ROH-set)

This symbolic dish, reminiscent of the cement the Israelites used for building as slaves in Egypt, is prepared differently by Jewish communities all over the world. Horoset makes a luscious dessert or delightful appetizer, depending how sweet or piquant you make it.

• *Options:*
Substitute white cornmeal if you cannot find matzo meal.
•
Sprinkle Fruit Mortar with finely chopped almonds or walnuts.

● ●

Makes 3 1/4 c. (800 ml)

Grind, grate, or blend in blender or food processor:

2 small apples, peeled
3 bananas, peeled
juice and rind of 1/2 lemon
juice and rind of 1/2 orange
15 dates
4 oz. peanuts, finely ground (125 g)
candied peel (if desired)

Mix with:

1 t. ground cinnamon (5 ml)
sugar to taste
1/2 c. grape juice or dry red wine (125 ml)

Shape into small balls or use as paste on matzo wafers, traditionally eaten at the Passover supper. To stretch amount of Mortar, or to make it easier to shape into balls, add a bit of matzo meal (optional), a special flour used for Passover baking. Matzo meal and wafers are available where kosher foods are sold.

—Florence Kreider, Broadway, Virginia

Mango Whip (India)

Ahm Phul
(ahm fool)

This dessert is so quick and simple—and has all the exotic flavor of fresh mango.

● ●

Serves 4-6

Select two ripe mangoes. Peel, then cut flesh from seed and puree in blender.

Mix thoroughly:

2 1/2 c. pureed mango (625 ml)
1/2 c. milk (125 ml)

Serve with dab of whipped cream on top.

• *Options:*
If mangoes aren't ripe enough, add a bit of sugar to sweeten.
•
Substitute canned, pureed mango pulp, available in Asian food stores. A 30-oz can (925-g) is about 3 c. (750 ml).

—Nav Jiwan International Tea Room, Ephrata, Pennsylvania

● ●

Baked Plantains in Orange Sauce (Guatemala)

Serves 6

375°F 190°C

20-25 min.

Plátanos al Horno
(PLAH-tah-nohss ahl
OHR-noh)

Plantains, common in tropical areas, are sold in many North American grocery stores. They look like large bananas. The skin of a ripe plantain has turned black and yields to gentle pressure. Store in the refrigerator. If you can't find truly ripe plantains, substitute 5 bananas.

Preheat oven to 375°F (190°C).
Peel and slice:

3 very ripe plantains

Place in greased baking dish and dot with:

2 T. margarine (30 ml)

Pour over plantains:

3/4 c. orange juice (175 ml)

Sprinkle with:

1 t. orange rind, grated (5 ml)

**1/4 t. ground cinnamon or nutmeg (1 ml)
(optional)**

Bake, uncovered, 20-25 minutes, basting occasionally.
Serve warm with dab of whipped cream, ice cream, or frozen yogurt (optional).

—*Nav Jiwan International Tea Room, Ephrata, Pennsylvania*

....

During one of the years we lived in Guatemala, we began our Christmas Eve celebration by attending an evangelical worship service with K'ekchi' Indian brothers and sisters. After the two-and-a-half-hour worship, we ate traditional steaming-hot corn tamales. Together we laughed, joked, and also shared our concerns.

When we left the church at midnight the whole town was exploding in sizzling, soaring, popping fireworks. The streets were nearly impassable for 10 minutes.

Before we reached home, a Catholic neighbor met us on the street and insisted we come to his home for tamales. We had already eaten our fill and were carrying more tamales home for breakfast, but we couldn't refuse his invitation. His house was filled with guests who greeted us with hugs and "Feliz Navidad—Merry Christmas!" Festive Spanish music played in the background as people ate tamales and visited.

Finally the host called for silence and invited the guests to gather at the miniature clay manger scene, spread beneath the Christmas tree. Everyone knelt for a short liturgy to welcome the babe in the manger.

When we resumed our walk home, hands piled even higher with the second generous batch of tamales, the streets were quiet and empty. We went to bed with full stomachs, and heads and hearts exhilarated with the evening's experiences.

A knock at the door wakened us on Christmas morning. A K'ekchi' friend of meager resources came to give us yet another plate of the ultimate specialty—hot Christmas tamales. In these celebrations of Christmas, so different from my own yet filled with hope and generosity, the reality of Christmas came alive for me.

—*Mary Jane Newcomer, Lake Wales, Florida*

Cranberry Whip
(Finland)

(ts)

Serves 6-8

●●●●●●●●●●●●●●●●●●●●●●●●●●●●●●

Vatkattu Marjapuuro
(vaht-KAHT-too
mahr-yah-POO-roh)

In Finland, where wild berries
are plentiful, this whip is
made with lingonberries,
similar in flavor and
appearance to cranberries. A
pleasantly light dessert and
easy to prepare.

● *Option:*
Instead of cranberry juice,
use apple, strawberry, or
raspberry juice along with
1 T. lemon juice (15 ml).

In saucepan, bring to a boil over medium heat:
   3 c. cranberry juice (750 ml)
When boiling, slowly sprinkle in:
   6 T. sugar (90 ml)
Stirring briskly, slowly add:
   1/2 c. uncooked cream of wheat (125 ml)
Reduce heat and simmer, stirring occasionally, until
thickened, 6-8 minutes. If using quick cream of wheat,
reduce cooking time to 3-4 minutes. When mixture is
thick, transfer to large mixing bowl and beat with electric
mixer at high speed 10-15 minutes, or until mixture is light
and fluffy, and has delicate pink color. Pour into serving
bowl or individual dishes. Serve within 2 hours at room
temperature.

—*Nav Jiwan International Tea Room, Ephrata, Pennsylvania*

Pineapple Pie
(Jamaica)

●●●●●●●●●●●●●●●●●●●●●●●●●●●●●●

Makes 1 pie

425°F 220°C (10 min.)

350°F 180°C (30-40 min.)

One fresh pineapple will
make one pie.

Have ready unbaked pastry for a 2-crust pie.
Mix in saucepan:
   4-5 c. tidbit-size unsweetened pineapple
   pieces, fresh or canned (drained, reserve
   juice) (1-1.3 L)
   1/4 c. flour (50 ml)
   1/4 c. sugar (50 ml)
   1/4 t. ground nutmeg (1 ml)
   1/4 t. ground cinnamon (1 ml)
   pinch of salt
   2-4 T. pineapple juice or water (30-60 ml) (as
   needed)
Cook over medium heat, stirring constantly, until mixture
thickens.
Remove from heat and stir in:
   1 T. margarine (15 ml)
Preheat oven to 425°F (220°C). Roll out half of pastry
dough and place in 9-inch pie pan (1-L). Fill with fruit
mixture. Roll out remaining dough; make several slits in
center and cover pie. Trim excess dough; seal edge. Bake
10 minutes. Reduce heat to 350°F (180°C) and bake
30-40 minutes, until crust is lightly browned.

—*Pauline Cousins, St. Mary, Jamaica*

Simple Watermelon Dessert (Korea)

Hwa Che
(hwah cheh)

Koreans add ci-da, a carbonated beverage similar to ginger ale, to watermelon for a simple dessert that complements the onion, garlic, red pepper, and sesame seed seasonings of their food. This dessert will be a pleasing finish to many international meals.

(ts)

Scoop chilled watermelon into balls or chop into cubes. Just before serving, sprinkle lightly with sugar (optional) and crushed ice. Pour a little ginger ale over and serve.

—*Mrs. Chung, Seoul, Korea; and Pat Yoder, Goshen, Indiana*

Wild Fruit Pudding (United States)

Menotse Inhino
(mihn-ohtz ih-NYE-noh)

The Cheyenne have long made a pudding, commonly called berry gravy, from wild fruit or berries they gather and preserve by drying in the sun. They crush and pound the berries, shaping them into patties for drying. Wild fruit is split open and placed in the sun.

 (ts)   M   *Serves 4-6*

Combine in saucepan:

2 c. dried wild sand plums, prunes, chokecherries, or other dried fruit (500 ml)
2 c. water (500 ml)

Cover and simmer until soft, 7-10 minutes.
Make paste of:

1-2 T. cornstarch (15-30 ml)
2-3 T. water (30-45 ml)
1 T. sugar (15 ml) or to taste

Stir paste into fruit. Simmer, stirring constantly, until thickened. Add 1/2 t. margarine (2 ml) to prevent a thick skin from forming on top. Serve warm or cold.

• Option:
Substitute fresh or frozen fruit or berries for half the dried fruit.

• Microwave:
In covered 3-qt. casserole (3-L), cook dried fruit and water on high for 8-10 minutes, until boiling. Make paste and stir into fruit. Cook on high 5 minutes.

—*Betty E. Hart, Clinton, Oklahoma*

 cheerful heart has a continual feast.

—*Proverbs 15:15*

Spiced Rice Pudding (India)

Payesh
(pie-ESH)

A thinner version of this flavorful rice pudding, without the raisins and cashews, is served at Annaprashanna, the Hindu celebration to mark the introduction of rice into a six-month-old baby's diet. During the ceremony, each guest has the opportunity to feed the child a spoonful of Payesh.

• *Option:*
Basmati, an aromatic, long-grain Indian rice, is especially nice in this dish.

●●●●●●●●●●●●●●●●●●●●●●●●●●●●●●●●

Serves 4-6

Place in saucepan:
1/2 c. long-grain rice (125 ml)
1 c. water (250 ml)
Bring to a boil, cover, and simmer 10 minutes.
Add:
3 c. milk (750 ml)
1/3 c. brown sugar, packed (75 ml)
2 bay leaves
2 cardamom pods
1-inch stick cinnamon (2.5-cm)
2 whole cloves
pinch of salt
1/4 c. raisins (50 ml) (optional)
2 T. unsalted cashews, chopped (30 ml) (optional)
Return to a boil. Cover and simmer over low heat 30-45 minutes, stirring occasionally so mixture does not stick to bottom of pan. When mixture is thickened, remove from heat and stir in:
1 t. vanilla (5 ml)
Chill and serve as dessert, snack, or breakfast food.

• *Microwave:*
In a 1-qt. glass measure (1-L), cook milk on high 6 minutes, or until hot, but not boiling. In 3-qt. casserole (3-L), combine milk, rice, and spices (omit water). Cover tightly and cook on high 6-8 minutes or until boiling, then on medium 25 minutes. Do not stir. The pudding will be very milky at this point. Uncover and add vanilla, raisins, and cashews (optional). Cook, uncovered, on medium 3-5 minutes or until most of the milk is absorbed and the rice is tender. Stir. Let stand 10 minutes to thicken. Chill.

—Cynthia Peacock, Calcutta, India

Sweetened Sticky Rice (Laos)

Khao Niew Varn
(cow NEE-oh vahn)

Usually eaten with mangoes or an Asian-type custard, Sweetened Sticky Rice goes well with fresh or canned peaches, or Bananas in Coconut Sauce (p. 295).

●●●●●●●●●●●●●●●●●●●●●●●●●●●●●●

Serves 6

Prepare as described in Sticky Rice (p. 144):
2 c. uncooked sticky (glutinous or sweet) rice (500 ml)
While still warm, mix rice with:
1 c. coconut milk (250 ml) (p. 280)
1/3-1/2 c. sugar (75-125 ml)
1/2 t. salt (2 ml)
Cover and let stand 15 minutes before serving.

—Linda Peachey, Lancaster, Pennsylvania

Lemon Cream of Wheat Pudding (Italy)

Budino di Semolino
(boo-DEE-noh dee
seh-moh-LEE-noh)

Italians make this custard especially for older people and as an after-school treat for children. Families enjoy it as a dessert with soup meals.

• Microwave:
Melt margarine in 1-qt. glass measure (1-L), about 30 seconds. Stir in cream of wheat. Add milk and cook on high, lightly covered, 6-8 minutes or until boiling, then on medium 8-10 minutes, until thickened. Stir every 2 minutes. Meanwhile, in a 1-qt. casserole (1-L), mix sugar, salt, lemon rind, egg yolks, and raisins. Combine with cereal mixture and cook on high 1-2 minutes. Fold in egg whites and bake in conventional oven.

M

Serves 4-6

325°F 160°C

30-35 min.

Scald in large saucepan:

1 1/2 c. milk (375 ml)

Keep heat low. Slowly pour in, stirring constantly:

1/3 c. uncooked cream of wheat (75 ml)

Cook 2-3 minutes until thickened. Remove from heat and add:

1/2 c. sugar (125 ml)
2 T. margarine (30 ml)
dash of salt
1/4 c. raisins (50 ml)
1 1/2 T. lemon juice (20 ml) or rind of one lemon, grated

Stir well to melt sugar and margarine.
Add and mix until smooth:

3 egg yolks

Fold in:

3 egg whites, beaten to stiff peaks

Pour into 2-qt. greased casserole (2-L) and bake 30-35 minutes in 325°F preheated oven (160°C). Top will be lightly browned and contents set like custard.

—Minnie Magro, Italy; and Naomi Fast, Newton, Kansas

In Laos, most festive occasions such as weddings, births, good-byes or welcomes, are marked by the traditional string-tying ceremony, *baci*. This is an intimate and community-oriented ceremony in which friends and neighbors gather in a home around a *baci* tree constructed of banana leaves and flowers, and adorned with candles and trails of string.

A community elder leads the ceremony with chanting, much like the chanting of Buddhist monks in the temple. Although the chanting begins in the familiar Pali language, the elder soon begins telling humorous anecdotes in the Lao language and gives well-wishes to the celebrants.

During the ceremony, the person being honored grasps a string trailing from the *baci* tree and holds it in his or her hands in a prayer position. The rest of the community link themselves to the string by gently touching the elbow of the person in front of them in an unbroken chain. In this way the elder's good wishes reach the outer edges of the circle where they are confirmed and showered back to the honored one.

To close the ceremony, the elder ties a string around the wrists of the honored member. Others in the community follow. Tying additional strings, they recite a blessing: "May you have a long life, good health, and 10 children. . . ." A meal featuring a dish called *lap* (luck) follows this affirmative and joyful ceremony.

—Lois Foehringer and David Merchant, Vientiane, Laos

Coconut Pudding
(Puerto Rico)

●●●●●●●●●●●●●●●●●●●●●●●●●●●●●●●●●●●

M

Serves 8

Tembleque
(taym-BLAY-kay)

*Contributor watched her
mother and grandmother
make this Christmas dessert
as she was growing up in
Puerto Rico.*

• Option:
Replace coconut milk with
8.5-oz. can of cream of
coconut (250-g) and enough
milk to make 1 qt. (1 L). Omit
sugar and salt.

Combine in saucepan:
   4 c. coconut milk (1 L) (p. 280)
   2/3 c. sugar (150 ml)
   3/4 t. salt (3 ml) (optional)
Use a little of milk mixture to dissolve:
   1/2 c. cornstarch (125 ml)
Add to rest of milk. Cook over medium-low heat, stirring
constantly, until mixture thickens. Lower heat and cook 5
additional minutes. Pour into serving dish. Sprinkle ground
cinnamon on top. Refrigerate and serve chilled.

• Microwave:
In 2-qt. casserole (2-L), combine salt, sugar, cornstarch, and
coconut milk. Cook on high 6 minutes. Stir. Cook on high
4-10 more minutes or until boiling and thickened, stirring
each minute to keep it smooth.

—*Elizabeth Figarella, Waterbury, Connecticut*

Coffee Custard
(Brazil)

●●●●●●●●●●●●●●●●●●●●●●●●●●●●●●●●●●

Makes 12 servings

350°F 180°C

35-40 min.

Pudim de Cafe
(poo-DEEN day kah-FAY)

Combine and scald in saucepan:
   3 c. milk (750 ml)
   1 c. light cream or evaporated milk (250 ml)
Stir in:
   3 T. instant coffee granules (45 ml)
   3 T. orange peel, grated (45 ml)
Simmer 10 minutes.
Add and combine thoroughly:
   5 eggs, beaten
   1/2 t. salt (2 ml)
   1/2 c. sugar (125 ml)
   1 t. vanilla (5 ml)
   1/4 t. ground nutmeg (1 ml)
Strain through fine sieve. Pour into 9 x 12-inch cake pan
(3.5-L). Set in larger pan of water in oven and bake at
350°F (180°C) 35-40 minutes until set. Cool, cut in
squares, and serve with dab of whipped cream.

—*Nav Jiwan International Tea Room, Ephrata, Pennsylvania*

The Nav Jiwan
International Tea Room is
operated by SELFHELP
Crafts of the World, a
Mennonite Central
Committee (MCC) job
creation program.
SELFHELP Crafts helps
low-income people earn a
living with dignity by
marketing their
handicrafts in North
America. The
International Tea Room is
located in the SELFHELP
Crafts store in Ephrata,
Pennsylvania.

Flan
(Spain)

●●●●●●●●●●●●●●●●●●●●●●●●●●●●●●●●●●●

Serves 5-6

350°F 180°C

35-40 min.

(flahn)

This delightful egg and milk dessert is popular in many parts of the world, especially where there has been Spanish influence. Latin American cooks add coconut for variety.

● *Variation:*
To make Costa Rican Coconut Flan (Flan de Coco), replace lemon juice with 2 T. water (30 ml) and a pinch of ground cinnamon. Reduce sugar in egg mixture to 1/4 c. (50 ml), replace 1 c. of milk (250 ml) with 10-oz. can evaporated milk (300-g) and 1 T. cornstarch (15 ml). Add 1 c. shredded coconut (250 ml) with eggs and sugar.

Syrup:
In small saucepan, heat on low until mixture is dark brown, like caramel syrup:
1/4 c. sugar (50 ml)
4 drops lemon juice
Don't worry if syrup burns a little. Place in flan mold, coating all sides and bottom. (Gelatin or individual molds work nicely.) Place in refrigerator while preparing Flan.

Flan:
Bring to a boil:
2 c. milk (500 ml)
1 t. vanilla (5 ml)
In separate bowl, beat:
4 eggs
3/4 c. sugar (175 ml)
Slowly add egg-and-sugar mixture to boiled milk. Pour into refrigerated mold and place in oven in another container that has about 1 inch water (2.5 cm). Bake 35-40 minutes at 350°F (180°C). Flan is done when knife inserted in center comes out clean. Cool and unmold. Serve chilled.

—*Mabel Pallares and Frances Penner, Madrid, Spain*
—*Luisa Cordero and Beverlee Ludema, San José, Costa Rica*

Trifle
(South Africa)

●●●●●●●●●●●●●●●●●●●●●●●●●●●●●●●●●●

Serves 8-10

Trifle dresses up leftover cake with pudding and fruit. Adding layers of green and red gelatin makes a colorful Christmas dessert. Trifle is often made for special occasions, such as the 21st birthday, an especially important day in the life of a young South African.

● *Option:*
Omit flavored gelatin layer and pour custard or pudding directly over crumbled cake.

Crumble into clear glass bowl:
cake, at least a day old (white cake is most common)
Pour over cake:
layer of half-set flavored gelatin, any flavor
Add:
layer of custard or pudding
Scatter over custard or pudding:
colorful combination of fresh, frozen, or canned fruit, cubed or sliced
Add to cover fruit:
another thin layer of custard
Repeat each layer a second time.
Top with:
whipped cream
Chill to set gelatin.

—*Olga Reimer, Mkuze, Natal, South Africa*

Chocolate Mousse (France)

Mousse au Chocolat
(moose oh shoh-koh-LAH)

A rich chocolate dessert.

• *Option:*
Garnish with whipped cream, shaved chocolate, or grated coconut.

• *Note:*
Traditional Chocolate Mousse often includes uncooked egg whites, beaten and folded in at the end. This recipe adds eggs earlier to avoid any chance of salmonella contamination.

Combine in saucepan:

3 oz. unsweetened baking chocolate squares (100 g)
2 c. water (500 ml)

Bring mixture to a boil over low heat, stirring constantly until blended.
Add:

3/4 c. sugar (175 ml)
1/8 t. salt (.5 ml)

Simmer 3 minutes, stirring constantly. Remove from heat. Combine in separate small saucepan:

2 envelopes plain gelatin
1/4 c. cold water (50 ml)

Mix well, then dissolve by heating. Add to chocolate mixture.
In separate bowl, lightly stir:

2 eggs

Add, 1 T. (15 ml) at a time:

4 T. of chocolate mixture (60 ml)

Stir until smooth. Add to remaining chocolate mixture and return to heat. Simmer until thickened; do not boil. Cool.
Add:

1 t. vanilla (5 ml)
1 T. wine (15 ml) (optional)

Whip:

2 c. cream (500 ml)

Fold whipped cream into mousse. Chill 3-4 hours.

—Melody Rupley, Akron, Pennsylvania

A friend took me to a village home in Jamama, southern Somalia. As quickly as we arrived, the hostess, who cooked on the earthen floor of her kitchen, began whisking eggs in an enamel bowl steadied between her feet. She added flour and cardamom seeds. After pouring the batter into a cake pan, she placed it into a larger pan resting over hot coals on the floor. Then she inverted a second pan over the top and spread hot coals over it. Before long we were enjoying a light, puffy sponge cake.

—Miriam Housman, Lancaster, Pennsylvania

Lemon Loaf
(Norway)

● ●

Makes 2 loaves

350°F 180°C

50-60 min.

Citron Kake
(sih-TROHN KAH-kah)

Potato flour, similar to cornstarch, gives this cake a smooth texture.

• Option:
If potato flour is not available, substitute cornstarch or rice flour, or increase white flour to 3 c. (750 ml).

Beat until thick:
  2 c. sugar (500 ml)
  3 eggs
Add and mix until blended:
  1 c. margarine, melted (250 ml)
  1/2 c. potato flour (125 ml)
  2 1/2 c. white flour (625 ml)
  2 t. baking powder (10 ml)
  1 c. milk (250 ml)
  rind of 1 lemon, grated
Preheat oven to 350°F (180°C). Pour batter into 2 loaf pans, greased and floured on bottoms only. Bake 50-60 minutes. Remove from pans. While still warm, glaze with thick paste of juice from 1 lemon and confectioner's sugar. Serve in slices with fresh fruit or sherbet.

—*Gerd Doroshuk, Dauphin, Manitoba*

Cheesecake
(Israel)

● ●

Makes 1 cake

350°F 180°C

35 min./10 min.

Cheesecake, a typical Sabbath dessert in Israel, is creamy rich, but not too sweet.

• Options:
Omit sour cream topping. Cool cake completely and top with fresh fruit (peaches, strawberries, apricots, or pineapple) and slightly jelled gelatin of the same flavor. Chill and serve.
•
Substitute a graham cracker crust for the pastry.

Have ready baked 9-inch pie shell (1 L).
Beat together until smooth:
  16 oz. cream cheese (500 g)
  2 eggs, beaten
  2 t. vanilla (10 ml)
  1/3 c. sugar (75 ml)
  1/8 t. salt (.5 ml)
Pour into baked pie shell. Bake at 350°F (180°C) 35 minutes or until set. Cool 10 minutes.
Beat until fluffy:
  1 c. sour cream (250 ml)
Gradually add:
  1/3 c. sugar (75 ml)
  1 t. vanilla (5 ml)
Spread over cake. Return to oven another 10 minutes. Chill and serve.

—*Esther Ben Yoseph, Israel; and Florence Kreider, Broadway, Virginia*

Anthill Cake
(Brazil)

Serves 20-30

350°F 180°C

45-60 min.

Bolo Formigeiro
(BOH-loh
for-mee-GAY-ee-roh)

The only ants in Anthill Cake are pieces of grated chocolate and coconut. This rich, dense cake should be eaten as Brazilians do—occasionally and in small servings. Burn off extra calories by beating egg whites Brazilian-style—with a fork.

• **Options:**
For lower-calorie cake, reduce sugar to 1 c. (250 ml), margarine to 1/2 c. (125 ml), cornstarch to 1/2 c. (125 ml); use 3 eggs.
•
Substitute flour for part or all of cornstarch.
•
Substitute milk for coconut milk.

Mix together:
   2 c. sugar (500 ml)
   2 c. flour (500 ml)
   1 c. cornstarch (250 ml)
   1/2 c. unsweetened grated coconut (125 ml)
   1 T. baking powder (15 ml)
Combine:
   4 egg yolks
   1 c. coconut milk (250 ml) (p. 280)
   1 c. margarine, melted (250 ml)
Mix dry and liquid ingredients.
Beat to stiff peaks:
   4 egg whites
Fold into mixture.
Add:
   1/4-1/3 c. semi-sweet chocolate, grated (50-75 ml)
   pinch of salt
Mix gently. Preheat oven to 350°F (180°C). Pour batter in greased and floured bundt, angel food, or 9x13-inch pan (3.5-L). Bake 45-60 minutes (depending on size of pan) or until golden brown on top and toothpick comes out clean. When cool, sprinkle with powdered sugar.

—*Doña Lourdes, Jardim Primavera, Recife, Brazil; and Mert Brubaker, Lancaster, Pennsylvania*

Traditional wedding ceremonies in northeast Kenya include a procession of four married men and four married women who take gifts to the house of the bride's mother. On their way, they pass through a set of symbolic gates. They pause at each to offer prayers of peace and blessing for both families, for all the livestock, and for the new couple. A typical prayer would be:

We are people of peace
Peace in the night
Peace in the day
Peace in the evening
Peace with animals grazing in the morning
Peace with animals grazing throughout the day
Peace with animals grazing at stock-folding time
Peace to the couple
Peace to their families
Peace in the north
Peace in the south
God bless the pasture with waters for our animals.

—*David Adolphe-Laroche and B. J. Linquist-Laroche, Kalacha, Kenya*

● ●

Old-Fashioned Stack Cake (United States)

This tall, moist cake, often made with dried apples, is a long-standing holiday tradition in southeastern Kentucky and other parts of the U.S. South. When people don't have five or six pans of the same size, they bake the layers two at a time, sometimes in iron skillets.

• Microwave:
To make filling, cook chopped apples in covered dish on high 5 minutes. Stir, cover, and cook another 5-6 minutes until tender. Stir in sugar and seasonings.

M

Serves 12-15

375°F 190°C

15 min.

Sift into mixing bowl:

4 c. flour (1 L)
1 c. sugar (250 ml)
2 t. baking powder (10 ml)
1 t. baking soda (5 ml)
1/4 t. salt (1 ml)
1 T. ground ginger (15 ml)
1/2 t. ground nutmeg (2 ml)

Stir in:

1 c. margarine, melted (250 ml)
1 c. buttermilk (250 ml)
3 eggs
1 c. molasses or brown sugar (250 ml)

Mix well to form stiff dough. Turn onto floured board and divide into 6 equal parts. Lightly roll each part and place in individual well-greased and floured 8- or 9-inch (1.5-L) round cake pan. Prick with fork to keep dough from buckling up as it bakes. Bake 15 minutes in preheated 375°F oven (190°C). When cool, stack layers with apple filling (below). Cake is best if stored in airtight container or wrapped well and allowed to stand overnight or longer to moisten layers.

Apple filling:

Combine and cook until smooth:

10-13 medium apples, pared and chopped, or 1-1 1/4 lb. dried apples, soaked several hours, drained (reserve liquid), and chopped (500-625 g) (about 11 c./2.8 L)
3/4 c. sugar (175 ml)
1 t. ground cinnamon (5 ml)
1/2 t. ground cloves (2 ml)
1/2 t. ground allspice (2 ml)

If using dried apples, add just enough reserved liquid to make a thick sauce.

—Dorothy Brogdon, Partridge, Kentucky; and Mary Score, Cumberland, Kentucky
—Emma Reed and Lori Weiler, Letcher County, Kentucky

....

*b*e who eats bitter things gets sweet things too.

—Swahili proverb

Appalachian Mountain Pudding (United States)

This fruit cobbler has been in contributor Emma Reed's family many years. It is the regular conclusion to a Sunday dinner of fried chicken, green beans, mashed taters, and coleslaw.

• Options:
Use self-rising flour; omit baking powder and salt.
•
Add 1/2 t. ground cinnamon (2 ml) to apples.

(ts)

••••••••••••••••••••••••••••••••

	Serves 8
	350°F 180°C
	30-35 min.

Preheat oven to 350°F (180°C).
Mix until smooth:
1 c. flour (250 ml)
1 1/2 t. baking powder (7 ml)
1/2 t. salt (2 ml)
3/4 c. sugar (175 ml)
1 c. milk (250 ml)
1/2 t. vanilla (2 ml)
Melt in 9x13-inch baking pan (3.5-L):
1/2 c. margarine (125 ml)
Pour batter into baking pan.
Place over batter:
3-4 c. fresh or canned fruit or berries, drained (reserve juice) (750 ml-1 L)
Pour over top:
1 c. fruit juice (250 ml)
Bake 30-35 minutes until light brown. Remove from oven and pour 1/2 c. fruit juice (125 ml) over top to keep pudding moist.

—*Emma Reed and Lori Weiler, Letcher County, Kentucky*

Ginger Pudding (Lesotho)

This steamed pudding, common in British-influenced southern Africa, is served at the Anglican Centre in Lesotho.

••••••••••••••••••••••••••••••••

	Serves 6-8
	375°F 190°C
	50-55 min.

Combine in 9-inch square baking dish (2-L):
2 c. boiling water (500 ml)
1/2 c. sugar (125 ml)
1/4 t. salt (1 ml)
1 T. vinegar (15 ml)
Stir until sugar dissolves. Set aside.
In separate bowl, combine:
1/3 c. margarine, melted (75 ml)
1/3 c. shortening, melted (75 ml)
2 c. flour (500 ml)
2 T. apricot, currant, or plum jam (30 ml)
1 t. baking soda (5 ml)
1 1/2 t. ground ginger (7 ml)
Mix well, adding a bit of milk if batter is too dry. Preheat oven to 375°F (190°C). Drop cake mixture by small spoonfuls into syrup. Cover tightly with lid or foil (so it steams) and bake 50-55 minutes or until set. Serve topped with custard, fresh or whipped cream, or milk.

—*Gillian Gator, England; and Rose Breneman Stewart, Lancaster, Pennsylvania*
—*Gudrun Mathies, Elmira, Ontario*

● ●

Fruit Torte (Germany)

Makes 1 thin cake

350°F 180°C

20-30 min.

Obstkuchen
(OHBSHT-KOO-kehn)

Obstkuchen delights both the eyes and the palate. It is a colorful alternative to heavily iced birthday cakes, and children can help arrange the fruit.

Preheat oven to 350°F (180°C).
Cream together:

1/2 c. margarine (125 ml)
1/2 c. sugar (125 ml)
1 egg
1/2 t. vanilla (2 ml)

Mix in:

13/4 c. flour (425 ml)
2 t. baking powder (10 ml)
1 c. milk (250 ml)

Beat until smooth. Pour into greased and floured 12-inch round flan or deep pizza pan (30-cm). Bake 20-30 minutes. Cool and turn out on serving tray. Arrange fresh or canned fruit on top (for example, bananas sliced lengthwise, pineapple rings, maraschino or bing cherries, apricots, or peaches). Cover with glaze (below). Serve with whipped cream or sherbet.

Glaze:
Combine in saucepan:

1 c. fruit juice (250 ml)
1 t. lemon juice (5 ml)
1 T. cornstarch (15 ml)
a few drops almond extract (optional)

Cook until thickened. Cool slightly; spread to cover fruit.

—*Hildegard Petry and Cathy Gingerich Stoner, Krastel, Germany*
—*Martha Miller, Bronx, New York*

Hungarians are sensitive to the ebb and flow of the seasons. Even urban dwellers in Budapest are compulsive about making pilgrimages back to their villages for harvest celebrations. They wittingly contend that if you scratch any Hungarian hard enough, you will always find a peasant underneath.

Autumn is a time of return and thanksgiving. Scores of Hungarians travel back to their roots. Villages celebrate the feasts of New Wine and All Saints' Day. Churches plan special harvest-home worship services. Family reunions, frolic, and worship become agreeably blended during the harvest celebrations.

—*Joseph Miller, Ephrata, Pennsylvania*

Fruit Meringue (New Zealand)

● ●

Serves 4-6

350°F 180°C

250°F 120°C (1 hour)

Pavlova
(pav-LOH-vah)

This unusual dessert demands high quality fresh fruit both for flavor and appearance. Make it when fruits are in season and at their prime—or when kiwi fruit is specially priced.

Preheat oven to 350°F (180°C).
Beat to soft peaks:

6 egg whites
1 t. cream of tartar (5 ml)
1/4 t. salt (1 ml)

Continue beating and slowly add:

1 c. sugar (250 ml)

When stiff, beat in:

2 t. cornstarch (10 ml)
1 t. vinegar (5 ml)
1 t. vanilla extract (5 ml)

Cut out 9-inch circle (22-cm) from brown paper bag. Moisten bottom of paper circle with water and lay on cookie sheet. Pile egg-white mixture on top of circle, forming depression in center. Place in oven. Reduce temperature to 250°F (120°C) and bake 1 hour, or until lightly browned. Cool. Slip knife between paper and moist meringue cake bottom. Transfer cake from paper to plate. Serve topped with fresh strawberries, raspberries, or kiwi fruit.

—*Carla Kaye Jones and George Switzer, Hampton, Virginia*

While my husband and I were graduate students at Virginia Polytechnic Institute and not yet married, we had the wonderful opportunity of living in Hillcrest Hall, an international residence. People from 27 countries lived in this hundred-person hall during our stay. We learned new languages, ate new foods, and began to feel a part of the global community. When we decided to marry, we asked our residence-hall friends to give us recipes from their home countries as wedding gifts. As we cook from our "Hillcrest Hall collection," we remember dear friends from all over the world.

—*Carla Kaye Jones, Hampton, Virginia*

When snow falls in the mountains of Lebanon, children gather clean snow and add fruit juice and sugar to make a favorite snack, *yuksuma*. On snowy evenings, large groups of young and old huddle around wood-burning stoves to eat *yuksuma*, tell stories and jokes, knit, and sing.

Stuffing and wrapping foods is a common theme in Middle Eastern cooking. Some people believe that a passage in the Koran which speaks about God being a hidden treasure is the inspiration for wrapping foods so that the tasty part is concealed. Egyptians stuff vegetables and fill leaves for a weekly main dish called *mahshi* (Arabic for *stuffed*). They also make sweets with a nut or piece of fruit tucked inside.

Baklava (Middle East)

(bahk-LAH-vah)

Commonly known as a Greek pastry, Baklava is a favorite festive dessert throughout the Mediterranean region. The contributor learned this recipe in the West Bank. It is easy to make, but takes a while. Allow plenty of time when you first work with phyllo dough. Serve this rich and sweet dessert in small pieces.

• *Option:*
Divide phyllo sheets into 3 layers and nuts into 2 layers. Delicious either way!

• •

Makes 30 pieces

325°F 160°C

1 hour

Stir together and set aside:
2 c. chopped nuts (500 ml) (English walnuts, almonds, pistachios, or mixture)
1 c. sugar (250 ml)
1 T. water (15 ml)
1 T. vanilla (15 ml)
1 t. ground cinnamon (5 ml)
Have ready:
1 1/4 c. butter, melted (300 ml)
Separate sheets and cut to fit bottom of 9 x 13-inch baking pan (3.5-L):
1 package phyllo dough (about 30 sheets)
Brush pan with melted butter. Layer half the trimmed phyllo sheets in pan, brushing each sheet in turn with melted butter. Spread nut mixture on top. Drizzle with melted butter. Place remaining sheets of dough on top, brushing each with butter. With sharp knife, carefully cut pan of Baklava lengthwise into 5 equal strips. Gently score the strips diagonally into small diamond-shaped pieces. Drizzle remaining melted butter on top. Bake in preheated 325°F (160°C) oven 1 hour or until golden.

Syrup:
Combine in saucepan:
1 1/2 c. water (375 ml)
1 1/4 c. sugar (300 ml)
Bring to a boil and simmer 10 minutes.
Stir in:
2 T. lemon juice (30 ml)
2 T. honey (30 ml)
Cool a bit. Pour over baked Baklava. Cool completely and finish cutting into diamonds.

—*Alice W. Lapp, Akron, Pennsylvania*

Scones with Cream and Jam (England)

A traditional English teatime treat.

• Option:
Add 1/2-3/4 c. raisins or currants (125-175 ml) after adding milk.

•••••••••••••••••••••••••••••••

450°F 230°C

12-15 min.

Makes 18

Preheat oven to 450°F (230°C).
Mix:

3 c. flour (750 ml)
1/2 t. salt (2 ml)
2 T. baking powder (30 ml)
1/4 c. sugar (50 ml)

Cut in:

1/2 c. margarine (125 ml)

Add:

about 2/3 c. milk (150 ml)

Knead well, adding more flour until dough is no longer sticky. Pat dough about 1/2-inch thick (1-cm). Cut out 18 circles with floured biscuit cutter or glass. Place on ungreased cookie sheets. Bake 12-15 minutes at 450°F (230°C). Cool slightly. Split in half. Top with butter, then a dollop of jam, followed by dollop of whipped, unsweetened cream.

—Leslie Book, Managua, Nicaragua

Banana Oatmeal Cookies (Jamaica)

•••••••••••••••••••••••••••••••

Makes 4 dozen

375°F 190°C

12-15 min.

Cream together until light and fluffy:

3/4 c. margarine (175 ml)
1 c. sugar (250 ml)

Beat in:

1 egg, beaten

Add:

2-3 bananas, peeled and mashed (about 1 c./ 250 ml)
31/2 c. rolled oats (875 ml)
1/2 c. peanuts or almonds, chopped (125 ml)

Mix thoroughly.
Combine in separate bowl:

11/4 c. flour (300 ml)
1/2 t. baking soda (2 ml)
1/2 t. salt (2 ml)
1/4 t. ground nutmeg (1 ml)
3/4 t. ground cinnamon (3 ml)

Add to banana mixture and mix well. Preheat oven to 375°F (190°C). Drop dough by teaspoonfuls on ungreased baking sheets, about 11/2 inches apart (3.5 cm). Bake 12-15 minutes or until golden brown. Cool on rack.

—Pauline Cousins, St. Mary, Jamaica

● ●

Sesame Seed Cookies (Nigeria)

Makes 4-5 dozen

400°F 200°C

8-10 min.

Zakin Ridi
(ZAH-kin ree-dee)

Children will enjoy cutting out these cookies and eating the crunchy results. A mildly sweet cookie with lots of nutty sesame flavor.

Cream together:

3/4 c. shortening or margarine (175 ml)
1 c. sugar (250 ml)
2 eggs
1 t. vanilla (5 ml) or 1/2 t. lemon extract (2 ml)

Add:

2 1/2 c. flour (625 ml)
1 t. baking powder (5 ml)
1 t. salt (5 ml)
1 c. sesame seeds (250 ml)

Stir until well blended. Cover and chill at least 1 hour. Preheat oven to 400°F (200°C). Roll dough 1/8 inch thick (1/3 cm) on lightly floured, cloth-covered board. Cut into desired shapes. Place on ungreased baking sheets. Bake 8-10 minutes or until very light brown.

—Martha Adive and Suzanne Ford, Jos, Nigeria

Christmas day in Jos, Nigeria, begins with a neighborhood food exchange. People prepare large pots of chicken stew and rice in advance. Then on Christmas morning, neighbors begin sending bowls of chicken stew and rice to each other.

In the afternoon women go dancing and singing from house to house, and people stop to visit. Each family has a large pot of a traditional grain drink prepared to serve their guests. They also serve meat, rice, and sweets on this occasion. Food is a symbol of joyful sharing.

---

*E*ating is sweet; digging is weariness.

—Swahili proverb

Grasmere Ginger Bars (England)

The recipe for this whole wheat bar with a snap of ginger comes from the village of Grasmere in England's Lake District, where poet William Wordsworth lived. These bars are more crunchy and textured than soft gingerbread.

● ●

Makes 24 squares

325°F 160°C

20-25 min.

Preheat oven to 325°F (160°C).
Combine in bowl:

2 c. whole wheat flour (500 ml)
3/4 c. rolled oats (175 ml)
3/4 t. baking soda (3 ml)
11/2 t. cream of tartar (7 ml)
1 T. ground ginger (15 ml)
3/4 c. brown sugar (175 ml)

Cut in until mixture resembles bread crumbs:

1 c. margarine (250 ml)

Stir in:

1/4 c. milk (50 ml)

Put in greased shallow 9 x 13-inch baking pan (3.5-L) and press down firmly with floured fork. Bake 20-25 minutes, until pale brown. Cut into squares while warm but leave in pan until cool. Keeps well when stored in airtight container.

—*Betsy Byler, Fairfax, Virginia*

Coconut Crunchies (India)

Bolinha
(bohl-EEN-yah)

These unique cookies made with cream of wheat instead of flour are popular in the Indian state of Goa. The original recipe uses yolks of six eggs; we substitute three whole eggs.

● ●

Makes 4-5 dozen

375°F 190°C

8-10 min.

Combine in saucepan:

1 c. sugar (250 ml)
1/2 c. water (125 ml)

Boil to make thin syrup, about 5 minutes.
Add:

3 c. fresh or packaged coconut, grated (750 ml)
1/4 t. ground cardamom (1 ml)

Cook over low heat 5 minutes, stirring constantly. Remove from heat and cool.
Add alternately to cooled coconut mixture:

3 eggs
2-21/2 c. uncooked cream of wheat
(500-625 ml)

Mix well. Preheat oven to 375°F (190°C). Drop batter by spoonfuls on greased cookie sheets and bake 8-10 minutes until golden brown.

—*Rose Chater, Bardez, Goa, India; and Cynthia Peacock, Calcutta, India*

Christians in the Netherlands have traditionally exchanged Christmas gifts on the eve of St. Nicolas Day. St. Nicolas, a Spanish-born, fourth-century bishop, traveled to the Netherlands by boat. He is remembered as a special friend of seamen and children. According to legend he secretly threw money through the windows of poor homes where families were going to sell their children into slavery, and down the chimneys of poor young women who needed a dowry.

Several contemporary customs have their roots in this story. Parents throw peppernuts (small spicy cookies) into the room and place presents under the chimney. Many families exchange gifts anonymously. They make inexpensive gifts and compose humorous poems that relate to an experience the recipient had during the year.

—Juliëtte Kuitse, Elkhart, Indiana

Dutch Spice Cookies (Netherlands)

Speculaasjes (spay-kou-LAHSS-yuhss)

Speculaasjes, known many places as windmill cookies, take their name from a spice mixture of ground cinnamon, ginger, cloves, and allspice marketed in the Netherlands. Traditionally associated with St. Nicholas Day, December 6, Speculaasjes are now a year-round favorite.

●●●●●●●●●●●●●●●●●●●●●●●●●●●●●●●●

Makes 3 dozen

325°F 160°C

10-12 min.

Cream:
  2/3 c. margarine (150 ml)
  3/4 c. brown sugar, packed (175 ml)
1 egg
Add dry ingredients, alternating with milk:
  2 3/4 c. flour (675 ml)
  1/2 t. baking powder (2 ml)
  1/2 t. salt (2 ml)
  1 t. ground cinnamon (5 ml)
  1/2 t. ground ginger (2 ml)
  1/4 t. ground cloves (1 ml)
  1/2 t. ground allspice (2 ml)
  1/3 c. milk (75 ml)

Knead dough with floured hands until smooth. Chill at least 4 hours. Roll out to thin dough on floured surface and cut into shapes or use cookie press. Bake on greased cookie sheets 10-12 minutes in preheated 325°F (160°C) oven.

—Juliëtte Kuitse, Elkhart, Indiana

The rural people of India love to have visitors; they extend their cordial hospitality even to strangers. Some even borrow money from neighbors in order to offer love and hospitality to their guests. On one visit to a village, we entered a house where a family offered us sweets and snacks with tea. Later we learned that, in anticipation of our arrival, the father had gone to the sweet shop and had purchased the food on credit.

—D. P. Poddar, executive secretary of West Bengal Voluntary Health Association, Calcutta, India

Almond Cookies (China)

Xingren Dangang
(shing-RUN DAHN-gahng)

● ●

Makes 7-8 dozen

375°F 190°C

10 min.

Cream:

1 c. shortening or margarine (250 ml)
3/4 c. sugar (175 ml)

Add:

2 eggs, one at a time
1 T. almond extract (15 ml)
2-4 drops yellow food coloring (optional)

Combine:

21/2-3 c. flour (625-750 ml)
1/2 t. baking soda (2 ml)
1/4 t. salt (1 ml)

Using fingers, mix dry ingredients with wet mixture into fairly stiff dough. Divide in half. On floured surface, roll each half with palms into 1-foot long, 11/2-inch diameter roll (30-cm, 3.5-cm). Wrap in waxed paper and refrigerate 3 hours.

Preheat oven to 375°F (190°C).

Beat lightly:

1 egg white

Cut cookies in 1/4-inch slices (3/4-cm) and place on ungreased cookie sheet. Press almond half in center of each cookie. Brush with egg white and bake 10 minutes.

—Nav Jiwan International Tea Room, Ephrata, Pennsylvania

....

For the last 400 years, the Hispanic people of northern New Mexico have celebrated Christmas with a blend of Spanish and indigenous customs and foods. A traditional New Mexico Christmas must include the lighting of *luminarias,* also called *farolitos.* People make these lights by putting a few handfuls of sand in brown paper bags and placing a small, slow-burning candle in the sand. At dusk they light the candles. Rows of these soft-glowing lights line the streets, sidewalks, driveways, and even the flat rooftops. People in the mountains sometimes light bonfires with piñon and cedar wood for the same ritual.

—Daniel Erdman, Lancaster, Pennsylvania

● ●

Chocolate Truffles (France)

Makes 25-30

Truffes au Chocolat
(troof oh shoh-koh-LAH)

These chocolates will melt in your mouth—and on your fingers, as you roll them by hand. Contributor writes that "in France and Belgium, someone is always making truffles at Christmas time."

Melt and stir together in saucepan over very low heat:

6 oz. semisweet chocolate (175 g)
3 T. milk (45 ml)

Add:

6 T. butter (90 ml)

Stir briefly until melted and well mixed. Remove from heat. Refrigerate 4 hours or even overnight. Form into small balls, using teaspoon or your fingers. Mixture may seem stiff at first, but quickly softens from heat of fingers. Roll balls in cocoa powder until totally coated. Truffles will keep about a week in refrigerator; a day or more at room temperature.

• *Option:*
Instead of cocoa powder, roll in shredded coconut, chocolate sprinkles, or chopped nuts.

—*Nicole Roose, Brussels, Belgium; and Sylvia Shirk Charles, Somerville, Massachusetts*

One night a young man named Dipu stormed angrily into the home I shared with friends in Bangladesh. He had exchanged harsh words with his father and was seeking refuge for a few days before leaving to make his own way in the world. He vowed never to return to his father's home.

The following night we heard music in the distance—a harmonica, drums, and singing. We wondered what the sounds of merriment were for, concluding there must be a wedding nearby. Then, suddenly, the celebrants came to a halt in front of our home.

As they crowded around, we recognized our guests—Dipu's father and several of his college friends. They slapped Dipu amicably on the back and pulled him into their circle as they sang and danced. "We're here to take you home," said Dipu's father. "School wasn't the same without you," his friends said. Dipu hugged his father and, with music and mirth, returned home.

Our eyes and hearts were full as the sounds of the party faded in the distance. Reminded of the biblical story of the prodigal son who returned home, I thought, This is what the kingdom of God is all about— loving people into the kingdom, replacing anger with joy.

—*Rebecca Pereverozoff, Akron, Pennsylvania*

─ *Notes*
1. Josef Pieper, *In Tune with the World: A Theory of Festivity* (N.Y.: Harcourt, Brace & World, 1965), p. 14.
2. Brenda and Rich Hostetler Meyer, *The Loads of Lesotho Travel on the Heads of the Women* (slide set produced by Mennonite Central Committee, Akron, Pennsylvania, 1986).

A Tourist's Prayer

O Lord, I don't want to be a spectator
A tour passenger looking out upon
  the real world,
An audience to poverty
  and want and homelessness.

Lord, involve me—call me—
implicate me—commit me—
And Lord—help me to step off the bus.

—Freda Rajotte, World Council of Churches, Geneva, Switzerland
    (used with permission)

Denis Sengualane, an Anglican bishop from Mozambique, told the following story to encourage international travelers to be environmentally aware and to recognize the needs of a hungry world even when on holidays.

The bishop had attended a church conference in Madagascar, held in a typical tourist hotel. One morning, waiting in line for a buffet-style breakfast, he happened to see the cook frying eggs. He watched him break each egg into the skillet, examine the yolk carefully, then invariably dump one or two or even three eggs into the garbage before he was satisfied with the quality.

The bishop became agitated as he watched, thinking how scarce food was in his home country; eggs were hardly ever available. Indeed, the parishioner who drove him to the airport for his flight to Madagascar had told about a special joy: her family had received six eggs as a gift, and they were keenly anticipating their gourmet meal that night. Remembering her, and all the Mozambican people who would have loved to have even one of those discarded eggs, this usually gentle bishop indignantly approached the wasteful cook.

"My son," he inquired, "why are you throwing so many eggs away? Don't you know that many people in the world are starving, and such wastefulness is sin?"

The cook, looking chastened, replied, "Oh yes, Father, I know it is wrong. But the manager says this is how I have to do it because tourists from far away refuse to eat eggs with broken yolks."

—Leona Dueck Penner,
  Winnipeg, Manitoba
  (adapted from Mennonite
  Reporter, January 22, 1990,
  p. 12)